Alexandros Lamprou teaches in the Faculty of Languages, History and Geography, Ankara University. He has formerly taught at the University of Crete and holds a PhD from the University of Leiden.

NATION-BUILDING IN MODERN TURKEY

THE 'PEOPLE'S HOUSES', THE STATE AND THE CITIZEN

ALEXANDROS LAMPROU

I.B. TAURIS

LONDON • NEW YORK • OXFORD • NEW DELHI • SYDNEY

I.B. TAURIS
Bloomsbury Publishing Plc
50 Bedford Square, London, WC1B 3DP, UK
1385 Broadway, New York, NY 10018, USA

BLOOMSBURY, I.B. TAURIS and the I.B. Tauris logo are
trademarks of Bloomsbury Publishing Plc

First published in hardback in 2015 by I.B.Tauris & Co. Ltd
This paperback edition published 2019

A catalogue record for this book is available from the British Library.

A catalog record for this book is available from the Library of Congress.

ISBN: HB: 978-1-7807-6876-2
PB: 978-1-7883-1394-0
ePDF: 978-1-7867-3940-7
eBook: 978-0-8577-3731-1

Series: Library of Modern Turkey

To find out more about our authors and books visit
www.bloomsbury.com and sign up for our newsletters.

Contents

Preface

Recep Tayyip Erdoğan has been the Prime Minister of Turkey since 2003. In his public contestation with the secularist opposition, the popular Islamist politician has repeatedly spoken with disapproving words about the single-party rule of the Republican People's Party (1924–46), condemning it on various occasions for many antidemocratic and authoritarian policies, such as for restricting the freedom of religion, for praising dictators like Hitler, for turning mosques into stables, or for introducing children to alcohol. Surely this constant condemnation of the 'single-party mentality' is a political tactic aimed at discrediting the main opposition of the Republican People's Party in the eyes of a conservative electorate that detests its secularist credentials. But it also expresses a genuine dissatisfaction with the authoritarian and antidemocratic rule of the single-party era and of later periods, something shared by many conservative Islamists but also leftists and liberals since the period in Turkey.

This negative narration of the single-party period has gained momentum with the rise of Islamist political parties and NGOs in the last two decades. It has initiated animated public debates about a part of the country's past whose critical exploration was until very recently considered almost taboo given that Mustafa Kemal Atatürk, the founder and first President of the Republic, was in charge during most of the said period. In this lively debate, discourses that emphasize the state repression of the population contrast with a highly positive narration of the period. In its most obstinate variation, this narration would declare the period and the reforms of Kemal Atatürk off-limits; more flexible variations would argue that the authoritarian and antidemocratic ruling was temporarily necessary for the establishment of a 'modern' state in the context of the population's 'backwardness'.

What is common in both narrations is their polarized view of state elites and population that treats them solely as opposing enemies. The people are portrayed either as country dupes to be enlightened or as the oppressed and resisting people; the state elites either as enlightened leadership or as degenerate oppressors. Neither narration leaves room for any degree of communication and negotiation between state and society. The period is equally portrayed either as the dark age of Premier Erdoğan's lamentations or the most illustrious period in Turkish history, the age of Atatürk. Neither could the reforming state elites be *totally* characterized by monolithic radicalism, nor could the population necessarily react *uniformly against* the reforms. Although both were quite legitimate options, they were also verging on the very extreme of practices of everyday life. They were rather highly ideological options and, in that sense, we might suspect that they were appealing to rather restricted social groups in the 1930s and 1940s in Turkey. Clearly less ideological and essentialist interpretations of the period are needed.

This book argues for a more moderate stance and offers an alternative picture of the period, based on the study of the People's House, an institution whose aim was to propagate the reforms to the population in the 1930s and 1940s. Without negating the authoritarian and antidemocratic nature of the political regime, I present a more nuanced account through the study of everyday moments of cooperation and negotiation between state and societal forces that occasionally resulted in the modification of state policies by local societies and populations. The period was until very recently studied with the help of rather restricted sources, mainly official publications, newspapers and published memoirs. The increasing availability of archival material since the late 1990s assisted historians in producing more comprehensive works on a period that is still widely considered a black hole in the history of modern Turkey, especially in respect to social history. I consider this book to be a part of a recent trend in Turkish historiography that emphasizes social and cultural history and alternative viewpoints in the study of state–society relations as it favours perspectives 'from below' or 'from the periphery' rather than the state centre.

This book started as a PhD thesis and since the beginning of the research ten years ago a number of institutions and several friends and colleagues have decisively contributed to its fruition. A scholarship from the State Scholarship Foundation of Greece (IKY) provided the financial means to complete my doctoral dissertation upon which this book is based. The bulk of the research took place in the State Archives of the Turkish Republic in Ankara. My deepest thanks go to the administration and personnel for their assistance and professionalism. I would also like to thank the personnel of the library of the Turkish Grand National Assembly, the Turkish National library in Ankara, the Beyazit and Atatürk libraries in Istanbul, as well as the libraries of the Leiden University and the International Institute of Social History in Amsterdam.

The writing of this book would have been impossible without the support of many friends and colleagues in the Netherlands, Turkey and Greece. I am deeply indebted to the supervisor of my thesis, Professor Erik Jan Zürcher, for his support and encouragement. I am grateful to professors Turaj Atabaki, Leon Buskens, François Georgeon, Lex Heerma van Voss, Jan Schmidt and Hans Theunissen for their commentary and suggestions. I owe many thanks to my friends and colleagues from Leiden and the Department of Turkish Studies: Özgür Gökmen, Umut Azak, İsmail Hakkı Kadı, Nikos Christofis, Mehmet Emin Yıldırım, Tryfon Bampilis, Guy Loth, Demet Varlı, Amber Gemmeke, Aris Perperoglou and Yiorgos Portokalides. I also thank my friends and colleagues at the History and Archaeology Department of the University of Crete, especially Antonis Anastasopoulos, Elias Kolovos and Marinos Sariyannis, for an unforgettable stay in Crete in 2010–11.

I am grateful to Aydın Ayhan, Ekrem Balıbek, Mustafa Durak, İbrahim Oluklu, Yakup Özkül, Zeki Özalay, Yakup Sahan and

Mehmet Sahin for their hospitality and assistance in Balıkesir. Yiannis Bonos, Özgür Gökmen and Yiannis Moutsis read and commented on draft chapters. Aydın Ayhan provided me with rare newspaper clips from local newspapers of Balıkesir, and Ahmet Yüksel of Sanat Kitabevi with the front picture from a rare periodical of the period. I would like to thank my friends for their continuous support for me and their contributions to this book: Lazaros Kazias, Dimitris Kouklakis, Yiannis Leventis, Georgios Loukas, Yianna Profiri, Onur Yıldırım, Oktay Özel, Damla Demirözü, Ulus Baker, Süha Ünsal, Özhan Önder, Nikos Sigalas, Evsen Yesert Akçay, Leo Moiras, Leo Karakatsanis, Sertaç Erten, Faruk Tuncay, Tansu Açık, Koutsoukos Vasilis, Özge Çelikaslan, Tolis Papaioannou and Bülent Varlık.

İrem has witnessed the making of this book from the very beginning. I thank her for her patience and kind support and for being there in Ankara, Crete, Edinburgh, Rotterdam, Leiden, and Ankara again.

Abbreviations

BCA	Prime Minister Archive of Republican Period (Başbakanlık Cumhuriyet Arşivi)
BJMES	*British Journal of Middle Eastern Studies*
CHFHT	Halkevi by-laws 1932 (*Halkevleri Talimatnamesi*)
CHPHCT	Regulations of Halkevi activities 1940 (*Halkevleri çalışma talimatnamesi*)
CHPHITT	Halkevi administration by-laws 1940 (*Halkevleri idare ve Teşkilat talimatnamesi*)
CSSAAME	*Comparative Studies of South Asia, Africa and the Middle East*
CSSH	*Comparative Studies in Society and History*
EJTS	*European Journal of Turkish Studies*
IJMES	*International Journal of Middle East Studies*
MES	*Middle Eastern Studies*
RPP	Republican People's Party (Cumhuriyet Halk Partisi)
Tebligat	Published Party communiqués *(CHP Katibi umumliğinin Parti Teşkilatına Umumi Tebligatı)*

Introduction

This book aspires to contribute to the study of change instigated by social engineering projects that were devised and executed by state elites upon targeted populations. These moments of social change flourished in the nineteenth and twentieth centuries in non-Western and (post-)colonial environments under the catchwords of progress, modernization and nationalism, and have been heavily studied since the 1950s within the modernization paradigm and dependency theory. Focusing on the Turkish case of social engineering in the 1930s and 1940s, the ambition of this book is to study such moments of change as an alternative to and as criticism of the above frameworks' perspective.

The need to study the 'Turkish modernization' from alternative perspectives has its origins in the growing dissatisfaction with the way this reform project has been viewed and studied hitherto. The bulk of the literature still chooses to study the Kemalist reform movement from a macro perspective, as a top-down project rather than a process of social change. This macro perspective is parallel to the literature's dependency on dualisms such as state/society, which conspicuously resemble the bipolar terms with which the modernizing ruling elite chose to define and represent itself and its enemies. It has been a common recent critique that the literature on the Turkish case does not leave room for the study of the everyday, micro aspects of social change or the 'life-worlds' of social subjects;[1] that it rarely takes into focus local social and cultural contexts or reflects on 'the emergence of new identities and new forms of subjectivity';[2] and that it fails 'to note those spaces where fact and fiction have met, where the project of modernity and those outside its walls have intersected and transformed one another'.[3]

The ambition of this book is to reply to these critiques and their request for alternative perspectives that would attempt to move beyond and problematize prevailing dualisms while studying such an instance of social change as a process that involved myriad moments of interplay between the reforms introduced by the ruling elite and their enactment and consumption by social subjects in concrete social settings, within local societies and power networks. My aim is to trace and situate the process of social change at the local level, within spaces where 'facts and fiction' meet, and to study how social actors made sense and use of the products of the state social engineering project. The broader context of this book can thus be defined as the social reform project written by the ruling elite, enforced and propagated mainly through the state and bureaucratic apparatus in the 1930s and 1940s in Turkey. The aim is not to assess the (extent of the) success or failure of such projects of social mechanics, but to study how actors coped with change, how this 'coping with' intersects and interrelates with power relations, local social and cultural contexts, and, ultimately, what it entails in terms of practices, discourses and representations by social agents, and what it might mean in relation to the shaping of social identities, personal and collective, to the 'emergence of new forms of subjectivity'.[4]

I address these issues by choosing to study the People's House, an institution created with the direct aim of propagating the reforms to the population of Turkey, through the circulation, application and enactment of a variety of 'modern' practices and discourses. The People's Houses were community centres opened and operated by the ruling Republican People's Party in most cities and towns of Turkey between 1932 and 1951. They were charged with the duty of disseminating Turkish nationalism and Western civilization through the introduction and practising of a set of novelties such as sports, cinema and theatre, Western music concerts and dance parties, and similar activities.

The Study of 'Turkish Modernization' and its Discontents

The political and social reform movement carried out in the early republican period has been extensively studied since the 1950s within the wider framework of modernization theory. Daniel Lerner's *Passing of Traditional Society* and Bernard Lewis's *Emergence of Modern Turkey* have been considered classic in that respect. Since its heyday in the 1950s and 1960s, modernization theory has attracted various critiques.[5] Works within the modernization paradigm have been extensively criticized for their institutional, legalistic and macro-level analysis and approach. Similar arguments have been raised in relation to Marxist (or Marxian) interpretations of the Turkish reform movement since the 1970s.[6]

With its emphasis on elites and institutional structures and change, literature within the modernization and dependency paradigms tends to favour one actor of change, 'the state', and view the social change primarily as a top-down process. As a consequence, society usually emerges as the recipient of change that can only accept or reject the prescribed order in its totality, being labelled Kemalist or reactionary, modern or backward. This stance does not allow for human agency or the capacity of men and women to interact with the imposed order in ways that move beyond a simple rejection or embracement of it.

A corollary assumption is that of an uncritical and unproblematic view of a substantialized, a priori and omnipotent state in oppositional terms with a similarly undifferentiated, set, static and resistant society, with both parts engaged in a one-way, top-down relation between a purposeful subject with power to enforce its will and a mute and occasionally resisting object. A clear-cut border is imagined dividing 'the state' from 'society', where the state stands for a unitary, monolithic apparatus or centre. This perspective results in an overestimation of the role, power and domination of an omniscient and omnipotent state over a passive society.

This standpoint is evident in studies within the modernization paradigm and works with a statist inclination. Heper, for instance, views state officials as a tight, homogenous and undifferentiated corpus of men with similar background and claims that 'the Turkish Republic seems to have inherited from the Ottoman Empire a strong state and a weak civil society', and that there is 'a tradition of a strong state and a weak periphery'. This approach differentiates between a strong 'arbitrary' state and an 'irresponsible' periphery or civil society.[7] Notwithstanding its insightfulness for understanding the centrality of the state apparatus in Turkey – something nobody with even a slight experience of Turkey today could miss – the state tradition approach overestimates the coherence and power of what we call the state to be and act as what it purports to be. It also overemphasizes the state's impermeability to and its lack of dialogue with society in general, allowing only for the bureaucracy's arbitrariness towards society and the society's irresponsibility towards state and bureaucracy. Thus, it implies a rigid, tightly delineated border between state and society. In the case of Ottoman–Turkish history, it is reminiscent of Ottoman political theories of governance where the borders between the ruling and ruled classes are tightly imagined.

Similar assumptions inherent in studies working within the modernization paradigm have been thoroughly criticized from a variety of perspectives. Kasaba's work on sedentarization and the relations of cities with the Ottoman central state lays emphasis on the multiple and not necessarily homogenous logics of the Ottoman state and reveals the multiplicity of state practices and the complexity of power relations.[8] A similar critique of the literature on the Tanzimat reforms (1839–76) argues that the state-led reforms have been studied and conceptualized solely as a top-down and rather unsuccessful reform movement that had minimal impact on the lives of the Ottoman subjects. Milen Petrov, for instance, has attempted to study the 'tangible impact of the Tanzimat reforms on the cognitive and epistemological world of the non-elite Ottoman subjects', something 'a large body of scholarly literature maintains [...] did not exist'.[9] Recent anthropological and sociological works on contemporary Turkey, exploring the social actors' understanding of such categories as 'state', 'modern', 'secular' and 'Islamic', move away from monolithic definitions and unproblematic dichotomies (secular/religious, state/society), highlighting the production of these categories by various social agents.[10]

My argument is that we need to employ similar perspectives to the study of the reform movement and social change during the first decades of the republic. Such perspectives should allow us to study as subjects of change the real people and their responses, address the 'everyday' and the 'life-worlds' of social agents operating within local social contexts, and ultimately reflect on the performing and shaping of social identities, issues not usually addressed in the relevant literature. There the subjects of change are either conspicuously silent or even mute in regards to their understanding and performance, or, even worse, assumed to react either totally for or against the implemented reform programme, a tendency that runs quite parallel, one might say even identical, to the regime's own discursive categories of 'reactionaries' vs 'Kemalists', of 'modern' vs 'traditional'. 'Transitional' stages are also devised for what does not fit into the neatly formed, unilinear movement from one end of the spectrum to the other, from 'tradition' to 'modernity'. This happens when a process is conceived solely in terms of a project, which in turn implies that the relation of the Turkish experiment in modernization is conceived as a 'copy' of a 'model'; the sense of failure to conform to the 'model' gives rise to notions of constant 'belatedness'. This belatedness to catch up with the Western model was and is still expressed, according to Ahıska, with a familiar metaphor, such as the bridge that connects East with West or the struggle to catch up with a moving train. Mardin has very eloquently expressed the Kemalist reformers' feeling of urgency when he wrote that they had 'to work for something which did not exist as if it existed and make it exist'.[11]

This tendency to focus on the programmatic nature of the social engineering projects obfuscates the agency of those subject to change, the capacity of people to react and respond, in numerous and various poetic, innovating and meaningful ways that go well beyond the 'modern' vs 'backward' division of the modernizing discourse and its echo in the secondary literature, to the 'new' spaces, mentalities, discourse and practices inflicted upon them. Another corollary consequence of this awkward reproduction of the modernizing elite's discourse is to ignore the ability of social actors to experience the meaning of such categories as 'modern' or 'reactionary'/'traditional' in various ways that might supersede or even challenge the official rhetoric.

If we are to move away from the constraints of dualisms and top-to-bottom, institutional perspectives towards a more open-to and inclusive-of-the-voices-of social actors point of inquiry, we have to 'bring society back'[12] and study the poetic, innovating and meaningful ways of understanding, (re)employing and making sense and use of the innovations brought upon their life.[13] We thus need an approach that detects the limits of 'the state' in implementing laws, rules and regulations, and privileges the study of the responses of the people to the state's involvement in their lives. In other words, what is required is a framework of analysis for the study of the people's understanding, appropriating and resisting the reforms the state was implementing and how these various acts and processes relate to the (re)shaping of social identities.

The aim is to have a clearer picture of (a) 'state and society relations' as a problematic, multidirectional, and multidimensional relationship, and (b) of the responses of the subjects of change and the ways these subjects consume, alter, appropriate, react, resist, avoid and manipulate the reforms introduced mainly through the state apparatus. In short, we need to focus on the various, myriad ways the subjects of change interact with each other and with state actors and agencies, and respond to the changes, and what this interaction might entail for the formation of novel forms of subjectivities, for the (re)shaping of social, individual and collective identities. This book attempts to tackle these issues by focusing on the People's House and treating it as a privileged locus for the study of the responses of the subjects of change to the changes the ruling elite was initiating, as a place wherein the new practices and discourses were meeting their targets, a 'meeting ground of fact and fiction'.[14] Placed within the above problematic and theoretical needs, this study is informed on the one hand by a corpus of recent works in anthropology and political science related to the study of the 'state', while, on the other, in its study of the way people use the state policies, this book employs a number of concepts and analytical tools borrowed from de Certeau's work on the 'practices in everyday life'.

The State in Society and Everyday Practices

In their introduction to *The Anthropology of the State*, Sharma and Gupta argue that states should be conceptualized as 'cultural artifacts, as multilayered, contradictory, translocal ensembles of institutions, practices and people'.[15] Following Mitchell and others[16] who have 'critically interrogated the assumption that "the state" is an a priori conceptual and empirical object', Sharma and Gupta view states as 'culturally embedded and discursively constructed ensembles', and call for the study of 'state construction', 'how "the state" comes into being, how "it" is differentiated from other institutional forms, and what effect this has on the operation and diffusion of power throughout society'. As a consequence, the assumption of statist approaches, that there is a border separating state from society, is also challenged. Mitchell has forcefully argued that the appearance of 'the state' as a discrete entity with an 'autonomous-from-society' status is itself a reification and an effect of power or, in Mitchell's words, 'an effect of detailed processes of spatial organization, temporal arrangement, functional specification, and supervision and surveillance'.[17] This argument leads many scholars 'to conceptualize "the state" within other institutional forms through which social relations are lived, such as the family, civil society, and the economy', but also to study the 'construction of the state' and its 'border' with society (a) in the everyday practices of its bureaucracies, its agencies and actors, and (b) in the representations of the state, 'in the realm of representations where the explicit discourse of the state is produced'.[18]

Starting with a broad perspective of the state that situates it within and not apart from or in opposition to society, this study conceives the state not in abstract or legalistic terms as an autonomous and unitary institution that operates independent of or even in contrast to society; it does not treat the state as a machinery of intentions or a subjective world of plans, programmes or ideas that excludes social agency. Drawing on Joel Migdal's state-in-society approach,[19] I follow his differentiation between the 'image of the state' and the 'actual practices of the state'.[20] For Migdal, what we call the state is 'a field of power marked by the use and threat of violence and shaped by the image of a coherent, controlling organization in a territory, which is a representation of the people bounden by that territory, and the actual practices of its multiple parts'. The image (discourse, representation) of the state projects 'a dominant, integrated, autonomous entity that controls all rule-making to make certain circumscribed rules'. This image 'posits an entity having two sorts of boundaries: territorial between states and social boundaries between state – its (public) actors and agencies – and those subject to its rules (private)'. Routine performance of state actors and agencies, such as ceremonies, the issuing of passports and visas, censuses, taxation, or the maintaining of police forces and armies, tends to reinforce this image of the state.[21] In a similar way, Mitchell conceptualizes the state as a structural effect, 'a powerful, metaphysical effect of practices that make such structures appear to exist'.[22] The everyday practices of state bureaucracies with the population may even be contradictory to the discourse of the state.[23] Thus, state formation has to be studied in the everyday practices of bureaucracies, the habitual performances of state agents and agencies in their interaction with social actors, as well as in the employment of the representations of the state by both bureaucrats and their clients.[24] The emphasis then should be laid on the spaces where this interaction regularly takes place. Migdal calls the places where state policies reach society and where they are performed, negotiated, resisted or appropriated[25] as 'junctures of state and society'.[26] I chose to study the People's House as a 'juncture of state and society', as a space within which the programmatic nature of the Turkish state elites' projects met the facts of concrete local settings and their appropriation by social actors.

Focusing on the concrete in provincial urban societies and Houses entails, on the one hand, a different level of contextualization of state–society relations than the one adopted or reproduced by the institutional and macro-level approach; on the other hand, it necessitates the employment of alternative theoretical tools. If we are to move society back to the picture and zoom in on local societies and actors, it is indispensable that we study the actors' use of the new laws, ideas, practices and discourses the centre strove to introduce among the population of the republic.

I address the issue of contextualization by favouring the micro level of analysis of case studies of the Halkevi space in provincial urban societies and by turning to the study of actors and processes. I consequently lay emphasis on the various levels and ways of interaction between the discourses and practices coming from the state centre[27] and the responses, resistance, accommodation, (re)appropriation, in short their *consumption* by social actors. 'The presence and circulation of a representation (taught by preachers, educators, and popularizers as the key to socioeconomic advancement) tells us nothing about what it is for its users.'[28] De Certeau's 'investigation of the ways in which users – commonly assumed to be passive and guided by established rules – operate' offers an alternative theoretical framework for the study of the Turkish reform movement. De Certeau introduces the term 'consumption' to refer to what consumers (or users) make with the products 'imposed by a dominant economic order' – the state, the army, the church, or even a corporation. This 'making' is a poetic activity – a production in its own right, as 'users make innumerable and infinitesimal transformations of and within the dominant cultural economy in order to adapt it to their own interests and rules'.[29] For de Certeau, this secondary production of the products of 'a rationalized, expansionist, [and] centralized production [...] is characterized by its ruses, its fragmentation (the result of the circumstances), its poaching, its clandestine nature, its tireless but quiet activity, in short by its quasi-invisibility, since it shows itself not in its own products but in an art of using those imposed on it'.[30] This book is an attempt to study the practices of consumption or else the (re) appropriation of the products of the social engineering project of the Turkish state in the 1930s and 1940s.

I choose to study this secondary production within the framework of the 'technocratically constructed, written and functionalized space'[31] of the People's House. This consumption does not take place in a socio-political and cultural vacuum. 'The procedures allowing the re-use of products are linked together in a kind of obligatory language, and their functioning is related to social situations and power relationships.' In order to study the practices associated with consumption while at the same time addressing the obvious power relations within which consumption is inscribed, de Certeau moves from a 'linguistic frame' to a 'polemological' one and distinguishes between two types of actions – strategies and tactics. 'Strategy refers to the calculation (or manipulation) of power relationships that become possible as soon as a subject with will and power (a business, an army, a city, a scientific institution) can be isolated. It postulates a place that can be delimited as its own and serve as the base from which relations with an exteriority composed of targets or threats (customers or competitors, enemies, the country surrounding the city, objectives and objects of research, etc.) can be managed.'[32] In contrast, a tactic 'is a calculated action determined by the absence of a proper locus ... The space of the tactic is the space of the other. It must play on and with a terrain imposed on it and organized by the law of a foreign power. It operates in isolated actions, blow by blow. It takes advantage of "opportunities" and depends on them. It must vigilantly make use of the cracks that particular conjunctions open in the surveillance of the proprietary powers. It poaches on them. [It] is an art of the weak.'[33]

Informed by de Certeau's concepts and perspective, this study addresses the consumption of the state policies of social reform; it examines the ways actors understand, (re/mis)use, (re)appropriate, resist and absorb the centre's policies and ideas, and the significance these secondary productions have for identity management – for the performance and negotiation of identities.

The bipolarity of strategies vs tactics refers to 'weak' and 'strong' subjects, used in studies of subaltern subjects[34] and resistance to domination. Here I treat resistance in a problematic way[35] and avoid substantializing it, in a manner quite similar to the conceptualization of the state.[36] I do not necessarily read *metis*[37] tactics as acts of resistance or as a medium to reach 'hidden transcripts' of domination.[38] Rather, this bipolarity of tactics/strategies is used not in oppositional or exclusionary terms, but as an analytical tool to view the consumption in hand in its productivity.

I thus view the boundary between strong/weak inherent in the strategies/tactics bipolarity as fleeting and unstable. Actors can be considered weak or strong in different socio-political and historical contexts and depending on their relations to different persons or groups of persons; their actions can be equally considered strategic or tactical depending on the context. Thus, it is the position of the actors within socio-political and cultural networks and relations of power that defines their status in any circumstance as weak or strong, and their responses as strategic or tactical. There is no place for an a priori subaltern within such a conceptualization. Notwithstanding the obviously ubiquitous relations of power, I feel it problematic to assign an overall subaltern status to those who produce the sources I use in this book, that is, the members of the People's Houses. In a similar way, I find it deeply problematic to read their responses as conscious acts of compliance, resistance or subordination to the policies of the centre. It would be too simplistic either to assume a given, essential(ized) subaltern, or to read his/her responses and representations solely through the conceptual repertoire of resistance/compliance. What is more, Halkevi members do not generally fall under the category of the subaltern subject as this is conceptualized in the subaltern studies literature, which is based on a distinction between elite and subaltern, that is, between literate and thus source-producing urban elites and illiterate, and thus silent, peasants. Most of the sources used in this book were produced by urban elites and the middle classes rather than subaltern, peasant or underclass subjects.

Nevertheless, the Halkevi sources, texts produced either by the centre or by Halkevi actors, were haunted by the presence of a collective Other that the Halkevi project was supposed to reform. This Other, which can easily be termed subaltern, was collectively referred to as 'the people' or the 'real people' habitually in contrast to the educated state elites. Whether reproduced in the texts of the centre or, more so in the texts of our Halkevi authors, the utterances about and representations of this Other were saturated with seemingly conflicting but also complementary images, that only make sense dialectically: the Turkish nation that was at once the sovereign people ready for 'modern civilization' due to their national qualities, but at the same time not ready yet to reach the level of modern civilization without extensive training; the peasant who was at the same time considered the repository of the true, authentic and celebrated national qualities but was also feared as the site of backwardness, tradition and religious reaction. The internal Other of the 'occidentalist fantasy', to use Ahıska's concept, was always present, and for those living closer to the border and in proximity with the Other (such as our Halkevi actors in the countryside and the provinces), even more so. The conceptualization of the internal other by non-Western elites reveals a number of tensions that have been identified and explored by authors within the subaltern/post-colonial tradition. These tensions are inherent in the discourses of reform and modernization and reveal an internalized orientalism. They surface in the images indigenous elites routinely employ to portray the absolute contrast between notions of the modern West vs the backward East or of the modern elites vs the internal backward population. The tension was clearly expressed in the rhetoric that celebrated the people as the 'almost modern' Turkish nation *and* condemned it at the same time as the internal backward Other. It is hidden in the polarized understandings of historical time in terms of space as it was habitually expressed in the images of the 'moving and modern' West and the 'stagnant and backward' East; in the ambiguities in the experiences and representations of being both modern *and* national; in a constant sense of belatedness expressed in various images and metaphors consistently voiced to express Turkey's position and quality of being a point on the map, but also in time connecting (and between) East and West: the waiting room of civilization, the time lag or the bridge between East and West, and the notion of running to catch a moving train.[39]

To sum up, starting with a broad definition of the state in terms of state actors and agencies situated within society (the state-in-society approach), and with a distinction between the 'image' and the 'actual practices' of the state, I study processes and everyday practices rather than institutional change through micro-level analysis of case studies of Halkevi activities and actors in provincial urban societies. My focal point of analysis is on the various levels of interaction between the centre's products and the responses of local actors, in short their consumption by social actors in situ, within local societies and a space – the People's House – operating within local politics and power relations. In this study, the People's House is treated as a space on the border or a juncture of state and society where the centre's policies interplay with social actors and groups in the concrete social contexts of provincial towns.

This book then is a study of the Halkevi, conceptualized as a space wherein the reforms were introduced and enacted in local societies. It is a study of (i) the Halkevi space in relation to the society and population within which it is situated; (ii) the Halkevi as an arena of power relations and local politics, a stage wherein local, state and non-state actors interact and fight each other in struggles implicating various actors and agencies; and, finally, (iii) the consumption of a number of state-imposed activities by

Halkevi actors. In the following chapters, I treat the Halkevi as an arena, a stage and a medium through, within and upon which social categories as well as related discourses and social practices were enforced, performed, contested, negotiated, evaded, reproduced and manipulated.

Organization and Arguments

The first chapter studies the Halkevi space as a state project, that is, as it was planned and articulated in the centre's discourse and intentions. It presents this juncture of state and society from the centre's point of view at its normative and programmatic level. It first offers a genealogy of the ideology upon which the Halkevi institution was established since the 1908 Revolution. It thus presents similar institutions whose primary aim was to train the Muslim population of the Ottoman Empire and Turkey into nationhood and 'modern civilization'. As an integral part of the Kemalist social engineering project, the goal of the Halkevi was to facilitate nation-building through the transmission of the elite's political and ideological products to the population. In analyzing the Halkevi in its ramifications for state–society relations during the 1930s and 1940s, I view it as an offshoot of the Kemalist single-party political regime and its mentality of tutelary popular sovereignty. I contend that the blueprint for the Halkevi institution reflected the ruling elite's political subjectivity, imbued as it was with contradictory feelings for both the 'modern' West (admiration but also fear) and the 'backward' and not-yet 'national' population (sympathy but also disgust).

The following chapters focus on the actual operation of the Halkevi blueprint as regards what it was supposed to educate and enlighten, that is, local societies and populations. Primarily drawing upon the examples of two Houses in the provincial towns of Kayseri and Balıkesir, the second chapter sketches a human geography of the Halkevi space, its cadre and members in provincial towns and among local forces. Halkevi statistics reveal that most Houses operated as elite spaces frequented and operated by educated middle- and upper-class civil servants, professionals, state officials and local elites. Texts by educated Halkevi members point to different patterns of participation in the Halkevi experiment and draw attention to the close connection of the Halkevi space and its performance within the dynamics of the symbiosis of local with non-local state elites.

It is the dynamics of this symbiosis – at once accommodating and conflictual – that Chapter 3 addresses by concentrating on local politics in an attempt to inscribe the Halkevi space and its actors in networks of power relations. Local politics involved various locals and outsiders, state and non-state actors and implicated central Party and state institutions in a dialogue with local state or non-state actors and agencies. The performance of local politics and conflicts in the Halkevi underscores its function as an intermediary space between the centre and local societies as it clearly confirms that the Halkevi functioned as an intersection linking state offices and personnel in the provinces and the centre to each other and to local non-state forces. In the Halkevi arena, the state, its local actors and their practices appear and function quite differently from what the image of a unitary, monolithic and distinct-from-society state projects. In everyday practice, local non-state elite actors were able to manipulate and occasionally control the Halkevi space and the manner in which state policies were implemented in practice.

The second part of the book (chapters 4 to 6) investigates the consumption of the centre's policies by Halkevi members. These chapters concentrate on three instances of consumption, namely of women-related Halkevi activities, coffee-house practices and Halkevi peasantist policies. In all three instances, I explore the performance of a wide set of tactics of accommodation, practices and discourses that attempted to alleviate the tensions that surfaced with the introduction of novel practices, and to 'tame' the practices that the centre was striving to initiate that were unfamiliar and even provocative to local realities. I employ the term domestication[40] to refer to these tactics of accommodation.

I view domestication as an imaginative and suitable concept to express the local actors' 'turning' and 'twisting' the Halkevi space and its activities into something more agreeable to local socio-political and cultural realities. Chapter 4 explores the ingenious inclusion in the Halkevi space of popular leisure and pastime activities that were proscribed by the centre. Local Halkevi actors employed poetic solutions to tactically evade and/or domesticate the centre's policies and discourse about leisure, exemplified in a number of activities associated with the coffee house (card playing, coffee and alcohol drinking). By cunning practices and the application of *metis* tactics in the intersection of the centre's plans with local practices, the space of the Halkevi seems to be inverted: instead of functioning as a space to colonize local society and people, it becomes itself colonized by local and popular practices of entertainment and leisure.

Chapter 5 considers the consumption of the centre's policies and discourses on women. I read complaint letters about incidents during dancing parties and theatre. In largely sex-segregated and patriarchal societies similar mixed-gender events were fraught with tension, and what the state was attempting to introduce in relation to women was openly rejected and habitually accommodated to local practices they were seemingly supposed to eradicate. The tensions, disturbances and confusions Halkevi members experienced upon the performance of such events were significant in terms of identity management,[41] as they provided stimuli for the negotiation of social identities.

The final chapter examines a highly systematized, prog-rammed, and tightly centre-defined Halkevi activity – the visits of Halkevi members to villages. I read the textual products of a series of village excursions of the Kayseri Halkevi against the programmatic texts the centre had crafted on the very same activity. I then locate the similarities and divergences between the centre's designs and their execution by Halkevi actors. Their failure to strictly conform to the plans and, thus, the weakness of the state in imposing its policies in the actual practices of its various parts and agencies is revealed. I ultimately read this

Halkevi activity as a border-setting operation, significant for the crafting of the mutually constitutive discursive and practical categories of peasant/villager and peasantist/urbanite but also the boundary between them. I see that boundary management as constitutive of the self-identification of the urban, educated and modern intellectual/citizen but also of his/her understanding of the village and villager. I uncover differing perspectives and argue that the Halkevi village-related activities ultimately facilitated the emergence of competing perspectives about peasantists and peasants alike. I am referring to a social realist narrative that would dominate Turkish literature and various discourses of the centre-left and left after the 1950s in its description of villagers and subaltern classes.

In summation, this book studies social change initiated by projects of social engineering, viewing it from the local level and from the perspective of those obliged to use the products of such state projects. I contend that the notion of the state as the fulcrum of change against society treated as a silent or resistant recipient of change is a simplistic dualism that cannot be easily substantiated by the sources. I search for the common ground, the meeting spaces wherein the state and its products were consumed and negotiated. The study of these everyday acts reveals a vast array of practices of accommodation and domestication of what the ruling elite attempted to initiate and, in the end, of the state itself. But as the state is accommodated and domesticated, the consumption of its products are themselves practices of identity management. In other words, as much as people alter state policies by just using them, they themselves change. More detailed studies, perhaps monographs of individuals or families across a wider continuum and span of socio-political change, are needed to explore this process. What follows in this book can offer an elementary context for prospective endeavours in that direction.

The People's House

1

Building on the experience and manpower of earlier associations, the People's House project was launched in 1932. It
was composed of cultural centres the ruling Republican
People's Party (*Cumhuriyet Halk Partisi*, henceforth Party or
RPP) was opening and operating in urban centres all over
Turkey. As the Party's cultural branches, the Houses were
planned to propagate the regime's ideology and policies to the
population through the circulation, application and enactment
of a variety of practices, discourses and activities. The Houses
were neither an independent institution nor did they possess
any legal identity of their own; they were part of a political
party. The fact that they were exclusively financed by the
state provided the justification for their abolition and the
confiscation of their movable and immovable property. When
the opposition came to power in 1950, it convincingly argued
that for 18 years the Houses and, thus, the Party had been
lavishly enriched by state funds, which had to be returned to
the state; as a result, in 1951 the Houses were closed down and
their property confiscated.

In what follows in this chapter I trace the prehistory of the
Halkevi institution from the 1908 Young Turk Revolution until
the Houses' establishment in 1932. I then describe in detail the
People's House structure, activities and administration, and,
lastly, I offer a reading of the Halkevi project within the ruling
elite's ideological make-up and the political context of single-
party rule in the 1930s and 1940s.

Young Turk Social Engineering and 'People's Education'

The 1908 Young Turk Revolution stands as a landmark in the history of modern Turkey. United by their opposition to Abdulhamit II and their concern to save the state from disintegration, a group of political dissidents and state officials – most of whom were graduates of the Western-type schools the Ottoman state had established to staff its administration and military – formed a secret organization, the Committee of Union and Progress (CUP), and organized the 1908 Young Turk Revolution that ended the autocratic regime of Abdulhamit II and restored the 1876 constitution. The same year, elections were held and the Ottoman parliament convened again. The years following the 1908 Revolution saw Ottoman politics polarize between the CUP and the opposition as the political antagonism gradually became even more bitter and violent against the background of almost continuous warfare that started with the Ottoman–Italian war over Libya in 1911. In 1912, the armies of Bulgaria, Montenegro, Greece and Serbia conquered the entire Ottoman Balkan territories in the First Balkan War. Until then, the CUP had never totally controlled the Ottoman government, as it had to compete with other power constellations and opposition in the parliament, the military and the bureaucracy. In January 1913 the CUP staged a coup deposing the government and took complete control, ruling as a single-party regime until 1918. In World War I the Ottoman Empire aligned with the Central Powers and lost at great demographic, financial and social cost.

Although ruling the Empire through continuous warfare, the CUP was able to introduce a number of sweeping changes in the administrative, educational and legal structures of the Ottoman state predating and prefiguring the reforms of the Republican period after 1923. The Ottoman state was made a constitutional monarchy and the sultan's prerogatives were severely reduced. The army was reorganized and provincial administration was put in order with the 1913 Provincial Administration Law. The position of the *ulema* (religious functionaries) was undermined. The highest religious official (*şeyhülislam*) was removed from cabinet; previously controlled by the *ulema*, religious schools, courts and foundations were reorganized and placed under state control, while the new inheritance (1913) and family (1917) laws, although technically within religious law, granted women more rights of inheritance and choices of marriage and divorce. Women were encouraged to study and participate in social life, and in 1913 basic education was made compulsory for girls. New schools for girls opened and women were accepted into university.[1]

Following the capitulation of Bulgaria, the Empire signed the armistice of Moudros in October 1918. The top Unionist leaders fled the country, but the military and civil administration was still in Unionist hands. In the aftermath of the armistice, a resistance movement organized and led by Unionist forces emerged in Anatolia. It gained impetus with the invasion of Izmir by the Greek army and the signing of the peace Treaty of Sèvres in 1920 which virtually erased the Ottoman Empire from the map of Anatolia. Ultimately, the nationalists fought and won a war to annul it and under the leadership of Mustafa Kemal the victorious nationalist forces signed the Treaty of Lausanne establishing the Republic of Turkey in 1923. Left with an independent but ruined country and a devastated population, the ruling elites around Mustafa Kemal have been since hailed for the extensive reforms they initiated during the 1920s and 1930s that gave shape to the modern Turkish state and society.

During its first years the Republic of Turkey went through a brief phase of multi-party politics. In 1924 an opposition party was formed in the National Assembly and the press was relatively free to criticize the ruling RPP. In 1925 the outbreak of a Kurdish rebellion in the east of the country offered the ruling party the pretext to silence and purge the opposition. To counter the rebellion, the government was granted extraordinary powers that were immediately used against the insurgents in the east but also against the opposition; the oppositional party and many newspapers were closed and a number of journalists prosecuted. The purges continued with the trials of prominent opposition leaders after a failed assassination attempt against Mustafa Kemal in 1926. As a consequence, after 1925, Turkey was in effect ruled as a single-party regime with a parliamentary facade. The government's extraordinary powers were kept in force even after the crushing of the Kurdish rebellion as a means to repress any resistance to the reforms or any potential opposition to the regime. In 1930, Mustafa Kemal decided to experiment with multi-party politics, entrusting the formation of an opposition party to a close associate and friend. Although envisaged as a loyal opposition, the Free Republican Party rapidly attracted much popular support and revealed the population's extensive dissatisfaction. After three months and the contemporaneous outburst of popular discontent, the Free Republican Party was dissolved by its own leader. A month after its dissolution, a small group of militant Islamists entered Menemen, a small town in the west of Turkey, and proclaimed the restoration of sharia, the Islamic law, in the local mosque. Then in front of the congregation and other assembled townspeople, they killed three policemen who tried to arrest them. The incident ended swiftly with the arrival of more policemen as in the ensuing fight some of the militants were killed and the remaining arrested. Alarmed by information that some among the crowd had applauded the militants' acts, the government's reaction was harsh: martial law was declared and tens of people were executed or imprisoned, while the fallen officers were declared heroes of the Kemalist reforms 'martyred' by reactionaries and enemies of the republic.

The Free Party experiment and the Menemen incident exposed the extent of the population's dissatisfaction. In response, the regime turned towards more authoritarian policies and for the next 16 years, until the end of World War II, Turkey was ruled as an authoritarian single-party regime exhibiting extremely limited tolerance even to the most subtle criticism. In the postwar period, Turkey aligned with the West, and as an ally of Western parliamentary democracies went through a gradual liberalization of its political regime. Political parties were permitted and multi-party politics established in 1946. The process was so successful that in the 1950 elections the Democrat Party could gravely defeat the Republican People's Party and end its uninterrupted rule of the previous 27 years.

Upon the political context briefly sketched above, the ruling elite of the republic embarked upon a comprehensive reform programme that followed and built upon the Unionist reforms of the period 1913–18. In the first years of the republic, the legal and educational framework of the new state was set up. The sultanate and caliphate were abolished and the country was declared a republic. The Islamic law was abolished and European legal codes filled the void. The Law for the Unification of Education in 1924 abolished all religious schools and established a unitary state educational system. The role and position of the religious functionaries were thus curtailed and they were closely controlled (as civil servants) by the state Directorship of Religious Affairs. Following the consolidation of the regime after the purges of 1925 and in effect under conditions resembling martial law, the political leadership went even further. In 1925 it abolished the Islamic brotherhoods (tarikat) and closed their places of worship. Next, the fez and other local headgear were prohibited and replaced by the Western hat, and the international clock and calendar were introduced in 1926. In 1929 a Latinized alphabet and Western numerals replaced the Arabic ones used in Ottoman Turkish. Western measures were introduced in the 1930s, and women were given the right to vote (1930) and be elected (1934).

In essence, the reforms consisted of the extensive discarding of a series of educational, administrative, legal and symbolic structures, from religious law, courts, schools and brotherhoods to political associations and pieces of clothing. In their place, 'modern' and 'national' ones were translated, adopted and invented from Western or local sources. The civil, penal and commercial legal codes that were to replace older and/or religious law were translated and adopted from Europe as was the case with the hat and Western numerals, calendar and measures that replaced the local ones. The language reform though was a more complex project involving, on the one hand, the adoption of a Latinized alphabet in place of the Ottoman-Arabic version, and, on the other hand, the extensive replacement of Arabic and Persian words with supposedly 'pure Turkish' ones retrieved among the people of Turkey or kin Turkic populations in central Asia, *but also* invented by linguistic engineers.[2] An official national history was also invented, downplaying the Ottoman and Islamic aspects of Turkish history while emphasizing the pre-Ottoman and pre-Islamic past of the Turks. To assist in the process of inventing the republic's national language and history, the Turkish History and Language societies were established in 1931 and 1932 respectively.[3] And to propagate the new national script, language and history, and to facilitate the regime's nation-building project, a series of educational and propaganda structures were established. The Village Institutes (1940–50), for instance, trained village youths and had them return to their villages as teachers and carriers of everything the new republic sought to instil in the villagers – the majority of the population which otherwise the state could not properly reach due to its infrastructural weakness. Planned to modernize and Turkify the villager, the state established 21 institutes that trained more than 15,000 village youths until their abolition in 1950.[4] The People's House was probably the most distinctive institution the interwar Turkish leadership established to propagate its ideology and policies, but it was not the first such attempt; in fact, Unionists and Turkish nationalist intellectuals had established a series of similar institutions since the 1908 Revolution.

There was a profound continuity in the ideological make-up, policies and cadre between Unionists and Kemalists.[5] These state elites were deeply influenced by the positivism and social Darwinism of the nineteenth century. They saw Western science as the means to reform society and save the state. In the course of imperial disintegration, they became Turkish nationalists unwavering in their resolution to instil national consciousness and create the Turkish nation out of the Muslim populations of Anatolia. As elitists they shared a deep distrust of the masses. They never believed in popular representation – in contrast to their declarations that their power was based on popular sovereignty – as they considered the masses to be backward and irrational. They were bent rather on enlightening and leading that population through the mobilization of educated elites like themselves into instructing the masses.[6] The need to educate and awaken the people into nationhood was probably one of the most consistent and ubiquitous motifs of the emerging Turkish nationalism since the late nineteenth century.[7] But it was the Young Turks, Unionists and then Kemalists who made it one of their key objectives.

With the 1908 Revolution, a conscious Unionist policy was to reach, discover and, ultimately, educate the people. The need to reach and educate the people was an idea pronounced in the thought and preaching of Ziya Gökalp. Considered the father of Turkish nationalism, he was one of the most influential thinkers and Unionist leaders of his era (he died in 1924). One of the recurrent themes of his writings was the need to awaken the people, and his famous distinction between civilization and culture is of great relevance. In his theoretical scheme, the Turkish nation would be the product of a synthesis of civilization, which he considered singular and essentially international/Western, and culture, which was national and intimate. For Gökalp, the elites were the carriers of civilization: 'the intellectuals and the thinkers of a nation constitute its elite [...] separated from the masses by their higher education and learning.' Culture, on the other hand, was to be found among the masses, the people. The elite's duty then was to reach the people in a move that was envisaged as a double act of instilling modern, that is, Western, civilization in the people, while also retrieving and reclaiming the 'true' national culture that was alive among them.[8]

Within their objective to mould the Muslims of Anatolia into becoming a modern and civilized nation, both regimes gave great emphasis to reform of the educational system, as it was seen as the primary means to modernize and nationalize society, but also to legitimize their power through the creation and widening of their constituency. But apart from improving state education and expanding schooling, both Unionists and Kemalists underscored the need to instruct and train the people. The CUP, for instance, embarked on a huge effort to propagate its ideology and policies through establishing or patronizing a number of clubs and societies,[9] among them cultural associations aiming at the 'people's training' (*terbiye-yi avam*)[10] or their 'civilizational training' (*terbiye-yi medeniyeye*); National Libraries;[11] female associations working for the promotion of women's rights in education, professional and cultural life, and the raising of their cultural level; paramilitary youth associations aiming to prepare the youth for war through sports, physical and military training (*terbiye-yi bedeniye*); societies to promote the national economy or carry out charitable work; and peasant associations to raise the educational, hygienic, cultural and civilization level of the villager. Hanioğlu has shown that the Unionists were well aware of their distance from the population and consciously created divisions to cater to key interest groups (women, the *ulema*, professional associations and youths). Special branches under the CUP Central Committee were created to supervise societies, unions and CUP clubs, while special attention was paid to the broadcasting of their message through the press and the monopolization of public space.[12]

The CUP opened Union and Progress Clubs (*İttihad ve Terakki Kulübü*) throughout the country with very much the same objectives; they were envisaged as places of political and social instruction. To take the example of a Unionist Club that is well researched, the Union and Progress Club of the town of Konya was predominately staffed by civil servants, teachers and local elites, and organized lectures for the education of the people and the youth and night courses for apprentices and jail inmates; distributed medicine and medically treated villagers and the city poor and assisted them in their dealings with state authorities; organized exhibitions of local products and attempted to promote the economic policies of the CUP; and connected its space and activities with those of a local private school opened by the CUP (*Konya İttihad ve Terakki Mektebi*), the local Turkish Hearth (*Türk Ocağı*), the local Unionist press and a local CUP theatre initiative named after the Unionist ideologue Gökalp (*Gökalp Tiyatrosu*).[13]

A characteristic trait of the Unionist fervour to educate the people was perhaps the establishment of associations that targeted distinct population categories. Next to the notion of 'the people', the youth, women and villagers also appeared as separate population categories targeted for instruction, disciplining and mobilization. The Unionist leadership organized and mobilized university students,[14] but also established paramilitary youth associations to promote military and physical training, prepare the nation for war, deliver conferences and courses, and visit villages to promote hygiene and physical training among the villagers.[15] Women's societies, on the other hand, although usually established as charitable associations, debated and promoted the participation of women in educational, professional and cultural life, while they struggled to raise the cultural level of women with lectures and through publishing newspapers and journals.[16]

Peasantist societies were also established in order to facilitate the scientific, educational, medical and agricultural progress of the villager. These were associations that would realize the Unionist vision and slogan to 'go to the people' to help, instruct and bring civilization, education, hygiene and modern science to the village, while working among them in 'a humanitarian [insaniyetkar] manner'.[17] Even paramilitary organizations such as the Müdafaa-i Milliye Cemiyeti (National Defence Association) and the Türk Gücü Cemiyeti (Turkish Strength Association) were supposed to visit villages to improve their living conditions.[18] Composing an integral part of the Unionist endeavour to reach the people, the peasantist trait was probably reinforced by the close contact elite members had with villagers and the countryside during the war. Consider the words Mustafa Kemal devoted, in a letter to a female friend, to his peasant soldiers in Gallipoli, at once demeaning and respectful: 'My soldiers are very brave. Their private beliefs make it easier to carry out orders which send them to their death. They see only two supernatural outcomes: victory for the faith or martyrdom. Do you know what the second means? It is to go straight to heaven. There, the houris, God's most beautiful women, will meet them and will satisfy their desires for all eternity. What great happiness?'[19] The villager and village life was introduced in the literary canon in essence during the republican period, a fact that by itself exhibits the elites' growing interest in the peasant.[20]

In short, the CUP created an umbrella of societies striving to enlighten the population in line with its ideology and mind-set. These societies placed special emphasis on the training (*terbiye*) of the people through publications, lectures, discussions, concerts and gatherings, the use of sports, theatre, cinema and music, through social assistance and charity activities, and visits to villages to medically treat and improve the living conditions of their inhabitants. Nevertheless, within the dire conditions of continuous warfare, the results could not have been but minimal.

In the republican period, few of the above associations survived, the Turkish Hearths (*Türk Ocakları*) being the most significant. Established in 1911–12, by 1913 the Turkish Hearth was receiving the full support of the CUP and opened many branches in the provinces that were closely cooperating with local CUP offices. The Hearths aspired to gather the youth and enlighten the people through publishing,[21] courses and lectures. They supported schools, assisted and guided villagers, and promoted physical training, sports, theatre and the participation of women in public life.[22] Re-established after the war in 1924, the Hearths adopted a more systematized structure than before, reflected in their programme of activities. With state assistance, they expanded enormously and the content of their programme and works became more concrete, as they had to work within a more stable political and ideological setting than before. From 71 branches and an 8,900 Turkish lire budget in 1924, they soared to 267 branches, over 32,000 members and a budget of 1.5 million lire in 1931. But in contrast to their spectacular growth, the Hearths remained an elite society. Most members were teachers, doctors, officers, lawyers and state functionaries, and it seems that there was a conscious choice to restrict membership to these occupational categories to the extent that by 1925 some members criticized the society's elite character and requested that the Hearths become the real 'Houses of the People' (*Halkevi*).[23]

The Hearths' goal was to reinforce national consciousness and promote Turkish culture, to facilitate the progress of civilization and hygiene, and the development of the national economy. According to their 1926 programme of activities (*Türk Ocakları Mesai Programı*), every Hearth would organize weekly conferences on Fridays to instruct the people about the economy, history, geography, local researches, fine arts and other relevant subjects; establish public libraries; collect photographs of the their region; set up lecture halls where journals and periodicals would be exhibited; organize exhibitions of local products and artefacts; work for the preservation of the Turkish culture by assembling and recording popular traditions, folk songs, dances and music; visit villages and examine the population, distribute medicine, fight against contagious diseases and help ameliorate the local means of production; teach foreign languages and open courses on commercial and agricultural techniques or technical specialties.

One of the Hearths' primary duties was the diffusion of the reforms to the masses and, thus, to act as 'the guardians of the revolution'.[24] Many Hearths established propaganda committees (*irşad heyetleri*) to enlighten villagers while their members taught thousands of citizens how to read and write in the new Latin script.[25] A continuation of the pre-war Turkish Hearth, the activities of the Turkish Hearths after 1923 were more canonized and systematized than before; we now observe the drawing of an organized operational plan in line with state and Party objectives. In supporting the regime, the Hearths tied themselves to the Party to the extent that by 1927 they were in practice controlled by it.[26] But only four years later they were closed down.

The year 1930 is considered a turning point in the history of modern Turkey. A series of events led towards a more authoritarian restructuring of the regime. More specifically, the repercussions of the 1929 crisis, the unsuccessful experiment at a loyal opposition with the Free Party and the events that occurred during its short life, exacerbated by the Menemen incident and ongoing Kurdish rebellions in the east, had a profound effect on

the Kemalist leadership.[27] Following the dissolution of the Free
Party, the ruling elite went through a period of 'soul-searching';
Atatürk embarked on a long investigative trip throughout the
country in search of solutions.[28]

One of the first changes was the 1931 Press Law, which severely
restricted the freedom of press and established its close control by
the government. The suffocation of the press continued in the
1930s. In 1934, for instance, the aims of the state Directorship of
Press and Publications (*Matbuat ve Neşriyat Umum Müdürlüğü*)
were to monitor the local and foreign press and see that they
functioned in accordance with the national aims, state policies and
the revolution's principles. The press was expected to propagate
the regime's principles while fighting against its enemies, helping
the government in its policies, and becoming 'the most modern
school in the political, economic and cultural education of the
people.'[29]

Along with the suffocation of the press, another feature of
regime policy was the expansion of the ruling Party's prerogatives
introduced with the Party reorganization, the drafting of a detailed
programme and the modification of its by-laws during the 3rd
Party Congress in 1931. These changes were especially related to
the elite's concern for the education and political indoctrination
of the people.[30] Responding to the Free Party debacle, the Party
leadership had many trusted Party elites investigate the issue; a
common thread in most of their reports was the Party's failure to
propagate its message and reach the population.[31] In parallel, the
Party leadership attempted to increase its control of the provincial
Party but also of society at large, a tendency that had already been
initiated with the first organizational attempt during the 1927
Party Congress. The new orientation was especially ominous for
the agents of civil society. Throughout the 1930s there was a long
list of non-state or non-Party societies that were either closed,
or joined – probably under pressure – state or Party structures
like the People's Houses.[32] Teachers' unions, amateur theatre and
Youth Unions, the Press Society, the Reserve Officers' Association,
the Union of Turkish Women, Masonic lodges and the National

Students' Union were closed down or merged with the Party under the slogan of 'unifying the forces of the revolution'.[33]

The Turkish Folklore Society (*Türk Halk Bilgisi Derneği*) is an illustrative example. Established in Istanbul in 1927, it was a non-state association whose aim was to open branches in the provinces to carry out research and collect folkloric material that they would then 'give back' to the people through lectures, shows, speeches and publications. Emphasis was also laid on the Society's duty to guide the people and organize activities that would 'make the masses feel the national self'. In 1932, the Society had to merge with the Halkevi of Istanbul and their journal *Halk Bilgisi Haberleri* became the *Eminönü Halkevi* journal.[34]

The tendency to limit the autonomy of social forces that were out of the regime's direct reach was also manifested in the centre's policy to establish a state organization of physical training that would centrally control and direct all sport and physical training associations and activities in the country.[35] The 1933 university reform was another example of how 'the aim to create a university that would support political power and defend the principles of the Turkish Revolution was realized'.[36]

One of the first casualties of this policy to curtail civil society was the Turkish Hearth.[37] During his inspection trip in January 1931, Mustafa Kemal informed the press of his decision to open 'Great People's Houses'.[38] In April 1931 an extraordinary congress of the Turkish Hearths was convened and took the decision to dissolve the society and transfer all property to the Party. In May 1931 the 3rd Party Congress ratified the transfer and conferred the duty to open People's Houses on the Party branches.[39] In less than a year a Party committee had prepared the Halkevi by-laws and in February 1932 the first People's Houses opened. They numbered 14 and most were established in the buildings of the dissolved Turkish Hearths.[40]

To sum up, an intellectual movement within the framework of the emerging Turkish nationalism in the Young Turk era preaching the need for the education of the people continued with clearer aims in the republican period. From 1912, the

Turkish Hearths society was the headquarters of an intellectual and political movement calling for the education of the people into Western civilization and Turkish nationhood. During the first part of their life, the continuous state of war and the collapse of the Ottoman Empire limited their activities, but with the establishment of the Republic of Turkey in 1923, the Turkish Hearths were restructured, and with Party and state support adopted a more organized make-up and activities' programme. They continued to expand throughout the 1920s and tried to operate as the regime's guardian and propagandist. However, when the regime turned towards more authoritarian policies at the beginning of the 1930s, the Turkish Hearths were closed and the political indoctrination of the regime came under total Party and state control. An immediate product of the regime's concern to propagate its message was the People's Orators Organization (*Halk Hatipleri Teşkilatı*), established by the Party in 1931. The People's Orators were to be chosen from Party members to address the population during state anniversaries, national and local elections and during village fests and open markets. Their by-laws stated in great detail how they were to address the people and even what clothes they were supposed to wear when delivering speeches about specific subjects, such as 'the Republican regime', 'the Party program and principles', and 'Turkish history, civilization and bravery'.[41] The Halkevi institution followed the next year and the pressing need for the political indoctrination of the population is already evident in the preamble to their by-laws:

> We have the obligation and duty to pull out from the deepest structures of society the roots of the institutions that already belong to the past, and clinch the principles of the republic and of the revolution in the form of the holiest provisions to all spirits and opinions. As we are not far away from the Menemen incident and other similar events, we are evidently obliged to quickly move away from negative developments. The power and speed the nations show in their way towards the road of life is parallel to

and commensurate with the work of guidance and education that is carried out.[42]

The People's House

All People's Houses were designed to have an identical structure and perform identical activities described in their by-laws.[43] Every House was directed by an administrative committee and had nine working sections headed by sectional committees elected every two years. The by-laws stipulated that the Houses were places of gathering and work and that all citizens could become members irrespective of party affiliation. Nevertheless, only Party members or state employees could staff their administrative and sectional committees, while schoolteachers in particular were recommended to join their activities.[44] The above stipulations offer a clear sight of the regime's blurred intentions: although directly owned by a political Party, the Halkevi was emphatically presented as a non-political structure. Thus, all citizens and civil servants, who were forbidden by law to join any political association, could become members, but only Party members or civil servants could become committee members. The method for the selection of the House executives confirmed the same paradox. The administrative committee was composed of the House chairman and one representative from every section elected among the sectional executive members; but while the sectional committee members were elected by those registered to each section, the chairman was directly appointed by the local Party structure, usually by its members.[45] The obvious contradiction was that a tightly controlled and hierarchical Party structure was presented as if it were a non-political cultural organization where free will and equality reigned.

The decision for the opening of a People's House was taken by the Party headquarters in Ankara, but it was the provincial Party branches that in effect established and controlled the Houses.[46] The local Party controlled the Houses' finances, ratifying and inspecting their budgets, which were provided by Party and state revenues,[47] while the House administrative committee performed the everyday management. It organized the public shows at national anniversaries; facilitated the execution of the House's programmes; preserved the working harmony between the sections and arbitrated in disputes; examined and ratified any sectional by-laws; kept the accounts and supervised the heavy equipment; prepared and carried through the budget;[48] and took disciplinary decisions and decided upon the employment and dismissal of the House's employees.[49]

A clear separation of responsibilities was introduced between local and central Party structures in relation to the monitoring of the activities of the Houses. The Halkevi administrative committee was to communicate with the local Party in relation to financial and administrative matters, and with the Party's General Secretariat about the House's activities.[50] In addition, every House had to report on its activities to both the local and central Party at set intervals.[51] The remnants of this communication between Party branches, Houses all over Turkey and the Party headquarters in Ankara are vast. Thousands of reports, communiqués, letters and all kinds of written material are preserved in the Turkish State Archives. Some are reports and letters sent by the provinces; others are the centre's orders and communiqués to the provinces. The central Party even published a section of these circulars in 21 consecutive volumes from 1931 to 1945 to function as a tool in its effort to control and direct the Party and Halkevi activities. Some of the circulars were clearly one-way, top-down requests, but there were also many responses of the centre to issues that had been raised in the provinces. This is revealed by some of the circulars but it is most clearly demonstrated by the sheer number of documents sent from the provinces to Ankara, which are preserved in the archives. Based on these data it is safe to argue that the Houses did not *solely* function as a mechanism for the top-down transmission of the centre's policies; on the contrary, as we will see in the following chapters, the communication functioned the other way around too, as local societies routinely exploited the Halkevi and its resources to further local aims and express local interests to the centre, which in no way can be considered immune to these 'signals from below'.[52] In this sense, the Houses should rather be considered as junctions in a two-way communication between centre and local societies, or as 'junctures of state and society', to use Migdal's terminology.[53]

The nine working sections were as follows: 1. Language, History and Literature; 2. Fine Arts; 3. Theatre; 4. Sports; 5. Social Assistance; 6. Courses; 7. Library and Publications; 8. Village; and 9. Museum and Exhibitions. In 1940 the first section became 'Language and Literature' and the last one 'History and Museum'.

The Language and Literature section was designed to execute propagandistic and educational activities, such as to organize lectures to raise the general level of knowledge and 'establish the principles of the Republic and the Revolution, and increase patriotism'. It was supposed to carry out research on history, language and folklore, collect 'ancient national fairy tales, sayings, proverbs, and traditions', publish the House's journal, and organize ceremonies to commemorate the 'Great Turks' in the fields of literature, knowledge and the arts. The section would also participate in the reform of the Turkish language through the collection of words and expressions in local use and through publications.[54]

The Fine Arts section would gather people active and interested in music, sculpture, architecture and the decorative arts; organize concerts and music events; ensure that 'the modern and international music is performed in its true nature'; increase the number of those interested in the fine arts through organizing courses if possible; help all the people learn the national marches; record the notes, harmony and style of 'national songs recited among the people'; promote national dances and incorporate them into its shows; encourage men and women to dance together; and organize painting and photography exhibitions.[55]

The Theatre section had to establish a mixed-gender theatrical group and stage plays that were either previously approved or recommended by Ankara. Men were explicitly prohibited from playing female roles. The section was also recommended to support popular shadow theatre and puppet shows. The popular *Karagöz* shadow theatre was considered so important in terms of propaganda that the Party commissioned, published and had the Houses stage new shadow theatre plays to bolster its image; traditional popular literary forms were used to lure the attendance and facilitate the absorption by the people of stories of the popular hero *Karagöz* giving his support to the reforms.[56] The centre thought of cinema the same way: the section could acquire a cinema projector and organize public, and free of charge, projections of the films the Party would send in order to 'raise the ideas and good taste of the People through the means of cinema'. In short, cinema and theatre were primarily seen as means to propagate the Party ideology rather than as arts in their own right.[57]

The Sports section was to mobilize gymnastics teachers and organize sporting events; 'teach citizens indoor gymnastics, which are the foundation of modern hygiene'; and establish spaces for physical training. Once a week it would organize a gymnastics event, separately for men and women. Certain 'national sports' were recommended such as hunting, horse riding and wrestling together with other, equally masculine, sports: fencing instructed by army officers, boxing, cycling, winter sports (skiing in particular) and sea sports, especially swimming. Although preparing the people for war was not mentioned among the section's objectives, one cannot but underline the affinity of physical training and war preparation as it was expressed in the Ottoman youth and paramilitary associations established during World War I. However, more so with the establishment of a nationwide state physical training association by the late 1930s, which resembled – and whose establishment was probably influenced by – similar institutions in European totalitarian regimes of the period.[58]

The Social Assistance section was to cooperate with charitable societies and doctors, and conduct philanthropic activities, acting 'as a guide for the transport of those who need medical treatment', and providing 'shelter to farmers and their families who come from the villages in need of medical treatment' and 'struggling to find jobs for the jobless'. The section was to materially and medically assist orphan students, the disabled and sick, war veterans and single women, the elders, and, with the cooperation of the Village section, the villagers.[59]

The Courses section was to organize courses taught by volunteers on various subjects, from reading and writing, foreign languages, sciences and art courses to history and local information, civilization, accounting and typing. Attesting to the positivist ideological roots of Unionist and Kemalist social engineering and of the Halkevi project, the section could also set up of physics or chemistry laboratories to introduce the exact sciences to the people.[60]

The Library and Publications section's duty was to establish and run a library that would be open to everybody free of charge. It could also establish reading rooms and book exhibitions.[61] The by-laws meticulously listed the prohibited books, offering a short but detailed description of the regime's own spectres: 'Books of religious nature, [books] that do not comply to the ideology of the Turkish Revolution, that depict foreign regimes and ideologies, spread superstitions against the general national and realistic opinions, propagate backward and reactionary mentalities, inspire pessimism, depict crime and suicide, works that increase the inclination for lust and greed and encourage the youth to harmful habits.' All foreign publications were to be sent to the General Secretariat before being placed in the House's library.[62] Halkevi libraries were seen not only as a means to raise the educational level of the people but to propagate the regime's ideology. For the Party secretary and Interior Minister Şükrü Kaya, the Halkevi libraries were 'nests of illumination and guidance' that would 'make the revolution of Atatürk take roots among the people.'[63]

The Village section 'works towards the material, aesthetic and sanitary progress and growth of the villagers, as well as towards strengthening the feelings of mutual affection and solidarity between the villages and the city dweller', 'by means of inviting the villagers of the nearby places to the Halkevi fests and the House members to the countryside festivals'. It would also cooperate with the Social Assistance section to expand their activities to the countryside.[64]

Finally, the Museum and History section was to assist in the establishment or enrichment of museums, organize exhibitions of works of arts and of 'national products and manufactures', and assemble ethnological and folklore material. All the materials to be collected were to be registered in an inventory to be sent to the General Secretariat.[65]

To give a picture of what the Party prescribed to all Houses, a look at the 'People's Houses' minimum activity plan' is enough. It is a large (80 x 60 cm) single-sheet annual timetable printed in red and black ink. Filled with the minimum activities the House sections had to perform within a year, the 'activity plan' was sent to all Houses. According to the plan, the House administrative committee convened to organize the elections of Sectional Committees, arrange the House activities during state holidays, ratify the House's budget and compile the two bi-annual reports to Ankara. The Language and Literature section organized lectures on various issues: 'training/inculcation' (*terbiye*) and 'child upbringing', 'hygiene', 'history and geography', 'popular literature' and 'folklore', 'agriculture', 'economy' and 'legislation', and 'revolution and republic'. The Fine Arts section organized ten family meetings, two musical evenings and two concerts, one with 'Western musical instruments' and the other with 'folk' ones where the collective singing and dancing of folk songs and dances were to be encouraged. The Theatre section staged one play every month from the Halkevi theatre repertoire of the Party; during the summer it staged plays in other Houses but also performed theatre, folk puppet and shadow theatre in nearby villages. The Sport section organized summer and winter sports, collective sport exercises and competitions, and participated in the 'Youth and Sport' public holiday. The Social Assistance section cooperated with charitable societies to help poor students and the needy. Once a year the earnings from one play and one ball were used to support the section's work. The Courses section taught Turkish to illiterates, and the Library and Publication section organized a book fair and operated a travelling book cabinet. The Village section organized visits to villages, travelling exhibitions and countryside fests, with wrestling and local sports competitions.[66]

The Halkevi by-laws seem to draw a very meticulous programme of activities and set very tight standards of what was permissible and what was not. From the use of the radio, the performance of sports, cinema and theatre to the publication and use of books and journals and the activities' reports the Houses had to send to Ankara, the by-laws seem to establish a very tight control of the Houses' activities by the centre. Due to their normative nature, however – as the blueprint of a social engineering project – the by-laws do not consider the local societies and conditions within which the Houses operated and thus portray a picture of uniformity and singularity. In the following chapters I trace the employment of the blueprint within local societies.

Up until their closure in 1951, almost 500 People's Houses were gradually established. During the early years of the 1930s, Houses were established in cities and large towns, usually in provincial administrative centres, but progressively smaller towns acquired their Houses as well. Although an urban structure, the Houses attempted to address the villagers through the activities of their Village sections, but for various reasons their potential was severely limited. By the late 1930s the Party endeavoured to overcome this deficiency by opening People's Rooms (Halkodaları) in villages. The People's Rooms were described as 'cultural institutions, like the People's Houses, that work and follow the Republican People's Party's principles' in villages. They were opened and controlled by the local Party 'in places not considered suitable for the opening of a People's House, due to economic, personnel and building-related shortcomings'. They had a much smaller organizational structure than the People's Houses. They were not divided into sections but were directed by an administrative committee elected among their members; their chairmen were elected among committee members but their appointment had to be ratified by the local Party. Although open to all citizens, their executives had to be Party members or civil servants. The Rooms were to communicate with the Party General Secretary regarding issues relating to their activities and with the local Party on administrative or financial matters. Necessary conditions for the opening of a People's Room were the existence of at least 50 members, a meeting and a reading room (or a reading cabinet), and funds for the first year's budget. As for the Rooms' expected activities, they had to 'be a clean place for gathering and discussions' on useful subjects that would 'arouse the interest of the people' and facilitate 'the reading of the journals and newspapers that the local Party administration deems appropriate'. Their libraries after all were to contain 'all the works that aim at the spreading, establishment and implanting of the principles of the Turkish revolution among the people'. To fulfil these aims they would invite lecturers from the People's Houses and organize the celebration of national holidays, exhibitions of local products, and the performing of sports like wrestling, hunting and riding, but also of local popular music and dances, shadow theatre, puppet shows and theatrical plays. The Rooms were also to provide social assistance to the local poor and ill.[67] In short, the status, administration, activities and aims of the People's Rooms were an abridged version of the Halkevi devised for the use of villagers. Although a few Rooms managed to develop and be turned into People's Houses, most were simply inactive. A contemporary witness wrote that although a teacher or a discharged soldier might occasionally run and enliven one, most Rooms were dormant, empty structures.[68]

Up to 1946, more than 4,000 Rooms were established, although most were not properly – if at all – functioning, as was openly acknowledged in the 7th Party Congress in 1946.[69] After 1945, and in all probability due to the emergence of multi-party politics, very few Houses and Rooms were opened. The liberalization of the political regime after World War II and the emergence of a vibrant political opposition transformed the status of the People's Houses and Rooms into a bitter political feud. The opposition accused the government of financing a Party organization from the state budget. The Houses and Rooms were not independent institutions; as a matter of fact they did not have any legal identity at all, as they were parts of the RPP and all the property they had accumulated through state funding was Party property. In 1947 the RPP tried to find a solution that would guarantee the existence of the Houses in a multi-party regime. During the 1947 Party Congress, a special committee prepared a report on the Halkevi institution. Accepted by the Congress, the report asked the Party leadership to turn the Houses into a legally recognized – and thus protected – foundation. Inertia or the bad old habits of single-party rule impeded that project. After their landslide victory in the 1950 elections, the Democrat Party passed law 5830 of 11 August 1951 that closed down the People's Houses and Rooms and transferred all their movable and immovable property to the state.[70]

Table 1: Number of Houses and Rooms from 1932 to 1950.

Year	People's House	People's Room
1932	14	-
1933	55	-
1936	103	-
1938	210	-
1939	373	-
1940	379	141
1943	394	231
1945	438	2,688
1946	455	4,068
1950	478	4,322

From CHP 18. Yıldönümünde Halkevleri ve Halkodaları (Ankara, 1950), 6–8.

Nation-Building and its Paradoxes in the Intellectual and Political Context of Interwar Turkey

The People's Houses were established by the RPP in 1932 as an institution of People's Education (*Halk Terbiyesi*). At the opening ceremony of the first People's Houses in 1932, the Party Secretary, Recep Peker,[71] explained the reasons for their establishment.

> We have firmly decided to raise the national unity in a painstaking work and assemble all the fellow citizens under the roof of the Halkevleri [...] The school is the classical institution a country has to prepare the nation for the future. However, in order to organize and educate the modern nation as an entity, the usual methods and the regular efforts are not sufficient; if you want to become a nation in this century and form a national community [*milletçe kütleşmek*], you'll have to establish a people's training in parallel and after the schools that will make the people work together as an unit.[72]

For an intellectual deeply involved in the Halkevi project, the first aim of *Halk Terbiyesi* was the attainment of national consciousness.[73] People's education strived 'to organize the nation and bring out our national values' by means of educating 'the individual in a way that is appropriate for the whole nation's ideal' and 'kneading the parts of [the] nation that have come apart due to different accents, levels of civilization and religious sects, into a social body, into the shape of a nation'. But it was not only about offering knowledge, as it had 'to stimulate the desire to move forward and become civilized'.[74]

There was agreement on the inadequacy of the educational system to instruct the people in the way the state leadership wished. People's education called for the instruction of those segments of the population the school had not reached – adults and, especially, the villagers. The contents and aims of this instruction were manifold, but the most urgent one was simply to mould the population of Turkey into a homogenous Turkish nation, the parameters of which – national language, history, folklore – had been and were still in the process of being set in the 1930s. The People's Houses' first objective was to facilitate the Kemalist nation-building project that was under way. The Houses and their activities were primarily attuned to that goal. Consider, for instance, the Houses' duty to teach the national anthem to the population, Turkish to non-Turkish speakers, or the participation of all Houses in the formation of the state-sanctioned Turkish national culture and history through linguistic and historic research and the collection of folkloric material, but also in the dissemination of this national culture through the Houses' activities or through public ceremonies.

But apart from solely being a form of civic education into nationhood, *Halk Terbiyesi* was at the same time aiming at 'raising of the level of civilization' of the people, as the jargon of the period had it. Its aim was to create a homogenous population that would possess both modern and national qualities. In Interior Minister Şükrü Kaya's words, 'the decisions and activities of the People's House must be carried out in an entirely Western, modern, and national mentality'.[75] In several cases, Kemalist intellectuals would prefer to call the work to be carried out simply and directly 'creation' or 'engineering' (*inşa*). The homogenous nation had to be engineered through 'civilizational means' (*medeni cihazlar*).[76] In that respect, the Halkevi by-laws gave special emphasis to the performing and teaching of Western music and musical instruments, Western types of physical training and sports, lecturing and courses on 'scientific' subjects (hygiene, economy, agriculture, etc.), but also a host of novel social practices that were identified as modern and civilized, such as, for instance, mixed-gender theatre, cinema, radio listening and dancing parties. In its attempt to realize the Gökalpian synthesis of national culture and international civilization, the aims and means of *Halk Terbiyesi* were obviously grounded upon the political practice and ideological universe of the Unionist and Kemalist leaderships.

Turning to the ideological connotation of *Halk Terbiyesi*, I would argue that the choice of the word *terbiye* was probably not entirely coincidental when it comes to describing the elite's desiderata: some of the term's meanings and connotations are 'upbringing', '(training in) good manners', 'civilized behaviour', 'learning through practice' rather than 'knowledge', 'education' and 'learning through teaching'. In Turkish, *terbiyeli* is a person with 'good manners', 'civil', while *terbiyesiz* is an uncouth and rude person, bearing close semantic similarities with words used to describe unsophisticated peasants and provincials (*köylü, taşralı, kurnaz*). In contrast to education that points to the enlightening of the educated, *terbiye* refers more to the process of instructing, controlling and disciplining its object.[77] Viewed from such a lexicographic perspective, *Halk Terbiyesi* appears a civilizing and disciplining operation, almost a colonial mission to civilize the indigenous Other of the country's periphery.[78] In a fashion parallel to the emphasis on *Halk Terbiyesi*, the civic training courses in Turkish schools were revised in the 1930s, replacing the liberal content of previous textbooks that emphasized the citizen's duties and rights with a more militant content emphasizing only the citizen's duties towards the state and the nation. For Üstel, this 'state-centred militant understanding of citizenship' was clearly aiming at producing homogenous single-type citizens through 'national training' (*milli terbiye*) in line with Party principles.[79]

For contemporaries, *terbiye* was consciously used as propaganda.[80] Most Halkevi activities were seen, reported and recorded as propaganda activities – the Halkevi lectures, publications, theatre plays, puppet theatre[81] and cinema projections were considered a useful means of inculcation (*terbiye/propaganda vasıtaları*). Music and fine arts were also considered in a similar manner, not as artistic forms but primarily as a means to propagate the official ideology. This was explicitly stated when influential intellectuals and politicians praised the potent use of the arts as propaganda in fascist Italy and the Soviet Union.[82]

Another characteristic aspect of the term People's Education emerges if we consider the collective actors *Halk Terbiyesi* presupposes and upon which it is based. How were the people defined? In a general sense, the term 'people' referred to the national whole, but more usually than not to the 'real people' (*asıl halk*), that is, the majority of the population defined in contrast to the elites, usually called 'intellectuals' in the sources of the period. *Halk Terbiyesi*, as a process and a concept, expressed a cleavage between the 'people' (*halk*) and the 'intellectuals' (*münevver*) situated at the core of the centre's discourse. The nation and the people was one, equal, 'the true master of the country', but there was also a differentiation between the 'real people' and the 'intellectuals', the gulf between whom had to be closed through *Halk Terbiyesi*, the essence of the Halkevi institution. This Kemalist (and Gökalpian) equation (*halk* + *münevver* = *halk terbiyesi*) expresses the centre's uneasiness and suspicion of the population that necessitates the people's training and disciplining through *Halk Terbiyesi*.

More specifically, the intellectuals were considered model citizens, educated in the principles of the republic, cognizant of their duties and rights, devotees of the reform movement; in a word, citizens able to act as representatives of the republic. They were called the 'guiding element' that would 'enlighten' the people.[83] They were described as modern and carriers of civilization, but potentially idle, snobbish, over-Westernized and not adequately national perhaps. These terms were habitually used to describe Istanbul and its supposedly corrupt, international and Levantine character. The mobilization of the segments of the population that had received a Western-type education within *Halk Terbiyesi* then resembled the celebrated[84] Kemalist journey from the Ottoman, old, idle, international and degenerate Istanbul to the young, modern, national and vibrating Ankara, an obligatory journey to the Anatolian wasteland conversely feared and experienced with despair by many bureaucrats and state employees.

Cantek has identified a quite similar paradox in newspaper writings of influential intellectuals about Beyoğlu, which very much projected the Turkish elite's 'love–hate' or 'admiration–fear' relation with the West. In the elite's discourse, Beyoğlu was considered the most 'modern' and 'Western' *but also* 'degenerate' and 'non-Turkish' or 'foreign' part of Istanbul as it was inhabited and frequented by minorities and foreigners. Here the equation of the West/Beyoğlu with foreignness, foreigners, hated minorities and (their) immorality is attested by the frequent contrast with other 'Muslim/Turkish' and 'moral' parts of the city – a very common juxtaposition among conservative intellectuals even today. Nevertheless, most of the modernizing elites who publicly portrayed Beyoğlu and Istanbul as the 'degenerate' West were frequenters of that same space and for many the idea of the West was surely formed through their contact with Beyoğlu and its non-Turkish and non-Muslim inhabitants.[85]

People's education was envisaged as a project to instruct the masses in being citizens of the Turkish nation-state through the mobilization of the intellectuals as trainers. But who were those in need of training? Elite perceptions portrayed the people as the bulk of the population and usually defined them in negative terms, as traditional, backward, reactionary, uneducated and attached to a past the elite had rejected. In the literature of the period, the 'people' were frequently equated with children, immature and in need of guidance. They were considered naive and empty, likened to 'raw material' or even 'dough' to be 'kneaded'.[86] The child metaphor presented the people and especially the villagers as mere objects to be handled by the elites. The people were the object of training in the same manner that children were the object of upbringing – in Turkish, *terbiye* means both education/training *and* upbringing. The reference to childhood immediately elucidates the disciplinary character of *Halk Terbiyesi*. They were also defined in relation to a set of deficiencies: a lack of civilization, modernity and nationhood – a lack illustrative of the distance between the elite's objective, or perhaps fantasy, and reality.

The reference to deficiency can be also be read in temporal terms, as belatedness, the status of 'not yet being there', the time-lag between West and East, or else between objective and reality. The regime's populist rhetoric proclaiming the villager the real master of the country, the singularity of the people and the nation, equality and the abolition of past oppression and privileges, was considered a target not a reality, an *aim* that had to appear like reality. As already noted, in Mardin's words, the Kemalists had 'to work for something which did not exist as if it existed and make it exist'.[87] Likewise, the people were celebrated as the repository of the national culture. But this celebrated national culture was not there yet; it had to be created through the compilation of national canons of folklore, language, music, and so on – again a proclaimed objective that had to appear like reality. Ahıska calls this 'as if' attitude of the indigenous elites as the 'phantasmatic performance of the nation' and considers it a key aspect of the performative discourse of Occidentalism.[88] The goal of People's Education and the People's Houses was to erase this gap between the reality and the ideal through the crafting of the national repertoire of folklore. National folklore was to be attained through an extensive operation to collect folklore and sanitize it from undesired elements into the national 'popular' canon, that is, into compilations of decontextualized folk dances, theatre, sports and music that could be enacted time and again in a unified national time and space.[89]

The reference to childhood also aptly conveyed this sense of belatedness, of still being unqualified for the task, which many intellectuals and bureaucrats presented as a cause or excuse for not treating this child-like and unprepared people as 'the true masters of the country'. The Party Secretary, Peker, for instance, was quite outspoken on this matter: 'Democracy is not a dogma, a paragraph of the Koran. It has a soul, a spirit and an essence. If what is necessary to be done [...] passes from a filter called reason in accordance with a necessity called place then it is useful and takes roots. Orange trees cannot grow on mount Zigana.'[90] Neither did the people possess the necessary reason, nor did the inescapable place (and time) they lived in make them ready for the luxury of the orange groves of democracy. The people had to be trained into citizenship, into becoming 'civilized' and 'national' by means of *halk terbiyesi*.

Peker's spatial metaphor can also be read upon the temporal axis. A prominent intellectual of the period, the peasantist Nusret

Kemal, offers such an example where the process by which the state educates the people can be easily understood in temporal terms. He wrote of the duty of the populist state to take the necessary measures in order to have the people reach a level of culture and consciousness that would then (and not before) enable them to participate in the administration. As a result, 'those among the people who reach this level will automatically be made partners in the administration of the country'.[91]

For Ahıska, this constantly invoked belatedness was a constitutional part of the hegemonic discourse of non-Western elites, which she terms Occidentalism. Drawing from Western and orientalist discourses, Occidentalism functioned as a discourse and a means of 'boundary management between East and West' and constructed the internal Others of the indigenous elites. In this way, the elites could differentiate themselves from the people that were supposed to inhabit an oriental and backward space-time by adopting a different historicity.[92]

The lack and belatedness of the people, and the different historicity between indigenous elites and population, was a method to disguise the paradox of an authoritarian single-party regime that declared itself populist. In Ahıska's words, 'the lack was the lacuna within which new sovereignty was to be erected'.[93] In practical terms, the discourse of the people's belatedness, childlikeness and lack of civilization was instrumental in legitimizing the political order, so eloquently expressed in the Kemalist slogan *halk için halka rağmen* ('for the people in spite of the people').[94] Simply put, those proclaimed by the elite to be the source of all power – the people – were denied political agency/subjectivity. In a way that betrayed the elite's patriarchal undertones, women and the youth – two other categories heavily addressed and manipulated by Unionists and Kemalists – were two groups that were also paradoxically denied political subjectivity. In the 1930s, the youth was consistently depicted as a vanguard force, always mobilized and on alert to defend the political order, *but* was neither considered (politically) mature, nor tolerated as an independent actor. Students and 'the youth' (*gençlik*), for example, although considered by the Party by-laws to be 'natural members' of the Party, were considered fit to enter the Party and politics only after having finished their studies and having 'reached an age of maturity'.[95] In a similar way, as we will see in Chapter 5, women were 'emancipated' and given full political rights, but at the same time were primarily expected to carry on their 'traditional' duties at home raising children.

The Halkevi was also in tune with the paradoxes of the Kemalist power discourse, as it was constructed upon and embodied the Kemalist elites' mentality of tutelary popular sovereignty. Consider, for instance, that the Halkevi by-laws stated that 'a sense of sincerity and brotherhood reigns under the roof of the People's Houses', and thus 'no separate place is reserved for individuals *except, in places with civil servants, for the governors, majors, village headmen, and the highest military commander of the region*'.[96]

The ideological proximity of the People's Houses to state power and the middle and upper classes, which can be sensed in the Houses' constitutive texts, was also manifested in a spatial proximity to the places these segments inhabited during working hours and after. The Houses were usually located in the centre of towns, next to or close to other centres of state or local power: the Party building, the Lycée, the main square, the Provincial Administrative Building (*Hükümet Konağı*), the Municipality, the banks and Chambers of Commerce or Industry. In a sense, the Houses were inscribed into the administrative, political and financial centre of the provincial town, a centre mainly inhabited by state and local elites that was habitually avoided by, or even kept clear of subalterns.[97]

Halkevi in Interwar Turkey: Single-Party Regime and State–Society Relations

The Halkevi institution was a product of its era, the 1930s. This can be read in their administrative and organizational build-up expressed in the normative texts of the period. The political system and regime of the period and the ruling elite's preoccupations, plans and aims were inscribed in the Houses' structure and the way they were designed to operate. By political system I am referring to the single-party regime and the two-tier electoral system in which the members of the National Assembly were handpicked by the state leaders to be then 'elected' by the people. In such a regime of tutelary popular sovereignty most MPs were (s)elected not because of their ties to their electoral constituencies, as most had been born elsewhere (usually in the Balkans or the Caucasus region), but due to their ties to the ruling elite, as friends, associates and colleagues from the military or bureaucracy.[98] The same held for other state and Party executive positions. In short, the political and executive power in the centre was held by a rather small group of people with similar educational, occupational and political backgrounds: graduates of the modern educational establishments of the Ottoman Empire and former CUP members engaged in politics at least since 1908.[99]

The textbook version of the Halkevi institution, its structure and modus operandi bears close resemblance to that political system. In a single-party political regime built upon the denial of parliamentary multi-party politics, the Halkevi was constructed upon the denial of civil society and the closure of a long list of independent societies. In a sense, the Halkevi seems to fulfil in the realm of culture what the single party had accomplished in the political sphere, that is, its contraction.

Likewise, the two-tier electoral system of the single-party regime that negated the essence of elections while keeping the facade of a parliamentary republic closely corresponded to the administration of the Houses: although everybody was eligible to register and vote, only Party members or civil servants were eligible for election; as for the Halkevi chairman, he was not elected but appointed by the local Party. The electorate, either for the parliament or the Halkevi, was deeply mistrusted, or, at the very best, considered not yet mature – consider the child(hood) metaphor above – for full citizenship. The centre's mistrust was not limited to the elusive Other, the childlike or backward people that was at once viewed as the 'real people' and the 'ignorant people' (*asıl/cahil halk*); this entrenched suspicion and the corollary need for control extended to virtually all existing social, political and financial associations not directly controlled by the centre, and the establishment of top-down, vertical control structures was a direct indication of this tendency.

From 1927 onwards, a tendency towards centralization was well under way.[100] A wide set of innovations and changes in the regime and the political system of the period attest to this growing attempt at organizational sophistication in the centre and the periphery with the employment of vertical, top-down control mechanisms. From the late 1920s, general inspectorates[101] were established in the Kurdish south-east and the western border of Turkey. They were given extraordinary executive powers and were staffed by bureaucrats or army officers very close to the state leaders. The Party reorganization in 1931 and 1935 led to the sophistication of its activities and structure that increased Ankara's control over the provincial Party. Part of this reorganization was the establishment of a hierarchical system to direct the management of petitions sent to Party and state[102] and the re-emergence of Party inspectorships[103] staffed by high-level bureaucrats selected directly by the upper echelons of the Party and state leadership to replace local Party bosses (*mutemet*) and control entrenched local elites. The Party inspectors, apart from their responsibility to investigate and report on the socio-political, cultural and financial life in the provinces (from Party and state structures and employees to newspapers, sports clubs and other associations, from the financial state of the regions and populace to the state of roads and popular grievances), had wide prerogatives to intervene in local Party and state politics and take decisions bypassing local authorities.[104]

Centralization became even more pronounced with the so-called merging of Party and state in 1936 in accordance with which the Interior Minister also assumed the office of Party secretary, and provincial governors also became local Party chairmen. It was an attempt to control the provincial Party and local elites by non-local state bureaucrats that reported directly to the centre.[105] In the centre, the top Party offices had always been occupied by state elites and cannot be understood as autonomous from the central state, at least in terms of its cadre. In general, the above policies should be seen as an overall tendency by the centre to expand its control over the provincial Party and society, a tendency that was paired with the ongoing state penetration in the countryside, through the establishment and expansion of networks of transport and communication, and various state agencies (educational, judicial, military, administrative and financial). But in order to fully appreciate these policies we must also consider the centre's proverbial distrust of the provincial.[106]

In principle and theory, this tendency and in general the policies of centralization and the increasing control of the provinces can be read as an attempt by the state to curtail, or at least seize, some of the powers and privileges provincial elites had traditionally wielded as middlemen between state and population. These middlemen were well-entrenched local notables constituting the backbone of the provincial Party leadership, exhibiting a high degree of integration into the political system through their status in the provinces, their Party credentials and vertical connections with state offices and men (in the provinces and in the centre) by virtue of their official and unofficial status and functions (tax farmers, court witnesses, municipal officials, members of chambers of commerce, ex-CUP and RPP executives, second electors, vote-mongers). They were able to mobilize the local population as they had done during the War of Independence.[107]

In practice, though, there was the other side of the coin. Beyond the centre's desiderata and the rationale behind the centralization policies, it is essential to acknowledge the centre's constraints in implementing such policies in the provinces. It was not only the local elites that benefited from their cooperation with the centre. The centre also had to rely on local elites in fulfilling its policies in the provinces. The structural dependencies of centre on local elites due to the rather low level of state penetration in the provinces (e.g. in terms of offices and personnel) necessitated the utilization of local elites. We also have to be wary of imagining that the centre – or the state – was one monolithic, integrated and autonomous entity above society, working to implement specific aims. Local elites had vertical relations with members and interests at the centre occasionally going back years, to the period when the CUP was in office or during the War of Independence. State employees and elites equally had familial and social ties and interests in the provinces.[108]

Two examples will suffice to illustrate the vertical links of provincial elites to the centre. One of the very few topics that raised objections at the 1931 Party Congress was the 126th article of the Party by-laws that stipulated that 'persons working in the Party cannot occupy more than one salaried position at the provincial or municipal assembly, or the chamber of commerce'. In the debate it became clear that the aim of the article was to increase the Party's social base and to open up its provincial cadre that was still in the hands of 'the twenty-five year old Committee of Union and Progress'.[109] The article was potentially threatening to the position of local power brokers, and the debate, rare as it was during the discussions, was a clear sign of their uneasiness but also of their ability to express it loud and clear in the centre. In the end, the article was accepted as it was, but in practice its provisions were habitually overturned.[110]

The second example comes from the memoirs of a Party inspector in the 1930s. His reports on the Party cadre of the town of Afyon were the reason he would never again be appointed a Party inspector, as they had apparently won him the enmity of a person close to Atatürk. Ali Çetinkaya, an MP and local of Afyon, was enraged to learn that the inspector had reported that the Party elites in Afyon were only thinking of their own interests.[111] The example reveals that the existence of vertical relations between provincial elites and state elites in the centre could frustrate the rationale of a project of that same centre.

This ambiguous relationship of local elites with the centre is evident in the names used to designate or denigrate the Party bosses in the provinces throughout the 1920s and 1930s: *mütegallibe* (usurper) and *mutemet* (trustee). Whether from the perspective of the centre or the provinces, the connotations of the latter term signify an entrusted local person representing the centre to the province and vice versa, while the former points to this person's illegitimate power to fulfil this intermediary role, to his usurping the power of another authority.[112] The centre's preoccupations with enlarging its constituency at the expense of entrenched local elites was also evident in relation to the Halkevi: in response to a letter by the Harput Halkevi, the General Secretariat replied to all Houses that relatives (father, wife or children) could not occupy more than one position in the Halkevi administrative committee, the same way 'the 79th article of the Party bylaws forbids more than one relative in Party administrative committees'.[113]

To recapitulate, two contradictory givens were simultaneously at play: the centre's predisposition to control the provinces and local party men it did not fully trust; and the reality imposing the need on the centre to employ these very same local elites to advance its policies. The dynamics of the power distribution and politics at the local level depended on and oscillated between these two conflicting traits, and must always be understood in relation to local socio-political conditions and circumstances.

Parallel to these two, we need to consider a third attribute, namely the centre's effort to broaden its influence, expand its constituency and propagate the reforms initiated since the 1920s. The establishment of a new set of institutions in the 1930s attests to the urgency of the ruling elite to broaden its base and propagate its policies. The People's Houses were among these institutions, preceded by the Turkish Language and History Societies and the People's Orators, and followed by the People's Rooms and the Village Institutes. In order to reach society, the regime could not but rely on local Party structures. The provincial Party organization was probably one of the few organizational mechanisms under the relative control of the centre that possessed the necessary expertise and authority to mobilize local resources. Both People's Houses and Rooms, as well as the *Halk Hatipleri* initiative, were conceived and activated through the employment of the Party's local resources. The oxymoron lies in the fact that the centre was trying to reach society and the populace through the use of the very same structures and people whose power, on a more general level, the centre desired to reduce, that is, the local notables and provincial Party elites.

In addition, a first step towards increasing its following, propagating its policies and attempting to attach the population – considered hostile – to the reforms was to consolidate what it considered its natural constituency, the parts of the population that had a Western-type education, a simple task if we consider that most were in easy reach, as they were predominantly urban and in state employment.[114] Occupational and cultural associations frequented by these strata were closed down, voluntarily or under pressure from the government, and their members were advised to join the Party or participate in Party-controlled associations. The civil servants were prohibited by law from becoming members of political parties. In practice, though, this prohibition did not cover the RPP as there was not much objection when civil servants were or became members of the ruling Party.[115]

The general aim was to tightly control or close down all non-Party and autonomous associations, while absorbing and mobilizing their members in Party or state structures. No source ever displayed any degree of ambiguity about the need to employ the 'intellectuals' in the Houses' activities. From the Halkevi by-laws to the communiqués of the general secretariat[116] and the speeches of politicians and bureaucrats,[117] the point was clearly made: the intellectuals had to be incorporated into the Party and the Halkevi project. Coercion and pressure was rife.[118] I read the regime's intention to mobilize civil servants and the educated within the Halkevi and Party structures as an *instrumentalization* within its social engineering project of what it considered as its most trustworthy constituency. The aim of the consolidation of kin forces was to employ them in the ongoing programme of 'reform diffusion' to be carried out through the People's Houses. From another point of view, the instrumentalization of the intellectuals was homologous with the centre's policies that were aimed at controlling the provincial Party branches and raising the Party (and Halkevi) membership figures,[119] or, more generally put, increasing the inclusion of the population in the Party structures and activities. The centre was, simply put, quite suspicious, uneasy, or at least not quite trustful of the provincial Party rank and file. In certain circumstances, especially when it came to propagating the reforms and novelties to the population, it rather tended to trust educated civil servants more than local elites, that is, the backbone of the provincial Party.

The above tenets (centralization through vertical, top-down control mechanisms; employment of local Party elites/notables and resources; and instrumentalization of intellectuals and state employees) were inscribed in the Halkevi institution's administrative structure and its underlying ideological framework, and thus have to be accounted for and problematized in any study of the Halkevi institution.

In terms of administrative structure, the dual control and administration of the Houses by the centre and local Party structures is an obvious example of the first two tenets. The Houses were to be established according to a centrally devised plan, run by local Party elites and through the employment of local resources, but also controlled by central Party and state authorities, such as Party inspectors and the General Secretariat. The local Party was also designed to go through the same vertical, top-down control by similar authorities. The 1936 resolution for further cooperation between Party and state, and its practical result in the provinces, that is, the presiding over the local Party structures by the governor in place of a local Party boss, is also a case in point. The centre's tendency towards more centralization through the employment of state employees and the mobilization of the intellectuals was also inscribed into the Halkevi by-laws. In the 1932 *Halkevi Talimatnamesi*, the Halkevi chairman was to be elected among the members of the local Party administrative committee, and the members of the Houses' sectional committees had to be Party members. However, there was no objection to civil servants becoming Halkevi committee members. The 1940 by-laws were more straightforward: Party members and/or civil servants could become committee members and even Halkevi chairmen. In practice that was the case even earlier in the 1930s, especially in the south-eastern part of the country where party structures had not been established as late as 1946, as demonstrated in the second chapter.

Conclusion

This chapter has contextualized the Halkevi within the emerging Turkish nationalism and similar institutions of 'people's education' after the 1908 Constitutional Revolution, and has thus placed it within the extensive socio-political reform and the ideological make-up of the Unionist and Kemalist state elites. As an important elite project to facilitate nation-building through the transmission of the elite's political and ideological products to the population, the Halkevi was an integral part of the Young Turk social engineering project. In describing the Houses' organizational framework, prescribed activities and modus operandi, this chapter has also shown that the Halkevi was planned to operate in a uniform way everywhere and be under close monitoring by state and Party officials. In prescribing a singular content and identical activities for all Houses while proscribing any divergence from this nationwide programme of activities, the centre betrayed the primary objective of the Halkevi, which was none other than to assist in the elite's nation-building project. A direct product of the Kemalist single-party regime and its mentality of tutelary popular sovereignty, the Halkevi blueprint reflects the political subjectivity of the Kemalist elite that oscillated between a 'love–hate' relation with an essentialized West and a 'disgust–sympathy' relation with an equally 'othered' local population which it considered at the same time naïve and deficient, national and backward. The state's social engineering project and the Halkevi as an integral part of it were located at the heart of this Occidentalist discourse, drawing from and reflecting its own ambiguities and paradoxes.

But for all the uniformity of their structures and organization, the singularity of their activities, and the tight hierarchical control their by-laws stipulated, the Houses were to operate within local societies where the uniformity and singularity the House by-laws projected was a desire not a reality. The textbook version of the Halkevi institution and the ideological and discursive conditions that shaped it as a *project* did not account for the dynamics of state–society relations and the political and cultural conditions within which the Houses were to operate in the provinces. The following chapters will try to recontextualize the Houses within local societies and concrete socio-political contexts.

People's Houses in Provincial Urban Centres 2

The previous introductory chapter presented and analyzed the textbook version of the People's House within the context of the regime's ideological and practical desiderata. Building upon but also moving away from the Halkevi images projected by the state in official texts, the following chapters study the House as a juncture of state and society in which the state's policies were employed and consumed. First, in this endeavour, this chapter attempts to view the Halkevi space as a part of local societies and local socio-political and economic networks. In what follows I broadly sketch a human geography of the Halkevi space and its clientele and manpower in provincial towns, where the majority of the Houses were established. I start by zeroing in on the Houses of Kayseri and Balıkesir,[1] and then juxtapose both their similarities and differences to available data from Houses in provincial towns across Turkey, occasionally exhibiting dissimilar socio-political, cultural, linguistic and ethnic characteristics. To do so, I use state and Party statistics, Halkevi sources and, lastly, the ever-growing secondary literature on provincial Houses. Next, I utilize the small case study of the Kayseri House as an elementary context in which to place a number of Halkevi actors, and embark upon a reading of their own voices in relation to the city, its population and their participation in the House and its activities. In this part, I read the petitions Halkevi actors sent to Ankara and the articles or books they published and relate these to their experiences in the Halkevi or in the provincial town of Kayseri.

Population, the Party and State Elites:
Halkevi in Provincial Towns

In 1935, Kayseri had a population of 46,181 with a 24.5 per cent literacy level (37 per cent male and 11 per cent female). Some 94.7 per cent of the female population was registered under 'no or unknown profession', while 29.4 per cent of the male population worked in 'industry and crafts' (34.4 per cent in textiles), 8.2 per cent in agriculture, 10.8 per cent in 'Administration, Public Services and the liberal professions', 6.2 per cent in commerce, and 3.1 per cent in 'Transports and Communications'. The rest (41.9 per cent) was not registered, and 6 per cent of both sexes were students (618 female and 2,158 male).[2]

Kayseri was always a town famous for its merchants. Established in 1896, the local Chamber of Industry and Commerce had 1,630 firms registered in 1938; among them, three banks, six factories and two printing houses. But most were craftsmen and small-scale tradesmen (grocers, plumbers, bakers, coffee house owners, barbers, etc.).[3] The Municipal Assembly of Kayseri was also crowded with merchants; between 1939 and 1942, 19 out of 30 members were tradesmen.[4]

In the 1930s a large part of the working population of Kayseri was employed in the industrial sector,[5] especially in two state factories employing thousands of workers: the airplane factory and the Sümerbank textile factory. Not just a factory, Sümerbank became a part of the city as it built a small hospital, apartment blocks for its employees, sports facilities and a 500-seat cinema.[6] By 1938 it had its own Party structure with 1,079 members, a considerable amount compared to the 4,455 members of the inner city. It was the only Party structure whose members were paying their Party fees,[7] although it is doubtful whether the workers were registered or paid their membership fees by their own free will.[8]

Perhaps such methods of involuntary recruitment contributed to a high membership figure in Kayseri. Between 1938 and 1944 it was reported that around 15 per cent of the local population were

Party members, well over the national average which was between 8.5 and 9.5 per cent.[9] However, these statistics do not necessarily say much and have to be treated with great circumspection. Consider, for example, the method by which they were compiled: numbers were reported hierarchically by the lower to the higher Party structure. Thus, from village/neighbourhood to district, sub-province, province and finally to Ankara, political interests could have increased the numbers significantly.[10] In contrast, in 1944, the educational background of the Party members in Kayseri was not very different from the national average. In a province of over 300,000 residents, the Party had almost 60,000 members but just 57 university graduates and a minor percentage of high and middle school graduates (0.2 and 2 per cent respectively) next to the vast majority (80 per cent) of barely literates and illiterates (16.8 per cent).[11]

More information is available only in regards to the local Party executive members. Their educational and professional distribution[12] clearly demonstrates that most educated Party executives staffed the upper echelons of the local Party structures, that is, the Party cadres of the province and sub-provinces of Kayseri. Moving downwards to the village or neighbourhood level, the majority was illiterate or barely literate (62 per cent). Equally, at the province level all executives were civil servants, professionals, landowners and merchants; at the sub-province level there was a clear majority of merchants and landowners; and at the lower levels, 80 per cent were farmers. The data indicates an urban–rural cleavage and offers a spatial dimension to the occupational cleavage observed by Öz regarding the overall Party constituency: 'At the summit of the pyramid the predominance of the professions, civil servants, teachers and merchants is evident. As we move downwards, the structure of the Party membership starts to overlap more with the general social structure.'[13]

A report submitted on 3 March 1940[14] offered qualitative information about the Party executives of the province and sub-province level. Half of the Party cadre of Kayseri were merchants. Some, such as the Party chief and the chairman of the local Chamber of Commerce, were quite wealthy but had not been educated in Western-type schools; the former had little education and the latter was strictly religious and a *medrese*[15] graduate. Most Party executives were merchants, civil servants and professionals, in addition to a few landowners from notable families.[16] Some were also members of the Municipal Assembly, the Chamber of Commerce and the Kayseri Bar.[17] To sum up, the local financial and political elites, mainly merchants, landowners and professionals from local families, staffed most local financial and occupational associations, were selected as MPs, and, as they constituted the local Party leadership, were responsible for the local Halkevi.

The People's House of Kayseri was established on 24 August 1932. Underscoring the Houses' close relation with the dissolved Turkish Hearths, the Kayseri House was located in the previous Turkish Hearth building (the old Armenian Church), benefited from the participation of schoolteachers, and drew its staff from local elites.[18] The Halkevi was directed by local Party elites.[19] Until its dissolution in 1951, the Kayseri House was chaired by 11 Party executives: five were teachers, two were merchants, two were lawyers, and two were Party executives who were to become MPs.[20] The Halkevi chairmanship was an influential local post next to other similar positions of authority (Party chairman or mayor), was widely considered a carrier-making position, and, as such, was occupied and contested by local elites.

Unlike its chairmen, the Kayseri Halkevi members were not recorded in a reliable fashion. The House reported that its members totalled almost 2,000 in 1937;[21] among them eight lawyers, eleven doctors, 200 teachers, 234 merchants, 515 workers, 227 farmers, and 165 belonging to the obscure category 'Fine Arts'. According to the list, all teachers of the Kayseri province, even those working and living in village schools far away from Kayseri, were Halkevi members.[22] The absence of civil servants is also rather strange given their noticeable presence in the sectional committees. Corroborated by contemporary sources, the ratio of 82 female to 1,891 male members is the only undisputed figure here.[23] The implausibility of the rest was revealed in 1940, when the Party Inspector Hilmi Çoruh reported only 253 registered members.[24] In contrast, the members of the sectional committees were well recorded. In 1934,[25] 1937,[26] and 1940,[27] a large part of the House's cadre was composed of teachers and other civil servants (65 per cent in 1934 and 87 per cent in 1940). The number of teachers in the committees increased from 10 in 1934 to 29 (66 per cent) in 1940. In 1950, out of ten members of the Halkevi administrative committee only the president was not a teacher.[28] Although teachers could be reappointed elsewhere, some remained committee members from 1934 until 1950; many were publishing in the House's journal *Erciyes*,[29] indicating a high number of teachers active in the House. Some were locals, like Kâzım Özdoğan (1901–61), member and chairman of the Museum and Exhibition section for many years, combining a number of identities: teacher, local scholar, peasantist and public orator.[30] Civil servants were the second largest category in the House's cadre (25–50 per cent) until 1940. In 1942 a Party inspector would even record their indifference towards the Halkevi activities.[31] There were a few workers and artisans, but mostly merchant executives during the first years (but none in 1940). However, they were not especially active; for instance, none of them published anything in the Halkevi's journal.[32] In 1940 they were eclipsed by a dominant teacher (29/44), civil servant and professional majority.

The Kayseri Halkevi gathered around it the majority of the local schoolteachers and professionals and a part of the town's civil servants and merchants. The House executives were mostly composed of teachers, as the presence of students also corroborates.[33] The Halkevi cadre then was primarily drawn from a very small part of the population of Kayseri; however, it was not the local Party elite, which had already been staffing the local socio-political and economic associations, that totally occupied the Halkevi cadre. Rather, it did so together with teachers and other educated civil servants and professionals, who carried out most of the House's activities. On the other hand, the financial control of the House was in the hands of the local Party structure, and part of its income came from the municipality, both structures controlled by local Party elites. One of them was habitually appointed Halkevi chairman. In short, although headed by local Party elites controlling the political and financial capital necessary for its operation, the Halkevi space was primarily inhabited and practically managed by educated state employees and professionals – a large part non-local – providing the 'scientific' capital: their technical and professional expertise. As for the people frequenting the Halkevi and following its activities (conferences, concerts, plays, meetings, library), the available data suggests that they were also from the same restricted parts of the local society.[34]

To turn to another example of a provincial urban centre, in 1935 the city of Balıkesir had a population of 26,699. The majority of the female (91.8 per cent) and 41.4 per cent of the male population was registered under the category 'no profession, profession unknown or uncertain'. What follows is based on the data given for men, unless otherwise stated. The largest occupational category was registered under the title 'Public Administration, Services and Professions'. It represents 20.9 per cent of the total male population, including all types of white-collar employees (civil servants, teachers, doctors, nurses, judges). 'Industry and artisans' formed the second largest category (18.4 per cent). The title, though, is misleading, since the city of Balıkesir did not have any large industries or any industrial workforce. Most registered were construction workers and artisans. Some 8.3 per cent was registered as farmer, 7.2 per cent as merchant, and 3.2 per cent in 'Transport and Communication'. Balıkesir had a rather large student population comprising 10 per cent of the town (almost 7 per cent of the female and 12 per cent of the male overall population). Teachers were the only major occupational category with a female majority (82 women to 41 men). Students and teachers were the only population categories that included substantial numbers of women.[35]

From 1937 to 1942 the provincial Party membership was almost identical to the national average.[36] No more information is available on the Party membership in contrast to the provincial Party cadre. In 1937 the backbone of the urban Party leadership in the Balıkesir province was primarily composed of merchants and artisans (54 per cent), bureaucrats and white-collar employees (16 per cent), 11 per cent professionals (lawyers, doctors, pharmacists, dentists), and just six farmers, four teachers and two workers.[37] Lastly, there were 27 executives described only as members in local associations; if distributed accordingly, the following picture emerges: 62 per cent merchants and artisans, almost 20 per cent civil servants and bureaucrats, and less than 15 per cent professionals; and just one female member. Although relevant sources are not available, cases of women Party executives in the lower and rural Party structures were probably extremely exceptional.

Another Party document dated from 1941 reported the occupational and educational distribution of the members of all, not just the urban, Party administrative committees of the province.[38] There, merchants, artisans and civil servants were reduced to a tiny 17 per cent, while farmers formed the majority (68.9 per cent) of the overall provincial Party cadre. Most (92.4 per cent) of the farmers, however, comprised the cadre of the smallest and relatively unimportant *ocak* Party level (neighbourhood or village). In contrast, the proportion of merchants rose from 44 per cent in the provincial centre to 58 per cent in provincial towns, 23 per cent in smaller towns and 10 per cent at the *ocak* level. In short, the upper echelons were staffed by urban elites, principally civil servants, professionals and merchants; the increase of merchants at the intermediary level of small provincial towns indicates the smaller number of state officials and educated professionals; at the lower level the Party executives (and probably membership) overlapped with the majority of the population.[39]

In contrast, the urban socio-political and financial associations of Balıkesir in the 1930s and 1940s were mainly staffed by members of local notable families, be it merchants or professionals, and, to a lesser extent, by state employees and teachers.[40] The majority were Party members, although a few were also Party executives.[41]

The Halkevi of Balıkesir first opened its gates in December 1932.[42] Within a month it had registered 577 members, of whom 97 were university graduates, 'fourteen from a European University.'[43] Within eight months, the Halkevi had registered 702 members. Amazingly, almost 80 per cent of the members were secondary school or university graduates,[44] while the remaining had primary education; no illiterate was registered. All Halkevi members were literate and four out of five Halkevi members were graduates of lycées or universities, an astonishing ratio compared to the educational background of the population of Balıkesir or Turkey. The Halkevi was drawing not only the executive but all its members from the educated minority of the town. The town hosted a Teachers' Academy (established in 1910), a lycée and numerous middle and primary schools; the 51 teachers of the Balıkesir lycée,[45] their colleagues in other schools, and the instructors and students of the Teachers' Academy offered the Halkevi a nucleus of energetic conscripts.[46] This is obvious if one examines *Kaynak*, the House's journal: most contributors were teachers.[47]

Thus, the People's House, at least upon its establishment, was appealing to the literate and educated parts of the local population. On the other hand, the illiterate of Balıkesir, some 62 per cent of the city's population (49.4 per cent for men, and 75.4 per cent for women),[48] were totally absent from the House's membership statistics. Women were also seriously underrepresented among the Halkevi members. Female members constituted only a minority (9.5 per cent of the House's members). If the female members came from the same social and occupational backgrounds as the female staff members (treated below), then all 67 women members were teachers or relatives of other, usually educated, Halkevi members. Either local or not (teachers or wives and daughters of civil servants appointed to Balıkesir), the female membership probably corresponded to an even smaller section of the local female population than male members. To drive this reasoning even further, a part of this tiny female minority was inscribed in the Halkevi, an act that was supposed to have an 'emancipatory' quality in relation to their domestic seclusion, in a fashion that refuted the very logic behind it; that is, as family members, wives or daughters, not just as women recently 'liberated' from the 'shackles of obscurantism'. The very small female membership was then a crude indication of the reception of the regime's women-related discourse and policies, a subject to be examined in a more detailed fashion in Chapter 5.

In 1933 the Halkevi cadre was heavily composed of state employees (mostly schoolteachers) and professionals.[49] Of only three merchant members, one was a local Party executive and candidate in the municipal elections of 1934,[50] together with four more Halkevi executives.[51] But besides their presence in the House's administrative cadre, the active engagement of teachers and, consequently, of their students in the Halkevi activities was reflected in the local press and the House's publications. During its first weeks, most executive members were teachers;[52] public speeches in the House were mostly delivered by teachers;[53] ten out of 14 actors and actresses of the first theatrical play were teachers;[54] teachers continued to stage plays and open courses for students[55] and women;[56] students and teachers from the lycée and Teacher's Academy recited poems at a Halkevi 'literature evening';[57] and students and teachers formed the bulk of the Halkevi library's users.[58] In general, most activities that were reported in local sources were carried out either by teachers (and students) or by a few doctors, lawyers and state officials, usually Party members. Notwithstanding the fragmentary nature of the sources, the available data reveals that half of the staff members of most local associations came from the same educational and occupational background, and, in many cases, they were quite often the same individuals. The other half were local notables (and a few female relatives), most of them Party executive and members.[59]

In short, the local social-political, financial and cultural associations were occupied by state and local elites, that is, state officials and professionals, but also merchants, artisans and landowners. The latter were locally based; state employees and professionals could be both local and non-local. What crudely differentiated the two groups was their educational background and the different pattern of participation in local structures. The People's House attracted those with a modern education (state officials and professionals) more than all other local organizations where Party membership and family credentials were deemed equally, if not more, significant.

In comparing the data on the population, Party and Halkevi of Kayseri and Balıkesir, the most striking difference was between the population and workforce of the two cities. Kayseri had almost twice the population of Balıkesir. In contrast, Balıkesir had more state employees and students but almost no industrial workers, compared to the growing industrial workforce of Kayseri.[60] These differences, however, were not reflected in the urban Party elite, which drew its cadre from the property-owning notable families (landowners, professionals and merchants) of the locality. In the lower echelons, the Party cadre was also incorporating artisans and small-scale merchants, while at the highest provincial level the influence of non-local state officials was also important. An equally important similarity was that neither farmers nor workers were Party executive members in either town.

Did the Houses follow similar recruitment patterns? Although local elites did register and an educated member of the local Party leadership was usually appointed Halkevi chairman, both Houses were staffed and practically directed by state employees, mainly teachers. In the 1930s, the Kayseri House had more merchant executives than the Balıkesir Halkevi, which, conversely, was staffed by more teachers, civil servants and professionals than Kayseri. In contrast to their pre-eminence in the Party cadre, the associations and municipality of Balıkesir, the local urban elites' presence in the Halkevi administration was rather weak. The existence of a greater state presence in Balıkesir, in terms of employees and educational, judicial, administrative and financial institutions, was clearly displayed in the Halkevi cadre, shaped as it was by the town's educated segments, by majority state employees.

This divergence suggests that the growth of the state apparatus in the periphery was inversely proportional to the peripheral elites' power over the local society and population. But if greater state presence amounted to a lessening of the local elites' power, how come all local associations were still in the hands of locals in Balıkesir? To evaluate such an assumption, more and definitively qualitative data on the symbiosis of state and local elites must be considered next to the study of the differing dynamics and structures of local societies in provincial towns, where most People's Houses were established.

The cadres of many provincial Houses seem quite similar, that is, teachers, professionals and educated state employees with the addition of usually a few, if any, local elites. Where data is available, teachers and state employees also constituted a large part of the overall membership.[61] This seems to be an unambiguous tendency although not easily applicable to all provincial Houses regardless of local conditions and the dynamics of the relations between local and state elites. The comparison between Kayseri and Balıkesir has already indicated that the size and strength of the state apparatus, especially the educational institutions, in a locality could account for differentiations in the Halkevi cadre. The prior existence of a Turkish Hearth or Teachers' Union (Muallim Birliği) greatly complemented – if not being the sole force behind – the opening and functioning of a provincial House. The Halkevi of Sinop, to cite just one example, was literally established upon the foundations of the local Turkish Hearth and Teachers' Union in terms of infrastructure (building, furniture, library, etc.), personnel and even financial resources.[62] The same applies to the Houses of cities like Istanbul, Izmir and Ankara, which had very different socio-cultural and economic conditions to those of provincial towns.

Apart from state presence and pre-existing associations, other factors have to be considered. To put it more explicitly, regions with extremely dissimilar linguistic, infrastructural and ethnic conditions cannot be treated equally with Houses in other parts of the country. In the south-east part of Turkey, the Houses' primary aim was to promote the state policy of linguistic and cultural assimilation of the local non-Turkish populations, which had been similarly promoted by the Turkish Hearts before 1932. Following the 1925 Sheikh Said rebellion, the Turkish Hearths increased their presence in the east and south-east of the country in an attempt to facilitate the assimilation of minorities, especially the Kurdish population. Needless to say, in spreading Turkish culture and language in cooperation with the state apparatus, the Hearths were sponsoring a state policy of assimilation primarily in the south-east but also among non-Turkish populations all over Turkey.[63]

Following the dissolution of the Turkish Hearths in 1932, the People's Houses inherited the duty to promote the Turkification of minorities.[64] A list of the People's Houses and Rooms that opened a Turkish language course in 1947 reveals that all 156 such courses were opened in 150 towns in 14 provinces that were all in the south and south-east, in places heavily populated by Kurds and Arabs.[65] In 1937 the Council of Ministers decided to transfer funds from the Interior Ministry to the Houses of the provinces of Adana and İçel in the south in order to assist in their teaching of Turkish to the Nusayri Arabs and facilitate their 'melting' with Turks through the payment of the expenses of their wedding with Turks.[66] The Houses' *mission assimilatrice* in the south-east becomes more evident upon looking at their profile and activities.[67] The Diyarbakır Halkevi, for instance, opened Turkish courses and attempted to increase the use of Turkish among villagers through lessons on Turkish language. Starting in 1935, it appointed villagers who could speak Turkish to teach those who could not; later it organized competitions and gave prizes to the best teachers and students.[68] Registering children to boarding schools[69] and thus placing them in a strictly Turkish speaking environment was another method followed by Halkevi and state authorities in their attempt to assimilate locals.[70]

The Halkevi's double duty to inculcate the people with Turkishness and civilization in order that they became both modern and national was more pronounced in areas populated by non-Turks. In the south-east, the Houses' *mission civilisatrice* was primarily and profoundly a *mission assimilatrice*: 'civilization' and 'Turkishness' were interchangeably used by bureaucrats.[71] The People's Rooms and Houses in the area were primarily conceived as a means of assimilation.[72] Party reports about the Houses of Diyarbakır, for instance, were clearly interested in and recorded the language of the local population and the Houses' performance in teaching Turkish.[73] At the same time as their attempt to 'civilize' and Turkify non-Turkish locals, the Halkevi members were also keen to record and ultimately consolidate the Turkishness of the region. Halkevi members were industrious in having non-Turkish place names replaced by Turkish ones and collecting folklore material in the Turkish language from an area essentially populated by non-Turkish speakers.[74]

Another characteristic of the eastern Houses was their direct and more pronounced (than elsewhere) link with the state apparatus. Most eastern provinces did not have Party structures throughout the 1930s, and until the late 1940s. As a result, the Houses were established, supervised and, to a very much larger extent than other places, staffed by state employees posted to the region; in some places they almost exclusively operated as gathering places for non-local state employees.[75] The Diyarbakır Halkevi was established by the higher bureaucrat in the region, General Inspector Ibrahim Tali. Its first chairman was the regional security officer Şükrü Sökmensüer, who had previously been the chairman of the local Turkish Hearth. The second and third chairmen were also bureaucrats who occupied the position until their appointment elsewhere. The majority of executive members were also civil servants, although the presence of local elites was also substantial.[76]

Conversely the Halkevi of the small town of Mardin was more isolated from the local society and population. Within a population that in 1927 displayed an almost 90 per cent illiteracy rate and whose mother tongue was 85 per cent non-Turkish, the local Halkevi was almost exclusively frequented and controlled by non-local civil servants.[77] In such cases, the existence of an extremely small (compared to other provincial towns with a larger state presence) number of non-local civil servants did not result in the presence of more local elites in the Halkevi.[78] Although relevant, the absence of Party structures that were habitually staffed by these urban strata was not the sole reason; rather, the linguistic, cultural and ethnic identities of the local population polarized the differences and the mutual incomprehensibility between state officials and the local non-Turkish population.[79] In Elazığ, for instance, the Halkevi was established by the governor who also became its first chairman. The next governor succeeded him to the Halkevi chairmanship as well. In addition, most executive members, library users and all House lecturers were teachers and bureaucrats. Most of the Halkevi's educational and entertainment activities unmistakably addressed the socio-cultural needs of non-local state officials: mixed-gender dance parties excluding those not dressed in formal wear (dinner jackets and ball gowns); tennis, volleyball and basketball exercises; foreign language courses; a kindergarten probably for the children of state employees; the circumcision ceremony for the child of the regional security officer; and teachers' professional meetings.[80]

Some of the educated state employees and professionals in provincial towns were not locals. In most cases the percentage of outsiders among civil servants was inversely proportional to the size of the provincial town. The south-east was the least integrated part of the country, whether in terms of infrastructure or state presence in general; had the lowest literacy levels; very few schools; and a very small number of educated individuals who could staff state services. More important, perhaps, was the explicit state policy not to appoint locals – that is non-Turks – to the state services of the region. Most state employees had to be drawn from other parts of the country. Unsurprisingly, most were unwilling to be appointed to the wasteland of the east and experienced it as an administrative exile.[81] It is not difficult then to imagine that the local Halkevi was appealing to them as an oasis in the middle of the desert, an inescapable centre of socialization for the educated non-local state employees. Equally unsurprising was the low quality of civil servants posted to the region and their lack of enthusiasm in fulfilling their duties: there was much grumbling by state leaders and senior bureaucrats who were requesting that more incentives should be given to state officials posted to the east.[82] In 1934 the General Inspector Ahmet Hilmi Ergeneli proposed similar incentives for the immigrants the state was settling in the east.

He explicitly called for better living conditions than those they had in their place of origin, 'financial rewards and advanced educational opportunities, high-quality housing, children's playgrounds and sport facilities' – all for 'our racial brothers', not the rest.[83] It was probably not a coincidence, then, that among the few activities of the Elazığ Halkevi, whose beneficiaries were clearly not state employees, was the support given to the over 4,000 immigrants the state had settled in the region.[84]

The above examples clearly designate the eastern Halkevi's propensity to become a space totally occupied by state personnel exhibiting a limited relation with local societies and populations. Allowing for exceptions and regional variations, the Houses in the Kurdish-populated east were definitely less – if at all – integrated into local societies than the Houses in the west and appeared to be isolated state colonies in the middle of the vast ethnic, linguistic and cultural otherness they were supposed to eradicate by facilitating the assimilation of its people and the colonization of its space through deportations and population settlement. An unambiguous part of such a state project over local society, the eastern Halkevi appears almost as a colonial state office or a recreational space for colonial administrators, a space built upon the differentiation and segregation between colonizers and colonized.

In the above general survey of the Halkevi human geography, and as a rule of thumb, Houses in large cities (Ankara, Istanbul and Izmir) and in a few provincial centres (especially Adana, Konya, Trabzon, Bursa, Balıkesir and Mersin, but less so Kayseri, Edirne or Eskişehir), that boasted a substantial state presence in terms of the educational, judicial, administrative and military sectors, were better staffed and usually (appeared) more active than Houses in smaller provincial towns where the state apparatus was weaker. There, as the available sources usually become fewer, the picture is less clear. In general, however, small-town Houses were less active and could be more easily claimed by, or be within the reach, or even the exclusive use of powerful local notables or state officials (a district governor or a police or military commander), as we will see in chapters 3 and 4. In other words, the variations of the Halkevi human geography and activities run parallel to local conditions and more specifically the interaction between local and state forces/ personnel, or else to the dynamics of state–society relations in the locality.

Since its inception, the Halkevi project called for and necessitated the mobilization of educated state employees and Party elites, that is, provincial notables of whom many were quite conservative. In practice, the interplay of state and local elites was a structural characteristic of the Halkevi space, as it was a project that was executed with state funds and the employment of state personnel but through the management of local Party elites. With the clear exception of the south-east, where it was solely a state project with minimal interference by local societies and elites, the Halkevi space, in essence, was built upon the symbiosis of state and local elites. By its nature, then, the Halkevi functioned as a juncture of state and society, a meeting ground of state and local men and women. Many of its functions and activities facilitated the communication between central state and Party and local societies and populations. Many Houses served as a medium between people and state offices, when, for instance, Halkevi members wrote the population's petitions and forwarded them to state/Party offices, or when House executives found jobs for the unemployed and provided assistance to villagers and those in need or those who had dealings with state offices. The Halkevi was obviously a node in that relation (a juncture in the relations between state and local societies), to the understanding of which a study of the Halkevi can contribute. And it is to the actors in this space that we must turn our attention in the endeavour to appreciate state–society relations.

Halkevi Members: Alienation, Segregation and Politics

A scribe in the department of Public Works, Sahir Üzel, was an active member and executive (1936–40) of the Kayseri Halkevi and published articles in *Erciyes*, the Halkevi journal, and *Kayseri*, a local newspaper.[85] In an article about local women, Üzel described the tradition of female veiling as ridiculous ('a sign of a sick soul'), vulgar and contrary to state laws, social life and the foundations of civilization (displaying a 'reactionary mentality'). The vocabulary he used to disprove a common practice was indistinguishable from the regime's discourse about its greatest enemy, religious reaction. Following the local ban on veiling, his aim was to refute the likely accusation that unveiling runs contrary to Islam, the national customs and the society's morality.

Nevertheless, although the article displays a polarized sense of time ('modern' vs 'backward') revealed by his juxtaposition of 'civilization' to 'reaction' (*medeniyet/taasup*), the stress of his argument shifted to the issue of honour (*namus*), a discursive and cognitive category that was primarily invoked by the those who rejected the regime's policies on women. In Üzel's piece, *namus* was not discarded as an obsolete or backward value; instead the argument that veiling safeguards the honour of women was rejected: 'The honour of the Turkish woman has always been clean; her forehead has always been clean and sinless. The veil does not protect honour, cannot act as the guard of honour.' On the contrary, veiling 'has always had a bad influence on the character and morality of women'. Thus 'the time headscarves had been dirtying this forehead has finally passed.'[86] Üzel was assaulting his opponents with their own weapons, by turning against them their own arguments.

In an article about a large state industrial complex in Kayseri, the Sümerbank factory, Üzel once more invoked modernity in

relation to local women. In a celebratory discourse he described
the modern factory and all its positive consequences: 'a brand
new and modern city has been created'. Something more than
a factory, it was also a school where young workers were taught
how to run the machines, a canteen where there was 'the subtle
sound of spoon and fork', and a sports field. 'Eat here, work there,
sleep in these modern apartments, take a bath, do sports in these
wide fields.' The addressees of the article were those that refused
to work in the factory and were thus deprived of all the above.[87]
By implication, these people were eating and working in the same
place, sleeping in 'backward' dwellings, did not wash or do sports.
The article's subtitle was more explicit: 'Why women do not take
advantage of such a blessing?' Although more productive than
men, a constant complaint was that local women were unwilling
to work in the factory.[88] Üzel gave three possible reasons for this
unwillingness, only to dismiss them as false: 'Some think it is a
result of your husbands' and your own fanaticism, others think
that you do not want to lower yourself by working, while others
speak of low daily wages.' What Üzel was refuting here are the
regime's expressed enemies, 'reactionary Islam' and 'communism'.
These were 'wrong and bad thoughts', but not the real reason for
the absence of women. For Üzel, the real reason was that 'you
and the people' have not yet been explained the lofty aims of
the factory: 'The factory in our region is a basis for the Turkish
industry, a source of livelihood for the workers, and a source of
work and honour [*namus*] for the women workers.'[89] Despite all
his rhetoric about 'the new and modern', Üzel, although refuting
it, or by the very act of taking it into account in order to refute it,
implicitly admitted what the factory director thought about local
women: they 'belonged to the most conservative [element] in the
whole country and were shocked at the very idea of working side
by side with men though they were living in dire poverty and
could well do with a few piastres'.[90]

An educated state employee and Halkevi member presented
two of the novelties introduced to Kayseri, the unveiling campaign
and the Sümerbank factory with its mixed workforce. In doing

so, Üzel entered into a dialogue with the 'other' these novelties were supposedly aimed at: the local people the elite habitually labelled backward or even reactionary. He incorporated their voices only to the extent necessary to refute them. The interest in this imaginative dialogue with the 'other to-be-instructed' lies in Üzel's inability to totally discard widespread popular categories as exemplified in the case of *namus*. Notwithstanding the obvious propagandistic nature of both texts, in addressing subaltern locals, Üzel was actually defining the meaning of both 'modern' and 'backward' by exactly drawing that same border that separated 'civilization' from 'reaction', and, thus 'us' from 'them'. However, Üzel's border-setting enterprise exposed a delicate *tension* inscribed on the core of his discourse, which is exemplified by the use of *namus* in relation to women. The position of women in society has been considered probably the primary indicator of being modern and has thus functioned as the foremost boundary dividing the discursive and cognitive category 'modern' from 'backward'. The exact same can be argued, from the other side of the fence, though, for the category *namus* – also related to women. *Namus* and its violation functioned exactly as the prime marker of difference, the reason why women were refusing to work side by side with men, or insisting on 'dirtying their foreheads' with the headscarf.

But for another Halkevi member, local teacher and scholar, the Kayseri of his time was almost not an issue at all. Born in Kayseri in 1908, Kemaleddin Karamete completed his secondary education in the lycées of Kayseri and Istanbul, studied chemistry and French at the universities of Lyon and Paris, and taught French at the lycée of Kayseri. As a local scholar, he published books and articles on local history,[91] and as a Halkevi member registered in the Language, History and Literature section, and taught French, delivered speeches and did research and various activities at the Kayseri House.[92] Next to that, Karamete aspired to be elected to the National Assembly. He applied at least twice, in 1943 and 1946.[93] The second time, in order to convince the Party, he wrote a five-page letter detailing all his achievements. His application offers the opportunity to see how a typical Halkevi member, that is, a local teacher and scholar, presented himself to Ankara.

He started by declaring that his family, as well as his wife's family, was one of the oldest families of Kayseri. He then presented his educational background, with studies in Turkey and France, and his mastery of four European languages. He mentioned his military service as an NCO, and his professional status as a teacher of French. However, the lengthiest section of his application was about his publications and research on local history, mainly on the local Hittite monuments. As he put it, 'I was not content with just teaching; I worked to make Kayseri and its inhabitants known to Turkey and the outside world.' This work was conceived as a national duty; one of his books 'ensured that a Turk before any foreigner made a number of historical monuments of our country known'. To reinforce this image of himself as the introducer of Kayseri to the world, Karamete stated that 'the person who for the last sixteen years is presenting Kayseri to all the Turkish and foreign scholars, ambassadors, and other visitors is me'. By emphasizing the intermediary role he customarily played between the locality and the state, Karamete was exhibiting precisely the very structural position and role of provincial urban elites as intermediaries between state elites and the local population.[94] His Halkevi work and his articles in local newspapers were mentioned in brief. Lastly, in the concluding paragraphs, Karamete, in the style of the regime's panegyrics – he was, after all, a public orator – confirmed his loyalty to the 'regime's great deeds and goals towards progress', that is, 'the numerous revolutions', 'the destruction of whatever was outdated and harmful to the nation', and the 'protection of country and nation in the Second World War'.[95]

In short, by presenting himself, Karamete referred to a number of attributes he considered essential for a prospective MP. A reputable family and educational background, an esteemed profession, active participation in the regime's social projects, interests in local studies, and authority to act as a representative of the region to foreign and Turkish guests, as well as a disseminator of the reforms to fellow citizens, all made a person eligible for the job. What is more, all the above characteristics outlined an ideal(ized) citizen of the Turkish Republic, instilled with all the qualities necessary to be part of what state and Party leadership referred to as the 'guiding element' or 'intellectual'.[96] Being an energetic Halkevi member was definitely considered desirable, if not a prerequisite. Karamete was not the only local teacher and Halkevi member who presented himself as a member of this group. At least four teachers and Halkevi members asked for the Party's nomination in Kayseri.[97]

Yet, however active he might have been in presenting Kayseri to the world, his speeches and books were conspicuously devoid of any reference to contemporary Kayseri. Although intimately familiar with local society and the population, he had almost nothing to say about modern Kayseri and its people. In his work on Kayseri[98] only a few pages were dedicated to the town's recent past, more specifically to its contribution to the War of Independence, and only a few remarks to the local achievements of the Republic. Karamete's Kayseri was a town with an illustrious national history, evident in the monuments of the distant past, but its present was absent. His reluctance to address contemporary Kayseri differentiated him from other educated non-local Halkevi actors whose texts wrestled with their present.

Mahir Şener, a foreman at the airplane factory in Kayseri and the chairman of the Fine Arts section of the Kayseri Halkevi, petitioned the Party headquarters twice, in 1938 and 1939. In his first petition, on 28 July 1938, he asked for a monthly salary instead of a daily wage.[99] In his petition, Mahir Şener wrote that he had been sent to Germany during World War I to be trained in arms production[100] and that since then he had been working for 23 years in various arms production units in Turkey. For the last six years he had been employed in the airplane factory in Kayseri and paid on a daily basis. In order to buttress his request, he also mentioned his engagement in the local House: 'Apart from my official duty, I have been working at various People's Houses in the Fine Arts section and their committees; moreover, I have been working for the publication and propagation of our national music together with my daughter in order to realize our Party's principles.' He continued in a fashion typical of similar petitions by stating his family's destitute financial situation: 'I am the father of six children and together with my parents and wife I provide the means of support for a family of ten.'[101] In an attached letter, the Halkevi chairman confirmed that the Fine Arts committee chairman, Şener, and his daughter, Ms Belkis, had actively participated in the House's annual programme of activities.[102] In his second letter, dated 20 May 1939, Şener asked to be promoted or transferred to the management of any other department outside Kayseri, as my family 'cannot get on well with the climate here'. Once more he played the Halkevi card, even implying that he was entitled to this 'reward for his numerous efforts'. He also named the MP Reşit Özsoy, the Halkevi Inspector Behçet Kemal Çağlar and 'the people of Kayseri' as witnesses that could vouch for him.[103]

Şener was the only committee chairman who was not a teacher or a civil servant. As a foreman from Istanbul with training abroad, he was not an ordinary unskilled worker like the industrial workers Lilo Linke described in 1936: 'most looked wild and uncouth, with faces burnt by the sun and clothes torn by age and hard work. Peasants and regular workers, hitherto living without any regular order, sleeping in hovels or, during the summer months, out in the open, half animals in their dumbness and ignorance.'[104] It is difficult to imagine them frequenting the Kayseri Halkevi.

Şener's petitions were forwarded through the Halkevi and local Party mechanisms; they portray the Halkevi as a mediating institution between state and local social actors, a node in local networks of patronage and clientelism. This constituted an obvious and widespread deviation from the way the Houses were designed to operate, something the sheer number of similar petitions sent to the Party Headquarters reveal. The tendency of Party bosses in charge of Houses to use their position to further their political status was so common that Party Secretary Recep Peker had to ask Halkevi executives not to do things that were not described in the by-laws, such as to 'engage in administrative works and listen to people's complaints, especially the ones followed by the Party or the government', or to work 'as if the Houses were an autonomous institution', but to engage 'only in cultural works'.[105] The centre envisaged the Halkevi as a cultural institution that would mediate and close the gap between the wider society to-be-enlightened and the educated segments of society. Petitions by Halkevi members presented a quite different picture of the Halkevi as a space frequented, manned and controlled by local elites and state employees, functioning as a means of negotiation and communication between local elite actors and the centre. In short, our sources display the Halkevi as an establishment that facilitated the communication between centre and urban elites, notables and state employees – not the coming together of elites and people.

The data on Halkevi and Party members show that only a handful of women – all relatives of local Party men – were members of the upper Party structures in Balıkesir and Kayseri. There was not even one female Party executive in the countryside, where the Party membership coincided with the nationwide occupational and educational majority (that is, illiterate farmers). In Kayseri, for instance, no more than four women appeared in a Municipal Assembly between 1930 and 1950, and only two women among the Party cadre between 1940 and 1946.[106] In contrast to the exceptionally low Party membership, women registered and became executive members in the Houses of both towns. Most were teachers (usually non-local), although there were some exceptional cases of relatives of local notables and state employees. The voices of a few have survived in their petitions.

A teacher and Halkevi executive, Nazlı Gaspıralı, asked for the Party's nomination for the national elections. She presented herself as the relative of important men ('the granddaughter of Namık Paşa, the daughter-in-law of the late Turkist İsmail Gaspıralı[107] [...] wife of Dr Haydar Gaspıralı [...] who chose to work for the fatherland in Anatolia'); a graduate of the Istanbul University; a teacher in Istanbul and Kayseri; a scholar and translator of Leon Brunschvicg's *Introduction a la vie de l'esprit* (Paris: Alcan,

1931); a member ('upon invitation') of the Municipal Assembly; the president of the House's Language, History and Literature section; the president ('upon the proposal of the Exalted RPP') of the Philanthropic Association of Kayseri; one of 'the twelve MP nominees of the Exalted RPP for Kayseri'; and a person engaged in 'a number of projects' on child care in Kayseri.[108]

Nazlı Gaspiralı was an exceptional and highly educated woman from a prestigious family who was also engaged in local politics. Lineage and education made her exceptional among local women (11 per cent literate), but also among Halkevi and Party members. This exceptionality qualified her for the parliament. Gaspiralı followed the same pattern as Karamete in stressing the characteristics that enabled her to represent the people: education, profession, engagement in social and political activities, and her family's long affiliation with the ruling and intellectual elite. Her gender, however, was not an explicit issue. Given the regime's expressed interest in the improvement of the social status of women, one would expect Gaspiralı to underscore the fact that she was an exemplar of the 'modern woman' the regime was aiming at. Nevertheless, she did not make a point of it, unlike another exceptional Halkevi and Party executive, Mamurhan Özsan.

Born in 1903 in Kayseri and a graduate of the local middle school for girls, Mamurhan Özsan presented herself as a housewife engaged in 'social services'. Married to the Party executive Osman Özsan and thus sister-in-law of Naci Özsan, Party boss, lawyer and Halkevi chairman, Mamurhan was a member of the Halkevi and local associations, and a Party executive, 'an enlightened of the Kayseri women and sociable', as Party Inspector Çoruh reported.[109] In 1943 she petitioned the Party for nomination in the national elections. She mentioned her participation in three Party Congresses; her active engagement in the Halkevi, the Red Crescent and the Society for the Protection of Children; and her father's membership of the *Müdafaayı Hukuk*[110] and the People's Party. Finally, she wrote, 'I believe that I'll be able to act and work towards the realization of the revolutionary role of women in Turkey as well as towards the spirit of the advances of the revolution in the National Assembly.[111] Family lineage, membership in local socio-political associations – her 'social and political services' – and attachment to the regime's ideals were again considered as qualifications for nomination.

On 22 February 1945 she petitioned the Party in Ankara for a salaried position in the standing committee of the provincial assembly in Kayseri because 'my house was broken into … my family has no other income except my husband's 100-lira wage, [and] I run into debt during the war years'. She again stressed her Halkevi credentials; her father's illustrious past in the Party; her membership in Party and provincial executive bodies; and the fact that she was the only woman in the Provincial Assembly.

> I was a member of the standing committee before and I worked flawlessly. As the only woman I was always in the minority. Because of various interests the male friends do not want to give me this job […] You will say 'why don't you get in touch with your seniors there?' I am a woman, if this issue lags behind, my reputation will be damaged. Besides, the interests excessively collide on this issue. The male friends always have the upper hand.[112]

Similarly to Gaspıralı, Mamurhan invoked the achievements of her family, or, more precisely, of her male relatives. In a sense, both women's commitment to the Party was testified not only by their direct involvement in its projects, but also by their husbands' and fathers' involvement. The attachment to male relatives here functions as proof of their attachment to the political elite and its causes, one of which was the emancipation of the Turkish woman. The oxymoron lies in the fact that the participation in politics of these very rare cases of 'modern' women could only be possible as wives to their husbands, daughters to their fathers, ultimately as parts of a family. That was probably in line with wider ideas about the proper position of women within the family and not in the open among unrelated men. In the local socio-political arena, they appeared (and chose to appear) not only or primarily as women but as daughters and wives. In her work on provincial elites,

Karadağ has shown that in the 1930s and 1940s local elite women were socializing with state elites in balls, receptions and concerts as 'status symbols', in an effort to enhance their families' cultural and social capital among state elites, but also to differentiate them from local non-elites. Thus, (some) elite women dressed in a modern fashion were engaged in philanthropic and cultural activities, and some exceptional cases – like Mamurhan – were even active in local politics.[113] Their voices spoke in favour of their husbands as well, but their public persona could also have the exact opposite effect. To buttress their denunciation of the Party boss Naci Özsan, two rivals informed Ankara that his sister-in-law Mamurhan 'is known among the people as a woman of low morals'.[114] The very few women active in Halkevi and local politics operated through and next to their husbands, whose political careers and prospects could potentially enhance but also harm.

Mamurhan – more explicitly than Gaspiralı – was playing the 'female card'. She emphasized that as the only female member she was 'always in the minority', while men were opposing her as they 'always have the upper hand'. She then pledged to work for 'the realization of the revolutionary role of women in Turkey'. Unlike Mamurhan, Gaspiralı did not mention such resistance to her involvement in local institutions, unless the phrase 'existing order of things' was a cryptic reference to any local opposition that was triggered by her gender. I contend that for outsiders with more loose connections to local society and its population, the opposition to female political participation was less relevant. For Mamurhan, on the other hand, her husband and family's status were crucial because of their position within local power networks. They would be competing with others in front of the eyes of the local public, rivals and clients. In her work on provincial urban elites, Özsan has argued that the figure of the 'powerful woman' of the local elite family, who was active within the family but also in philanthropic or cultural activities, was also supposed to advance the family's status and authority. In that sense, 'their subjectivities and gender statuses were overlapping with their families' history and social class'.[115] Admirable as it might have been in the eyes of the Party leadership in Ankara, a politically active woman in a provincial society that was largely sex-segregated could easily invite opposition and threaten her and her husband's position in the local political equilibrium. Mamurhan's letters have to be understood within the framework of local politics and the resistance to the participation of women in politics being instigated. Within that context, Mamurhan's petition was an attempt to enlist the centre's assistance against the opposition she and her husband were facing from local rivals within a society that was not that supportive of innovations regarding women. But what if politics was not the sole concern of female Halkevi members petitioning the Party?

An 18-year-old from a poor family of Romanian Muslims recently settled in Kayseri, Zatiye Tonguç, was engaged in the activities of the Kayseri Halkevi, but not in local politics like Mamurhan or Gaspıralı. Until her dismissal in 1940, Zatiye had been employed in the Halkevi Library. On 21 August 1940 she petitioned the Party Secretary General:

> Your humble servant, I come from the immigrants from Romania, a girl of eighteen years old. We came to Turkey two years ago and were settled in Kayseri. My family consists of eight members. I take care of the education of my four siblings. I also have an aged father and mother. It is me who provides the livelihood for all of them. A year ago[116] I was employed at the library of the Kayseri Halkevi for a salary of thirty liras. For a whole year I had never left my duty, working every day till eleven at night. The other day I was ill, I took two days' leave from the Halkevi secretary and after being treated for two days I returned to my duty. By that time the Halkevi chairman had fired me [...] Now they reject me and a family of eight has been impoverished. This is why I write to you [...] I cannot work anywhere else because I am a girl and we cannot go anywhere else once we have been settled in Kayseri. That's why I ask for your mediation to get back to my post.[117]

Zatiye Tonguç was probably one of the girls the Party Inspector Çoruh was referring to in 1940: 'two girls are employed with a 30-lira salary as library clerks. They are supposedly working in the theatre section as well.[118] It is not right to assign this job to them as they do not have a legal license.[119] Although probably active in the Theatre section,[120] Zatiye did not mention it to buttress her petition. In contrast, Karamete, Mamurhan and Gaspıralı did not neglect to mention their Halkevi credentials – and for something more significant than a petty job request. This difference underscores the distance between Zatiye and most Halkevi members. For a girl from a poor immigrant family, stating the obvious – their destitution – might seem sufficient to make her seniors feel sorry and help her, rather than bragging about her commitment to the Party's high ideals and her participation in the reform projects, typical of most petitions. The oral/colloquial character of the letter's language – something I tried to maintain – its spelling mistakes and the absence of any punctuation marks immediately contrasts it to the more grammatical texts of the elite women treated above, but might also have made Zatiye's destitute case even more apparent. Zatiye's moving piece seems to have touched the Secretary General, who personally wrote for the re-employment of 'our little girl' in her former position or in a 'suitable job outside the House'.[121]

Zatiye was a rare case of a low-class woman in the Halkevi whose voice has survived, albeit in a fragmentary form. She was an exception among the Halkevi women, but also among the women of Kayseri, a recently settled outsider. Professor Karpat, himself an emigrant from Romania to Turkey in the 1940s, has expressed the differences of identity that separated the Muslim community of Dobruca in Romania from that in Turkey and himself 'as an individual, from the natives'.[122] Perhaps a similar 'identity difference' enabled Zatiye to participate in something 'the natives' considered inappropriate, to say the least, for women.

The divergent patterns of participation in the Halkevi space and the different ways that Halkevi membership was experienced between local-elite and state-elite (i.e. non-local bureaucrats and white-collar civil servants) actors point at the divergent network of relations both sets of actors had with the local society. In other words, their position and interests in the local society and politics differentiated the Halkevi members. What Üzel wrote about local women, for instance, conveys what many educated civil servants faced upon arriving at their place of appointment in a provincial town. Karpat eloquently described it as differences of identity between the immigrants and 'the natives'. How then did educated outsiders who constituted a significant part of the Halkevi clientele and operatives experience and account for their life in the provinces? The following authors, all writing about Kayseri in the 1930s, hint at boredom, or even alienation from the provincial space, time and inhabitants.

Four days in Kayseri in March 1936 were enough for the novelist Nahid Sırrı Örik to publish a short travelogue.[123] Mostly attracted to the remains of the past, the author described in detail old monuments and buildings, mosques and libraries, but also past poets, scholars and rulers. The contemporary Kayseri was ill- and under-treated, with a few not very flattering comments. Upon arrival he visited a coffee house, for him the best way for a stranger to quickly feel the general character of a town. He entered the one across from the lycée building, as he was told that it was the most suitable and clean one. 'This coffeehouse, though, the cleanest of coffeehouses of the ninth largest city in Turkey, was a place that would not give the right to any provincial town to praise itself.' What was wrong? It was crammed with customers, the tables were not covered with any tablecloth, most customers were playing backgammon, and the only available newspaper, *Cumhuriyet*, was moving from table to table. 'The atmosphere was heavy, smoky and suffocating. Small local civil servant and tradesman types.' The voice of the radio, the backgammon and chat noise, the sound of the door being closed and opened, even the waiter's torn jacket, seemed to annoy the author.[124] His description continued in the same unflattering vein. In contrast to his praise of the old monuments, the roads and houses of contemporary Kayseri 'very much display an Arabistan picture', its central square 'full of small, ugly and ruined buildings ... full of mud in the winter and dust in the summer', and its cinema 'very expensive and crowded'.

It is difficult to find a single word of praise about modern Kayseri. All the places were ugly, unsatisfactory and always lacking, all presented as deficient and unable to match the grandeur of the monuments of the past. Locals were treated in a similar fashion: 'Their frock coats with their grey backs resembled ... the robes of the *ulema*. They rarely wore collars or ties, while some had caps. As the *çarşaf* had been abolished, [women] were all dressed in coats, but some wore black coats and gloves, holding their black umbrellas in such a way, that it would have been impossible for anyone to see their faces.'[125] In describing the locals, the author ironically was again referring to the past; not the illustrious past of monuments, but the breathing past, the 'backward' present of 'Arabistan'. A short remark on a picture the author saw in a shop illustrates this point. The picture was of a city by the sea, 'just like Istanbul'. 'Who might have been the painter coming from which place in Europe, passing who knows where from to come all the way up to *this place!*'[126] Apparently for the author, contemporary Kayseri was not a place where activities such as painting were meaningful.[127] But Örik was not writing for a local readership, in contrast to another educated non-local, writing in a local newspaper.

Although not local, Murat İğneci lived and worked in Kayseri. In an series of articles published in a local newspaper in March 1939, he described the visit of a friend from Istanbul, a state employee travelling through Anatolia to compile some kind of report. İğneci confessed to feeling ashamed to show a city full of mud and dirt to his friend, who had studied city planning in Europe, and warned him not to expect much. Like a self-fulfilling prophecy, his friend fell into a ditch full of mud and had to change clothes. They then walked through the market, which was 'full of mud and dirt', village women, elders and local tradesmen who were shouting and annoyed the author. The goods were displayed in baskets and open bags 'open to microbes in the mud'. The author posed a series of 'whys': why so much dirt, why no price labels, 'why do they have to shout, why do they deceive the customers, why don't the authorities do something?'[128] In a manner similar to Örik, he described the central square in harrowing terms[129] and mentioned a series of deficiencies: for example, the absence of public toilets, the broken town clock. They then visited the cinema where they were annoyed by the furniture's bad condition and the audience's whistling, shouting, cursing and applauding; something that 'directly shows the social and psychological manners of the spectators.'[130] 'We walked around Kayseri, step by step [...] through the poor streets full of mud and dirt, rubbish and dirty water [...] We saw how people throw their garbage [in]to the streets and [...] how these poor people live in houses [...] impassable due to animal dung.'[131]

Unlike the silence of the local teacher Karamete, Örik and İğneci present modern Kayseri as a set of deficiencies. Even when they whined about something *that was there* (dirty roads or ugly buildings), they actually invoked the lack of what *should have been there* (cleanliness or beauty). Certain things were totally absent (public toilets, ambulances, newspapers) but others were there (restaurants, coffee houses, hotels, the cinema) but devoid of certain qualities the authors were apparently expecting, be it beauty, hygiene, cleanliness, table cloths, and so many other characteristics that would not evoke the orientalist image of 'Arabistan'.

Locals were evaluated in a similar way: they lived under awful conditions, were coarse, and lacked in manners. Their cloths were not Western but suspiciously resembled the cloths of the 'other-to-be-abolished', the cloaks of the *ulema* or the *çarşaf*. Both authors communicated feelings of shame, mistrust and disgust for the local people. Both texts convey a polarized sense of time and place,[132] a historicity to be found in the Occidentalist discourse of non-Western elites that complained about the 'lagging behind' of their countries and fellow citizens, and constructed, in this way, their internal oriental Others.[133] What these educated elites expressed was a sense of embarrassment and mistrust for the very people they were supposed to educate in the Halkevi.

The distance and alienation from the 'real people' was expressed – but also criticized – in a novel by another contemporary. Cevdet Kudret used his experience as a literature teacher and Halkevi member[134] in the 1930s in Kayseri as the main source of inspiration for his novel *Havada Bulu Yok*.[135] Born in Istanbul in 1907, Cevdet Kudret studied law and between 1936 and 1938 taught literature at the Kayseri lycée.[136] Kudret, an Istanbul intellectual, went to Kayseri with hopes to 'transmit an interest in literature open to the Western civilization' but soon came to understand the 'very painful realities' of the province upon seeing 'students without coats, with holes in their shoes during the winter ... doing their homework under street lamps'. Soon his engagement in the Halkevi's Social Assistance and Village sections 'opened the way to a number of whispers' about his supposed left(ist) leanings.[137] Kudret (and the novel's hero) was described as an idealist teacher of left leanings coming for the first time to the provinces and wishing to enlighten his compatriots.[138] Local realities, however, were not accommodating to his desires.

The first thing Kudret's alter ego, the teacher Süleyman, faced upon arriving in Kayseri was the monotony of the lives of teachers and civil servants. Alienated from the local population, they stuck to themselves, passing their long after-work hours in the coffee house (perhaps the one Örik visited) and tavern playing backgammon and drinking. One of them summarized their boring life:

> What are you going to do every day from 15:00, when you leave school, till 23:00? If you are thinking of books, they don't come here; if you are thinking of newspapers, when they arrive here it's already old news. If you are thinking of cinema or theatre, there are no such places here. Not even a decent brothel exists [...] you are single. How will you spend your free time after 15:00, or, when you have no lessons, from morning till evening? It's easy for one or two days, but what about one, three, five years, every single day after 15:00? You are obliged to go to the coffeehouse, play backgammon, then to go to the restaurant and drink till you go to sleep.[139]

If Kayseri was the intellectual's wasteland, then the People's House must have been a refuge intellectuals could not refuse, a place to socialize among peers. To evade boredom, Süleyman registered in the Halkevi. The chairman was an ambitious lawyer wishing to become an MP and saw the Halkevi as an instrument for his political advance.[140] Obsessed with reporting his achievements, he habitually sent reports on completely fictitious activities.[141] Another teacher also had political ambitions and became a Party Orator[142] to the ridicule of most locals. In contrast, Süleyman took a real interest in the Halkevi but soon understood that only activities that could yield an arresting report or a newspaper picture were executed. However, when famine struck during World War II, a Halkevi committee visited the rich to gather money, and the city's poor to distribute food,[143] giving Süleyman the opportunity to meet the local poor and rich. In Kudret's description, the people whose progress the House was supposed to work for had no relation with it and some had not even heard of it. The local rich, however, were aware of the Halkevi solely as a place of entertainment. Kudret's Halkevi was the playground of teachers, civil servants, local Party men and merchants, each group being there for different purposes, be it sincere interest, a solution to boredom, political ambition or entertainment. With a shared sense of identity, teachers and non-local officials socialized among themselves and became active in the House out of boredom and obligation. Local elites appeared to be only superficially interested in the Halkevi's activities, participating for their own reasons, whether political ambition or the House's opportunities for entertainment.

Conclusion

Next to the socio-political order that established it, the Halkevi project has to be contextualized within its operational environment, that is, provincial urban centres. By outlining a human geography of the Halkevi space, this chapter has attempted to place provincial People's Houses within local societies and socio-political and economic structures, and thus draw an elementary context within which to read the voices of social actors and study state–society relations and the consumption of the centre's policies. The data consulted above indicates that the People's Houses were able to mobilize the educated segments in provincial towns: professionals, students and teachers, bureaucrats and state officials. They were the Houses' writers, lecturers, actors, musicians and library users. More long-established local elites – merchants, artisans, landowners and Party cadres – were also part of the project albeit in fewer numbers and in a different capacity to that of teachers and state officials who were responsible for most Halkevi activities. Local elites seemed more interested in the House's political potential, which they tried to harvest by placing themselves in its cadre. For many of its members and cadre, the provincial Halkevi was clearly functioning as an opportune space within local politics, an aspect of the Halkevi treated in detail in Chapter 3. Teachers and bureaucrats were unofficially pressed to join, but many definitely experienced their participation as an idealist enterprise to 'enlighten' the people. But again, as the example of Cevdet Kudret shows, many felt alienated from the very people they were supposed to educate. The alienation and boredom of non-local teachers and bureaucrats probably increased the likelihood that the Halkevi was used as an exclusive space for socialization by state elites, segregated from the locals, a potential generated by the Halkevi space's political nature. Chapter 4 studies Halkevi free-time activities and focuses on the Houses' function as spaces of elite socialization.

Whatever the Halkevi by-laws, or whatever the Party might have envisaged, neither the cadre nor the operation of every House across Turkey could have been identically uniform. Depending on various factors, the Halkevi cadre, membership and activities exhibited major differences from place to place. Local socio-political and cultural conditions, such as population and literacy levels, the size of state offices and educational institutions, the number of state employees, teachers and students, and the magnitude of local cultural, charitable and professional associations, significantly contributed to the Houses' make-up. Building on the experience of the local Turkish Hearth and a considerable state presence, the

Balıkesir Halkevi, for instance, was able to marshal a significant part of the large student and teacher population of the town into its activities and thus considerably increased its output and correlation with local society. The opposite was probably the case for Houses in smaller towns whose populations' educational and cultural status obviously left much to be desired. At the other extreme, in provincial towns with no Party structures, a minimal state presence primarily limited to repressive forces, and the existence of large non-Turkish populations, as was the case in the Kurdish-populated south-east, the Halkevi tended to become a space of segregation, unmistakably and exclusively occupied by non-local state officials with little or no relation to local society.

In contrast to the many disparities observed between People's Houses, the female membership was probably one of the very few common attributes of all provincial Houses: it was minimal and limited to schoolteachers, the relatives of civil officials and, in some exceptional cases, the relatives of local elites. Similarly exceptional was the case of their voice being recorded in the archives. Nonetheless, those very few texts by women were alike, saturated with the uneasiness of moving across contradictory demands, something to be considered in Chapter 5.

People's Houses and Local Politics 3

On 8 March 1940, Muammer Köksal went to the Trabzon Halkevi to compose music for a school play. Upon arriving, he took the piano to the Fine Arts section and started working. Hearing the piano, the Halkevi chairman called Muammer to his room.

- You asked for me, I said.
- By whose authority and with what right do you open the piano?
- If I do not open the piano, who is going to open it? As a matter of fact there is only me and one other friend who play the piano, isn't that so?
- Sir, the piano was closed.
- If the piano is closed, I have the keys.
- Did you ask my permission? In that case you might as well open the House's safe.
- You cannot compare the piano with the safe. It is my right to open the piano, not yours. You won't insult me for a piano and you have no right to shout at me.
- You have gone too far, I will shout, not only won't you open the piano without my permission, you won't be doing anything here. Otherwise I should resign and you should take my place.
- It won't be bad; it would be better if you resign, that's what the youth wants after all.
- You talk too much, get out, and don't come here again, he yelled.
- Just don't forget this is the People's House; no power can throw me out, not even yours.
[Some days later] I went to the orchestra room. Ten minutes later the chairman was calling me.
-You have called me, I said.

– No, I haven't called you; they have (with his right hand he showed the police officers standing by the door).

There were five of them. He was supposed to have me taken to the police station.

– Look, am I a murderer? Can anybody be driven away or sent to the police station from the House of the People?

It has now become clear that the chairman and the Halkevi accountant, who assists in this kind of business, have not yet understood what the People's House stands for.

Muammer ended his letter writing, 'I think that today the House's activities will be crippled because of the chairman and the accountant' and asked for the Party's intervention.[1] Muammer's letter is one of many complaint letters that describe similar conflicts erupting in the Houses. Numerous denunciations of Halkevi chairmen[2] were exposing local feuds. These struggles were usually revealed when one of the sides, usually the overpowered one, asked the centre's mediation to get the upper hand or strike back at its opponents. The conflicting sides could be as diverse as the occasions and pretexts leading to the denunciation. Provincial and sub-provincial governors, police and army officers, Party leaders, judges, mayors, civil servants, teachers, tradesmen and professionals might appear on one side or the other of a power struggle set in a provincial town, bringing internal and inter-institutional enmities and alliances into the open.

Occasionally surfacing in the Halkevi halls, these conflicts, seemingly ubiquitous in local societies, form the subject of this chapter. What follows is an attempt to place the Halkevi within local politics through the study of a number of clashes between elite actors enacted in a number of Houses. In the cases to be treated below, the People's House served as an arena within which local feuds were staged and fought, and in relation to which local actors unfolded their narrative. The study of these narrated moments of conflict will help us inscribe the Halkevi space into local societies and view how the Halkevi related to other elite spaces and congregations.

Building on the study of local politics, this chapter will also address the issue of state–society relations in provincial urban settings. The centre was implicated in these fights from the very beginning either through the direct participation of its agents in the feud and/or through its involvement in response to requests by the feuding parties. The study of local conflicts provides the micro level of analysis that is indispensable for the observation of state practices within society and, thus, for the production of nuanced arguments on state–society relations. Perceived as arenas of conflict, the People's Houses constitute a privileged site for the study of local politics and state–society relations.

Local Politics and Halkevi

The state archives contain thousands of complaint and petition letters compiled by Halkevi and Party members, state officials and, less frequently, anonymous writers or those using fake names. In many cases the letters were the result of a minor dispute between Halkevi or other local Party leaders and a state functionary, such as a police officer.[3] The chairman of the People's Room of Belveren, for instance, requested the Party's intervention against the local police officer,[4] who came to a Halkevi show that was staged by students 'with three–four policemen and threw the students out with curses and improper language. He ruined the merriment and leisure of the people by shouting insults (I am the security officer. I can do whatever I like).'[5] Elsewhere, disputes often had deeper roots, as in the town of Buldan where the Halkevi chairman was brought to court by the local policeman who accused him of being 'an ordinary theatre man'[6] because he had invited two actresses from a travelling theatre company to participate in a play staged by students. The police officer ordered this to stop because 'the coming together of these sick women with the youths would supposedly give rise to a number of negative feelings among the youths'.[7] The officer's determination to produce a document to be used against the Halkevi chairman in court suggests a deep-rooted enmity between the two actors.

Clashes between influential individuals or groups were rather typical in local settings, and the public space of the Halkevi could not but have been a typical venue for them to surface or be staged. Consider the following denunciation of a provincial police officer in the Black Sea town of Pazar: 'In the afternoon of 12 December 1943, during a Halkevi concert, the police commander was seen publicly on stage engaging in immoral acts with Ms Necmiye, who was singing.'[8] This is an extract from an official record signed by the secretary and the accountant of the Halkevi, and four citizens, with the request for a formal investigation. The Party investigation that followed concluded that the officer had embraced and kissed Naciye, 'a woman of low morals who goes with everybody'. Following exchanges with the locals, though, the Party investigator reported that 'apart from any legal and disciplinary action necessary, [the officer's] removal from Pazar would be appropriate [because he] is known as an enemy of morals and has attracted the people's hate and disgust'.[9] The report disclosed something the initial letter had not mentioned: the relations between the officer and the locals had been pretty bad even before his 'acting on stage'.

The police officer was not the only state official to attract the Halkevi chairman's rancour. The Aydın Halkevi chairman (and local Party boss) requested the removal of the commercial school's principal ostensibly because he did not allow one of his students to participate in a Halkevi play out of vengeance for the Halkevi's refusal to give him chairs for the ball he had organized. The chairman's letter escalated into a polemic: 'he does not value the local people and intellectuals; engages in questioning issues he is not justified to question; speaks against our Party disputing in detail the results of Party meetings and tries to initiate gossip'; 'downgrades the enormous achievements of the great Turks'; and 'is the grandchild of the Kurd Cemil who, together with the last ottoman sultan and caliph, tried to strike the Turkish nation in the back'. Although written in 1948, when political opposition was officially permitted, the letter did not accuse the director of being a member of the opposition party, but of being from a treacherous Kurdish family and a foreigner to the region and the locals: 'From the very first day he came to Aydın, we never discovered this person's nature. He has been opposing any kind of association; he has not entered the Teacher's Society and prevents his teachers from entering. In this way, he has damaged the solidarity of the region's cultural family.'[10] The letter hinted at ethnic and cultural differences between the local denouncer and the non-local teacher. If not the sole reason for the conflict, such social, educational or ethnic differences – a rather common phenomenon in the provinces – could, without doubt, stimulate conflict. By means of education and occupation, outsider state officials were considered part of the local elite and were positioned among existing local power relations and, thus, potentially within competing factions and alliances, and their feuds. This was more noticeable in the case of more influential state officials than schoolteachers. The sub-provincial governor (*Kaymakam*), for instance, appears equally, if not more, vulnerable to denunciations by local actors.[11] Consider the following denunciation.[12]

The sub-province governor has covered himself behind the government's authority and exploited his position and influence to satisfy his personal desires. In that sense he does not refrain from doing exactly the opposite of [the Halkevi] principles. He is also plotting against civil servants and persons from the people he dislikes using official dealings as a pretext. He tries to succeed in satisfying his desires by complaining about them and by using his powers to open investigations against them. Those under his influence, both civil servants and individuals from the people, are hindering the communication between the people and the rest of the civil servants. Unfortunately, the people of our sub-province lag behind in the realms of culture and knowledge. As a result, they think that his acts are in concert with the government's wishes and for this reason the people, as it is normal, have started to harbour a concealed disobedience towards our institution.

Moreover, the people, unable to tolerate these unlawful acts, have appealed to various official authorities and have made complaints even to ministries [...] Nowadays [the governor] has even attacked me and has thus started to impede the activities of our House.

The *Kaymakam* of Bulanık was denounced for similar reasons. He was reportedly reducing 'the people's interest and the region's esteem towards our House and, as a consequence, he is preventing the realization of our aims'. But at the end of his denunciation, the Halkevi chairman admitted that the issue was (also) personal and requested what most denunciations usually requested, that is, the removal of the opponent: 'if this *Kaymakam* stays, there will be no possibility to continue with our activities. Because I am a civil servant, he wants to damage my record and tries to discredit me to my superiors'.[13]

Another comparable incident occurred in the town of Çan. The problem erupted when a visiting theatre company performed on the Halkevi stage. The Halkevi officials stopped the play because 'it was observed that the play was running contrary to our bylaws', as many among the audience were consuming alcohol although they had been requested to stop drinking. The theatre company secured the support of the local Party boss, at whose hotel they were residing, but his mediation – 'to safeguard his own interest' – was unsuccessful. The Party boss turned to the *Kaymakam* who had the police enforce his decision. 'In this way the players performed in the evening of 3 March 1947'. But again, as in most letters, such incidents usually offered only the pretext for the outburst of an ongoing feud, whose details the Halkevi chairman subsequently presented in terms of a series of consecutive incidents involving the *Kaymakam* and the Party boss: 'In the past I wrote numerous letters to the Party inspector and the provincial Party about the national and local elections. The *Kaymakam* is definitely aware of that and is continuously trying to create problems and accuse me. Once again I prepared a report to the provincial Party about the last village elections that contained a paragraph about the *Kaymakam*. The Party boss took a copy to the *Kaymakam* saying "again he writes against you" and the paragraph was erased.' The offended Halkevi chairman asked for the Party's intervention: 'In case this situation is not ameliorated, I'll decide to resign from the local Party and Halkevi.'[14] Perhaps due to the last sentence, or probably because the chairman was also a Party member and executive since 1928, a Party inspector was dispatched. His report focused on the ongoing conflict between *Kaymakam* and local dignitaries, not on the initial incident with the theatre company.

> There is complete disagreement between the Kaymakam, the Party chairman and local Party executive members. This Kaymakam is constantly creating problems for the Party friends and acts in an oppositional manner. He looks down on the Party friends, considers them incompetent and thus prevents all the achievements they want to realize in the name of the Party and the Halkevi. In fact, the Kaymakam feels insulted by the Party and the government because he was made Kaymakam to this sub-province from the position of deputy-governor. As a matter of fact, during the previous national and municipal election he betrayed our Party. I consider his immediate dismissal from this region as quite appropriate.[15]

Let us take a step back: a trivial Halkevi theatre play provided the stimulus for the surfacing of a local feud. The chairman's letter and the inspector's report revealed the conflict between *Kaymakam* and local power brokers, and explained it as a reaction to his administrative exile to a small town. This might seem sufficient to account for his 'betrayal of the Party and the Government' but it does not fully elucidate the relation between the *Kaymakam* and the local Party boss. Given the existence of many denunciations of state officials by local Party executives, an explanation pertaining to less personal and more socio-political attributes appears more reasonable. My argument is that local socio-political conditions and power networks, as well as the place reserved for, but also claimed by, the non-local state official within that local order of things can provide a broader interpretative framework of analysis for the study of the relations between state officials and local elites. In many cases this relation must have been conflictual from the very beginning; as agents of the centre in the periphery, the duties of state administrators naturally collided with the interests of local elites, whose wealth and status was based on their position as middlemen between state and population.

Cultural differences also must have increased the propensity for conflict. Many educated and non-local civil servants were definitely likely to 'read' local habits, accents, food and clothing as signs of 'backwardness', something we have detected in the texts of non-locals who were visiting or living in Kayseri in the 1930s. Here it suffices to recall a motif in the texts produced by modernizing elites, namely the canon of the 'idealist' teacher or *Kaymakam* struggling against all odds to bring civilization to an indifferent, or even hostile, populace.[16] From a local perspective, however, as many denunciation letters recorded, the 'idealist *Kaymakam*' of the modernist national literature was described as a tyrannical and ignorant foreigner constantly causing problems due to his inability and indifference to adapt to local conditions or perhaps because of his resentment of his exile there.

On the other hand, adaptation to local conditions meant cooperation with local socio-political and economic elites, by and large the local Party elites. This cooperation might at the same time mean that the state official was taking sides in ongoing local feuds. Unbenhaun's monograph on the small town of Datça on the Aegean coast has shown that the local elite families were establishing a set of relations with state officials, offering cheap housing and other services to non-local bureaucrats while staffing local Party structures with family members. Within such a setting, the bureaucrats' footing in the locality was critically dependent on and roughly corresponded to their relations with the local elite families, a relationship that could be both conflictual and conciliatory. In a number of cases a strategic alliance was concluded, as with the three sub-provincial governors who married the daughters of local elite families; but the opposite was also possible, exemplified in the case of two *Kaymakam*s who opposed the power of local leaders.[17] Michael Meeker's work on the town of Of on the Black Sea coast has also demonstrated the potentially troubling symbiosis of the outsider bureaucrat with local elites. In the 1930s the *Kaymakam* of the region forcefully replaced the town's mayor – a power broker from a local elite family – with the deployment of policemen, but then artfully entered into negotiation with him to select his successor.[18]

Although rarely offering a complete picture, denunciation letters hint at the problematic symbiosis between local elites and the ongoing feuds that implicated the Halkevi space and clientele, and expose the inscription of the Halkevi space into the geography of local politics and rivalries. In most cases, the People's House provided a stage for the conflict or was the space for control of which the rival sides were battling.

In many cases of a local feud that was revealed by denunciation letters, the archive usually contains fragments of the voices of the implicated, but occasionally, as in the following case, the report of an outsider, usually a Party inspector entrusted with the investigation of the issue. In 1942, three complaints against the Halkevi and Party chairman of Artvin brought about an investigation. The first letter was a direct denunciation of the Halkevi chairman. On 12 September 1940 the plaintiffs went to the Halkevi to listen to the latest war events on the radio 'as always', but the Halkevi chairman came with a group of civil officials 'in a cheerful state' and ordered the janitor to change the radio to a music channel. They complained that the chairman had behaved similarly many times in the past, in a way contrary to the principles of 'our honoured Republican government' and of the Party.[19] In essence, the letter narrated a verbal confrontation between two groups of civil servants in the garden of the Halkevi. One group denounced the Halkevi chairman, offering a reason or pretext for his dismissal.

A year and a half later, the chairman again became the target of denunciation with the second letter. The complainant was a Halkevi executive who refused to sign the decision for the dismissal of Hasan, the chief of the Halkevi orchestra, because the chairman had written on the Halkevi decision register that Hasan was dismissed 'due to his continuous immoral behaviour'. Following his refusal to sign he was never again called to the Halkevi meetings and later received a letter from the Halkevi chairman informing him that he was considered resigned from the House, something he never accepted. The complainant then accused the Halkevi chairman of refusing to fix irregularities in the House's account books; for the bad condition of the Halkevi furniture; for tyrannical behaviour; for drinking alcohol in the Halkevi garden; and for being 'an ignorant person who cannot understand what he is reading'. The structure and narrative of this denunciation is typical of many complaint letters, from the description of the critical event that led to the confrontation, to the climactic delirium of accusations, some of them seemingly inflated, to the request for redress.[20]

A third denunciation followed: 'The Halkevi chairman is a man with much influence in the region, but worthless. Although worthless, his supporters form the majority and thus he is powerful. He became the Halkevi chairman, although he was the local Party leader as well ... The Halkevi shows no activity due to his unlawful and unplanned activities.'[21] The Halkevi chairman was evidently the target of an orchestrated assault by a group of people who were related to the Halkevi.

The Party inspector's report added a lot of information. The last complainant was described as 'an abnormal man' who had also sent 'anonymous and meaningless letters' in the past and had 'no relations with the Party and the Halkevi, unable to understand anything of the region's problems'. In fact, the inspector continued, he was actually used by the other complainant, Mehmet Bilgetürk, and Hasan Şener, the chief of the Halkevi orchestra. Both had been removed from their duties in the Halkevi by the chairman and had henceforth been acting against the Halkevi executives. The report exonerated the Halkevi chairman of the fake charges of the complainants who were removed from the Halkevi due to 'the improper execution of their duties and their unpleasant behaviour that was distressing the region'.[22] The report uncovered the dynamics of a conflict staged in the Halkevi between the chairman and a group of ex-members and revealed the tactics of the complaining group.

In the time span of two years, the same Halkevi chairman was denounced on three occasions, but such denunciations were neither unusual nor limited to Artvin. The Halkevi chairmanship was a position of power and influence and it was usually filled by the local Party elites. The House's physical closeness to Party and state buildings underscored the Houses' place within state and Party power structures,[23] something evident in official ceremonies, where the Halkevi chairmen figured next to bureaucrats, army officers and Party leaders. Hence the position was a political one and as such naturally attracted opposition, making the Halkevi a nexus of local politics and power relations. The story of the first chairman of the Balıkesir Halkevi is indicative of the place the Halkevi occupied within local politics and state–society relations.

An iconic figure in the postwar left,[24] in 1934–5 Esat Adil Müstecaplıoğlu was a Party executive and chairman of the Halkevi in Balıkesir. His case is illustrative of the integration of the Halkevi space and clientele into local politics. Born in Balıkesir into a local notable family – his older brother, Haydar Adil Müstecaplıoğlu was MP between 1923 and 1927[25] – Esat Adil finished his primary and secondary education in Balıkesir; graduated from the Law School of Ankara; and acquired a PhD in law from the University of Brussels. During his studies he was active in student associations and published poems and articles on various issues (financial institutions, villages, folklore and local history).[26] Upon his return to Balıkesir in 1932 he made an assertive entry into the local socio-political scene, registering in almost every existing local association. He became a Party member and was immediately appointed chairman of the newly founded Halkevi, but he was also an executive member of the Sports Administration of Balıkesir (*Balıkesir İdman mıntıkası müfettişliği*) and the Balıkesir Physical Training Society (*Balıkesir İdman yurdu*); founding member of the Balıkesir City Club; Party executive; elected member of the Standing Committee of the Provincial General Assembly; and he might have been a member of any one of the five remaining associations of Balıkesir. However, within two years he had to resign from the Halkevi chairmanship and the local Party cadre and accept administrative exile in the east of Turkey.[27]

Esat Adil was remembered as 'a populist Halkevi chairman'. Apparently he was very successful in drawing people from lower social strata into the House's activities. An observer in the summer of 1934 was astonished to see the Balıkesir Halkevi crowded with students, peasants, workers and poor people. Some had come to see the doctor and receive medicine gratis, others to have their petitions written, or to participate in the House's theatre plays, but above all to meet the chairman because as a lawyer he gave legal advice and represented the poor in court free of charge.[28] Similar news about activities in favour of villagers and the local poor were announced in the first issue of the Halkevi's journal in February 1933.[29]

The chairman's vivacity did not end with these activities; Esat Adil was also the editor of and a regular contributor to the Halkevi journal, with articles on literature and folklore.[30] His political opinions were reserved for Savaş, a 'daily Political newspaper',[31] which he owned and directed. With their egalitarian and populist overtones,[32] his editorials on local and national socio-political issues did not refrain from being critical of government policies and performance. Within just one week, in July 1934, Esat Adil signed three articles that condemned the condition of the country's education,[33] penitentiary system[34] and labour law.[35] These articles probably ignited some kind of reaction in the local political arena because a week later he wrote a polemical article addressing those 'using a dirty lens against the publication of Savaş'. There he openly accused his opponents of being with the regime only to serve personal and material interests.[36] A response to accusations by local Party rivals,[37] this article was a clear indication of local rivalries and opposition to Esat Adil. Some years later a local and ex-MP[38] would denounce him to the Party headquarters as 'a friend of Nazım Hikmet'.[39]

This opposition could have been caused by Esat Adil's rising popularity; in the 1935 municipal elections, just three years after his return from Belgium in 1932 and among a candidate list full of local Party executives, Esat Adil received 5,025 votes, second only to the mayor, Ismail Naci Kodanaz, and well ahead of the elected 24 local Party executives.[40] His work as Halkevi chairman and lawyer in favour of the local poor and villagers had probably won him a local constituency that alarmed local contenders. His articles in *Savaş* most likely increased both support and opposition in the region. For instance, he wrote against the prices charged by the local electricity company, succeeding in having them reduced.[41] But most importantly, in 1934 Esat Adil supported the miners on strike at the Balya-Karaaydın mines. Almost 16 years later, Esat Adil recalled: 'The newspaper I was publishing supported the strike. I was depositing the newspaper's profits in the strike's account. The workers left their destiny in my hands. The Party chairman of the district of Balya was at the same time the legal consultant of the mining company and was naturally against the strike. As the company refused all fourteen requests of the miners, there was no other solution but [to get] the support of the government and the Party.' With the assistance of the regional army commander, Esat Adil went to Balya and 'made the Party chairman resign. The strike committee accepted my proposal for a hunger march to Balıkesir. The next day the governor Salim Gündoğan grasped the serious effects that such a march could have. He showed his shrewdness when he called the representatives of the company to Balıkesir and informed them, as an order from the government, of the necessity to have the miners' demands accepted.'[42]

If Esat Adil's work for, and his growing popularity among, the local poor had worried local rivals, his overtly political activity undoubtedly won him enemies among local political and financial elites, such as the Party executive in Balya or the owners of the electricity company, that is, local wealthy elites and usually fellow Party executives. It is in that sense that what followed does not appear coincidental. On 23 July 1934 the public prosecutor, following orders from the Justice Ministry, opened a court case against *Savaş* and Esat Adil. The prosecutor considered that five of his articles had breached the 30th and 40th articles[43] of the 1931 Press Law.[44] The hearing began in August and ended with Esat Adil's acquittal, but, nevertheless, it was the first time he was openly branded as a communist.[45] The interesting element in this story is that with the 1931 Press Law, the government could easily close down a newspaper with no need to open a court case. The Press Law of 1931 very harshly curtailed the freedom of the press and established very strong government control over it.[46] Even a governor could close a publication, as in the case of the opposition newspaper *Mücadele*, which was closed by the provincial governor after its first issue was published in Istanbul in 1931. The governor was warned by Party Secretary Recep Peker, who had been informed by an anonymous denunciation letter.[47] But in the case of Esat Adil, his newspaper was not administratively closed but instead he was openly brought to court and then acquitted.

We cannot be absolutely sure whether his local rivals incited the intervention of the Justice Ministry, but their involvement was both possible and probable given the threat Esat Adil was posing to their position in Balıkesir. Only two months after the court trial and his acquittal, in the municipal elections of October 1934, Esat Adil received the second highest number of votes, but then had to resign from the Halkevi chairmanship.[48] A few months later, during the February 1935 elections for the standing committee of the provincial General Assembly,[49] Adil and another Party executive member resigned from the Party executive in protest at the nomination of candidates in direct contravention of Party rules.[50] Although prohibited by Party regulations, local elites would habitually have their own clients and protégés elected by declaring them official Party candidates,[51] an ordinary phenomenon within a political culture of patronage.[52] What is more, the nomination of candidates was also a tactic to outflank rivals and their clients, as Esat Adil's resignation indicates.

But then the Justice Ministry opened another court case against him. Esat Adil had studied law in Ankara with state funding and, in return, had to perform obligatory state service. However, after graduating in 1928 he continued his studies abroad instead of accepting his appointment as Deputy Prosecutor at Kemah in east Turkey. In October 1935 the court case was closed with Esat Adil's acceptance of the appointment and, in response, the ministry dropped the charges.[53] The timing of the court procedure can very well raise questions about the motivation behind it; three years had passed since his return from Belgium before Esat Adil was asked to pay his debt or accept his appointment to Kemah. On the other hand, upon his return, Adil entered into a number of activities – publishing and politics – as if unaware of his appointment in Kemah. Or, perhaps, he intended and managed to circumvent this appointment up until the moment he started to intimidate local rivals, who were able to enforce his administrative exile from Balıkesir through their own ties to the centre. Both trials against Esat Adil were instigated by the Justice Ministry. His removal from his position in the local power structures and finally from Balıkesir then probably came as a result of the combination of local initiative and the centre's intervention. The almost contemporaneous reaction by rival local power brokers and state structures suggests a degree of collaboration.

Esat Adil's reaction was also to seek the centre's backing. A denunciation letter sent to the Party headquarters suggests that he requested to become a Party candidate in the 1939 national elections.[54] Although his 1939 applications could not be found in the archive, Esat Adil had probably applied, as he did in 1943, as attested by his application for election as MP for Balıkesir. Until the liberalization of the political regime and the establishment of opposition parties in 1946, MPs were selected by the Party leadership and then elected by electors, themselves elected by the population. The two-tier electoral system and the existence of candidates only from the Republican People's Party meant that the MPs were in practice appointed by the Party leadership. So, getting the Party's nomination amounted to election to the National Assembly. For Esat Adil, then, becoming an MP would have decreased his vulnerability to administrative exile and enabled him to return to the local political scene from a more powerful position. To achieve his return over his local rivals as an MP necessitated the centre's approval and active support, and this was the strategy Esat Adil followed in 1943 and, in all probability, in 1939.

To sum up, in Esat Adil's case both centre and local elites appeared able to incorporate into their structures an elite member as long as (s)he did not threaten (a) the local equilibrium of power and (b) the centre's politics with dissident activities. Esat Adil's case indicates the point when this inclusiveness shattered for both local rivals and the regime; it should also be appreciated within the framework of local politics and at least within two sets of relations, horizontal between local elites but also vertical relations between local elites and the centre. The case of Esat Adil points to the centre's limited ability to control the provincial Party and monitor society independently of local elites, let alone to change society through an institution (the Halkevi) controlled by those very same elites. Consider, for example, the role played by the centre and its agents in local politics. All sides at one time or another were petitioning the centre to request its mediation to get the upper hand in the conflict (Esat Adil and many local elites requested to become MPs). Esat Adil made two state agents, the governor and the local army commander, intervene in favour of the strikers and against a Party boss. As for the trials, the Ministry of Justice presumably did not act autonomously of local rivals, as the timing of both trials seems to indicate. The centre's intervention was of a secondary nature, moulded by local politics and dependent on the local elites' vertical and horizontal relations with state agents. This is an indication of the limits of the centre's scope for action independent of peripheral elite forces.

But, again, the centre's intervention was not sweeping, but rather co-optive. Although exiled, Esat Adil was not marginalized or excluded from state employment and its payroll. Such an attitude might be explained by the relative scarcity of people like Esat Adil, well educated and relatively supportive of the regime – those deemed 'reactionary elements' or minorities were thought more dangerous and were not treated with the same leniency.[55] Esat Adil was surely not the only leftist to join the People's Houses or other Kemalist projects, such as the Village Institutes.[56] Many intellectuals and politicians with different and conflicting ideas and political agendas were among the founders, executives and active members of many cultural projects and associations. Party and state cadre lists included extreme nationalists and Turkists, ex-communists,[57] liberals,[58] conservatives,[59] even hard-line admirers of totalitarian regimes.[60] Given a minimal, at least, acceptance of the regime's basic premises, this cohabitation was normal; as state employees and part of the extremely few citizens with a modern education, the political and intellectual elites of the 1930s and early 1940s did not have many legitimate political, intellectual and occupational options outside the state and regime's reach. Only with the liberalization of the regime after World War II did new options emerge. Centrifugal tendencies led to a shattering of the Kemalist block, and the diverse ideological groups that until then had spontaneously joined the only legitimate power block could now claim more ideological and political free space. In other words, up until then the centre did not (or did not have to) totally exclude (by way of imprisonment, for example) persons under its relative control, such as civil officials, but rather attempted to incorporate and re-employ them elsewhere. Occasionally, and depending on the degree to which they challenged the equilibrium, they might need to be intimidated one way or another. In Esat Adil's case, this happened with the first court trial. This carrot-and-stick method rather changed after 1945. The end of the one-party regime and the emergence of (and the potential for) alternative political and social structures – from liberal to socialist – altered the centre's options towards dissidents, as the closure of Esat Adil's Socialist Party of Turkey and his imprisonment in 1946 and 1950 demonstrate. But until then the options offered by the single-party regime were limited, and the People's House was unmistakably among them. This scarcity of legitimate opportunity spaces increased the propensity of the Halkevi to be a space and a means of and for politics; as such, it invariably operated as a stage for conflicts as the above cases and letters have disclosed. But what were the mechanics of actual conflict, of its staging and receptions, and how did they relate to the People's Houses, their members and activities in provincial societies?

Dramas of Conflict

Complaint letters rarely offer extensive accounts of ongoing conflicts. In a few cases, though, the antagonism escalated into open fights and even physical violence, into dramas of conflict[61] between local actors competing on the Halkevi stage. The selection of the Halkevi for the staging of the conflict was not always accidental. First of all, it was usually the control of the Halkevi that was contested; and, second, in the tactics of the confrontation, the Halkevi and its clientele offered an opportune stage and audience for the public discrediting of rivals. The Halkevi of the small town of Silvan, the administrative centre of a sub-province linked to the province of Diyarbakir, became the stage of two consecutive clashes between two of the House's chairmen and a group of civil officials. Both cases are relatively well recorded, enabling a more in-depth reading and analysis of cases of conflict than the incidents treated above. At Silvan in 1935 and 1936 the existing antagonism between local power brokers twice escalated into actual verbal and physical confrontation on the Halkevi stage. This eruption of violence offers an opportunity to study the conflicting discourses produced about the hostility and its escalation into an actual fight, but also to 'read' the tactics the actors followed, before, during and after the fight.

Stage one: 'Tevfik! You shameless rascal'

On 17 January 1935 the pensioner Rahmi from Silvan denounced the Halkevi chairman Tevfik to the *Kaymakam*.[62] In five handwritten pages, Rahmi accused Tevfik of as many as 17 faults; nearly all were of a financial nature. For instance, he accused Tevfik of embezzling the House's income; denying control by accountants; not paying the Halkevi janitor; purchasing a number of items for the House at inflated prices; moving furniture from the Halkevi to his own house; and other similar charges. Lastly, he accused Tevfik, who was also the school principal, of neglecting his teaching duties and treating his subordinate teachers badly. Most accusations pertain to financial misconduct, indicating the complainant's skilfulness in accounting, while the two separate handwriting styles of the letter denote that at least two persons wrote and were aware of the accusations, and thus can be considered as Tevfik's opponents. Three months later, Rahmi wrote another denunciation of Tevfik, this time to the governor of Diyarbakır 'because my last denunciation had no result'. This time the letter was shorter and charged Tevfik with breaking the harmony between high and low officials, reporting that he assaulted the *Kaymakam* and the district revenue officer (*Malmüdürü*) under the influence of alcohol, an event that necessitated the intervention of the police. Lastly, Rahmi reiterated the accusations pertaining to Tevfik's occupational negligence and incompetence.[63]

Tevfik's own narrative followed; he informed the Party that the *Kaymakam* had been publicly denigrating the People's House for a long time and that, as a result, some 'drunkards' had attacked his house some nights before and 'had cursed the spiritual personality of the Halkevi and the committee that had the holy duty to organize the Red Crescent evening'. Tevfik accused the *Kaymakam* of the events during that evening, when 'our beloved people participating in the show had to flee their own House'.[64] Tevfik ended his letter with a request for the removal of the *Kaymakam* from Silvan.

A final document revealed what had happened at the Red Crescent evening. It was the result of an investigation by the Education Ministry into Tevfik that was sent to the Party General Secretariat. An 'ill-tempered and heated person', Tevfik

was born in Siv[e]rek in 1901. He graduated from the Diyarbekir Teacher's College in 1915 […] Lately his relations with the Kaymakam and some of his followers have been bad. As a result, on 30 March 1935 during the Halkevi Red Crescent show, a group composed of the revenue officer, tax collectors and civil servants from the financial departments entered the House. The tax official shouted, 'this one did not pay'; then he closed the gramophone playing music for the people and started checking the tickets. When someone suggested that the control should be done at the entrance, he started shouting. Tevfik then said 'don't break the good order of the Halkevi'. In reply to this it was uttered, 'Tevfik! You shameless rascal' [*Ulan namussuz Tevfik*]; according to some present even harsher words were exchanged, such as 'Don't make me say what I'll do to yours and to the Halkevi's good order'. Next the district revenue officer said, 'My officials know what they'll do'. He declined the intervention of the head of the conscription office. As a result, the assailants were taken out by the police. The aforementioned civil servants were dispatched to other areas and Tevfik was removed from the Halkevi chairmanship by the provincial authorities.[65]

The report disclosed the conflicting sides: the *Kaymakam* and a number of officials from the financial services against the principal and Halkevi chairman Tevfik. The reason behind the antagonism was not given. If we believe Rahmi's letters, the dispute was due to Tevfik's unlawful administration of the Halkevi, his professional negligence and tyrannical behaviour, but it could have been personal grievance or antagonism over the use of local resources such as the Halkevi. It could also have been a clash caused or augmented by cultural and ethnic distinction. Most civil officials in the area (the south-east) were outsiders, in contrast to Tevfik; he was from the region, a native of Siverek, a town in the province of Diyarbakır populated by Zaza Kurds and (still) controlled by the powerful Bucak tribe, a clan traditionally supportive of the Turkish state. The letters indicated that the actual incident at the Red Crescent evening was a public eruption of hostility that had been dragging on for quite a while, a clash that was probably staged by Tevfik's opponents in order to retaliate for his insults against the *Kaymakam* and the district revenue officer.

In his work on social conflict, Victor Turner introduced the term 'social dramas' to designate conflicts during which public eruptions of hostility occur. He argued that 'social dramas' are social events identifiable in every human society, and analytically dissected them into four distinct phases. The drama starts, signalled by an act that makes the feud visible, by a public eruption of hostilities, a 'breach of regular norm-governed social relations'. It is followed by an *escalation* of the crisis, where the conflicting sides become polarized, making it difficult for others not to take sides. *Redressive action* aimed at the resolution of the crisis usually follows. This may take the form of institutional or unofficial arbitration and, as a result, the last phase of the drama ends with the *reintegration* of the sides within the social format or with an *irreparable schism*.[66] At Silvan, open hostilities probably commenced with the incident at the Red Crescent evening, a staged public breach of regular social relations. The public character of the breach was crucial, not only for probing the centre's involvement, but also in order to create a public *fait accompli*, an event that would make the return to the status quo ante difficult, if not impossible. In that sense, the humiliation of Tevfik was a tactical move. This direct, visible and public attack on his personality and public persona rendered his ability to execute the responsibilities of the positions he occupied (teacher and Halkevi chairman, state and Party representative) curtailed in front of the eyes of both local clients (students, Halkevi audiences, local public) and superiors (Party and state). It is not accidental then that the accused side, Tevfik, described the incident as an attack on the 'spiritual personality of the Halkevi and its executive members' that made the people 'flee from their own House'.[67]

If the public eruption was the first stage of the conflict, the petitioning and denouncing 'communication battle' that followed – here it had already started before the actual incident – was the second, successive phase of the ongoing feud. Bearing similarities to Turner's second and third phases, these communicative skirmishes can be explained as an attempt by both sides to win the war by successfully instigating the centre's involvement. The Red Crescent event and the denunciations were probably meant to bring about the intervention of supervising state authorities. In this sense, both the eruption of the incident and the communicative war that followed were structurally interwoven and complementary in nature. The provoking of a public incident was an act with communicative value, a 'play' staged for an 'audience' – both central and local – whose involvement it was aiming at.

Probably a large part of this communicative battle is missing. In his telegram, for instance, Tevfik acknowledged that he had also petitioned the local governor. Notwithstanding the fragmentary nature of the evidence, the letters to hand hint at the tactics employed during this entrenched battle of petitioning. Tevfik was denounced as a drunkard and accused of occupational incompetence and negligence, financial misconduct and embezzlement, and of injuring the accord between civil servants. The accusations were directed to the complainants' superiors, that is, the highest state bureaucrat in the region, the governor. All but the last accusation against Tevfik pertained to issues that fell under the direct responsibility and interest of the state administration. In a sense, they were accusing their opponent of impeding the state's authority and work, thus aiming at – or even trying to manipulate – the state's sensitivity towards these issues and the governor's duty to intervene.

Tevfik followed a similar tactic. As the head of the Halkevi (a Party structure), he chose to address the Party and, in a similar vein to that of his opponents, accused them of damaging the 'spiritual personality' of the House and its executive members, causing 'the People' to flee from their 'own House' – and, thus, impeding the realization of the Halkevi's aims. Not accidentally, these were the aims and policies of the Houses' owner and the letter's addressee, that is, the Party, and, by extension, the state.

In their attempt to gain the edge, both sides denounced their opponents to different parts of the centre (Party and civil bureaucracy), setting one part of the centre against another, in a curious civil strife between state and Party offices. This civil strife among state actors *at the local level* has been rather overlooked by approaches that overemphasize the state's effectiveness in the periphery, pitting a monolithic state against a passive society. These perspectives conspicuously resemble, to the point of repeating, the discourse of the official sources from the period and consequently reproduce the image of the state, not its practices.[68] It suffices here to say that the view from the periphery, with its ubiquitous conflicts between state and non-state actors setting state offices against one another, which occasionally erupt in social dramas, renders such approaches quite simplistic. The situation in situ was evidently far more complex.

The governor's involvement produced a resolution of the crisis with the removal of Tevfik and some civil servants, although the implicated *Kaymakam* was, as we learn below, made Halkevi chairman, perhaps until a suitable candidate could be selected. However, this proved not to be a lasting solution.

Stage two: 'he slapped his face in reaction'

Almost a year and a half year later another similar incident erupted in the Silvan Halkevi. The chairman described it in his letter to the Party headquarters in Ankara:

In the evening of 26–27 November 1936 I was at my place together with the teacher Aydost, Saadet and Esma from the family of the retired Rahmi. Sergeant Ali, the municipality's tax officer, came and told me that the Kaymakam was calling me to the Halkevi. I went with Aydost. The Kaymakam, the Halkevi executive Hulki, captain Doğan and inspector İbrahim Omay of the land registry were present. There was a picture of Premier İnönü that has been sent at the time of the old chairman, the Kaymakam İzzet Kılavuz. This picture was left in the book cabinet, the best place in the House. They attacked me using as a pretext that the photograph was not put on the Hall wall – as if there was not a bigger one on the wall – and taking advantage of the picture to further their secret aims with the inspector, with whom they had spent their last days and nights together. I was insulted and slapped in the Halkevi Hall, where we struggle every day to enlighten and guide our people. They had opened the Hall with no authorization, they had sent the janitor away, and had put a policeman at the entrance.

I barely managed to escape and save myself. The life of your child was in danger today at Silvan, where I honestly promote the exalted ideal of Turkish culture. Let my records be examined. For the last ten years I have been working as teacher, principal; I have always been struggling in cultural duties and there is no stain on my reputation.[69]

A few days later it was the *Kaymakam*'s turn to report the event to his superior, the provincial governor. His report was not significantly different from the chairman's. The actors remained the same as in the chairman's account of the event. Nevertheless, indirectly he admitted that what they did that evening was to a certain extent premeditated. He wrote that even before the chairman's arrival they had prepared an official document, where they explained the state of the Premier's photograph. The Halkevi chairman argued that the photograph was a pretext for the assault of the *Kaymakam* and the land registry inspector. The *Kaymakam*, on the other hand, maintained throughout his letter that the starting point for the dispute was the Premier's photograph. However, the premeditated nature of their acts, as well as what he wrote about the chairman and the judge of Silvan, unveiled a deeper animosity between these regional elites. The *Kaymakam* reported that a week later a picture of Atatürk that was sent to the Halkevi as a present was found in the school 'in an ugly state, with its cadre made of common wood, full with glue stains, and [a] newspaper as back cover. I took this picture to put it in a proper cadre.' The *Kaymakam* then turned to Ömer, the Halkevi chairman:

The aforementioned Ömer was not insulted; it was he who insulted these photographs with his acts. This person was beaten in the middle of the market in public in the towns of Lice and Osmaniye where he used to reside. In what sense then is this person referring to self-esteem? He is a bad person and I think that just the event that took place above is sufficient to give an idea about his morality.

The letters revealed that the incident was just the beginning; both actors now tried to respond. The chairman wrote to the Party; the *Kaymakam* to his superior. Moreover, as the *Kaymakam* reported, the chairman enlisted the assistance of the local judge, who opened an investigation against the Land Registry inspector. The *Kaymakam* accused the judge of partisanship and of trying to take revenge. However, he did not explain the reason for the judge's behaviour. 'The people of our region were living in order and peace for two months because the judge was on leave [...] Starting from a small issue he magnified it to the point that state authority is being broken.' He called the judge a 'leader of bandits' and deplored that he had not been removed from the region after so many complaints and 'letters sent to official authorities', but instead had been increasing 'his influence among the ignorant people'. The *Kaymakam* ended his letter by requesting the removal of both judge and Halkevi chairman to another area. As he put it, 'because a teacher that has been beaten cannot instruct and teach manners to the local children (*ders ve terbiye*) [...] he must be appointed to one of the nearby districts'. Moreover, he recommended the district revenue officer for the Halkevi chairmanship. If his requests were not to be carried out, he asked for his own reappointment elsewhere.[70]

Both letters clearly demonstrate that the clash – orchestrated in all probability – between the two bureaucrats and Ömer in the Halkevi was just one round in the fight between the two sides. It also becomes clear that many more people – bureaucrats and teachers – were implicated directly or indirectly by either side: the judge, the Land Registry inspector, a couple of teachers, the wife of the retired Rahmi, the revenue officer. We have to keep in mind that the persons mentioned, even if not directly implicated, were in all probability not named in vain, but rather as potential witnesses in the (likely) case of an investigation, which was usually requested by one or both sides. In that respect, it is highly probable that they were allies of one side or the other.

There were striking similarities with what had taken place a year before at Silvan, again involving the principal and Halkevi

chairman, the *Kaymakam* and a number of state officials. Even
if the revenue officer was not the same person, the match in
terms of posts was almost identical; a retired Rahmi, for instance,
was implicated in both cases. In this sense, the existing sources
indicated an enduring local feud. Was there a 'locals vs outsiders'
character to the fight? Tevfik was not from Sivan but from the
region; Ömer had been employed in the region. From the opposite
side, the *Kaymakam* was always a foreigner to the region, as well
as the Land Registry inspector and the army officer. The same was
also likely for the revenue officer. Many more aspects of the actors
might have contributed to the schism – for instance ethnic origin
and language, social and educational background and lifestyle –
even though they were not mentioned in this case.[71]

Another factor that might have contributed to the conflict
was the limited number of power positions open to local power
contenders in small towns, but especially in the south-eastern
parts of the country. Party structures, for example, did not exist in
most of the south-east provinces up until the late 1940s.[72] Within
such an environment of scarcity the struggle for one of the few
available positions, such as the chairmanship of the Halkevi, must
have been much more intense.

In accordance with Turner's four-phase scheme, this second
successive social drama at Silvan publicly erupted with a breach
of social protocol – the public slapping of the Halkevi chairman.
As a consequence, the feud became public, the implicated persons
polarized, and the opposing sides entrenched. What is more,
audiences, both local and external, were established by the very
same public, and thus communicative, act. The communicative
trench warfare that followed the event can be identified as part
of the second and third phases of Turner's processual analysis
of social dramas. This communicative warfare involved the
petitioning of higher authorities. Both the tactics they followed
and the arguments they offered were similar to what had occurred
in Silvan during the previous conflict. Both sides petitioned their
superior authorities: the *Kaymakam* wrote to the governor, the
Halkevi chairman to the Party. In order to have his rivals, the

Halkevi chairman and local judge, dismissed, the *Kaymakam* tried to exploit the state's concerns in relation to what was considered the proper functioning of civil bureaucracy. He accused his rivals, especially the judge, of damaging the cooperation of state officials, endangering the 'peace and order' in the region, and breaking the 'state authority' by 'increasing his influence among the ignorant people'. These were all catchwords for state officials and power, probably carefully selected to make an impression: speaking of '*sükünet ve asayış*' ('peace and order') and '*cahil halk*' ('ignorant people'), the *Kaymakam* played with the state's most serious preoccupations, suspicions and fears in general, especially in this largely Kurdish-populated area that had witnessed and would continue to witness armed uprisings. Not afraid to admit the violence against the Halkevi chairman, the *Kaymakam* hinted at his opponent's anti-regime stance and questioned his morality because he had twice been publicly beaten and, thus, dishonoured. Here the *Kaymakam* turned away from criteria of administrative efficiency and state preoccupations, resorting to socio-cultural values. Although not directly pertinent to state discourse, the widespread and intrinsically gendered notions of 'honour and shame'[73] were ironically shared by both bureaucrats and the very same 'ignorant people' the *Kaymakam* was ruling and trying to keep aloof from at the same time.

The tactic followed by the Halkevi chairman on the other hand was to petition the Party headquarters and accuse his opponent of damaging the ideals and policies of the letter's addressee, the Party and regime, and failing in his duty to enlighten and guide 'our people', which were again aims the Party and state had assigned to the Halkevi. In respect to the incident, he presented himself as the 'unjustly treated', a narrative tactic typically employed by non-state social actors petitioning state authority against a regional state representative.[74] In short, both sides in their discursive tactics made allowances to both state preoccupations and societal values, addressing both centre and local society, a necessity as it seems, once the 'social drama' was staged for and in front of a double audience, the soon to intervene state authorities and the implicated, gazing and evaluating residents of Silvan, whether locals or outsiders, family members or students of the attacked schoolteacher, local clients of the implicated state actors, or even 'the ignorant people'.[75]

Conclusion

This chapter studied the power relations within which the Halkevi, its personnel and activities were inscribed and had to operate; demonstrated the simultaneously conciliatory and conflictual nature of the relations between local power brokers and state officials, and the dynamics of local politics, socio-political networks and relations within which the Halkevi space was entirely inscribed; and argued that local and central state mechanisms operated in conjunction with local elites, while the centre seemed to favour co-option rather than confront local power brokers. In Esat Adil's case, the state did not react pre-emptively and independently of local elite actors, but only after the local power equilibrium had been shattered, opting for a solution that would not entirely exclude the 'exiled' power broker from the state's employment and reach.

In studying local politics, then, the picture of an 'imperial state society' – to quote Meeker – emerges; in the 1930s and 1940s local elites continued to function as connecting ties between the centre and local societies as they formed the backbone of the Party cadre, interacting with bureaucrats, and maintaining connections in the centre, which they habitually used in case they needed to outmanoeuvre state employees or local rivals. Similarly, state officials habitually enlisted the cooperation of local power brokers, whose hostility could endanger their position but also their reputation and standing in the eyes of their superiors.

It is thus difficult to speak of a clear line of separation between state and society, between state and non-state social forces. As we shall see in the next chapter, state officials expressed the need to segregate themselves from the local population and constructed such segregated spaces, the Halkevi space functioning as such. That was consistently the case where the cleavage between state officials and the local population was greater and state presence limited, especially in the Kurdish-populated areas. But even there, as the case of the Artvin Halkevi has demonstrated, the state appeared and functioned quite differently from what statist conceptions of state–society relations can account for. Its activities and habitués situated the Halkevi within an interrelated web of social spaces, institutional structures and a vast array of formal or informal networks that filter through local societies and move across the state–society divide. The study of local politics renders the differentiation between an omnipotent and monolithic state or bureaucracy and an equally undifferentiated and potentially hostile society, against which the state operated, quite simplistic. Such conceptions fail to question the 'image',[76] or the 'discourse of the state',[77] either in its Ottoman version of the divide between rulers and ruled, or in the persistence of a similar state discourse and mentality among the republican bureaucracy, as exemplified in the suspicion of the periphery that was hidden behind the regime's populist slogans.[78] Nevertheless, to assume that this state discourse and mentality can account for or explain the vast array of interactions between state and non-state actors without taking into account the actual everyday 'practices of the state' is rather simplistic.

Local politics and the place of the Halkevi space in it point to a different conceptualization of 'state–society' or 'centre–periphery' relations, one that draws on Migdal's state-in-society approach and Meeker's conception of the old imperial system's survival and functioning in the republic, wherein peripheral elite forces cooperated with state officials, occupied state offices, functioned as intermediaries between local society and state, and occasionally acted as representatives of the centre to the local population and vice versa by utilizing their position in the local society and their relationship with central state and Party offices and officials.[79]

An elite space itself, the Halkevi was – in a literal, that is, spatial, sense as well – in the middle of local politics, a node in interrelated webs of social-political relations. This also reflects the circumstances within which the aims of the Halkevi institution were (supposed to be) understood, enacted and contested, not least by the larger populace, those habitually excluded from it, as we shall see in the following chapters; what happened at the Halkevi was 'heard by our people' as the letters frequently mention. The study of the Halkevi and the various ways its discourses and practices were employed by social actors cannot be appreciated without reference to this indispensable substratum of local politics.

People's Houses vs Coffee Houses   4

In this chapter I study the Halkevi as a space of socialization and leisure-time practices in relation and contrast to the rival social space of the coffee house, its clientele and activities. My ambition is to read the consumption of novel free-time activities the Halkevi intended to promote in local societies. I study how these novel practices were applied and consumed by local actors, but most importantly how they interrelated with pre-existing male socialization and free-time practices and spaces, among which the coffee house occupied the most prominent place. Reading the Halkevi space and activities through the coffee house space and its dominant male homosociality will enable us to view the local consumption of the products of the Kemalist state in more depth. The association between the two spaces offers a more nuanced perspective because it builds upon popular spaces and everyday practices. In addition to the historical depth of the conflictual relations with state power since its appearance in the sixteenth century, the coffee house was immediately (and customarily in the 1930s and 1940s) contrasted to the Halkevi as an antagonistic space, a direct threat and rival to the regime's and Halkevi's aims.

The first part of this chapter offers a brief history of the relations between state and coffee house and a short presentation and analysis of the official discourses about the coffee houses in the 1930s and 1940s. The second part of the chapter focuses on the performing and consumption of everyday activities of free-time socialization in the Houses. Drawing from letters of complaint and Party documents, I encounter extensive grievances about the turning of the Halkevi into a coffee house, through the habitual performance in the Houses of a set of social activities that were typically related to the coffee house, such as gambling and drinking. Lastly, I dwell on the accusatory practices of supplicants who, excluded from the Halkevi space, utilized tenets of the official discourse in an ingenious articulation of narratives that employ a vocabulary and imagery which in the following decades would heavily permeate the conservative populism of the discourses of the Turkish right, namely, that of the 'undeservingly oppressed' and 'righteous' subject.

State, Coffee House and Halkevi

There is a long history of tense relations between coffee houses and the Ottoman/Turkish state.[1] Since their first appearance in the sixteenth century, coffee houses became the targets of oppressive state policies and a negative discourse uttered by state and religious authorities. Kırlı has demonstrated that this negative discourse was framed in terms of morality, albeit not in the modern sense of the word. Rather, it was a political discourse signalling the transgression of social boundaries between rulers and ruled, a transgression the coffee house was supposed to generate by bringing together a heterogeneous clientele and becoming the hotbed of subversive popular political discourse. The coffee houses were places the state was suspicious of, not without good reason one might argue: a number of rebellions resulting in the sultan's deposition were reported to have started in coffee houses.[2] The Ottoman state occasionally closed down coffee houses or attempted to control them by means of exemplary punishments. By the middle of the nineteenth century, though, the reforming Ottoman state established a system of surveillance of public spaces, like coffee houses, through the employment of spies.[3] Kırlı has argued that by the 1840s a change had occurred in the way the state viewed the coffee house, passing from methods of disciplinary punishment to surveillance, a change underscoring the emergence of the concept of public opinion and its significance for state power, but also of a gradual change in the way the state treated and managed its subjects, in short, of 'a new governmentality that underlined the Ottoman polity towards the mid-nineteenth century'.[4]

The nineteenth century witnessed another momentous change that transformed society and the coffee house space in particular. With the introduction of the printing press and the publication of the first newspapers, the coffee house would also function as a reading room. As a result, a new kind of coffee house, the *kıraathane*, was established. Books and newspapers were to be found, bought, read (out) and discussed in such coffee houses; in Istanbul, frequented by state officials and intellectuals, some coffee houses started to resemble modern-day clubs and associations.[5] Notwithstanding the revolutionary changes of the late nineteenth century, coffee houses continued to function as communication centres that men frequented to socialize, discuss, learn the news, read or hear the newspaper read, and meet friends and strangers. As public spaces, coffee houses were also used for explicitly political purposes. Prominent intellectuals during the last years of the Ottoman Empire gave lectures in coffee houses while Unionist agitators used the network of coffee houses and *kıraathane*s for propaganda purposes. Nationalist forces also used coffee houses as propaganda and mobilization centres during the War of Independence.[6]

From the second half of the nineteenth century, there was a shift in the way the coffee house was represented and thought of, with intellectuals starting to criticize the coffee house on different grounds from before. Emulating the discourse of Westerners on the Oriental coffee house, intellectuals started to compare it to the café of European capitals and criticized it as 'the nest of the idle and the ignorant'.[7] In the past, the coffee house had been primarily accused of being a hotbed of seditious talk (*devlet sohbeti*) and the site of the transgression of the accepted borders between rulers and ruled. But as new concepts achieved prominence, the coffee house began to be criticized with reference to the lack of hygiene and physical training or the obstacles it was supposed to pose to the population's productivity. A new discourse was coming into being that would represent the coffee house as a nest of filthiness and laziness, drinking and gambling, moral and physical decay that adversely affected the well-being of the family, the nation and the people as a whole.[8]

The early republican period was not devoid of negative representations of the coffee house, mostly to be found in newspapers, but also in the writings of intellectuals and politicians of the period.[9] Coffee houses were depicted as places 'hurting family life', 'lodges of the idle' (in reference to the abolished dervish lodges) and 'nests of gossip'. They were also identified as almost antagonistic to the ongoing reform programme. It was lamented, for example, that 'our coffeehouses' did not resemble the cafés of European capitals, Vienna being the most popular example. In addition, a number of plans to reform the coffee houses were articulated and, to a small extent, attempts to modernize some in Ankara and Istanbul were realized.[10] Voices recommending more aggressive policies, even the total closing down of coffee houses, were heard in the 1930s and 1940s. In some rather rare cases, it was not the central state but provincial state and municipal authorities that applied repressive policies such as the closing down of coffee houses, the prohibition of the opening new ones, and the strict control of the existing ones through the employment of hygienic and administrative regulations.[11] Due to their sporadic character, similar repressive policies did not seem to have any substantial impact on the coffee houses. The sizeable amounts of tax revenue that coffee houses were producing probably constituted the most significant reason why the state did not apply any heavy-handed measure against them.[12]

Notwithstanding the absence of any comprehensive repressive policy against urban and rural coffee houses alike, this moralistic discourse about the shortcomings and the harmful consequences of the coffee house persisted well into the 1930s and 1940s. The centre's suspicion of the coffee house space continued, exemplified in occasional suppressive policies[13] and sporadic attempts to correct the coffee house space through the input of novelties, such as hygienic regulations, sports, state or Party propaganda, film projections and theatre plays. However, imbued with Orientalist overtones about the backwardness and slothfulness of the coffee house, this discourse still shared with the Ottoman state the old fear of coffee houses as uncontrollable and potentially subversive spaces. The republican leadership continued to be suspicious of the coffee house for the same old reasons. The coffee houses of ethnic and religious minorities were seen as spaces promoting identities antagonistic to the unitary national identity the regime was striving to enforce: following the closure of their lodges, dervish orders were suspected of secretly operating in coffee houses; during the Free Republican Party experiment in 1930, coffee houses were considered spaces of subversive propaganda and gossip, whether 'communist' or 'reactionary'; and during the Sheikh Said rebellion in 1926, they were suspected of sheltering brigands, vagabonds and lowlifes, and the police were ordered to monitor and even prevent the discussion of politics in coffee houses.[14]

The regime's anti-coffee-house moralistic discourse contrasted the new spaces the state and Party were establishing to coffee houses and their 'dirty atmosphere'. When, for instance, a Halkevi journal criticized local people for still visiting coffee houses, the author exclaimed that 'today the coffeehouse of the Turks is the Halkevi'.[15] The People's House emerged as an alternative to the coffee house, endowed with qualities, infused with activities and ideas supposed to be contrary to those of the coffee house. In a parallel fashion, the People's Rooms were portrayed as spaces that were in contrast to village coffee houses and village rooms.[16] With the establishment of the People's Rooms, these village rooms were considered outdated,[17] while the images employed to describe the two spaces overtly corresponded to the incompatibility that was supposed to exist between them: village rooms were 'filled with smoke, nasty smells and foggy', in contrast to the 'clean and educational order' of the People's Rooms.[18] The People's Reading Rooms (*Halk Okuma Odaları*), another regime project to establish free-time socialization spaces under state control, were presented in an analogous way as 'hearths of education and ideas for the people of every class and type, [aiming] at satisfying the students' need for reading and saving them from dirty places like the coffeehouse and the night club'.[19] The Education Ministry presented the Reading Room as 'an upright place people can visit instead of going to the coffeehouse'.[20]

According to this official moralistic discourse, the people and the youth were the coffee house's primary victims in need of the new spaces the state and Party were establishing for them. For a Party boss seeing that 'the village lads' visiting a provincial town's market were filling the coffee houses and drinking alcohol was a very good reason to request the opening of a People's Room to save 'these youths from bad habits'.[21]

Occasionally even the intellectuals suffered from the lack of Reading Rooms, sports clubs and People's Houses and, of course, the activities these spaces were supposed to offer. Nevertheless, the principal beneficiaries of the new spaces and their activities were reported to be the youth and the people. Here, the separation of the educated and state elites from the rest of the people of the Gökalpian synthesis and the regime's project of people's education[22] was reproduced verbatim in this moralistic anti-coffee house discourse. There, the coffee house was portrayed as a space of the people and possessed all the people's vices and deficiencies to be treated with people's education; a space of filthiness and laziness in need of hygiene, sports, national culture, civilization, theatre and arts. The divide between people and intellectuals and the concomitant contradiction of the official discourse with its populist rhetoric, as analyzed in the first chapter, permeated the regime's rhetoric on the coffee house. Only two years before the establishment of the People's Houses and only ten days after the establishment of the Free Republican Party in 1930, the Party issued a communiqué prohibiting gambling and the consumption of rakı in Party buildings and Turkish Hearths. The reasoning behind such a prohibition is interesting: 'these activities [drinking and gambling] will not be tolerated by the people'. Nevertheless, drinking and gambling were not prohibited in general, as 'in reality drinking is not at all prohibited by our principles. Everybody is free to exercise this pleasure', but 'it is forbidden to give the impression of a drinking tavern'.[23] The centre's preoccupation with appearances here is comparable to the Ottoman state's attitude towards the coffee house: it was not against the consumption of coffee, but against the uncontrollable socializing in coffee houses, the concomitant trespassing of the borders separating population from state officials, and the subversive popular political discourse, the *devlet sohbetleri* mentioned in the police reports Kırlı has studied.[24]

Considering the position and functions these two spaces had (or were supposed to have) in local societies, the rivalry that the official discourse claimed to exist between them seems reasonable. Notwithstanding their differences in many respects, both were spaces of free-time, after-work socialization. In contrast to the coffee house, though, the Halkevi was designed as a heterosocial space, although female participation in the Halkevi space and activities was rather low.[25] This overlapping of activities together with the pervasiveness and long history of the coffee house as a popular male socialization space immediately established the Halkevi as a competitive space and rival to the coffee house and vice versa. This rivalry becomes evident if we consider a few activities that were customarily carried out in both places. The Halkevi theatre and musical events, the Houses' radio sets and cinema projections, were in direct competition with the performances of traditional storytelling (*Meddah*), popular and shadow theatre (*Karagöz* and *Orta Oyun*), and of wandering theatrical troupes, but also occasional cinema projections, radio listening and newspaper reading – all commonly taking place in coffee houses.[26]

The letters used here amply employed the moralistic discourse when referring to the coffee house or coffee house-related activities (gambling, drinking coffee, gossiping and sitting idle).

Gambling, Drinking and
Elite Segregation in the People's House

Probably one of the most prevalent aspects of complaint letters was the gambling and drinking of coffee and alcohol in People's Houses.[27] Gambling and alcohol drinking were strictly prohibited by the Houses' by-laws. The drinking of coffee was not; nevertheless, the complaints employed the vocabulary of coffee and coffee-drinking to project the negative image of the coffee house inside the People's House. Many petitioners employed this tactic in stressing the (unattained) difference between Halkevi and coffee house, such as the 18 people signing as the 'the Youths of Sarıgöl' on 3 April 1940: '[T]his holy nest you have opened with the aim to enlighten and save us, the youth, from the dirty atmosphere of the coffeehouse.'[28] Salim Çanga from Bahçe complained that the Halkevi chairman was hiding the House's books and newspapers so that 'our people lead a solitary life in the coffeehouse corners'.[29] The image of the coffee house with all its negative characteristics, gambling and drinking, was frequently mentioned in order to stress the gravity of the situation: 'It has become entirely a place of gambling completely resembling a coffeehouse';[30] 'you cannot distinguish between a coffeehouse and the reading room. The Halkevi is having a catastrophic effect on the region, as its secretary drinks a lot of booze';[31] or, 'on its tables the gamblers play from dusk to dawn and have turned this beautiful place into a common gambling coffeehouse'.[32]

The letters drew from the ready-made moralistic discourse circulating in newspapers and Party publications and described the coffee houses as dirty and unhealthy places that promoted laziness and spread evil ideologies. But, this time, the same rhetoric was also implicating the Peoples' House. A civil servant complained that the youths 'are damaged in the corners of the coffeehouse, in dirty places' because of the local House's idleness.[33] Signing as 'a Party member', the anonymous author of another letter played with the state's old fear of the coffee house as a centre of seditious talk. He lamented that the local House's Sports section had done nothing to attract the youth and, as a result, 'the youths will be surrendered to very catastrophic ideologies in the coffeehouse corners. Whose duty is [it] to save these youths from the coffeehouse corners?'[34] Our authors, clearly copying the official jargon, contrasted the People's Houses and Rooms with the coffee houses and reminded the Party that the Houses were established to save the people and the youth from the coffee house. They gave various reasons for this failure. The letters usually invoked the negative image of 'the [dirty] corners of the coffeehouse' in two circumstances. The first, as we saw above, occurred when, deprived of the space and the activities of the Halkevi for a variety of reasons, the complainants and those they purportedly represented (most commonly 'the people' or 'the youth') were left with the only available option, which was to assemble at the coffee house.

But secondly, and most importantly, complaint letters cited the coffee house when they disclosed that popular practices of male socialization which were associated with the coffee house (gambling and drinking) were also commonly taking place in the Houses. As a complainant reported, 'coffee and tea are served to the visitors of the Halkevi library, while they can also play domino, chess and similar games. Now this nest of culture functions like a coffeehouse; it is impossible to read a book or a newspaper because of the noise.'[35] Another letter protested that 'some civil servants, thinking highly of themselves and despising the local population, are customarily and in front of the local youths exercising immoral deeds, such as gambling and drinking, in the Halkevi.'[36] Drinking coffee or alcohol, gambling and playing other games, activities the letters related to the 'dirty corners of the coffeehouse', were reported in the People's Houses of Bozcaada, Biga, Osmaniye, Bayramiç, Arhavi, Tortum (Erzurum), Kemalpaşa, Kuşadası, İnebolu, İzmit, Kızılhisar (Denizli), Kula (Manisa), Kızıltepe (Mardin), Sinop, Erbaa (Tokat), Bingöl and Amasya, and the People's Rooms of Ceylanpınar (Urfa) and Bozova (Urfa).[37]

Next to accusations of immorality, the exclusion of their authors from the Halkevi was probably one of the most common themes of the letters.[38] Sometimes it was the sole reason for complaining; sometimes it emerged as a corollary to the situation or event described. In their attempt to report their exclusion from, or inability to enter, the People's House for a variety of reasons, not a few authors resorted to the argument that 'unable to go to the House, the people or the youth spend their time in the coffeehouse', which the letters describe of course in negative terms, employing the regime's moralistic discourse.

A village teacher complained that the gendarmerie corporal had occupied 'the People's Room and its garden.[39] When the doors of our People's Room closed for our villager fellow citizens, everybody, the youth and the elders started to waste their time in the coffeehouse corners.'[40] In a similar vein, Rifat Kayral 'from the people of Buldan', denounced the 'illiterate' and 'ignorant' Halkevi janitor who was the reason 'our people and our youth are refused the access to knowledge [and] spend their time in the coffeehouse corners.'[41] In a different tone, the chairman of the Sports section of a provincial House complained that 'it is difficult to assemble the youth to do sports, because there is no space for such activities, which means that the youths stay behind in life as they generally spend their time in the coffeehouse corners.'[42] More inspired reasons were also given for the youth's estrangement from 'their own House'. According to an anonymous letter, the youths of Doğubeyazit were filling the coffee houses playing poker because the Halkevi chairman could not speak Turkish, while the hobby of the 45-year-old Halkevi secretary 'has been for a long time now to defile youths, that is, he is a sodomite [kulampara]'.[43] 'Lack of proper administration' (idaresizlik) and apathy were, on another occasion, the reasons the youths of Bilecik were left with no choice but to 'spend their time in the coffeehouses and in the streets gossiping.'[44]

But most of all the exclusion was once more expressed in terms of the all-pervasive divide between 'the people' and the 'intellectuals'. This divide, and the exclusion it signified, apart from the rhetoric scheme of the letters, denoted certain social and discursive practices enacted by our actors customarily, but also in response to the centre's policies and their implementation, and prominent among them was the establishment and operation of new social and institutional spaces, such as the People's Houses. More specifically, many letters complained that, although prohibited, coffee-house activities were performed in the Houses, expressed in terms of the omnipresent 'people' vs 'intellectuals and civil servants' divide. The letters commonly denounced the civil servants and intellectuals for monopolizing the Halkevi space and for excluding their authors ('the people' and 'the youth') while practising what the centre was vehemently criticizing the people for performing in coffee houses. Two tailors from Biga, for instance, complained that the Halkevi chairman and executives were playing cards and poker in the Halkevi, while 'the youths spend their time in coffeehouses'.[45] In simple words, the argument went as follows: '[T]hey gamble in the Halkevi, when *we* are asked not to visit the coffeehouses in order to gamble.'

Consider the following incident as described, on the one hand, by six complainants, and explained, on the other hand, by the local Party chief. On 3 November 1944 'the undersigned youths' – a farmer, a tailor, a shoemaker, a municipal porter, a caretaker in the state dispensary, and a grocer – denounced the *Kaymakam* of the small Aegean town of Kuşadası for cursing and expelling them from the People's Room while slapping one of them in the face. 'Is the People's Room the civil servants club? The people are rejected there.'[46]

In his letter to the provincial Party branch (Izmir) on 1 April 1944, Dr Sezai Yavaşça, chairman of the local Party branch, recounted the event quite differently.

Our district is small and there are no suitable places for our civil servant friends[47] to sit. In order not to have them visit unsuitable places but in order to gather [in a place] together, one of the rooms of this building, which belongs to the municipality, was allotted to them. Those from them [civil servants] who desire to study and exchange opinions pass to the People's Room, which is a separate room, while those wishing to play common games enter the other room. So the incident took place in the civil servants' room, which has no relation to the People's Room. As for the incident:

When the Kaymakam Fevzi Hamurculu entered the civil servants' room, the complainants were playing parafa [a card game] on one of the tables. The Kaymakam addressed them in the following words: 'why do you follow us, there are eighty coffeehouses, this place belongs to the civil servants. There is no reason to be impolite, just go there.' Then, according to rumours, he entered the room a little later and, seeing them there again, he slapped Kenan Önder in the face. All of them are about eighteen–twenty years old. They are *not intellectuals, but immature youngsters, some of them wishing to pass for rowdies and toughs [külhanbeyi].*[48]

The way the local Party chief described the plaintiffs is telling of the way categories that were exalted in the official discourse, such as the 'youth' or the 'intellectuals', were used in the local context. He reported their youth as a handicap rather than an asset, attesting to the fact that they were not intellectuals. This contempt for their youth conformed to popular norms regarding seniority. In that sense, the complainants were depicted as trespassing on a space they were not fit to enter due to status (non-intellectuals or civil servants) and age restrictions. Needless to say, these restrictions were not to be found in the Halkevi by-laws; quite the contrary, they were prohibited. What is more, in discrediting the complaints, Sezai Yavaşça moved away from categories employed by the official discourse (intellectuals/ the people) and invoked the image of the *külhanbeyi* of the neighbourhood. In popular representations, the *külhanbeyi* was an ambiguous figure, the local 'tough guy' who would 'protect' the 'honour' of the quarter and its residents (especially its women) against the outside, but at the same time was the local bully. In the eyes of a centre, which aspired to penetrate and 'modernize' the locality that this local 'tough guy' was protecting against outsiders, the *külhanbeyi* was translated into an outdated negative type that obstructed the very 'progress' of the region the centre was aiming at with the People's Houses. In the eyes of educated and usually non-local state officials, the *külhanbeyi* was seen as a low-class primitive vestige, an 'immature youngster wishing to pass for rowdy and tough'.

The manner in which gambling was accounted for by the implicated is also telling of the way the distinction between civil servants and locals was expressed and performed. Here, the complainants mentioned nothing about gambling. Instead, their accusation was based on the argument that they were expelled by the *Kaymakam* because they were from 'the people' and not civil servants. The accused side, on the other hand, admitted that they were denying access to 'non-civil servants', albeit not from the People's Room but from an adjacent room that had been allocated for the exclusive use of civil servants. Moreover, upon explaining the reasons for reserving a room for exclusive use by civil servants, the local Party chief used a tone somehow assenting or accommodating to the accusations of exclusion. As they desired to assemble by themselves, and since their district was small with no suitable places for them, an adjustment was necessary. Eloquently yet quite simply expressed, they considered themselves entitled to be segregated from the people and the 'unsuitable' coffee houses they frequented.

As for the complainants, the *Kaymakam*, who was accused elsewhere[49] of playing backgammon with the bank's vice-chairman in the Halkevi, was reported explaining where the complainants – that is, not the 'civil servant friends' – should assemble, that is, at the coffee house. The problem, thus, was not playing cards *per se*, but playing cards in the wrong place, in the People's Room, where gambling was prohibited. And, as one can plausibly assume and the Party chief's letter implied, the civil servants were playing cards or – as Dr Sezai Yavaşça put it – 'common games' in the Halkevi. Instead of excluding the low-class 'others' from the People's Room then, as the complainants protested, the local Party chief responded that a separate space was created for that same purpose within, or next to, the People's Room. True or false, this arrangement was an ingenious solution on the part of local Party and state elites, an answer to two seemingly incompatible demands: on the one hand, to spatially segregate from local non-elites without monopolizing the Halkevi and thus excluding the 'other', while, on the other hand, to be able to perform privately and away from the public gaze (coffee house) activities prohibited in the People's Houses.[50] In the terms of the Ottoman state's political discourse (not necessarily its practices), this solution prevented the transgression of the border between rulers and ruled by safeguarding distinct spaces of socialization for state officials. But from another point of view, current state practice regarding the relationship of important state officials with the population of the places they were appointed to was also based on a similar rationale: high civil servants, judiciary, police and military officials were not usually appointed to their place of birth or residence and would be optimally reappointed to a new area after some years so that they would not establish relations with locals that would compromise their duty to the state. In a similar fashion, the Party delegated the duty to inspect local Party structures to non-local MPs or Party elites. So, a certain distance from locals was both solicited and expected. The ingenious method of creating a segregated space within the People's Room to separate from the locals while gambling was excused on these grounds.

A letter from İnebolu revealed an analogous method to keep the border intact and achieve the segregation of the gambling and drinking intellectuals from the rest by a similar act of exclusion.

> We are of the People's Party and since its establishment the Halkevi of our district has been divided into two parts; the large hall is reserved for studying, theatre plays, and all kinds of meetings; the other part is a small room where the Halkevi administration has permitted [the drinking of] coffee, and the playing of billiards. Everybody could sit in both rooms. In the evening of 22 March 1949 we, children of this country, went to the Halkevi that we know to be open to everybody and sat in the small playing room that is used as a coffeehouse. Upon ordering two coffees and the domino, the person making

coffee replied that he will neither give us the domino nor make
coffee because, as it seems, the Halkevi chairman had said that only
Halkevi members, lycée graduates, and civil servants could enter this
small room used as a coffeehouse and open to all the people over the
age of eighteen. If lycée graduates and civil servants are considered
to be from the people, then aren't we – non-lycée graduates or civil
servants – from the people?[51]

Both practices revealed by the letters (elite segregation and card and
game-playing) were in particular invoked in popular grievances
against the City Club (*Şehir Kulübü*). City Clubs were established
as places of socialization for local and state elites, usually educated
professionals, civil servants and bureaucrats. Some were supposed
to operate as a 'scientific and social institution in the region'[52] –
to quote the by-laws of the *Şehir Kulübü* of Balıkesir. Outside
Istanbul, Izmir or Ankara, City Clubs started to appear in the
1930s and it seems that most City Clubs of Anatolian provincial
towns were established in the late 1930s and 1940s. Right from
the beginning, they were spaces established and frequented by
state officials to the effect that they were alternatively called 'civil
servants clubs'.[53] Consider, for instance, that in 1934 the Party
Secretary Recep Peker informed the Party organization that youth
unions and 'clubs under other names' could function as nuclei for
the forthcoming establishment of a Halkevi. For this reason, he
recommended that such institutions be protected and controlled
by the local Party through the registration of Party members and
supporters.[54]

At the same time, though, the City Club was commonly
targeted by both complaint letters and newspaper articles[55] using
the same rhetoric and discursive terms as was applied to the coffee
house. They were accused of hosting 'high gambling parties'[56] and
discriminating against non-elites.[57] But the City Club was also
negatively associated to the People's House and its activities by
both complaints and Party investigations. In an interesting and
rare case from the island of Bozcaada, for instance, state officials
had turned the local People's Room into a City Club; they even

had a sign put at the Room's entrance: 'City Club, entrance only for members'. The ensuing investigation by the Party confirmed the accusation and ordered a return to the previous state of affairs.[58]

Zühtü Durukan, MP for Samsun and Party inspector of the Bilecik area, related the indifference of some civil servants towards the Halkevi to the existence of a City Club. According to the inspector, Bilecik was a small and neglected province and the former governor did not care about anything, waiting as he was to serve his last five years until retirement. The situation was aggravated by a number of civil servants who, instead of facing prosecution for previous offences, had been administratively exiled in Bilecik. These civil servants 'were taking advantage of the governor's indifference, have lost their discipline to the state, and were assembling in a place called City Club, where they were gambling until morning, sometimes even abandoning their service and continuing gambling at daytime'. As a result, the Halkevi 'remained stagnant', and 'as some of the addicted to gambling high-level civil servants were not visiting the Halkevi, they became an obstacle to the participation of the junior civil servants as well'.[59]

Muhsin Adil Binal, MP for Konya and Party inspector of Seyhan, offered a more general assessment of the 'City Club' phenomenon, its causes and results:

> In fact, one of the first things a governor is thinking of doing in the cities and towns is to find a building for the civil servants in particular to assemble in order to relax, and to manage it as a Club. In such a place, they come together to chat and read newspapers and journals; depending on the place, in a small or large scale, gambling is accepted as a natural fact. Our People's Houses are obliged to benefit from the efforts of the intellectuals and the expertise of the civil servants. After all, in small towns the success of the activities of the People's Houses depends solely on the civil servant members. From this perspective, the existence of such Clubs is naturally preventing the activities of the Houses. It is also needless to explain

how much damage to our social body the gambling in the Clubs and
the creation of lazy and vagabond types produces.[60]

Although criticizing the fostering of gambling, and while he
recognized the potential impediments to the Halkevi activities
these clubs might produce, the Party inspector did not seem to
consider the idea behind the creation of such clubs – that is, the
carving of an autonomous space for the exclusive use of civil
servants – harmful, unless perhaps used for gambling. This is
reminiscent of the Party's position on drinking and gambling
in Party buildings and Turkish Hearths in 1930, when a Party
communication stated that these activities were not prohibited
in general, but only inside Party buildings in order not to give
the wrong impressions to 'the people', who 'will not tolerate
them.'[61] Appearances again were paramount. The need to sustain
the border was silently expressed, but the civil servants within
the border should not *appear* provocative to the excluded. The
ambivalence was once more conveyed: drinking, gambling
and playing games, although condemned as inappropriate and
unpleasant in the official discourse, were not always evaluated the
same way regardless of where and by whom they were performed.
The documents available do not directly voice the opinions of
the main users of such spaces – the civil servants – but Muhsin
Adil Binal partially conveyed them. The civil servants were
tacitly granted the right to assemble together separately from
the rest of the people and, if not becoming 'lazy and vagabond'
or 'preventing the activities of the Halkevleri', 'gambling, big or
small, is considered a natural fact', almost acceptable.

Similar grievances were raised by complaint letters as well.
A letter from Tosya attempted to direct the centre's attention
to the local City Club 'because I consider it to be opposing
the government and Party principles'. The anonymous author
informed Ankara that all the regional civil servants, including the
public prosecutor, judge, mayor and the Halkevi chairman, were
members and paid membership fees. As a result, the civil servants
became totally indifferent to the Halkevi and the gap between the

people and state officials was further widened. The complainant continued that the Club was doing nothing for the region or the common good: 'It is just a nest of gambling and drinking for three or five civil servants and their superiors. For the judge and prosecutor's sake Party and Halkevi members say nothing and have fun together.'[62]

Three years later, a communiqué of the interior ministry reiterated almost identically the charges of the above letter against the City Clubs. The document admitted that the City Clubs were established and run in opposition to the People's House; that the Clubs had obtained a number of privileges in comparison to other public places; that because of these privileges they had become gambling and drinking centres; that they were obstructing the 'coming together' (kaynaşma) of people and intellectuals; and that they were preventing the interest and participation that was necessary for the People's Houses and Rooms.[63] Considered together with the above report by Muhsin Adil Binal and numerous letters from Party chiefs and civil servants, the Party communiqué revealed the existence of various perspectives among Party and state personnel regarding the place the People's House and state officials should have in the provinces. State and Party institutions and actors in the centre and the provinces were expressing a set of needs and aims that were mutually exclusive. On the one hand, silently or not, the need of civil servants and bureaucrats to separate and keep themselves segregated from the rest of the local people was voiced; equally expressed, on the other hand, was the primary aim of the People's Houses, to realize the 'coming together' of intellectuals and people. A number of ingenious solutions to these two conflicting demands were devised by Halkevi elites and consequently denounced by those excluded from the Halkevi space.

Several Houses could circumvent the Houses' programmatic openness through the veiled segregation of civil servants, teachers and students. 'Teachers' evenings', students meetings and civil servant meetings were employed to this end.[64] However, the most common and commonly denounced method of segregation was the issuing of invitations. The system of invitation cards (*davetiye*) to Halkevi events, such as theatre and musical performances, was devised by Party and Halkevi bosses to regulate the entrance to Halkevi activities but also to restrict the entrance only to the people receiving the invitations. In this way the entrance to many – perhaps most – Halkevi activities was restricted and the Halkevi executives could limit entrance, enforcing rules of partial (spatial and temporal) inclusion of some and exclusion of others. Not unreasonably, then, the *davetiye* was one of the most popular grievances of those excluded from the Halkevi Halls. Several letters mentioned or complained about the invitations needed to enter the Halkevi during a theatre play or general show,[65] a concert,[66] or a ball.[67] In Zonguldak, as an anonymous writer protested, a system of coloured tickets was applied to regulate the entrance to the Halkevi cinema. The Monday evening shows were restricted to high-level officials holding white cards; the Tuesday evening shows to the rest of the civil servants with the pink card; the Wednesday shows to executives of the state Mining Company with the blue card; the Thursday shows to low-level company employees with grey cards; and, finally, the Friday evenings to workers.[68] In another example, the chairman of the Izmir Halkevi printed invitation cards for the Halkevi programme on 12 July 1943, entitled 'Cultural Evening'. The card was for two persons and informed that students and other minors would not be admitted.[69]

To sum up, the complaint letters and the reports – be it from a local Party man or an (external) Party inspector – referred to two practices already present in a number of spaces and occasions even before the creation of the People's Houses. One was the practice of segregation of the educated and elite segments of local societies from the rest of the population. The second was a wide set of leisure socializing activities the centre had been suspicious of for centuries, including the space within which they typically took place, that is, the coffee house. These practices intersected with the new space of the People's House and its activities; encountered and contrasted with the Houses' aims; and interrelated with, reflected and became reflected in conflicting but also parallel discourses employed both by the regime and social actors. We have seen how the accommodative discourse employed by civil servants and Party men in relation to their need to segregate from the rest of the people was contrasted with the accusatory discourse of those excluded from or denied access to the Halkevi.

The letters complained about many deficiencies, wrongdoings and the exclusion of their authors from the Houses. Willing but unable for a number of reasons to enter according to their account, these complainants used the official discourse in a tactical and ingenious way; turning, stretching and even mutating without totally and outwardly refusing it, using its own contradictions and ambiguities in order to further their accusation and, ultimately, their request. I read these grievances as the result of a continuous struggle that was waged by our actors (included and excluded) upon the Halkevi border. By Halkevi border, I do not refer to the Houses' spatial characteristics alone, but to the totality of the discourses describing, the practices connected with and the values attributed to the Halkevi, and to the contenders or refuters of such discourses, practices and values; that is, the men and women situated in, on, outside but also far away from the Halkevi border. I chose to view these twists and turns and the accommodation tactics and discourse involved as acts of domestication of the practices the centre was striving to introduce. Domestication here refers to acts by social actors that attempted to render the policies of the reforming state familiar to local needs and interests, and to the socio-political and cultural realities of local societies.

Drawing on Meltem Ahıska, I employ the term boundary management to designate but also to explore this process of domestication, of that continuous turning, twisting, resisting and accommodating the centre's projects on the real, practical and discursive border of the Halkevi.[70] Ahıska studies Turkish radio broadcasting in the 1930s and 1940s in order to explore the continuous boundary management the Turkish elite was practising in relation to twin concepts such as foreign/national, elite/people, men/women, or authentic/artificial. Employing the term to point to the inclusiveness/exclusiveness of the representations of such notions in radio broadcastings, Ahıska notes the ability of the representations to recognize the existing boundaries and thus draw new ones, while stressing the association these operations of boundary management had to relations and practices of power. I use boundary management in a broader sense, to denote the struggles social actors were engaged in at the boundary of Halkevi space, but also to include – next to its representations – the discursive practices that constituted the boundary separating the Houses and what they were supposed to stand for from their exterior that they were intended to 'nationalize' and 'civilize'.

Employed by their authors to enhance the expected result of their petition, the letters' vocabulary drew from the official discourse but also reflected their authors' perceptual and cognitive panoply. Even upon a quick reading of the letters, it becomes immediately apparent that their authors were aware of and utilized the official negative discourse about the coffee house.[71] The extensive use of the anti-coffee house moralistic discourse, first of all expressed the authors' ability to identify the regime's fears and preoccupations and manipulate them to advance their own demands and interests, and claim the Halkevi space, its resources and the facilities and status it might offer to contesting sides in an ongoing local feud, such as the ones analyzed in Chapter 3.

On a more general level, petitioning the Party meant that the author was likely to start and conclude the letter with some kind of reference to the ideals of the Party and the People's Houses. In their attempt to demonstrate their commitment to the regime and ensure a positive reaction to their demand, many authors imitated the Party's vocabulary to show a degree of ideological affinity. A tactical move disclosing the supplicants' ability to acknowledge and utilize (fragments of) the regime's jargon, 'speaking Kemalist'[72] was something expected but probably not as common as 'speaking Bolshevik' in the Soviet Union.[73] The utilization of the Kemalist jargon did not automatically mean that the underlying discourse was readily accepted; rather, the employment of the official discourse was a conventional way to address authority. After all, denouncing the regime's principles would not have been a productive way to protest or request anything from that same power; thus the letters needed and tried to phrase their demands in the appropriate language.

Notwithstanding the letters' affinity with the official discourse, from another perspective they deviate from the centre's discourse. Apart from just copy-pasting the regime's vocabulary, many authors' tactical use of it overturned some of its propositions. That was evident in the authors' frequent employment of the distinction between intellectuals and people, but also of key words from the Kemalist lexicon ('intellectuals', 'people' and 'youth', in particular) in a fashion that radically differed from the official populist discourse. In their reuse, the terms were transformed to denote different attributes.

The supplicants' exclusion, for instance, was voiced in terms of 'we' against 'them';[74] the 'them' included were 'the civil servants', 'the rich', 'a few rich merchants', 'oppressors', and 'landlords' (*mütegalibe, zengin, ağa*).[75] The complainants depicted themselves as (of) 'the people' or 'the youth' and as conscious supporters of the regime's ideals. In doing so, they consciously employed the regime's own categories of the celebrated youth and people, whom official ideology was proclaiming as the source of sovereignty. However, the complainants reversed the official discourse by presenting themselves as the oppressed, suffering and disempowered people or youth, something that was emphatically invoked when complaining about their constant exclusion from their 'own House', that is, the People's House. And it was here that their self-presentation as the people both separated from and built on the official populist discourse. In the official discourse, the people were trained into civilization, nationhood and equal citizenship by the intellectuals; in a way evocative of the official jargon, the complainants contrasted themselves (as the people) with the intellectuals, but only to protest their exclusion from the 'training' they were supposed to receive from these same intellectuals.[76] The celebrated 'people' of the official populist rhetoric then was turned into the humble or the unjustly treated subject – a common motif in petition letters – who was despised and oppressed by the officials.[77]

In another resourceful employment of the official discourse, some authors – even those signing as 'from the people' – repeated the 'child metaphor' of the discourse of social engineering and people's education. Their presentation of the people as a passive and naive child easily surrendering to coffee houses, gambling and drinking was a device to stress the exclusion from the House and the oppression by state and local elites, whom the letters denounced as 'civil servants' and 'landowners', the 'high class', the 'usurpers' and 'oppressors'. What is evident is the authors' ability to acknowledge and manipulate the official discourse in a tactical attempt to safeguard their interests.

But as we have seen in a number of cases, when Party and state elites had to respond to the accusations of exclusion, they likewise portrayed the plaintiffs as 'from the people', 'non-intellectuals', 'non-civil servants', or 'immature youngsters'. Within the context of multi-party politics after the postwar political liberalization, RPP and government elites felt less restrained by the official populist discourse when denigrating the supporters of the opposition as 'plebs', a 'mob', 'lowlifes', 'bad breeds' and 'flat-cap wearers' (*kasketliler* – referring to the popular headgear the lower classes and villagers wore as opposed to the more expensive brimmed hat of civil servants and urban elites).[78]

Another salient trait of the accusatory discourse of complaint and denunciation letters was the constant invocation of/reference to morality. As exemplified in the complaint about coffee-house activities (gambling, laziness, drinking, etc), the supplicants' exclusion from or aversion towards the House, but also the more general theme of the oppressed people's suffering at the hands of oppressing elites, was expressed in terms of immorality. Just like the civil servants in the City Club, the Halkevi executives and state/local elites who excluded 'the people and the youth from their own House', were not only 'thinking highly of themselves and despised the local population', but were also 'customarily performing immoral deeds in front of the local youths, such as gambling and drinking'.[79] In popular discourse and grievances, oppressiveness of the accused went hand in hand with their immorality. The oppressed, on the other hand, were frequently rendered as moral and righteous.

In more general terms, the letters' language did not revolve on the axis of modern/backward but moral/immoral. Simply put, the authors did not complain that local Party and state officials were backward or reactionary, but that they were acting in an immoral fashion. The vocabulary the letters resorted to typically invoked the morality/immorality divide; certain words appear regularly, such as '(im)moral(ity)', 'upright', 'proper', 'clean' (*nezahet, nezih, ahlak, gayri ahlaklı, ahlaksız, feci, temiz, hayasızlık, rezalet, namuslu/suz*). A commonplace rhetoric means that what many letters conveyed was the image of the coffee house, the gambling house, the drinking tavern and the brothel, all signifying a moral and social decay.[80] On the other hand, this emphasis on morality was very rarely expressed in words that had a religious connotation.[81] In most cases, religiously flavoured words were infrequently paired with (and in praise of) a Party institution or idea, as in the banal references to 'our Party's sacred aims', or 'the sacred Halkevi stage'.[82]

But if the authors were astute in not referring to Islam when denouncing a Party executive to the Party, they also appeared – rather unexpectedly – incapable of using ready-made anti-regime categories in their denunciations. The letters very rarely accused their adversaries of being 'reactionary' or 'backward'. The vocabulary the regime used to identify its enemies (*yobaz, irtica, murteci, şeriatçi* and so forth) was hardly ever employed in these letters. This was probably due to their lack of relevance within any widespread frame of reference outside the official discourse. Otherwise, our authors would have been quick to use the Party's catchwords to blame their adversaries, as, for instance, in the contemporary Soviet Union where accusations such as *kulak* and *Trotskyist* were extensively used.[83]

Irrespective of the motive behind the complaint, the validity of the grievance or the identity of the petitioner and his/her real feelings about the reforms and the Halkevi activities, all letters converged in the language/rhetoric within which they were framed and with which they expressed their grievances. The most employed references in this accusatory discourse were to immorality and oppression; and it was upon these two grievances that the differentiation between denounced and denouncers, elites and people, was erected. Oppression was surely a very common rhetoric element of grievances in Ottoman history, but also before and elsewhere. It was a central element of the legitimizing discourse of many pre-modern states in the Middle East, in the official discourse of which the ruler dispensed justice by protecting his subjects from the oppression of state officials.[84] But the pairing of oppression with (im)morality was (and still is) to be found at the core of conservative populist discourses and of the Turkish right since the 1950s. The imagery and cultural scenarios[85] our letters depicted have been identified in the works of influential conservative intellectuals in the 1940s and 1950s,[86] but also in the discourse of politicians and political parties since then.[87] For Bora and Erdoğan, for instance, the subject of conservative populist discourses is the people: their suffering, undeserved misery and oppression at the hands of immoral and over-Westernized elites constitute the backbone of such discourses. The archetypical scapegoat is the ethnic and religious Other, the Westernized woman and man, the foreigner and the communist. They were responsible for the suffering of the righteous people, who, in turn, are characterized by common sense as opposed to the superficiality and ignorance of the intellectual and oppressor elites.[88]

The imagery of the letters exhibits a number of similarities with the discourse of Turkish Islam that Açıkel has studied from the perspective of the 1980s and 1990s. For Açıkel, the discourse of 'sacred oppression' (kutsal mazlumluk) conveys feelings of oppression, disempowerment, insult, loss of status and reputation, alienation, but also the longing for the restoration of dignity and power of the undeservingly suffering moral subject. Paired with the immorality of the oppressor, the suffering almost appears sacred – a common motif in all three Middle Eastern monotheistic cultures.[89] In that sense, the undeservingly oppressed and righteous subject awaiting retribution was a readily available and popular narrative and a cultural scenario constantly reproduced in popular literature and songs, music and cinema.[90] I view this scenario of the 'oppressed righteous subject' as a discursive and cognitive category through which the narration of socio-political relations and collective identities was performed and renegotiated.

But whose identities? For Açıkel, the subjects of the discourse of 'sacred oppression' were the millions of disoriented and destitute peasants that had been leaving their villages to settle in shanty neighbourhoods in Turkish cities since the 1950s. But our authors were neither displaced peasants nor could they be considered to be from the illiterate masses. On the contrary, based on the information provided by the authors,[91] most letters were compiled by middle-class, predominately male, and educated, or at least literate, urbanites, such as Party and Halkevi members and executives; teachers, lawyers, civil servants, merchants and artisans. In short, the excluded or indignantly observing complainants were none other than those the regime considered its own constituency in provincial urban settings.

The use of petition-writers cannot be ruled out – after all, many Houses assisted illiterates and villagers in their dealings with the state, and writing petitions was a typical activity.[92] Nevertheless, I view petition and complaint letters as negotiated cultural artefacts produced within specific political and literary contexts[93] and argue that, even if a number of letters were co-authored by public scribes and supplicants, that by no means suggests that the supplicants' voices and their discursive and cognitive universe were not reflected or reproduced in the end product. On the contrary, the letters are selected from an array of discursive resources: the Party jargon they were mimicking (perhaps the input of a professional scribe or a Halkevi petition-writer); the moralistic discourse of newspapers and intellectuals about the coffee house's smoky environment of gambling and drinking that promoted an unhealthy and lazy lifestyle; and a populist conservative discourse that bemoaned and protested the exclusion and/or oppression of the people by state and Party elites who were performing immoral deeds (gambling, drinking, and womanizing) in the Halkevi, the City Club and elsewhere. It was upon struggles for the management and definition of the Halkevi boundary (that is, what the proper Halkevi and its activities were or should be like) that these discursive melanges were produced by dissatisfied middle-class urbanites. In that sense, I view their narratives of insult, oppression and immorality as constitutive of the way they comprehended the Halkevi experiment, the reform movement in general, and their own position inside or outside it. But, as we have already seen in the previous chapter on the Halkevi space within local politics in provincial urban settings, this was inevitably a discourse of politics as it was ultimately about the political empowerment of its carriers.

Conclusion

In this chapter we have seen how social actors coped with novel habits, discourses and practices of free-time socialization, while at the same time making allowances for local popular practices and discourses as well as their personal and group interests; and how both in terms of discourse and practices the actors of the stories narrated in the letters managed to domesticate the Halkevi practices of leisure by means of manipulating the ambiguities of the reforming state's practice and discourse, as well as through a number of ingeniously crafted adaptations of the activities the centre had planned. More specifically, although prohibited by the Halkevi by-laws and despised in the official discourse, activities habitually performed in the homosocial space of the coffee house – a *bet noire* for the Kemalist modernizing discourse itself – were routinely performed by state and local elites in the Halkevi space. Moreover, Halkevi actors devised a number of ingenious techniques to keep the space of the Halkevi segregated while performing coffee-house practices. I view this as an act of domestication of the space and the activities the regime was attempting to initiate. The domestication refers to the way the centre's ideas and plans – without being rejected – were blended with activities, perceptions and practices they were supposed to eradicate, or to which they were discursively opposed.

By studying the accommodation and domestication of the reforms by social actors, my aim is not to assess the success or failure of such reform projects.[94] Rather, I am interested in viewing the consumption involved as a *process of boundary negotiation* indispensable for identity management. It is upon and within the continuously negotiated boundaries of the local socio-political and cultural milieu that men and women operated and produced meaningful representations of themselves and others.

The complainants, for instance, while recognizing and employing the official anti-coffee-house discourse, were able to employ elements of the regime's discourse in a fashion that cleverly manipulated its ambivalences to enable them to turn it without refuting it entirely. The way the word 'people' was employed in complaint letters to denote the powerless and unjustly treated is telling of their authors' ability to draw on a key element of the official discourse and use it to signify something completely different from its former meaning – the hallowed people of the populist rhetoric. In addition, the accusatory discourse of the letters exhibited imagery and characteristics that were employed by conservative populist discourses of the Turkish right after the 1940s. Interestingly, their writers were not those the Kemalist regime considered its arch-enemies. The authors were neither uneducated nor illiterate villagers, nor religious reactionaries; they were none other than what the regime considered its constituency in provincial urban settings.

Women on the Halkevi Stage 5

The 'woman issue' formed an essential component of the Kemalist modernization and nation-building project.[1] In the Republic of Turkey, women were propelled into the public domain. They were given civil rights and educational and professional opportunities, but at the same time they were expected to continue performing their 'traditional' duties as mothers and wives; women, thus, assumed the double burden to be active in both public and domestic spheres, being both modern and traditional. Women made forays into society but were simultaneously 'restricted by moral and behavioural codes that were considered essential to the preservation of their families' respectability and honor'. Although promoting women's education and professional life, Kemalism did not alter or seriously challenge 'the patriarchal norms of morality and in fact maintained the basic cultural conservatism about male/female relations'.[2] While, for instance, polygamy was abolished and women were given extensive legal rights, men were still legally considered heads and representatives of the family while women had to get their husbands' permission to work outside the house. The Turkish Penal Code acknowledged the association between women and the honour of their male relatives, as it accepted that in the case of adultery or rape, the honour and prestige of their husband or father could be hurt.[3] Although placing great emphasis on the education, occupation and public appearance of women next to men, the state leaders were adamant in stressing women's primarily domestic duties and the requirements for chastity of the 'emancipated but unliberated'[4] Turkish women. As Kandiyoti argues, this preoccupation with moral behaviour would in effect impose a 'new veil' on the recently 'unveiled' women: sexual repression.[5] Thrust into a male-dominated public sphere, women faced 'unprecedented problems of identity management', having to negotiate their public presence without compromising their respectability.[6] This chapter studies practices of identity management through the examination of the consumption of the women-related activities of the Halkevi space.

The People's Houses were among the loci wherein and through the activities of which the new 'Turkish woman' was going to be realized. The Halkevi executives were charged with the duty to introduce women into the public sphere by bringing them onto the theatre stage, into the concert and lecture hall, and onto the dance floor among unrelated men in urban settings where such novelties were widely considered wrong and rendered immoral, and where women were as a rule domestically secluded and heterosocial interaction was restricted to the family. Women were given the privilege and at the same time the duty to register in the Houses, give lectures to mixed audiences, act on stage, play and enjoy music, socialize with men in 'family meetings', concerts, cinema and theatrical plays, dance with men at festivals and parties, visit villages and participate in various courses as both instructors and students. Halkevi activities undermined homosocial norms and the traditions of female domestic seclusion, especially in provincial urban settings, where the majority of the Houses operated. Drawing on complaint letters and investigative reports by Party men, I study the presence of women in the People's Houses and their activities. In what follows, I review the tension produced by the introduction of mixed-gender entertainment and social interaction within largely sex-segregated local societies; study the practices men and women performed and the discourses they articulated in responding to such moments of tension; and consider their significance as practices of identity management.

Women, Party and Halkevi

To what extent and in what capacity were women included in the reform project of the nationalist elite? The data on the female Party membership reveals that only a handful of women – all wives or sisters of local notables or bureaucrats – were members of the upper Party structures in Kayseri and Balıkesir. Not even one woman seemed to be a Party executive of the lower structures in urban or rural areas, where the Party membership tended to overlap with the nationwide occupational and educational majority. This tendency confirmed wider social perceptions situating women in the domestic sphere, something the Party itself was purportedly struggling to change. The exceptional presence of women in urban Party structures and their routine absence in the rest of the organization, even if we allow for possible exceptions, indicates the rather minimal appeal of the regime's policies about women in Turkish society.

Nevertheless, next to the virtual non-existence of women in Party structures, women did register and become active in the People's Houses. Almost 10 per cent of the members of the Balıkesir House, for instance, and six out of its 43 executives were women in 1934. Most female members and executives were teachers.[7] The same picture holds for Kayseri and the majority of Houses, where, apart from very exceptional cases of the wives of local notables, the majority of women were teachers or wives and daughters of state officials, a large number of whom were not locals.[8] Teachers probably made up most of the female state employees in the provinces while some came from larger cities, such as Istanbul or Ankara. The rest of the female members were the wives, daughters and sisters of usually non-local state employees and local Party bosses, although the vast majority of the female family members of local urban elites were absent from Halkevi and Party registers.

The choice of local notables to enlist (or not) their women into the Party or Halkevi was a deliberate move that could have direct consequences for their political and social standings.

In enlisting and having their women participate in Party and Halkevi activities, the expected addressee was the Party and state leadership. Such an open and personal act of adherence to Party ideals and policies was expected to generate a positive reaction when presented, as we have seen with the case of Mamurhan Özsan's petition letter in Chapter 2. A denunciation letter against her brother-in-law and Halkevi chairman, on the other hand, plainly demonstrates the reasons behind the choice to keep women away from public, and away from the Halkevi or Party spotlight: he 'is almost blind, his sister-in-law has no potential to be elected and is known among the people as a woman of low morals'.[9] The accusations of immorality help explain the reasoning behind the decision of most local Party bosses and members alike not to expose their women to local public life. I am referring to the probable discrediting that such an act might entail for the 'liberating husbands' in the eyes of local society, whose value system assigned women to the domestic and family sphere and obliged men to protect their honour by safeguarding their women's seclusion and chastity. Thus, publicly and openly 'emancipating' his womenfolk to earn Ankara's endorsement or support during a local feud could damage a notable's standing among the local population and in local politics.[10] Having his wife or daughter engage in politics, a notable could 'injure his honour', losing face with local clients, and hurt his position as middleman and power broker, risking the denunciation of local rivals. Surprisingly or not, one of the most frequent accusations in denunciation letters (second only to corruption) was that of immorality, increasingly in relation to the accused persons' womenfolk. As Najmabadi has shown in the case of twentieth-century Iran, political discourse could easily translate into a contest about women and the discourse of morality as rumours about women's behaviour 'did a great deal of political work'.[11]

The above example offers a clear indication of the opposition to women-related policies and the tension produced by their application at the local level. But local societies and actors were not alone in expressing uneasiness towards the increased visibility of women; the centre also exhibited a rather ambiguous stance in regards to women and (Party) politics.

More specifically, for all the data the information-hungry centre was requesting from the periphery, figures on women were only requested in relation to the People's Houses. Every six months the local Party structures were asked to report on the Party membership figures, and Ankara also habitually requested information on non-Party associations; Party and state inspectors regularly reported on local societies, Party branches and staff, the local press, non-state and non-Party associations, the Houses, and even state offices and personnel. But for the majority of the Party papers, gender was not an issue; among this deluge of material the centre was seeking information about women only in relation to the Halkevi.[12] I explain this by considering the centre's emphasis on the 'cultural' rather than 'political' nature of the People's House. This preoccupation with the institution's non-political nature was probably related to the centre's desire to mobilize the educated segments of society – including the majority of state employees who were prohibited by law from engaging in politics – but also to establish an institution that would be more inclusive of the population than local Party structures and, thus, lure those who for a variety of reasons did not desire – or were not considered fit – to enter (Party) politics, such as students or the youth.[13]

The same applied to the place women were considered to occupy in a broadly segregated, homosocial and patriarchal society wherein different roles and spaces were assigned to different sexes. Politics as a public activity was not only considered the domain of men but it was in practice: leaders and decision-makers were exclusively male. This perception of gender roles was implicitly reproduced in the centre's silence and indifference when it came to women's participation in Party structures, and in its explicit interest in having women participate in the Halkevi activities. Paired with the emphasis on the 'cultural' rather than the 'political' character of the Halkevi, the centre's discourse appeared to favour the engagement of women in 'cultural' activities and to assign women to the domain of 'culture', which can be conversely read as an implicit disinclination to have women perform more 'political' – widely considered 'masculine' – roles. This understanding of the regime's discourse clearly conflicts with the celebrated discourse about the liberation of women from the shackles of tradition and their incorporation into the nation's life.

Considering another relevant example, it seems that the issue of women registering with the Party became an issue during the short period of multi-party politics in 1930. More significantly, the issue did not seem to appear as an initiative of the centre but arose from provincial Party branches and in response to the registering of women with the opposition party.[14] It was local Party branches that informed Ankara that women were registered in the Free Republican Party and asked whether they could or should do the same. The matter was considered and the Secretary General accepted the registration of women, as they had been given the right to vote in municipal elections only a few months earlier. This is another indication of the difficulty in accepting women as political subjects not only by a patriarchal society, but also by an intellectual and political leadership that was at the same time 'liberating the Turkish woman'.

What is of interest here is not the place of this contradiction or its function within the centre's discourse,[15] but the tensions it gave rise to and the responses to these tensions by social actors, both men and women. These tensions surfaced in the provinces.

Although our corpus of letters deals with a variety of subjects, certain themes predominate, and immorality was probably one of the most frequent charges levelled against Halkevi and Party figures. Accusations of immorality were mostly related to the presence, absence or activities of women in the Houses. The Halkevi theatre stage[16] is an important site for studying the attitudes, ideas and reactions regarding the presence of women in the Houses. The majority of letters referring – even vaguely – to women were related, one way or another, to the theatre, either in the context of visiting theatrical groups or the Houses' own groups.

The Halkevi Stage and Women

The Party regarded theatre, as well as cinema and radio, as a powerful means of education and propaganda. The Kemalist regime intended to popularize and employ theatre as a medium to propagate the reforms,[17] and the People's House was one of the key instruments of that policy through its Theatre section. In that sense, and instead of artistic value, the Halkevi theatre aimed at 'the emotional merit of one or more men dying for their country and the survivors waving the flag just before the final curtain', to quote an eyewitness of the Halkevi theatre.[18] It was expected to propagate the 'principles of the revolution' and 'satisfy the modern, cultural, and national feelings of the local Turkish society'.[19] To facilitate the implementation of its intentions regarding theatre as a propaganda means, the Party commissioned the writing of plays, organized play-writing competitions and published a series of theatrical plays for use by the People's Houses.[20] The Party also issued a catalogue of plays[21] appropriate for the Halkevi stage and even promoted theatrical groups to perform in the People's Houses.[22] Plays not included in the list had to be approved by the General Secretary.[23] Most important, men were forbidden to play women's roles.[24] This created a real problem for the Halkevi officials. It was openly admitted that there were very few, or usually no, women willing to put themselves on the Halkevi stage in front of the local public.[25] Within a largely segregated and patriarchal society, theatre in general, and women on stage in particular, were broadly considered to be immoral.[26]

In view of this restriction, the Party asked writers for plays with only a handful of female characters. According to the instructions of the 1938–9 Halkevi theatre-play competition, for instance, the prospective plays had to have few female roles; in the 1945 competition, the Party requested plays with three female roles at the most.[27] Yet, plays with few female roles did not automatically or necessarily resolve the practical problem. The lack of women willing to take part in the Halkevi theatre experiment was a common secret, something Halkevi chairmen mentioned in letters to the Party, either as an excuse for the bad performance of their House's stage, or as a reason for the Party and/or state's intervention, mostly by pressing female teachers to 'go on stage'.[28]

Faced with women's refusal to act on stage, Party and state officials developed an array of responses. Although prohibited by the Halkevi by-laws, there were some cases where Halkevi executives had men play female roles.[29] But probably the primary method that most Party and state officials applied was official and unofficial pressure on female teachers. Ankara continually urged local Party branches and Houses to mobilize teachers[30] and even had the Education Minister issue a dispatch that strongly recommended that teachers participate in such Halkevi activities.[31] Party executives habitually reminded teachers of the minister's recommendation to join the Halkevi.[32] Autonomous teachers' associations were also under pressure to join.[33] Women students were perhaps also under pressure as an article in the journal of the Ankara Halkevi indicated when it urged Halkevi officials to overcome the exceptionally low number of women registered in the Houses' sports sections by turning to the girls 'who play together with their boy classmates in the school courtyards'.[34]

But women teachers were also subject to everyday unofficial pressure to climb the stage, as numerous Halkevi officials disclosed in their reports.[35] In 1939 the overzealous governor of Denizli was after those teachers who were sceptical about 'coming on stage'[36] and neglected 'their duties in our Houses', as he wrote to the Party to inform that women teachers could not be convinced to act on the Halkevi stage, although the 'theatre section's chairman is a woman teacher and has asked for their participation and despite the intervention of the director of education and of the governor-cum-Party chairman'.[37] Another form of pressure was to force women teachers to sign an official paper stating that 'although recommended to play the female roles in the plays to be staged in the Halkevi, the women teachers informed that they would not be able to accept'.[38] These documents were usually sent to their administrative superior, the local director of education, governor, or even the ministry, and were presumably expected to intimidate those refusing to participate and act as a warning to the rest. A probable way to mobilize women was through pressure on their male relatives. Although I could not find any explicit reference to such pressure, there are numerous examples of women climbing the stage only after getting the permission of their fathers or brothers. There are likewise indications of women acting together with their husbands or brothers.[39] The first woman on the Halkevi stage in Ordu was the chairman's sister. Another one of the first volunteers was a teacher who participated with her brother – also a teacher and the director of the play – who had previously asked for their father's permission for her acting on stage.[40]

Another widely applied method to overcome the ubiquitous lack of women volunteers was to lure women through material offers. Although in direct contrast to the logic of the Halkevi by-laws, according to which participation in the Halkevi activities was considered to be a voluntary action and not in return for money, financial compensation was a rather common practice.[41] Women working in the Houses were probably informally obliged to act on their stages or at least were more prone to submit to pressure. When, for instance, she was asked to take a role in a Halkevi play, the former secretary of the Edremit House told the Halkevi chairman: 'I am not the Halkevi secretary any more. I cannot go on stage.' She had found a job in a local bank, as the angry chairman complained.[42] In Kayseri, a young girl, Zatiye Tonguç, was employed in the library *and* acted on stage until she was dismissed on the orders of a Party inspector.[43] The chairman of the Elazığ House even openly asked Ankara (5 February 1937) whether they could employ actresses as the Halkevi of Bursa had already done.[44] A member of the Bursa Halkevi Theatre section asked that the ten liras his 12-year-old daughter had twice received for the Halkevi plays she took part in be given on a monthly basis, as was the case with two more female members of the section. In his words, 'taking into consideration the problems encountered in the procurement [*tedarik*] of ladies, you [RPP] have ordered that necessary expenses are to be given especially to women in all Houses'.[45]

The Party's attempts to procure women for its stage were illustrative of the negative perceptions of women on stage. The Party correspondence offers considerable insights into the perceptions and attitudes towards theatre and women on stage and on the desegregated space of the Halkevi in the provinces. Many Halkevi mixed-gender events like theatre were quite novel and challenged cultural beliefs and socially constructed expectations of male and female behaviour within a largely homosocial society. For many, theatre was not a morally upright form of entertainment, given the presence of women on stage. Previously it had not been that common to have Muslim women on stage, and thus female roles were usually enacted by non-Muslim actresses, Armenian, Jewish and Greek.[46] In traditional Turkish theatre, men played the female roles. It should not come as a surprise then that complaints about the Halkevi stage rarely discuss anything but women and (the breach of) morality;[47] their grievances were directed at the low morality not the low quality of the Halkevi stage. Next to the coffee house and the drinking tavern, complaint letters used the theatre stage and its practitioners – Halkevi or not – to lament immorality and its grave consequences for society.

To a large extent the experience people had of theatre in provincial towns in the 1930s and 1940s was that of the itinerant theatre companies, especially a stage performance called *tulûat* theatre. *Tulûat* theatre typically combined music and songs with a large degree of improvisation. Originally it drew upon plots from Western plays and techniques from the traditional Turkish theatre *Orta Oyun*. *Tulûat* theatre created its own characters (the villain, the fool, etc.) and had one or more women sing and dance on stage usually making appropriate gestures to the lyrics.[48] Among intellectuals it was considered a low-quality and even vulgar entertainment. Its coarse vocabulary and obscene scenes even resulted in brawls and police-related incidents.[49] In most cases it is not certain whether many of the letters were aimed at wandering theatre troupes performing *tulûat* theatre in the strict sense or not. What is unambiguous, however, is the widespread negative connotation of the word: *tulûat* was typically used as a metonym for performances the complainants considered obscene or immoral. In Güntekins's travelogue *Anadolu Notları*, an artisan in a small Anatolian town painted a vivid picture of the effect of theatre on Anatolian men: 'May Allah punish them, once in a while theatre players come here. There are inappropriate [*uygunsuz*] women among them. They take the country's money, but they also seduce families.' The author explained that the only thing local men 'can see of women during the day is a ghost lost inside a large *çarşaf*,[50] a tight veil. The young know of no woman except their mother and sister.' The effect of theatre could be devastating: 'they enter a crowded place in the middle of the night. A little later, a colourful wall is lifted among sounds of drums, violin and bells. Women dressed in golden cloths glimmering under the lamps' flashing lights appear, with their faces, hair, and arms uncovered, their chests open. What are these men then supposed to do if not go crazy and abandon their wives and children?'[51] Theatre in general, but in particular *tulûat* and the 'inappropriate women',[52] was conceived as a calamity threatening family and moral values, commonly evoked in most letters with the employment of the term 'theatre girls' (*tiyatro kızları*).[53]

Either in order to supplement their meagre budget or perhaps even to circumvent the absence of local women actresses and thus manage to stage plays in the Halkevi, many Houses leased their stage to touring troupes. At times called *tulûat* or 'common theatre' (*adi tiyatro*), these groups constituted a frequent target of complaint. Mazar Gençkurt from the Theatre section of the Bursa Halkevi denounced the section's chairman for – among many other wrongdoings – having acted in *tulûat* theatre companies and for inviting such a theatre company to perform its 'obscene acts on the Halkevi stage'.[54] A member of the Kütahya Halkevi Theatre section described the people's reaction to the *tulûat* group performing in their Halkevi: 'The Halkevi Hall was used by a *tulûat* group and for days the people had been coming to the House with the only purpose to watch naked legs. Some people did not even refrain from gossips like "Well done Party! At last by showing naked legs they managed to assemble people at the People's House." A couple of years before, the author wrote, the Halkevi stage had been given to a *tulûat* theatre again and a sign had been placed on the Halkevi wall stating that 'It is prohibited to pass words to the girls'. The author did not feel the need to comment on a sign he probably considered explicitly improper for the Halkevi 'sacred building'. The sign was a clear indication of how women on stage were perceived and what kind of words men were more or less considered entitled to toss, and indeed did toss, at them.[55]

Another letter, sent from Izmit in February 1942, was even more expressive. Signed by 'an officer and his family', the anonymous author claimed that he loved theatre:

> But only theatre and not the gang of prostitutes and vagabonds that has brought shamelessness, immorality, disgrace and all the consequent calamities to our city. In short, these supposed theatre people made their third visit here and this time after drinking in taverns they tried to deceive the region's youth by poisoning them with propaganda, by having an almost naked 13–14 year old girl on stage drinking from the bottle. Is it the aim of the People's Houses to entertain the country's drunkards and womanizers in the lowest way, by having prostitutes perform in their Halls? Is our House going to enlighten the people in this way, with belly dancing?[56]

Two more letters from the same city, Izmit, criticized the *tulûat* group performing at the Halkevi. The first, sent on 18 June 1943, complains about an incident that was 'completely contrary to the sacred aims' of the Halkevi:

> A well-known Armenian,[57] the person under the nickname Attila, together with Muhlis Sabahattin and some ill-famed women he had gathered from Istanbul, have been performing şaklabanlık

[performance by a stand-up comedian usually considered of low quality or obscene] for a fortnight in the – sacred for us – Halkevi stage; we also saw them bringing a live donkey on stage and becoming the cause for a number of repulsive events.

The author then offered a colourful description of his annoyance at the way the Halkevi loudspeakers advertised the event:

For the last fifteen days the Halkevi loudspeakers have annoyed thousands of citizens with extremely boring and irritating broadcasting. 'Hello, Hello, Dear citizens. This is the People's House. One of our country's most famous artists, Kamil Tekin now on our stage [...] From this to that date he is going to amaze you for ten days with his strange tricks [...] Don't miss it. Skeletons speak, living people become skeletons [...] Cheap tickets, simple 35, balcony 50 cents.' Two miserable gypsy kids with bells wander around the town carrying a billboard and shouting: 'run to the People's House tonight [...] watch, be amazed.' [58]

The second letter, sent on 16 November 1943 by one of the members of the Theatre section, bemoaned the repercussions of 'the vulgar and low expressions of a *tulûat* group [performing on the Halkevi stage]. The plays we have been staging for years now with the school theatre group have stopped, just as the affinity we had with our House has ceased. A family girl that has closed her ears with great self-sacrifice to all kinds of gossips and has participated in the Halkevi Theatre would now feel the necessity not to take once more any role on the Halkevi stage.'[59] In a similar vein, in a letter from Boğazlıyan published in the newspaper *Tasvir*, Hüseyin Öney complained that 'the Halkevi chairman and members have surrendered this nest, which is our own House, to worthless theatre people who only work to fill their stomachs'.[60] The *tulûat* wandering theatre companies performing on the Halkevi stage were mentioned as one of the misfortunes the local society was facing. Most complaint letters placed immoral theatre next to gambling and drinking and usually related all three calamities to non-local bureaucrats and civil servants whom they contrasted with their oppressed subject – the people. I have argued in the previous chapter that this was a structural element of a popular conservative discourse expressed in both letters and the texts of popular conservative intellectuals like Peyami Safa and Necip Fazıl Kısakürek. In criticizing the leasing of a provincial Halkevi stage to *tulûat* groups *and* the gambling taking place inside the House, a Party member related these wrongdoings to 'the essentially poor children of our deprived town' being robbed of 'the few cents they have to feed themselves and thus leave their families destitute'.[61]

The letters above demonstrate the association of stage, theatre and especially *tulûat* with immorality. In that sense, they explain the disinclination of women to participate in Halkevi plays and their families' reluctance to permit them to act on stage. Struggling to enlist women for the Halkevi theatre stage, the chairman of the Karahisar Halkevi reported, for instance, that one woman teacher 'tried to sabotage our efforts [to recruit female teachers] by referring to the wickedness of acting on stage and spreading her propaganda towards other women'.[62]

The Halkevi stage and other instances of heterosociality in the Houses constantly produced grievances about the breaching of public morals. Clearly the desegregated space of the Halkevi created tension. A sensitive issue the letters touched upon, for instance, was the reported sexual and/or emotional relationship between Halkevi members. Such relationships were deemed inappropriate and immoral, ultimately damaging the Houses' esteem among the population, or in the words of five witnesses to such an event, 'it badly affected the families and the region'. One incident occured in the town of Pazar, when the gendarmerie officer hugged and kissed Necmiye, a lady 'singing on stage' during a Halkevi concert. The Halkevi secretary saw them and 'the following day it was heard by everybody'. Party Inspector Kemal Çelik and five witnesses identified the incident as an 'ugly event', inappropriate for an upright 'nest of culture that is always open for our People'. As for the lady involved, 'according to the result of my inquiry, she is a woman of low morals going with everybody'.[63]

The Bursa Halkevi staged a similar event. The chairman
of the Bursa Halkevi explained that Ms Saadet was dismissed
from the Theatre section because of her affair with another
member of the section, Mr Turgut: 'This lady lives together with
Mr. Turgut as his mistress. As a result, Mr. Turgut has abandoned
his family' and 'this affair has affected our House and stage',
necessitating their resignation. The affair, the chairman wrote,
gave rise to allegations against the rest of the female members,
although 'the allegations directed towards them belong altogether
to another woman'.[64] An anonymous letter from Izmit bemoaned
another Halkevi relationship. A teacher and president of the
town's Charity Union (*Yardım Sevenler Birliği*) was denounced as
the Halkevi chairman's mistress, but also because 'she and some
other loose women invite some local ill-fated women teachers
and girls to the Halkevi and introduce them to men of her kind.
Therefore, the Halkevi has become a house of theft, gambling,
rendezvous and prostitution, unlike the People's Houses that,
everywhere else, are cultural and moral institutions.' This is why,
the author added, the 'honourable families and family girls' had
withdrawn from that 'dirty place'.[65] Complaining about the same
relationship, an army officer also wrote that the Halkevi 'hall is a
place where our boys should assemble under conditions of firm
inspection and supervision with regards to morals and social
life, and where moral people have to be employed'. The officer's
problem was the Halkevi employee Namık, who 'is a bachelor
and corrupts the youngsters'. As for 'our girls, the situation is
more tragic. Our girls, lycée students who wish to continue in the
music, fine arts and theatre sections are frightened by the attacks
of that immoral employee. I state with regret that a keen on art
young girl working at the Monopolies [*Tekel*] Administration
became the subject of gossip because of that disgraceful scum.'
The list of 'immoral' persons in the Halkevi goes on: apart from
the above, 'famous for his immorality uneducated and bachelor
jerk', the chairman is a grocer, and his girlfriend teacher corrupts
the rest of the female teachers with the help of a third teacher, 'a
licker and a stain for the lycée and our Izmit'.[66]

A similar complaint was filed in January 1939. The Party chairman in Tercan in the province of Ağrı denounced the regional *Kaymakam* for taking Emine – 'a woman performing on stage' – to his house to 'live like husband and wife'. Due to this 'immoral' relationship, the complaint continued, the *Kaymakam* insulted some moral families and even threatened with a pistol and had beaten someone.[67] The accountant of the Giresun Halkevi and his reported immoral character and acts became the cause of yet another anonymous denunciation letter:

> Naci Laçin [the Halkevi accountant] comes close to the women and girls during the rehearsals drunk in order to get to touch and watch them if possible. He has managed to dishonour some of them and as a result no girl or woman is to take any role in the Halkevi stage any more. This man, who is a catastrophic disease for the Halkevi, said a number of improper things to my sister too. He said to her 'we want to stage a play and if you take a role I'll give you a pair of shoes, in the second play I'll give you a skirt' and so on [...] Although many girls and women could take advantage of the Halkevi's activities, no one approaches because of this man's immoral behaviour.[68]

The unresolved tensions of the desegregated space the state elite was attempting to establish during Halkevi theatre plays, concerts, balls and family meetings would find their proper expression in popular discourse. There, the words 'jazz', 'jazz band' and 'tango' signified moral decay and decadence, but were also used as signifiers of the border between the elite and the people.[69] While for the bureaucratic state elite listening to the jazz band and dancing tango with their women was an expression of their being modern, among the lower classes the word *tango* 'meant the wicked woman who did not love her religion or her nationality, who rebelled against her neighbourhood and her family, who sold her virtue and honour, and committed every sin'.[70] For mainstream intellectuals in the 1940s, jazz was leading youths to immorality, degeneration, alcohol-consumption and prostitution.[71] Following the postwar political liberalization of the regime, the popular denunciatory discourse could be expressed even within the ruling Party. During the 1947 Party Congress, for instance, delegate Abdülkadir Karamürsel complained that the youth had abandoned the People's Houses because the Party had banished Turkish music and brought the 'jazz band into the Halkevi', which 'is lust music worse than alcohol' and 'a means to destroy morals and culture'.[72] In the works of conservative intellectuals, the employment of the image of the immoral and over-Westernized woman was habitually contrasted to the upright mother and wife at home. Our letters also reproduce a similar imagery, juxtaposing the 'theatre girls' to the moral 'family girls'. What is more, the immoral woman of the accusatory discourse of both letters and conservative intellectuals was used as a scapegoat of social dissatisfaction:[73] elites were commonly depicted as corrupt and immoral. One example suffices to demonstrate the point: one Party document contains summaries of more than 100 denunciation letters against MPs and provincial elites who asked for the Party's nomination for the 1939 national elections. After corruption and oppression, the letters' most favoured accusatory category was that of the immorality – commonly associated with Westerness or ethnic otherness – of the accused bureaucrats, officers and notables, and of their wives.[74]

The referent of the letters' popular discourse was the people. But even in the discourse of Halkevi and state executives, public opinion was invoked. Although the letters' complaints of immorality might have been integral parts of local feuds, the habitual employment of common elements of a popular conservative discourse (immorality, gossip) suggests that popular reactions to such events were taken seriously (or even feared) and attempts were made to avoid them. An official investigation of the allegations, for instance, was an explicit indication of the centre's interest. This interest is also attested to by the issuing of directives in response to complaints. On 26 March 1949, for instance, after a number of complaint letters reached Ankara, a directive requested information about touring troupes performing on Halkevi stages: 'The Halkevi executives must consider the impressions and influences these theatrical plays will have on the area.[75] This represents an explicit rejection of the nationwide singularity of the Halkevi project, with the centre accommodating local reservations and even negative responses to its policies, and instructing the local Party to take into account *local* conditions. The Party's half-heartedness on this matter might have been connected to the changing political landscape after 1946: with the introduction of multi-party politics, the ruling Party had to win the people's votes, and some kind of acknowledgment of popular sentiment was surely needed. After all, the existence of opposition parties and the vibrant antagonism had provided people with an officially legitimate cover to voice hitherto silent/ silenced grievances against the regime and its policies. Theatre as a metonym of immorality and the public presence of women was one of them.[76]

I read the omnipresence of these images about women on stage as an indication of the wide circulation of a social script[77] about what was expected during heterosocial activities: outside the control and protection of male relatives, women on stage and the dancing floor were supposed to lead (and, as a self-fulfilling prophesy, occasionally led) to 'immoral' acts, draw male sexual predators, and give birth to 'ugly incidents' and uncontrollable behaviour, and political, cultural and sexual trespassing. Constantly performing boundary management, men and women in the People's Houses had to act in consideration, rejection, or even circumvention of the expectations and fears that were contained and expressed in social scripts about public and visible women in a patriarchal society and a predominantly homosocial public space.

Boundary and Identity Management

Given that most letters were written by men, it is interesting to read what Saadet – accused of being Mr Turgut's mistress – wrote about her dismissal from the People's House:

I am a housewife with a family of two male children. In 1930 I finished the second class of the Teachers School for Girls in Bursa and I began working. For some time now I am obliged to earn my livelihood myself as I shouldered the responsibility to cover the expenses of my children myself. So, I live a modest family life by sewing. On 15/12/1937, after the numerous pressures and requests of my friends at the Theatre section of the Bursa Halkevi, and in spite of the intense critiques and objections of my environment and especially of my family, I joined the Section, which I regard as a work for the country in a holy nest. The very negative ideas of our people and especially of my environment and my family about the theatre stage left me in serious speculation. But I was not discouraged. [After a while] they understood that the stage is not a bad place and that the people on stage are clean and honourable/moral as a teacher is. I worked for two years for 15 liras.

First of all, Saadet remained silent about the reported immoral affair with Turgut Simer[78] and stated that she was laid off 'without reason', although she admitted that she knew that 'in order to save the day' her opponents in the Halkevi would 'stain her name'. To describe her and her opponent's acts, Saadet repeatedly employed the discourse of morality, which was also used by her family, environment and even 'our people'. She 'served under the roof of the Halkevi with honour and good name [namus ve şerefimle] for two years' as 'a clean and honourable family woman'. She described two women performing on the Halkevi stage on similar terms: one did not have a good reputation, was twice arrested drunk in taverns, and, as a result, was dismissed from her job in a factory. The second one was dismissed from the Halkevi after 'a similar ugly incident'. Then 'I unfortunately regretted acting on that stage and swallowing all the things said against me'.[79]

In expressing identical social beliefs and expectations on gender relations, Saadet's and, as a matter of fact, most women's voices did not differentiate from the voices of men.[80] The most visible difference between a female (exemplified in Saadet and probably most women who had to publicly voice themselves)[81] and a male voice was not in the discourse but in the tone used. Although accused and in direct contrast to the angry pitch of most men who happened to complain or defend themselves against a denunciation, Saadet's voice was not belligerent towards her denouncers but almost apologetic.[82] The archive contains extremely few documents produced by women – this scarcity is probably the most striking disparity with the countless narratives by men. But in those exceptional cases where women were obliged (by officials or perhaps by a male relative)[83] or felt themselves obliged to speak, the volume of their voices appears low – almost a whisper.[84]

In a similar manner, whereas men usually boasted about their involvement in the Halkevi or Party, women's voices were again more subtle, evoking feelings of uneasiness next to self-sacrifice. Obliged to break her silence and sign an official statement with her refusal to participate in the Halkevi stage, a woman teacher articulated her uneasiness, adding that 'I cannot participate, I feel uncomfortable'.[85] One of the first actresses on the Halkevi stage in Bolu, a teacher, recalled her experience with pride but also as a price (*bedel*) her generation had to pay in order to give an example to younger generations.[86] Notions of self-sacrifice were quite common and used extensively by men as well, but the uneasiness was primarily mentioned by (or in relation to) women and reveals the tension of public heterosocial interaction.

A variety of discursive practices were devised and employed to alleviate the uneasiness and tension. Compiled by both men and women, almost all archival documents employ the vocabulary of kin when touching the issue of women. In declaring herself 'a clean and honourable family woman', Saadet used a quite typical formula to express her morality. The letters use the word 'family' as synonymous with 'womenfolk', and the expression 'family girls' pointed to family as the epicentre of morality and moral women in contrast to 'common women' and 'theatre girls'. The employment of the vocabulary of kinship was a common way to negotiate the tension of an encounter between unrelated men and women that otherwise would be considered inappropriate. When asked about their relation with fellow Halkevi actresses in the 1940s and about society's ideas about them, two amateur actors of the Halkevi of Balıkesir resorted to the vocabulary of family: 'We respected all the girls acting on stage with us. They were like our sisters.'[87] In explaining an 'ugly incident', a Party inspector would excuse the Halkevi executives for having such an 'immoral' woman on their stage because initially 'she was presented as a relative of a schoolteacher, that is, of an intellectual.'[88]

Family relations were also used to resist the pressure to participate in the Halkevi: in Diyarbakır, single women teachers refused to act on stage because, they argued, it would impede their efforts to get married, while those who got married refused because their husbands did not allow it.[89] But again, as we have seen before, many women participated through their family, either together with, or after receiving the permission of, their husbands, brothers and fathers. The employment of family relations and the vocabulary of kin facilitated some women's evasion of Halkevi activities, but also justified the participation of others as it attempted to de-sexualize the Halkevi heterosocial interaction by discursively rendering it in terms of inter-family relations. I view this as a resourceful, inventive and tactical act of boundary management that aimed at alleviating and addressing the tension produced when a social boundary was breached – in our case, cultural beliefs and social expectations regarding gender relations and practices.[90]

A further function of the kin vocabulary and discourse was to enable the public scrutiny and control of women's public behaviour and presence. In a sense, with women's increased presence in a male-dominated public domain, next to male relatives the monitoring of women's proper behaviour was practised by state agents but also society at large, as teachers, doctors and bureaucrats scrutinized female students' attire and behaviour. Berktay has argued that since the reforms of the nineteenth century, society has been shifting from an Islamic towards a Western or nation-state patriarchy.[91] Kandiyoti, on the other hand, calls this public control and the (in many cases self-inflicted) sexual repression it entailed the 'new veil' of the Kemalist reforms.[92] The vocabulary of kin facilitated the performance of these 'new veiling' practices by state agents and women themselves. In refuting Saadet's allegations about the immorality of the Halkevi amateur actresses, for instance, the chairman of the Halkevi of Bursa presented the relationship between Halkevi administrators and Halkevi female members in very familial terms: as if between male and female relatives. These women, he reported, were moral 'because we have followed their actions step by step, materially and spiritually protected them, and even looked after the future of one of them by having her married.'[93]

A similar tactic employed by Halkevi actors to alleviate the pressure was to differentiate between Halkevi and 'common theatre', the distinction being expressed in terms of morality/immorality. The distinction between moral and immoral theatre was also expressed with reference to the vocabulary of kin, exemplified in the contrast between 'family girls' and 'theatre girls'. This distinction indicates the production of, what I choose to call, an accommodative discourse about theatre, that is, about the participation of women. It attempts to accommodate the regime's policies on women with widespread reservations about theatre and women on stage. These reservations were occasionally expressed when the distinction was openly refuted, as in the case of the mother of the ex-secretary of the Edremit Halkevi, who was reported as publicly declaring that 'there is no difference between common theatre and the Halkevi stage and that all those girls on the Halkevi stage are, at the end, nothing more than theatre girls.'[94]

The usual conveyor of this accommodative discourse was the Halkevi chairman, a member, or a habitué. The chairman usually tried to refute the allegations of immorality, while a member or a frequenter would whine about the transgression of that border between 'common theatre' and the Halkevi stage. An incident underscoring this difference between 'common theatre' and Halkevi stage took place in 1943 when the Buldan Halkevi chairman employed two actresses from a troupe to perform the female roles in a school play at the Halkevi. This arrangement provoked the reaction of the gendarme commander, who deemed this cooperation inappropriate, because 'the staging of a play by the youths together with sickly women [has resulted] in numerous gossips and is going to create a number of negative feelings among the youths'.[95] The incident could have been used as a pretext for action in the context of a local feud. Nevertheless, the commander based his arguments on the precept that school theatre was different from the theatre of the itinerant company with its 'sickly women'. My argument is that the carving of this distinction between 'moral' Halkevi theatre and 'immoral' *tulûat* theatre or 'theatre girls' was a tactical move to accord with society's gender relations, perceptions and practices, in a more general sense a tactical response to the tensions produced in local provincial settings upon the establishment of a Halkevi theatre stage and the participation of local women.

Probably the most employed practice to manage the tension the Halkevi heterosocial interaction generated was the tactic of limited inclusiveness. Numerous complaint letters, as we have seen in the previous chapter, denounced the entry restrictions imposed during mixed-gender activities – especially 'family meetings' and dances. On the basis of the identity of the complainants, as well as of the replies to such complaints by Party and Halkevi officials, it becomes obvious that the inclusion of some and the parallel exclusion of others was both desired and applied in practice, although no normative text or Party directive stating such a stipulation seems to exist.[96]

An afternoon family meeting took place in the House of Erzincan on the Halkevi anniversary. The governor, all of us, and all the civil servants' families were there. The army orchestra was playing. In the meanwhile, some youths came; although without [their] family, they were allowed to enter because their social position was considered. At 24:00 hours the meeting ended in an upright way. A little later, these youths asked [for] rakı [an alcoholic drink] from the buffet. Although they were told that rakı is prohibited in the Halkevi, they insisted and the whole issue went on and they started to dispute with the waiters. At that moment, an employee of the Forest Department grabbed his pistol and fired twice at the ceiling. The officers next to him took his pistol and […] the issue was taken to court.[97]

Numerous letters complained about drinking, gambling and immorality in the People's Houses. In reporting that 'the meeting ended in an upright way' and that alcohol, although asked for, was not served, the above Party executive was actually defending the Halkevi against charges of immorality. But he also reported those included in the family meeting – the governor and civil servants, 'all of us' with their women, and by contrast he suggested who was supposed to be excluded. Although men unaccompanied by their families, that is, women, were normally excluded, the 'youths' above (probably bachelors) were accepted because of their 'social position' – they were civil servants. As we have seen in the previous chapter, non-elite locals were routinely excluded from the Halkevi space. This being the case, in the event of well-established men of the town bringing their women, people of lower 'social position' and bachelors tended to be excluded, while the civil servants' entrance seemed acceptable.

Among the numerous works published on Halkevi activities (theatre plays, village excursions and studies, folklore collections, etc.) there was no – to my knowledge – publication or directive on how to conduct mixed-gender activities like family meetings or balls. Nevertheless, the letters indicate that there were tacit rules that were employed especially when members of local and state elites were present. The most evident one was the exclusion, or limited inclusion, of certain persons. Those whose presence was not desired among elites and their women were single (and young) men unaccompanied by their family, *and* of lower social status ('non-intellectuals', 'non-civil servants', 'from the People').

In response to a complaint by two men who had been expelled from the Bitlis Halkevi,[98] for example, the governor's report explained the method by which a family meeting was directed:

There is a small recreation room in the Bitlis Halkevi. On Saturday evenings […] family meetings […] take place there. All those desiring to participate with their families will be accepted. As for those from the people (*Halktan*), they can stay in the library room if they wish so. A letter announcing the above had been placed at the Halkevi entrance and Hall. Despite all these, those sitting there had not left the room at the proper time. Rifat Güney […] argued that the announcement was not signed. Upon hearing that, the Halkevi chairman signed it leaving no room for any warning to Rifat and his friends. Rifat's claim that they were thrown out is wrong.

Although the recreation room was appropriated for the family meeting and they do have a family, these people desired to stay there among families unaccompanied and in this way use this family meeting as a pretext for wandering around.[99]

In short, the governor confirmed what the Party inspector implicitly suggested above: men unaccompanied by their family, or bachelors, 'from the People', that is, low-class men and youths, and 'persons wishing to stay among the families' to gaze at the elite women present were not to be accepted at family meetings. Here we first of all witness 'the widespread perception that young men in unregulated spaces were social pariahs, sexual aggressors who destabilized moral boundaries'.[100] Occasionally, even a bureaucrat could fall into the same category. Invited to a family meeting, 'the *young and single* Kaymakam' had to be 'reminded' by the Halkevi chairman that 'the consumption of alcoholic drinks in the Houses is prohibited by the bylaws'.[101] Conversely, the presence of female relatives was probably supposed to defuse the nature of men as sexual predators. What was then feared, and had to be avoided, was the coming together of undesired and/or uncontrolled (by the presence of their family, for instance) men and 'family girls'. It had to be avoided and it was feared because it might lead to incidents that would 'have a bad influence on the area' leading 'honourable families' to abandon the Halkevi. Consider the case of Nafia Izli. Accompanied by her husband, she attended a ball at the Gelibolu Halkevi and had to 'share a table with the school principal Ahmet, his wife, and his sister. While watching those dancing, I noticed Ahmet was insulting my honour under the table. At once I came to myself [and] I showed my husband. Faced with this calamity, my husband told me to show this to his sister. Prodding her with my hand I told her "Don't you see your brother Ahmet's dishonourable action?" But Ahmet continued behaving this way.' Her husband protested to the Party chief and after receiving no reply they wrote to the Party.[102]

In addition to bachelors, the governor revealed another regular target for exclusion that the letters routinely complained about. Stating who could participate in these 'family meetings', he differentiated between 'families' and those 'from the people', that is, non-civil servants and non-elite locals without their families. Thus, these acts of segregation were precipitated by the double concern to safeguard the chastity of female relatives from potential sexual aggressors on the one hand and, on the other, the Halkevi as an elite space from non-elite locals. These two categories were usually conflated. Those from the people, as the governor categorically stated, did not bring their women to the Halkevi, but rather attempted to use it as a place of male socialization, in a way similar to the coffee house, a place nobody attempted to inhabit with women in direct contrast to the wider society's practices and perception about the position of women.

To prevent unwelcome incidents and to keep aloof from those who might endanger their status and social position, the Halkevi officials and frequenters employed a system of limited inclusion in activities where families were present. This segregation was usually regulated by the use of invitations (*davetiye*), an issue which produced frequent complaints as we have seen in the previous chapter. By these acts of exclusion/inclusion, a distinct stage of social interaction emerged where selected women could participate on certain occasions. I view this stage as an 'implicit, hidden form of segregation', an ingenious and tactical solution to address the confusion and tension created when novel forms of mixed-gender interaction were introduced to a largely segregated patriarchal society. The creation of such a segregated space within the 'modern' space of the Halkevi underscores the paradoxical circumstance wherein the 'unveiling' of the 'Turkish woman' 'has mandated new forms of puritanism' – and seclusion we might add – 'in a society where femininity was incompatible with a public presence'.[103] In a 'family meeting' or a dance party, a girl seemed to be at the same time located outside and inside the culturally prescribed space, not *in* the family but *with*, or under the supervision of, the family, and within an extended family formed for the occasion. In another sense, she was residing in a space located somehow between the public and the domestic world, a secluded space denoting class and gender difference.

But this implicit form of segregation was also accompanied by more open moments of sex segregation in the Houses. A number of provincial Houses either organized or requested the permission to organize explicitly gender-segregated activities. In response to petitions by local citizens, the chairman of the Halkevi of Elazığ inquired whether women and men could be invited separately during wedding and circumcision ceremonies in the House.[104] In a similar request, the chairman of the House of İnegöl was even more illuminating: 'From time to time we permit weddings in the Halkevi in accordance with the 61st article of the bylaws. Some families though ask for ceremonies to be attended only by women, with which men would not interfere.' Even after being told by the chairman that such ceremonies do not accord with the 'Halkevi principles and the rules of civilization', the citizens insisted on their requests, relying on the absence of any clear explanation about this issue in the by-laws: 'In order to give a final answer we ask you to issue a clarification.'[105] The strains produced in the heterosocial space of the Houses, especially in the dark of the audience hall, could even appear in the journal of the Ankara House. An article in *Ülkü* mentioned that when the executives of the Adana House debated the discomfort of the female students that had to follow the House's works among men ('80 per cent of them young men'), some members proposed to use the balcony as a segregated space for women and girls.[106] In smaller provincial towns such segregation was probably taking place in the Houses.[107]

Some courses in a number of Houses were another silent form of sex-segregated activity and, interestingly, it did not attract any rejoinder from the centre. Among the various courses delivered in the Houses, some almost explicitly addressed women, such as courses on dressmaking, embroidery, decoration or hat making.[108] In petitioning the Party for employment in a Halkevi, a person signing as 'Halkevi teacher of fine arts' enumerated the 'courses necessary for every lady' he had taught in various Houses: 'women's hat, flower, bag, gloves, knitting'.[109] The governor of Kayseri reported that the House was organizing a three-days-per-week course on hat-making and flower decoration 'only for women'.[110] Elsewhere even music courses were organized separately for men and women.[111] We might even guess that internal homosocial segregation was practised during heterosocial Halkevi events, where women – often teachers or students – unaccompanied by family males would flock together, establishing subtle spatial and temporal arrangements of sex-segregation that could decrease the potential threat of sexual aggressor males but also the uneasiness of women among unrelated men.

I view all the above as discursive practices of continuous boundary management by social actors negotiating the proper place of the 'modern-yet-modest'[112] woman in the public domain. These practices would sometimes put 'new experiments into the old package',[113] with the subtle application of sex-segregation within the supposedly desegregated Halkevi space; on other occasions, such practices would be performed in order to safeguard the customary spatial and social segregation of elites from the non-elite population.

Conclusion

In a small town on the Black Sea in the 1970s people still remembered with astonishment the 1930s as the 'era of the waiting girls'.[114] An amateur actor on the Balıkesir Halkevi stage in the 1940s recalled that 'then there were coffeehouses where girls were serving, something you won't see anywhere today'.[115] For others today,[116] as was the case in the 1950s,[117] having waitresses and local women on stage was received with disapproval. Even today divergent memories of the period are indicative of the tension produced by the introduction of similar women-related novelties to local societies.

Designed to publicize the changes the regime had initiated in that respect, the People's House, its hall and stage, were planned as desegregated spaces of heterosocial activities. But only a handful of women, mostly schoolteachers and some relatives of state officials, were engaged in the Houses' activities. What is more, men and women habitually devised a variety of responses to the Halkevi activities, employing numerous tactics to resolve the tensions of its novel space of heterosocial interaction. Although under constant pressure, direct or through their male relatives, women evaded or outrightly refused to participate. Others experienced their commitment with uneasiness *and* pride as a self-sacrificing duty or a 'price they had to pay'. Obliged to deal with accusations of immorality, Halkevi executives and clientele made allowances for popular conservative perceptions by establishing a distinction separating Halkevi theatre from 'common theatre'. Similarly, the moral character of the Halkevi was safeguarded through the internal segregation of its heterosocial space. In another sense, the sex segregation the regime was ostensibly fighting re-emerged in the form of a new segregation within the Halkevi. This novel segregation was attained through acts of exclusion of low-class bachelors, or unaccompanied low-class males – widely considered potential sexual transgressors – but also during the performing of sex-segregated practices – courses or gymnastics solely for women. Lastly, even a desegregated space or occasion could be internally semi-segregated and 'familiarized' by the habitual clustering together of unmarried women, such as teachers or civil servants, and of family womenfolk with male relatives.

I view such practices of men and women on the Halkevi stage as performances of boundary management and contend that they, as signifying acts, ultimately (re)produced discursive and cognitive categories such as the 'theatre girls' of our letters, women of 'low moral disposition' in contrast to 'upright women' and 'family girls', or 'self-sacrificing', 'uncomfortable' and 'proud' modern women as opposed to secluded and 'backward' ones.

In so far as the 'woman issue' became a public one, the proper place, behaviour, attire and sexuality became increasingly public issues, as both state and society encroached upon practices, idioms and norms which had been predominantly within the domain of kinship.[118] The letters amply articulate this point by asking for the Party and state's intervention to uphold public morality and the chastity of women.[119] In doing so, they placed women within the discourse of morality, whose persistence in the letters points at its significance as a cognitive and performative category, a way through which people viewed the People's Houses and the new ideas and habits they were introducing.

The place of women was crucial for, and, in a sense, brought together, high-modernist and popular conservative discourses. The 'woman issue' was the place where societal and state discourses intersected, as both were conservative and patriarchal with regard to women. This is testified to by the vocabulary employed in letters and Party/state reports. The letters' accusatory discourse and the more sober tone of Party reports were both saturated with the vocabulary of morality, reproducing the cultural script of the 'ugly event' that was generated by the woman who behaved immorally. Patriarchal discourse and practice did not run contrary either to Kemalist 'modern civilization' and 'national culture' or to societal conservative values that might otherwise have been in confrontation with the Kemalist reforms and ideas. Nationalism smoothed this convergence as it met both at the same spot in relation to gender: for nationalist imaginary and everyday letters alike, being (or accused of being) a foreigner or a minority member almost equated to being immoral. Minority or Western women were habitually depicted as immoral (or, plainly, whores) in nationalist literature and denunciation letters. Turkish nationalism and Kemalist modernizing and conservative-patriarchal discursive practice intersected smoothly and fed one another in relation to representations and practices about women.[120] In a similar manner, Kandiyoti argues that there is 'one persistent concern which finally unites nationalist and Islamist discourses on women in Turkey: the necessity to establish that the behaviour and position of women are congruent with the "true" identity of the community and constitutes no threat to it. The prime area or potential threat centres around women's appropriate sexual conduct and its control.'[121]

People's Houses in the Countryside 6

In one of his short stories, Mahmut Makal[1] recounted the story of a 'Village Evening' in a provincial Halkevi.

> Last year the chairman of the village section of the Halkevi came to the teacher: a decision was taken to organize 'villager's evenings' once a week. In the beginning the administrative committee objected. They ridiculed this activity saying 'The villagers are occupied in their own works [and they won't] attend your meetings.' They found the idea funny. 'What does a villager understand of meetings; a lesson on military issues might be suitable ...' they said.
>
> Nevertheless, out of curiosity, out of interest in this novelty, the Hall was very crowded on the meeting days [...] These meetings were an opportunity for the villagers to see the inside of a structure they had been seeing for years from the outside. During these evenings, dances, popular songs and wrestling events, all familiar to the villagers, were organized. The customs of each village were introduced to others. An attempt was made to give the villagers some basic knowledge. This was a part of the activity described as people's education. The villagers were coming in great numbers. But then the complaints began. 'The hall is full of lice, get rid of the villagers!' This voice came from the eminent merchants, the grocers and the 'bosses', as well as from those who had taken the decision to organize these meetings.[2]

The Halkevi was established by the ruling Party in order to disseminate the reforms and the state's policies to the people. This reform diffusion being one its most significant objectives, the People's House was envisaged as a converging point where the people would meet and be instructed by the intellectuals, those the Party regarded as its natural followers: state officials, Party elites and educated professionals. All the relevant sources, however, present the House as the playground of state elites and local notables, a space of elite socialization built upon the parallel and habitual exclusion of non-elite locals – the very same people they were supposed to train into civilization and nationhood.

Makal's story above vividly summarizes the attitude of urban elites and Houses' executives towards villagers. A number of texts by both local and non-local members of the Halkevi of Kayseri treated in Chapter 2 offer a similar picture. Their texts are usually devoid of locals, especially low-class ones; and when they mention them – usually in response to a complaint – a sense of embarrassment and discomfort emerges, signifying in a sense the social distance separating these elites from the rest of the people. The limited inclusiveness of the Halkevi and the social and gender segregation of state officials and regulars was in all probability coupled with the indifference, even repulsion, that some of the excluded people felt for the Halkevi.[3] The People's House then appeared less as 'the house of the people', but rather as the 'intellectual's house' (*aydınlarevi*), a term coined by an eyewitness of their activities.[4]

There was, however, a richly recorded Halkevi activity, which, in contrast to the rest of the Houses' activities, and by its very nature, demanded the coming together of intellectuals and people, although not in the People's House and under a given limitation of time and space. The village excursion (*Köy Gezisi*) can be broadly defined as an expedition of a group of Halkevi members to nearby villages in order to carry out a number of activities, most of them stated in the Halkevi by-laws and expressed in detail in more technical texts.

In this chapter my aim is to study this moment of fusion in order to explore the consumption by Halkevi actors of the regime's village(r) policies. In a similar way to the 'Turkish woman', the 'Turkish villager' was an explicit target of the regime's discourse. The People's House was one of the means employed to enlighten and educate the villager, but also constitutive of the way(s) the villager was perceived and accounted for. The Halkevi was expressively designed to execute village(r)-related activities. In what follows I explore the (re)appropriation by social actors of the village-related categories, discourses and practices the regime had produced and attempted to introduce through the Halkevi network. I argue that it is upon this (re)appropriation that the categories 'villager' and 'village' were (re)created and (re)defined, the same way the relationship between (and the border separating) the villager and the state, its offices and personnel, between the countryside and its inhabitants and the city were also constantly shaped.

In the first part of the chapter, I try to give a brief outline of the emergence of the village issue, offering a historical background of the organizations aiming at changing the village since the 1908 Young Turk Revolution. Drawing on Party publications about the activities of the Village section of the People's Houses, the second part of the chapter presents the textbook version of the Houses' village activities and proposes an analysis of the Halkevi village operation. Next follows the study of the execution of this Halkevi activity based on a series of village excursions of the Kayseri Halkevi in the late 1930s.

Village Operation: Prehistory and Theory

The Halkevi institution was not the first cultural and political structure to conduct village and villager-related activities in Turkey. A steadily increasing interest in villagers had existed, in a more or less organized form, at least since the Young Turk Revolution in 1908. This interest took a solid form within the ideological framework of the emerging Turkish nationalism and especially within the era's cultural and certainly political associations, as part of what was later to be emphatically referred to as the people's education (*halk terbiyesi*).[5] The growing interest in the villager and the village life that had appeared by the end of the nineteenth century was also echoed in the literature of the period. Village actors and themes started to make their appearance in the Turkish novel from the beginning of the twentieth century, although it was not until after the 1920s that the village and villager became mainstream themes of contemporary Turkish literature, with the works of a number of urban intellectuals.[6] But this early interest in the village cosmos remained an urban phenomenon, a movement of educated urban elites with very minimal impact on villagers. Due to the precarious conditions of the period until 1923, peasantist activities remained extremely limited in nature, scope and outcome, never really surpassing a missionary-like enterprise with no clear aims and programme. This lack was partly covered by the expansion of the Turkish Hearth association within a more stable socio-political environment after 1923, but even more so with the establishment of the Halkevi institution, one section of which was specifically designed to execute activities aimed at the 'material, aesthetic and sanitary progress and growth of the villagers'.[7]

As the headquarters of the Houses' village-related activities, the Village section was guided by a series of Party publications that functioned as a set of directives and instructions on the application of village-related works, from the collection of folklore material to the speeches the Halkevi visitors were asked to deliver to the villagers.[8] Starting in June 1933, *Ülkü*, the journal of the Ankara Halkevi, was the first to publish instructions and examples of village studies with an article series entitled 'Village Survey'.[9] More articles on the Houses' village activities followed.[10]

Published in 1939 by a member of the Village section of the Ankara Halkevi, *Köy Kütüğü* (Village Register) is an example of such publications. The booklet offered guidelines on how to carry out studies of villages: 'Our House's village section has created a "village register" for every village with the aim to render the cause for village progress, to which our Party has given great importance and value, easier as well as in order to achieve more positive results in practice.' The booklet is essentially a list of all the information the Party deemed necessary to be recorded for its programme of village development. Starting with a sketch and photographs of the village before and after the Republic (aptly called 'old and new village' – *Eski ve Yeni köy*), the prospective authors of such 'village registers' were asked to collect and register information divided into a number of sections: geographical data (climate, water, natural difficulties and beauties); population statistics; cultural situation (schools, number of students, teachers, literacy statistics, stories and tales); historical information and folklore (dances, musical instruments, songs, customs, stories about the village's name and history); administrative situation (number of gendarmes, households, public services); public works (the state of roads, gardens, parks, ponds, bridges and state monuments); hygienic conditions (general hygiene, cleanliness, Turkish baths, laundry, swamps, stables and manure, water, diseases); economy (agriculture, crafts, and commerce); and social situation (family life, family budget, living conditions).[11]

The People's House of Kütahya published a similar booklet about village studies that proposed a similar list of subjects to be studied. The Halkevi peasantist was advised to study and record information about the village's geography, position and waters, its economy, agriculture and products, its houses and transportation means, but also its folklore (fairy tales, sayings, folk songs and stories). Next came information about the village's literacy rates, schools, teachers, books and newspapers (if they existed, of course), and its cultural and social situation, that is, information about gambling and the use of drugs or alcohol, the existence of reactionary and superstitious customs, men and women's clothes.[12] In stressing the scientific nature of the village study, another peasantist book, titled *How should a village be studied?* and published by the Istanbul Halkevi, very much presented the villager as pure matter or an object of nature: 'the village and the villager are distinctive beings, just like all the objects and aspects of nature and society. In relation to them, [we] have to be as objective as possible, as if we were to study an "object", staying away from any personal interests, objective, calm and with no resentment.'[13]

Most similar publications stressed the importance and seriousness of the operation to be conducted in the villages and upon the villagers. Villagers and villages were objects to be counted, described, photographed, transformed and instructed; they almost emerged as matter, parts of nature, in contrast to what the visitors embodied, which was by contrast implied: subjecthood, the city and civilization, the state and power. Both texts inscribed relations of power between researchers and researched (in contrast to the populist rhetoric of the regime that declared the villager to be the master of the country). 'The peasant subject is produced for non-peasant consumption,' Mitchell reminds us.[14] This becomes apparent when we look at who was bestowed the right to speak about whom. What these books on how to conduct research on villagers described was an operation over a mute or silenced Other; an object created within the framework of the ongoing socio-political change but also inherited by local scholars, peasantists and Halkevi members from the Turkish Hearths and previous institutions such as the Peasantist Association (*Köycüler Cemiyeti*)[15] and the Peasant Information Society (*Köylü Bilgi Cemiyeti*),[16] both established by Unionist elites – some of them deeply engaged in the Halkevi project as well – in 1918 and 1919 respectively. Drawing from de Certeau, I view the Halkevi village excursion as a meticulously designed strategic operation the Halkevi members had to execute over the villager.[17] The village operation, but more generally the centre's power to operate upon the villager, was sustained and at the same time justified by the rationalist and expansionist discourses of science (hygiene, architecture, rural planning, medicine, statistics, etc.) that were employed to represent and legitimize it, and, as such, it also signalled the change of the state's perspective on the villager. In place of the Sultan's subject, treated solely as a resource for the extraction of taxes and conscripts, the villager was proclaimed a citizen of the Republic and, in the populist rhetoric of the period, was hailed as the 'true master of the country'.[18] The populist overtones of the nationalist Republican regime clashed with the old mentality and practice of the Ottoman state, as the villager, previously an object of contempt and ridicule by urban elites, was saluted as the most authentic part of the nation, a repository of the true national culture uncontaminated by foreign influences.[19]

Nevertheless, the discourses articulated in relation to the village operation revealed an objectified villager, a mute, silenced object, upon which the state's increased interests and aims were to be enacted by state mechanisms and personnel (in a variety of fields, from education, the military and the economy to culture). So, if we place the village operation or, more broadly, the state's new discourse about peasants, within the unchallenged relations of power existing in the countryside, we can speak of a continuation of the old state mentality that saw itself above society and the populace in direct contrast with the otherwise expressed policy of populism, a paradox exemplified in the Party slogan 'halka rağmen halk için' (for the people, in spite of the people). In a nutshell, the change in the regime's perspective and wishes for the villager did not seem to significantly alter the mentality and practice of social demarcation that functioned within an effectively uncontested system of power relations. Instead, the regime's peasantist discourse and practice was a clear manifestation of the mentality of tutelary popular sovereignty of the single-party period, exemplified in the concept of the people's education, that is, the foundational principle of the Halkevi institution and its village activities.

Village Excursions of the Halkevi of Kayseri 1936–9

The Kayseri Halkevi organized a series of village excursions between 1936 and 1939 with the active encouragement and involvement of Adli Bayman, the then governor of the province of Kayseri.[20] The first one took place just two months after Bayman's arrival at Kayseri,[21] and more were to follow.[22] Bayman informed the Interior Minister that the aims of the excursions were to promote the progress of the villager, carry out research and enlighten the villager. For Bayman, the local situation made these needs even more pressing: 'Kayseri, as you also know and recognize, is one of the most underdeveloped parts of our country.'[23] So, every Sunday, a group of Halkevi members and state officials, headed by the governor himself, walked to nearby villages. A contemporary report described these activities in the following manner:

1) The village excursions program continues with the participation of women. We are working towards the strengthening of feelings of mutual affection and cooperation between village and city men and women.

2) A doctor and a nurse participate in the excursions and examine the ill villagers. Medicine is distributed free of charge by charitable associations.

3) Research on the cultural, social, and financial situation as well as on the history and hygiene of every village is carried out and an attempt is made to publish a brochure about every village visited.

4) During the excursions orators from the section deliver speeches on various issues in a language that is simple and comprehensive to the villager. (The subjects of the talks are Revolution, Independence, infectious diseases, village cooperatives, improvement of products and animals.)

5) Our villagers are invited to the House on holidays and wrestling competitions are organized between village wrestlers.

6) Our section is trying to organize courses for the people by contacting village teachers who are considered natural members of the section. Our section also assists the villagers who apply to the Halkevi in writing their letters and petitions.

7) During the excursions, members of the theatre section stage plays [that aim at] the inoculation of the revolution and independence while the Halkevi band plays national songs.[24]

The Kayseri Halkevi members performed philanthropic, propagandistic, cultural and educational activities, as well as the more scientific work of studying the village(rs) and collecting a broad spectrum of information about the village, from folk songs and material to financial and agricultural data. The villages were thus counted, registered and studied, medically treated and politically instructed, and received amusement and charity. But this report recounted the activities of the peasantists of the Kayseri Halkevi in a canonical way, that is, in a manner almost identical to the relevant Party peasantist literature. In what follows, I read a number of narratives by participants in an attempt to move beyond the lip-service many Halkevi sources pay to the Party canon and locate diverging perceptions of the above activities. In doing, so I explore the ways the Kayseri Halkevi members performed and recounted their participation.

The participants in these visits were, according to all accounts, the same urbanites who staffed and frequented the provincial People's Houses. The authors of all texts were either teachers or bureaucrats. What is more, most of the participants named in the texts were also teachers or state officials. For instance, a Halkevi publication named the 27 men and women taking part in the visit to the Germir village.[25] Of 11 women, three were teachers and the rest were accompanying their husbands or fathers: the governor's wife and daughter, the wives of two local Party men, of the local military commander, and of the director of the local state factory. The male participants were, in addition to the influential figures already mentioned, three schoolteachers, a lawyer, a merchant, a doctor – all Party members – two civil servants (a scribe and a nurse), an army officer, the president of the Sümer Sports Club, and an unidentified man. The governor's reports and the rest of the accounts mention the same people: the Halkevi peasantist group drew its members from the urban elites of Kayseri, mainly civil servants, teachers and local Party men, plus some female relatives.[26]

In a sense then, the group represented, or at least was perceived as representing (certainly in the eyes of the villagers), not just the People's House, but primarily the power of the state and of the ruling Party. After all, all three institutions were considered, not at all unjustifiably, very similar if not identical. But from another point of view, the participants were not only visiting the countryside as agents of state power and of the city as the site through which state power descended upon the countryside, but also as carriers of (the discourses of) civilization, science and nationalism, that is, of what the city possessed to excess and of what the countryside was in shortage and desperate need. To the regime's understanding and discourse, the village and its inhabitants appeared to reside out in nature, in a space and time far away from and in need of what its Halkevi agents were to 'inoculate' them with.[27]

If for some of the participants – especially non-local state officials – the village excursion was an opportunity to come into contact with villages and their inhabitants for the first time, provincial elites had already been in contact and had a wide set of relations with villagers. Urban elites had functioned as tax-farmers, provided credit and help when needed, absorbed part of the villagers' product, and, in general, mediated between villagers and state officials. In short, the local urban financial and political elites, who usually staffed the local Party and supervised the Halkevi, shared a complex set of deep-rooted patron–client relations with the village population, extending from financial to political and cultural ties. The regime's peasantist discourse emphatically referred to the need to 'enlighten', 'civilize' and 'liberate' the villager from 'ignorance' and 'oppression', usually exemplified in the personae of the 'sheikh' or 'dervish' (şeyh, derviş, mürit) and that of the local 'despot', 'overlord', 'exploiter' or 'oppressor' (ağa, mutegallibe, zorba). And so a paradox emerged: the village operation was partly executed by members of a social group whose structural relation with the countryside and the villager population was supposedly one of the prime targets of that very same operation. This paradox is illustrative of the meagre possibilities the village excursion, but also the overall village-related programme of the regime, ever had of realizing any substantial change in villages, as it had to rely on what local elites, that is, the same people that were usually considered the villager's 'oppressor', could offer and mobilize: local knowledge, expertise, and even manpower. It was apparent that the regime did not aim at any foundational transformation of social relations in the countryside; instead, the education and enlightenment of the villager by the intellectuals was considered the panacea that would change the life of villagers. These features of the Halkevi peasantist operation become clearer in the texts of the participants.

On 13 January 1937, Adli Bayman reported to the Party headquarters in Ankara about the visit to the village of Reşadiye. 'A group of twenty-nine people from the village, sports, music and social assistance sections of the People's House, we went on foot to the Reşadiye village.' After assembling in the village mosque, 'we discussed with the villagers for hours. Speeches on social issues were delivered in a language intelligible to the villagers.' The governor then reported the problems the villagers were facing: the lack of a road, school, mill, and the dispute between the villagers of Reşadiye and a nearby village about grazing space. The visitors also compiled a list of the village's orphans and poor children in order to distribute books to them gratis. They then distributed sweets to the village children. The Halkevi's music group sang national songs to entertain the villagers and, finally, the doctor examined the villagers and wrote 28 prescriptions. The medicines were to be distributed free of charge at the Memleket Hospital and the American dispensary in Kayseri.[28]

In a second report, the governor described the excursion to the Mimarsinan village.[29] The structure of the report, and probably the work done, was similar: they (40 men and women visitors) 'listened to the villagers' problems', 'discussed' with them, delivered speeches on appropriate issues,[30] distributed sweets to the village children and books to poor children and orphans, played music, 'entertained' the villagers, carried out medical examinations and distributed medicine. Once more, as in the previous report, the governor mentioned only problems related to infrastructural issues, such as the (bad) conditions of roads, schools and drinking water. He also gave examples of the excursion's 'achievements': 'five Liras were given to a disabled man who had lost his foot in a work accident. Quinine was distributed free of charge to the poor malarial. Hacı's wife, the poor and blind Halide, was to be operated on thanks to the support of the local administration. Finally, the Halkevi gave a gift to all houses of the village: gilded photos of Atatürk and Mimar Sinan. Bayman sent the reports in his double role as governor of Kayseri and local Party chairman.[31] As the leading bureaucrat supervising all state affairs in the province, he was interested in problems of infrastructure, such as the state of roads and bridges, education and school buildings, the local economy and agriculture. On the other hand, as head of the local Party and, thus, of the local Halkevi, he presided over the House's and Party's 'cultural' activities and the regime's attempt to disseminate its reforms and ideas to the local population. Therefore the village excursions he had initiated gave him the opportunity to combine these two functions: on the one hand as a bureaucrat inspecting the villages and solving problems falling under his administrative jurisdiction, and on the other as Party leader promoting Party and Halkevi activities in the villages. Bayman's reports were composed for the eyes of his superiors. They were, in a sense, texts explaining his actions and achievements, reports of a work in progress concerning the development of the region.

In addition to his reports, the governor also commissioned the publication of a series of booklets, one for every village that had been visited. These booklets were envisaged – as the title suggests – as a series of research notes about the villages visited, and five such booklets were published in 1937–8.[32] Fahri Tümer, the teacher who headed the Village section of the Halkevi, published another two village studies in 1938 in the House's journal.[33] These works, although more or less following the norm set by Party and Halkevi publications-cum-directives concerning Halkevi activities, also deviated from standard practice in some respects. The booklet about the Germir village, for instance, was divided into two parts. The first part was a short account of the village excursion, presenting the participants and describing their journey from Kayseri to the village and the acts of the peasantist group (medical treatment of villagers, distribution of books, speeches, hearing of complaints). The second part of the booklet took the form of a short village study that followed the pattern the Party had already set, with the description of the village's geography, economy, its social, cultural and educational state, and lastly its hygienic conditions. The text was supplemented with photographs of the peasantist group of men and women in suits and Western clothes; village women, and even men, are hard to spot.[34]

Tümer's articles in *Erciyes* conformed more to the Party's archetype of a village study. These articles were in essence a set of answers to a research questionnaire, such as the ones featured in the publications about village studies. Starting with a description of the village's physical appearance and its surrounding area, and a few notes on the legends from the village's past and history, the author continued with population data, and figures about households, men and women. He then commented on the water supply and springs used in the village. Information about schools, libraries, reading rooms, students and local poets and songs (if any) were subsequently presented under the subtitle 'Cultural situation', while a short presentation of the village's agricultural and pastoral products and artefacts was made under the heading 'Economy of the village'. The next part reported on the sanitary conditions of the village, providing data on diseases, cleanliness, child death rates and child care. The 'Social situation' was then considered, the smallest and least descriptive subcategory of the village study. It was actually a brief summary linked to the regime's own preoccupations. Obviously reflecting the response to certain questions, the author reported that 'the village law is applied normally and the assembly of elders has been established. There is no oppressor [*mütegallibe*] in the village and civil servants visiting the village do not face any kind of problem. The villagers are devoted to the Party and the Republic.' These replies exposed the regime's mistrust of the villagers as possible 'reactionaries' who might reject the new laws of the Republic, but essentially they reveal the lack of information and feedback from the provinces and the state's fear that local elites might usurp its power and authority.

These studies say very little about the actual meeting of the Halkevi visitors and villagers. They are extremely impersonal and tightly structured as they follow a set framework in providing information requested by the Party headquarters. As a result, they portray the village almost as a part of nature, isolated from and having sporadic encounters with the city and state, their laws and functionaries. As for the villager, (s)he appears as a mute object, a number in the population or education statistics, a healthy, or not, body, an agricultural producer, a passive carrier of national culture, such as music, songs, dances, folklore, or even undesired attributes, superstitious beliefs or reactionary ideas. Finally, the villagers emerge as recipients of laws, instructions, propaganda, medical aid and charity, all 'they' (the villagers) *lacked* (and thus *needed*) and the visiting city dwellers *possessed* and *offered*.

But what both Bayman's reports and the other publications fail to express, because of their specific aims, is the atmosphere of the village excursion and the impressions of the participants. In contrast, a newspaper article about a visit to the village of Erkilet depicts the merry atmosphere of a group of friends and colleagues going on a weekend trip to the countryside. Four schoolteachers and Halkevi members are mentioned in this account of a joyful journey.[35]

> Even before departing the jokes had started [...] As the time passed the jokes continued and everybody started throwing snowballs to each other. Mr. Nevzat took a broken violin and tried to fix its strings. Ms. Erkmen then said, 'Children! Hit [with snowballs] Mr. Nevzat!' [...] Once in a while, Mr Karamete and Mr Özdemir were joking to each other; we also participated sometimes and continued walking with joy. At the end, Mr. Nevzat managed to repair the violin and we started singing. Some of us sung songs, some folk songs [*türkü*], but we were all very happy.

After resting for a while at the village, the merry atmosphere of the journey returned once more: 'The jokes became more intimate and the souls more calm.' The article thoroughly reflected the joyful mood of the participants. The author did not overlook yet another occasion for laughter: when they entered a village house and took their shoes off, 'everybody looked at Özdemir's torn socks and started laughing. At the end there was no end to our happiness, we were dancing, laughing, singing and having fun.'[36]

Another element of the article was the constant reference to nature coupled with the sense of joy, as seen in the above passage. Elements of nature, such as the weather or the landscape, clearly touched the senses of the writer: 'The sun was very nice and the horizon bright'; 'a cool wind was caressing our hair'; 'sitting proudly on the crest of a grey hill, boastful of its clean air and its abundant water, the village of Kıranardı has a delightful view. Like a magnified picture, a number of villages could be seen spread on the hillsides below.'[37]

Özdoğan's brochure also conveyed the same feelings of joy together with a celebratory reference to nature. The brochure offered an almost impressionistic picture of the journey: 'We went ahead following the Sivas highway under an autumn sun pouring out from the clouds. After five kilometres we arrived at the beginning of the road leading to the village. [We] passed through grey fields.' After reflecting on the pleasure of the journey and the merry atmosphere among the visitors, the author described the village, its houses and its location amidst a beautiful landscape.[38] Not much was said about the villagers or their problems, apart from a reference to their healthy appearance and nature:[39]

Most important, the bodies of the village people are healthy and robust. The doctor of our group, Behçet, after examining the villagers, said that there was only one sick, in fact crippled, villager [...] There is not even one skinny and weak person among the villagers.[40]

Then, after a self-gratifying comment ('the affection and applauding of the village people towards us made our pleasure grow'), came a blatant flattering of the governor who was rendered as 'mixing with the people, listening to their problems, thinking of solutions, and showing the way towards their progress'.[41] Apparently the narrative choices and the unabashed flattering attracted the criticism of the centre. More specifically, Nafi Atuf Kansu,[42] head of the fifth bureau of the General Secretariat of the Party, that is, the office responsible for the monitoring of the Halkevi activities,[43] politely criticized the booklet in a letter to the Kayseri Halkevi chairman on 6 April 1937.

> Our Party received two of the booklets published by the Kayseri Halkevi under the title 'Village Excursion Series'. It is surely necessary to praise the village excursions and studies. It is also proper to recognize such activities. Nevertheless, it has been concluded that the two brochures we have in our hands *are overstating the work done enormously, while reducing the seriousness and significance of the work*. I am sending you the account of a village study published by the Ankara Halkevi. It is useful to publish the results of village studies in this way. But publications like the ones of the Kayseri Halkevi leave bad rather than good effects while they cause expenses.[44]

Kansu's letter is significant because it expressed the disapproval by the official Party department charged with monitoring the Houses of the way the Halkevi village activities were presented and, obviously, executed. For the centre, the village excursions and the research to be carried out in the villages was an important and serious work – a scientific activity. For Halkevi urban actors in situ it was depicted above all as a pleasure trip to the countryside in complete contrast to the centre's desiderata. What is more interesting, and at the same time illustrative of the limits of the village operation within the existing socio-political conditions, was what followed Kansu's letter. The governor reacted and wrote to Şükrü Kaya, at the time both Interior Minister and Party Secretary General, to protest about Kansu's letter.[45] Kansu had to reply to the governor that the criticism was not personal but aimed at the improvement of the Halkevi's performance.[46] Nevertheless, one month after Kansu's last letter, the journal of the Halkevi of Ankara[47] would praise the village excursions and these very same publications of the Kayseri Halkevi the centre had previously condemned in private.[48] This incident offers an exceptional picture of the multiplicity of agents involved and the environment within which the Halkevi had to operate. It also demonstrates the centre's awareness of and its limitations in mending what it conceived as erroneous Halkevi performance. Similar, but usually polite, disapproval of the activities and publications of various Houses was presented in a series of articles in the journal of the Ankara Halkevi. The most recurrent advice was that the Houses should carry out and publish research on their localities instead of publishing theoretical works or the poems, short stories and translations of 'a small group of friends'. What is more, they should do that in 'a more methodical manner' and after 'reading the Halkevi programme of activities'.[49] But again, neither Kansu nor *Ülkü* were alone in criticizing the unscientific and shallow nature of Halkevi publications and activities.

A similar viewpoint was expressed by Arman Hürrem, who, as a university student, participated in one of the first research missions to villages in the 1930s.[50] Together with a group of students from the Gazi Pedagogical Academy and other Halkevi members, the author had settled in a village near Ankara in order to conduct research. One day a group of men and women came from the Ankara Halkevi to the village and within a short while managed to destroy the relationship the researchers had painstakingly created with the villagers and, thus, the results of their research. They stayed for some hours and a feast was organized to celebrate their meeting with the villagers. Arman severely criticized their superficial interest in the villager and described them as 'foreign tourists', resonant of Fay Kırby's portrayal of Halkevi peasantist groups as 'foreign tourists who tried to discover the dark corners of Africa'.[51] Here we bear witness to the clash of two different elite perspectives regarding the villager. Arman's group of students indeed believed in the seriousness and importance of their work for the enlightenment of the villager, which they saw as a scientific or populist (or both) endeavour. They were annoyed by the light-heartedness and disinterest of the rank and file Party and Halkevi members in changing the villagers' lives and criticized the unchallenged patron–client relations between villagers and local elites.

In his novel *Havada Bulut Yok*, Cevdet Kudret recounted a similar village excursion of the Kayseri Halkevi. The novel's hero, Süleyman, was an idealistic literature teacher with left leanings from Istanbul. Appointed to the local lycée, he came to Kayseri with great hopes of educating and helping his fellow citizens to improve their life and actively participate in the Halkevi activities.[52] Kudret himself was a literature teacher in the Kayseri lycée in the 1930s, actively participating in the local Halkevi, and drew from his personal experiences to write this novel. In describing a village excursion, in which his hero and alter ego participated, the author was narrating a semi-fictitious event.

A group of almost 20 people, among them teachers, the municipality doctor, the hospital dentist, the public works engineer, the amateur folklorist teacher of German, the Halkevi secretary, some members of the Social Assistance section and some from other sections, started their excursion on a Saturday morning on a hired bus and after a while reached a village of the region. They then rested at the village headman's house for an hour, waiting for the villagers to assemble in front of the village's People's Room (*Halkodası*).[53] Then the House members stood in front of the Room facing the villagers.

The chairman ordered,
– Sit!
Everybody sat where they stood. Then the chairman said,
– Brothers, villagers! We came here to listen to your complaints. The times have changed; in the old days you would stand in front of us. Nowadays it is we who stand in front of you. Look, the Halkevi

chairman, the doctor, the dentist, the teacher, the engineer, great men came all the way to this place. Parties existed in the old days too, but this would have never taken place. The People's Party decided that the villager is the master. You do understand, don't you? Let us see, tell me, what are you?

A villager replied,

– We are villagers.

– Yes, you are villagers, but you are also masters. Impress this on your mind. You are now our masters.

Turning to the secretary,

– Suphi Bey, give me this sign. See what is written here.

THE VILLAGER IS OUR MASTER

– We will hang this on the wall of the People's Room, you will show it to your visitors and you will read it yourselves.

Kudret's irony is again at work; the villagers were pompously given a sign they probably could not read, as one of the Halkevi members noted.

Then the chairman asked the villagers to express their complaints.[54] Some villagers complained that neither doctor nor veterinarians had ever visited their district while another whined about the taxes the village headman was asking them to pay. The chairman instructed the secretary to write down these complaints in order to show the villagers his interest in their problems. Then he informed the villagers that they had brought books for them, triggering a teacher's sarcastic remark about the absence of any village school or literate villagers. Next, the villagers were examined by the visiting doctors who treated them with manifest indifference and cruelty. The villagers were given useless prescriptions because there was no pharmacy in their village, and when a villager started screaming because the dentist was pulling his tooth out without administering any form of anaesthetic, the dentist told the novel's hero not to worry at all because 'these people have been used to a great many troubles'.

After having their meal at the headman's place, the chairman addressed the villagers again.

– Villagers, brothers! In the morning we heard your complaints. Now let's hear your songs, let's watch your dances.

Five villagers started dancing and singing. [Th]e amateur folklorist teacher was writing down the words. The chairman said to the music teacher,

– Şadan Bey, write their notes. We'll use them in our concerts; we'll also send a copy of them to Ankara.

Then they departed to visit another village. The place they were heading to was unsightly. The dentist commented on how people could set their village in such a remote place behind these rocks. A teacher showed off, explaining that the villagers always tried to hide from tax collectors and state officials. Citing old Ottoman authors, such as Evliya Çelebi and Koçu Bey, the teacher's comments underscored the way the educated viewed and comprehended the villager: as a page from a book or an object of literary and academic research, completely alien to their lifestyle and mentality. The dentist openly expressed his indifference and dislike for what they were supposedly doing. 'Why are we going to such remote villages? It's a corner of hell. These are damned places. It suffices to improve the nearby villages and leave the faraway villages for our successors.'

Upon arriving at the village, the group rested at the house of the village elder and enjoyed the luxurious dinner prepared. Then they slept, and the following day, after lunch, they gathered the villagers.

The same speeches were given; the same sign was hung in the People's Room. The chairman addressed the villagers,

– Come on speak, let's hear your problems.

Nobody said anything.

– Why don't you speak? Don't you have any problems?

A villager responded. It was not clear whether he was smiling or not as his mouth was hidden underneath his moustache.

– We don't have any problems, sir. Before you, a group of people came here – may they be well – with pens in their hands. They wrote down all our problems. We are grateful; we have no more problems.

– A village without problems? How can this be real? Tell a few problems to us as well.

– There aren't any, sir. Who's the problem, who are we? [Dert kim, biz kim?] You have troubled yourselves to come all the way here. There is no road coming to our village, but yet you managed to find it.

The peasantists were very sad to return empty-handed from that village. They wanted to pay their debt for twice eating and drinking there by writing on a piece of paper their problems, but it didn't happen.[55]

In contrast to the official rhetoric, which stressed the importance and seriousness of this Halkevi activity, Kudret's description of a village excursion almost borders on parody.[56] But notwithstanding the differences in narrative style or perspective, what was narrated was very much the same: Kudret's excursion was not much different from what other accounts portrayed. The participants were the same (teachers, bureaucrats and urban Party elites) and the activities they carried out were reproduced almost verbatim in most accounts, that is, speeches, medical treatment, folkloric research and listening to grievances. The significance of Kudret's story then lies not in its refutation but in its complementarity with these accounts. For instance, the indifference – even antipathy – with which the peasantists treated the villagers in Kudret's novel corresponds to the disappearance of the villager from the rest of the accounts. In the novel, the villager was treated as a mere object of study, a quotation from a book, a text to be read, a music to be recorded, and a body without an intellect or emotions to be treated. Kudret ridiculed the encounter between the city visitors and their 'villager brothers' as it was usually recorded in official publications: the Halkevi chairman ordered the 'masters of the country' to sit and listen. The contradictions between the regime's statements about and the actual treatment of the villagers by Party and state men and women were sketched with bitter irony.

Apart from the participants' apathy, Kudret also hinted at the power relations between the visitors and the villagers, as well as the coercion and violence the villagers occasionally faced, in the hands of the Halkevi visitors. The doctor's indifference to his patient's screams is an example. The villagers were ordered throughout the village excursion. Lilo Linke described a quite similar incident that took place in Samsun in 1935. A 17-year-old adolescent participating in the village excursions of the Samsun Halkevi told her about a villager with venereal disease in need of medical treatment: 'He had defied the previous orders of the visiting doctor. Talat [the Halkevi youth] warned him that he would be fetched by a gendarme and had told the village headman and the teacher to keep an eye on him.'[57] The gendarme was the villager's *bête noire*, the villain of numerous complaint letters.[58] A form of a brutal semi-military countryside police, the gendarmes were mostly employed for the extraction of taxes, conscripts and compulsory work. In a number of cases, though, they apparently contributed, in their own capacity and way, to the satisfaction of more cultural needs of the state and Party elites in provincial towns by fetching villagers from nearby villages to sing, perform, dance and play music for the entertainment of high guests[59] but also in fests, holidays[60] and folkloric events.[61]

But the treatment of the villager as an object was primarily revealed in the way (s)he was described and quoted. In all accounts, the villager was portrayed in a limited way: as an object of study, a number in population statistics, a body in health-care accounts, a producer of agricultural goods and a cultural container – of music, songs, and similar folkloric ingredients of a national culture in the making. Images that corresponded to, or perhaps derived from, the above way of looking at the villager emerged as well. The villager was portrayed as happy, good looking and healthy;[62] bearing a heroic appearance (*kahraman yapılı*); and proud and full of national and military qualities: 'I see in front of me a middle-aged villager with a thin beard. He is wearing a casket with the crescent and star on it saluting me militarily. "I am the village watchman sergeant Osman!"[63] What all texts agreed upon was the Turkish villager's hospitality, presented as a national quality. Moreover, the villager was definitely a treasure and a history (or text) they – the intellectuals – had to read, study and evaluate.[64] Invoking the characteristic category of the producer or the resident of nature were the metaphors of the field used to describe villagers: 'their hands were like fields', 'her breasts resembled a productive field, a dried out spring'.[65]

However, the villager could also be a repository of undesired, negative qualities. The irrational villager who had faith in superstitions was also a common stereotype, a theme found in the manuals on research in the villages, in literature[66] and in the village studies: in the village of Hacılar, as a Halkevi peasantist wrote, 'a number of dervishes' tombs exist [...] two or three meters high. The people believe that the dervishes were equally tall and attach long colourful wish-cloths to the tombstones. Some even attach silk veils and handkerchiefs [...] The social life of this village, which is near Kayseri, has not yet been raised. Blood feuds persist.'[67]

The villager appeared as an active subject only when (s)he was reported speaking or when quoted, which usually happened when the peasantists recorded their complaints and requests. But what the villagers were reported requesting was what the Halkevi members would have deemed necessary, such as information about child care, a school, road, or a reading room, instead of the municipal coffee house, and the demolition of the dervish tombstones. Neither taxes nor compulsory work on road construction and other state projects were discussed. Such requests had been voiced in the Party Congress of Kayseri[68] a few years before and, timidly, by Kudret's villagers. Given the nature of such texts,[69] it is unreasonable to expect popular requests and issues arousing popular distress to be recorded. Village studies did not refer to such complaints, an indicator in itself of the authenticity of the villager's voice in these studies. In a given confrontation with the state and its agents (gendarmes, tax collectors, conscription officers and the Halkevi members), the villagers were reported to nod even when disagreeing or, more likely, understanding nothing of the things said. On the other hand, the peasantists' indifference, evident in Kudret's text and easily sensed in the rest of the accounts, precluded any possibility of a dialogue between the two sides – and dialogue here is defined as an exchange between two sides that desire to communicate and *speak the same language*,[70] which was definitely not the case.

In a very few cases the villager was permitted to say a few words. The exceptionality of such direct quotations signifies the low intensity of the dialogue between city-dwellers and villagers, while it also reveals the lack of importance Halkevi members attached to searching for and recovering the villager's own voice. Not that direct quotations by their nature and especially within the authoritative discursive space of Halkevi and Party publications carried any guarantee of authenticity, or that the quotations were real and spoken word for word. They are important, however, in disclosing the way(s) the writers viewed their object.

In most narratives the villager was not quoted at all. Just once, when excitement was caused by the presence of a 131-year-old village woman, a more extended quotation than usual was allowed. Because of the interest shown towards her by the governor and other Halkevi visitors, the old woman was reported crying and saying the following: 'May Allah give you a life as long as ours! But I do not know, are these words for us a wish or a curse?' When asked about her reminiscences, she was reported mentioning her husband's prolonged military service: 'My husband was a soldier for 12 years in the lands of Arabistan. I was waiting for him for 12 years in this village. I will not be able to forget this pain till I die.' The author's assessment of this statement is quite telling of the way a villager's word might be read by a Halkevi member: 'She said with tears in her eyes, still feeling the pains of the old regime.' The third and last direct quotation came at the end of the article: '"I haven't seen anything. That's it, I came, I will go." She described with one sentence in an open, absolute and eloquent way the philosophy of her long life.[71]

This article was subtitled 'Impressions from village excursions' and thus was neither about the village excursion, nor a village study. It was almost totally about the old woman. But out of four and a half pages about this woman, the three quotes above were the only few words she was allowed to utter. Her words were rendered meaningful only within the frame in which they were uttered, that is, the rest of the text. In the first quotation she expressed her gratitude to the governor and the visitors for their help and interest. This should also be read as an endorsement of the current state activities in contrast to her condemnation of the old regime's deeds, which was the author's reading of the second quotation of her words, as well as its function in the text. As for her last words, they complemented the metaphors the author used to describe her: the words of a simple person, of an object, or else, of a '*bridge* connecting the beginning of the previous century with the current one', 'a *field*', 'a valuable *history* to be read', 'a *spring* feeding fifty-four grandchildren', 'a *residue* tossed from the previous to this century', and 'a precious *treasure* that has to be studied', all of which constituted the conceptual imagery the modernizing subject employed to imagine, apprehend, study and operate over its object, a mute or silenced Other, much celebrated as the repository of national culture and simultaneously feared as a potential core of reactionary opposition. Even when directly quoted, then, exceptional as such instances were, the villager's words did not amount to anything more than a part of the author's discourse.[72] The villager simply reiterated with his own words what the rest of the text expressed about him/her, which was nothing more than an overt denial of the villager's subjecthood.[73]

The differentiation between Kudret's account of the village excursion and the Kayseri Halkevi texts about the same excursions exemplify a shift in the representation of the villager that took place in the 1940s. Popular novels and early Turkish films of the 1930s and 1940s offered a romantic idealization of village life,[74] very similar to many Halkevi-produced peasantist texts. Although criticisms of the superficiality of the Halkevi village policies might surface even within such popular novels, it is from the 1940s that the critique of the single-party village operation became more comprehensive as an overall social critique of the villagers' living conditions. The description of the village excursion in Kudret's story, but also in general the way he presented the meeting between urban intellectuals and villagers, was typical of authors writing within the current of social realism since the 1930s, but especially from the 1940s onwards.[75] Probably the first to write village-related short stories based on direct observation of villages was Sabahattin Ali. A friend of Cevdet Kudret but also of Niyazi and Mediha Berkes – sociologists engaged in village research in the 1940s[76] – Sabahattin Ali's short stories relate the encounter of villagers with urban elites in an almost identical way to Kudret's account. In his short stories, Sabahattin Ali ridiculed the peasantism of intellectuals and disclosed the insults and cruelty peasants were subjected to by urban elites and state officials.[77] Later on in the late 1940s and 1950s, writers like Sadri Ertem, Orhan Kemal, Yaşar Kemal and Orhan Hançerlioğlu would offer, in a realistic way and often with the use of humour and irony, an overt social criticism of the poverty and injustice the low classes and the villagers experienced.[78] The divergence between Kudret's social realist account of the village excursion and in general of Halkevi activities, and the celebratory and romantic tone of official reports and Halkevi publications, was not just a rivalry about narrative form, but rather highlighted the emergence of a discourse that was critical of the superficiality and indifference of urban intellectuals and the state towards the villagers' plight in the face of poverty and hardship but also at the hands of oppressive notables and state officials. This critique would become vociferous by the 1950s, with the first generation of village-born writers – most of them Village Institute graduates. The publication of Mahmut Makal's *Bizim Köy* in 1950 is a landmark in this respect.[79]

The shifts in the discourses about the villager were definitely influenced by various factors. The hardships during World War II and the emergence of a class of wealthy landowners; the gradual postwar mechanization of the agricultural economy; and the increased village-to-city migration by the late 1940s were unquestionably important factors. The Village Institutes were also quite influential in the emergence of a generation of village-born writers by the late 1940s. Journalistic writing was probably another area within which such social critique could materialize. At least three novelists started their career writing newspaper reports about the life and hardships of working men and women, a motif they elaborated on in their novels (Yaşar Kemal, Sadri Ertem and Reşat Enis).[80] Next to these factors, I argue that the Halkevi village operation and the thousands of village excursions that took place within a span of 19 years (1932–51) fostered the emergence of this critique of the hitherto hegemonic discourse and customary practice of urban intellectuals and state over the villager. To be more specific, if Mahmut Makal, Fakir Baykurt and Talip Apaydın were Village Institute graduates and teachers-cum-authors writing village novels, there was also another group of teachers-cum-authors writing about villages who were either engaged in or familiar with the Halkevi activities, such as Cevdet Kudret, Sabahattin Ali[81] and Mükerrem Su.[82] Again, Yaşar Kemal's first published work was a collection of folklore for the Adana Halkevi.[83] There were also other writers familiar with or engaged in Halkevi activities who carried out research and published academic works on village issues, such as Niyazi Berkes, Mediha Esenel and Hürrem Arman. Village sociologists were definitely aware of the Halkevi and the enormous amount of published material on folklore and village issues – irrespective of its quality – the People's Houses had been publishing for almost 20 years. For studies of village sociology that started to appear by the late 1940s, the Halkevi village excursion and study experiment functioned as a substratum of works, literature, attitudes and accumulated experience to draw upon and stand critical against.[84] My argument is that the same applies to non-fictional works that articulated a social critique of the mentality, discourse and practice of peasantism in the single-party period. In a somehow paradoxical way, the Halkevi experiment introduced villagers and Anatolia to middle-class intellectuals and in that sense contributed to the emergence of a discourse that was critical of the mentality, discourse and practice of peasantism and populism the Halkevi had been built upon. Apart from works of literature, this criticism also surfaced, albeit timidly and rarely, in official publications like *Ülkü*. In one of the village studies *Ülkü* published, the authors wrote that the villagers were maltreated and deceived by state officials; that they were not accepted in the town hospital; and that village teachers were not active in enlightening the villagers.[85] This article provoked the local governor's reaction and in a letter to *Ülkü* all complaints were rejected as unsubstantiated.[86] The village studies that were subsequently published in *Ülkü* did not contain such sharp commentary.

Conclusion

Although publicly proclaiming the Turkish peasant to be the true master of the country, the reforming state did not (nor did it probably have the necessary means to) carry out any major transformation of the country's villages.[87] In that respect, the village excursions were not considered to have made any contribution to bringing substantial change to the countryside.[88] Nevertheless, the village excursion was probably the only Halkevi activity wherein villagers met with Halkevi members. This short moment was planned in detail by numerous publications on peasantist activities and produced a large number of publications about every aspect of life and culture in villages. In examining a number of such texts, I first of all argue that this peasantist literature ultimately produced and defined its object, the villager.

From even a cursory glance, it is apparent that the Halkevi village operation was huge. During the 19 years in which the

Houses were active, thousands of villages were visited[89] and thousands of books were published.[90] The Halkevi journals regularly featured items on folklore and village studies for almost 20 years.[91] I argue that this concentration of material and representations of the 'Turkish village' was constitutive of the categories of villager and village as reservoirs of the supposedly authentic popular culture of the Turkish nation. The consequent formation of a national literary and folkloric canon was built upon the de-contextualization and 'death' of its research object.[92] The formation of the 'Turkish villager' can be also seen as a redefinition of what the villager had been for the ruling urban elites. The village operation reflected and contributed to the shift of the state and elites' perspective on the villager, transformed from an object of taxation and conscription to the citizen of a nation-state.

Secondly, as part of this process, I argue that the Halkevi peasantist operation was also constitutive of the discourse and identity of the carriers of that perspective, that is, urban intellectuals.[93] Apart from being an exercise in boundary management between urban and rural, peasant and peasantist, performing but also repudiating the Halkevi peasantist activities constituted a meaningful social experience, something to be mentioned with pride in their memoirs and their petitions to the Party for some; something to provide an opportunity for social criticism for others. For Halkevi members, participating in the village excursions entailed the performance and realization of the border separating them from the Other they were supposed to enlighten. The village operation either established or reinforced existing relations between urban elites and villagers, as it replayed the power relations between them. More precisely, borrowing from F. Barth's ideas on the significance of borders for the (self-)identification of ethnic groups,[94] I argue that by virtue of their participation in this boundary-setting operation, the Halkevi members involved can be described as establishing and performing their membership in this missionary-like social group that aimed at transforming the lives of villager-Others.

In a sense, this meeting of urbanites with villagers underlined and strengthened the existing distance between them, the same paradoxical way that the 'liberation of the Turkish woman' led to the creation of new forms of – hidden or public – segregation.[95] The social distance between urban elites and villagers that was once partially based on spatial distance was now (re)established and defined by those few moments of temporally, spatially and socially restricted proximity that was performed during village excursions.[96]

Finally, although the existence of the boundary was not challenged, its range was contestable, as demonstrated by the differing perspectives over, and images of, the villager. All peasantist narratives presented the villager as a passive and silent object, a pervasive Other to be operated upon as the village operation by its conception and upon its execution produced discourses *about* the villager and not *of* the villager, however different they might be in style or authorial perspective. Nevertheless, this same operation ultimately contributed to the formation of competing perspectives and discourses about peasantists and peasants alike. Next to the romantic narrative of the idealist peasantist and the idealized villager from earlier depictions of village life, the village-related discourses were enriched with rival narratives that presented a social critique of the hardships and oppression the villagers faced at the hands of notables, state officials and idealist peasantists. A social realist narrative would become dominant in literature and among the centre-left and left after the 1950s. From the villager and peasantist of the romantic Kayseri Halkevi publications to the realist depiction of villagers in Sabahettin Ali's short stories; from the authoritarian description of a Halkevi village excursion by a leading bureaucrat to the irony of that of a participating teacher like Cevdet Kudret, or to the criticism of village monographs by a social scientist like Mediha Esenel,[97] the village operation and its discursive products functioned as a substratum that was necessary and beneficial for the emergence of varying and competing interpretations of peasant and peasantist. The

Halkevi village operation and its products provided in this way a medium for constant boundary management of and about social and political identities.

Conclusions 7

Years before the establishment of the Turkish Republic, a young staff officer of the Ottoman Army stationed in Yemen bought a gramophone from a French engineer and Western music records from an Italian diplomat. Many years later he recounted his first impressions upon listening to these records. Although he and his fellow officers had never before listened to such music, they considered it to be good music because it was European and modern. Nevertheless, their first impressions were utterly negative and they were annoyed that they could not appreciate these arias and operas. It was difficult to 'endure the noise of the pieces we did not know and sense'.[1] Having no other records to listen to, they listened to these records again and again every evening until some of them managed to appreciate it. The officer was İsmet İnönü, later to become one of the founders of the Republic of Turkey, its second president and a staunch advocate of the Kemalist reform movement. He would later become a regular at classical music concerts at the Ankara Conservatory, apparently succeeding in appreciating Western music.

Notwithstanding the happy ending to this story, in İnönü's recounting of the event years later, the initial difficulty of enduring alien music was still remembered, an indication that this was at first a painful experience. This anecdote indicates that the path to 'modern civilization' was not a straightforward one, devoid of complexities, even for Western-educated elite Ottoman officials who were convinced of the necessity to reform in accordance with Western European patterns. The experience of having first to learn to endure and then to appreciate was disturbing and demanding even for those who were successful in the process and cherished the memory of it. The path was full of ambiguities and contradictions even for its most steadfast supporters like İnönü. A convinced believer in the separation of religion from politics, İnönü was apparently quite religious and privately prayed and fasted until the end of his life. Even Atatürk, the founder of the modern Turkish Republic, privately enjoyed traditional songs he was so adamant about banning from state radio because he considered them inferior to Western music and not adequately modern for the Turks.[2]

Moving away from the founding fathers of the Turkish Republic to social actors in provincial urban settings, whose voices I have tried to listen to in this book, a number of questions arise. How did *they* endure listening only to Western music on the state radio, or wearing the 'infidel' hat instead of the fez? How did they cope with the tensions that compulsory introduction of such innovations in their lives apparently gave rise to? Was their understanding and management of such moments of tension similar to İnönü's steadfast resolution? And ultimately what can such tensions and their management possibly tell us about (i) state–society relations during a social-engineering project and (ii) how the consumption of these reforms within local socio-political and cultural contexts can be related to the (re)shaping of social identities?

To explore this 'coping with', I draw on Michel de Certeau's work on everyday practices and employ the term 'consumption' or 'usage'. Consumption designates the myriad ways people consume the cultural products that institutional orders such as states, corporations or churches impose upon them. For de Certeau, this consumption is never a passive process: in consuming the cultural products of a dominant order, users ultimately transform and adapt them to their own rules and interests.[3] I have tried to view the application of the novelties the Turkish state introduced in the 1930s and 1940s as a cultural production in itself that took place within local socio-political networks in both conflict and accommodation with state power.

Instead of analyzing the introduction of novelties such as theatre or dance balls as an exact enactment of what the state initially prescribed, I choose to view them – to use a theatrical metaphor – as numerous 'rehearsals' and 'stagings' of the original state 'scripts': every 'staging' was unavoidably different depending on the socio-cultural and political diversity of the local 'stages', their 'theatrical scenery' and 'actors'.

In order to study the consumption of the reforms, this book has focused on the People's House institution and has resorted to an analytical perspective that led to an end-product that can be described as a *multi-locale* historical ethnography.[4] Starting with an analysis of the textbook version of the Halkevi *locus*, the book turned to the study of specific social *loci* – the Halkevi in provincial urban centres. Then moving away from the Houses' ideological-discursive and socio-political *loci*, the book jumped to thematic *loci* and read the responses social actors in provincial urban societies produced upon consuming three sets of policies the centre attempted to introduce through the People's Houses.

Established in 1932, the People's House was a product of its era – the interwar period of single-party authoritative rule – and directly reflected the ruling elite's approach of tutelary popular sovereignty that denied political agency to the same people the elite declared to be the 'real master of the country'. An integral part of the Kemalist social engineering project, the Halkevi's primary aim was to facilitate nation-building through the transmission of the elite's political and ideological products to the population. With branches in most urban centres in Turkey, the Houses were to assist in the state project of nation-building whose explicit goal was to mould the 'modern' and 'civilized' Turkish nation out of the people of the Republic of Turkey. Until their closure in 1951, the Houses performed activities of adult education and political indoctrination, ranging from music concerts, sports and folkloric research to the regime's propaganda. All Houses had an identical structure and their activities were performed in an identical fashion everywhere, while their operation was tightly and hierarchically controlled by local elites and state and Party officials.

The primary consumers of the Halkevi activities were the urban middle and upper classes. The People's Houses were in general able to mobilize the educated segments and the elites in provincial urban settings. Doctors, lawyers, teachers and state officials were in most cases the active cadre of the Houses, those who carried out most of their activities. Although, in general, these educated segments were considered as sharing – and indeed shared – many identity traits, such as a modern education, a Western outlook and complete adherence to the reform movement, a look at the sources also reveals significant differentiations among them. Teachers and other state employees, especially women, were habitually coerced to join the Halkevi, something many despised and resisted. Others used their participation as leverage to further their personal or political interests. But there were equally many idealists who wholeheartedly participated in the Halkevi activities in order to 'enlighten' the people, however alienated they felt from the very people they were supposed to educate. Most sources indicated that feelings of alienation and boredom were quite common among many Halkevi members in the provinces as the cultural and social life of provincial urban centres could hardly offer much to satisfy the needs of educated state officials or professionals, that is, the bulk of Halkevi members.

In contrast to educated Halkevi members, long-established local elites (merchants, artisans and landowner Party cadres) participated in smaller numbers and usually in a different fashion. Local elites were mostly interested in the Houses' potential as opportunity spaces for the enhancement of their political standing. It is for this reason that they were usually appointed Halkevi chairmen, which was a position that was considered to possess political capital. These local power brokers came from notable families, dominated most local social, political and financial structures and functioned as middlemen between population and state, as Party executives, mayors, vote-mongers and MPs.

These variations in the way the Halkevi project was experienced point to differences in the educational, professional and social outlook of the Halkevi members, while they also confirm the existence of conflicting interests and ultimately divergent perspectives regarding the People's Houses and their activities, as well as the reforms they were supposed to propagate. Another factor that directly contributed to the nature of each House was the environment within which it operated. In contrast to the singularity of the Halkevi seen as a project, local socio-political and cultural conditions greatly affected the various Houses' activities and clientele. Factors such as literacy rates, the volume of state institutions and employees, and the magnitude of local associations significantly contributed to the local Houses' make-up. The previous existence of cultural associations that had fostered 'modern' activities (theatre, concerts, courses, balls, etc.) or a large student and civil servant population, for instance, could considerably increase a House's yield and its correlation with local society. That was usually the case in a few provincial urban centres that hosted major state educational, administrative, judicial and financial institutions. The opposite was usually the case for Houses in smaller towns whose populations' educational and cultural status obviously left much to be desired. The People's Houses in the Kurdish-populated south-east was at the other end of the spectrum, where the cultural and ethnic rift between local population and state employees was reflected in the Halkevi space, exclusively occupied by non-local state officials who maintained minimal association with the locals. Obviously this diversification in the Houses' output and character was related to the level of relations between state institutions and local societies.

But despite the variations in the activities of various Houses and in the modes of participation among their members, there was a structural characteristic shared by all Houses, namely their unmistakable *political nature*. As a space of socialization for the urban upper and middle classes, the Halkevi was an elite space itself; it was located at the centre of local politics and operated as a node in interrelated webs of socio-political relations. As such, the People's House was habitually and literally turned into a stage and an arena within which local feuds were played out. The study of the Halkevi space and actors within local politics immediately projects an image of state–society relations very akin to Meeker's conceptualization of an 'imperial state society' wherein 'local elites composed a tiered state society, the uppermost tier being inside and the lowermost outside the state system'.[5] In the 1930s and 1940s, local elites continued to function as a link between the centre and local societies. They formed the backbone of the Party cadre and formed alliances with state and Party officials locally but also in the centre. They habitually used their patrons in the centre to outmanoeuvre state employees or local rivals. State officials likewise enlisted the cooperation of local power brokers, whose hostility might otherwise have endangered their position but also their standing in the eyes of their superiors and the local public. As the playground of both local and state elites, the People's Houses were situated in the middle of various other social spaces and institutional structures, and a vast array of formal or informal networks that filtered through local societies and moved across the state–society divide. This picture of state–society relations at the local level is at variance with what statist conceptions of state–society relations can account for and renders the limits between state and society, state and non-state social forces, rather hazy. What is more, it de-emphasizes the centre's ability to enforce its wishes while it conversely stresses the capacity of local forces to dilute or even prevent them. State institutions and officials were not 'society-proof' even in places like the Kurdish-populated south-east where the cleavage between state officials and local population was greater and state presence limited; although to a smaller extent even there locals were able to contact and influence them, and, thus, convert the execution of the centre's plans.[6]

This ability of local actors to negotiate and alter state projects, and to accommodate them to local socio-political and cultural realities was also manifest in the way they consumed a number of Halkevi activities. I have argued that Halkevi actors were able to do so by means of manipulating the ambiguities of state discourse and practices, as well as through a number of ingeniously crafted adaptations of the novelties the centre had planned to introduce through the Halkevi. For instance, local actors were able to devise resourceful techniques in order to perform in the Houses the exact same 'coffee house' practices (drinking, gambling, idle gossiping) the state was struggling to eradicate through the introduction and promotion of 'modern' socialization practices (concerts, sports, lectures, balls, etc.). Another example of this negotiation and ultimate fine-tuning of the state's products was the local actors' ingenious reuse of the official discourse. In their texts, Halkevi members 'turned' the celebrated 'sovereign people' of the official discourse into the 'unjustly suffering people', utilizing the image of the righteous subject who is undeservingly tormented by immoral oppressors and usurpers of state power. Such imaginative narratives employed a vocabulary and imagery that would, in the following decades, heavily permeate most discourses of conservative populism on the Turkish right. What is more, those who articulated these discourses in petition and complaint letters were neither illiterate peasants nor religious zealots, but what the regime considered its own constituency, that is, the urban middle classes. Although the image of the oppressed subject had been a norm of petition-writing for centuries, the stress on the immorality of the oppressor was something novel; it was increasingly related to or plainly established by his/her participation in 'modern' activities performed in the Halkevi, such as the theatre, concerts, mixed-gender meetings and courses, and so on.

The blending of the image of the oppressed subject with the discourse of morality was emphatically pronounced with respect to women-related activities. In their attempt to resolve the tensions produced by the introduction of heterosocial activities in a substantially homosocial society, Halkevi members devised various strategies. For instance, when Halkevi executives organized or reported Halkevi activities, allowances were made for popular conservative perceptions of morality and 'proper' gender relations.

Low-class bachelors or unaccompanied men were deliberately denied entry to avoid the potential harassment of the women present. The exact same fear of sexual harassment of women by unrelated men was obviously the reason behind the practice of sex-segregated activities, such as courses and sports for women only. But even more subtle and everyday practices internally segregated the heterosocial space of the Halkevi, such as when women habitually flocked together during theatre plays, cinema projections or village trips. In short, the widely homosocial nature of local societies was subtly introduced into the Halkevi, a space with which the state aimed to introduce heterosocial socialization and facilitate the 'liberation of the Turkish woman from the shackles of obscurantism'.

The consumption of the regime's village policies by Halkevi actors was another activity whose results did not always conform to the state's aims. Thousands of village excursions and village studies published by Halkevi members contributed to the shaping of village-related discourses that openly contested the manner in which state and Party portrayed the villager and state–village relations. The volume of the products of the Halkevi village operation, in terms of the number of villages visited and texts produced, was immense. More importantly, this production contributed to the emergence of discourses of social critique that did not hide the hardships of villagers or their oppression by notables and state officials. Many writers and intellectuals engaged in or at least cognizant of the Halkevi village policies, but others also directly influenced by the state's village policies, such as Village Institute graduates, produced social realist narratives of villagers and village life that were to become dominant between the 1950s and 1970s.

In summation, I argue that the local consumption of the Halkevi space and its activities was unquestionably an act of domestication of state policies. By domestication I refer to the regular renegotiation, accommodation and adaptation of the centre's products by local agents, 'turning' those products into something more agreeable to local conditions and more meaningful for their users. The centre's ideas and plans – without necessarily being rejected – were blended with activities, perceptions and practices they were supposed to eradicate. Given the novelty of many state-sponsored practices and ideas and the expressed goal that they replace 'older' or 'backward' ones, their consumption in the Halkevi was also a process of negotiation of contested categories – modern vs backward, Western vs national/ local – but also of the identities of both their carriers and refuters. It was upon and within the continuously negotiated boundaries of the local socio-political and cultural milieu that Halkevi men and women operated and produced meaningful representations of themselves and others.

I view the consumption of the political and cultural products of the state on the Halkevi stage as performances of identity management. With their performances, social actors negotiated and defined the boundaries of what could socially and culturally be considered proper; and it is due to their function as such that I view these practices as signifying acts that were inevitably practices of identity management, ultimately (re)producing discursive and cognitive categories. The experience of heterosociality in the Houses, for instance, was articulated with the conflicting images of 'immoral theatre girls' and 'moral family girls'. Many women habitually expressed uneasiness upon their participation in the 'modern' activities of the Halkevi and associated the experience of being 'modern' with 'self-sacrifice'. Many male Halkevi members also described themselves as altruistic missionaries propagating a just cause. The (re)appropriation of the village-related discourses and practices of the regime by Halkevi practitioners was another example of the performance of boundary and identity management as it entailed the continuous negotiation of the categories 'villager' and 'peasantist' (that is, urban intellectual) but also the boundary and the relations between villager and state, village and city. The Halkevi village activities and, more generally, the village-related state policies and their discursive products provided a medium for the constant management of social and political identities. It gave birth to and reproduced the images of the idealist teacher struggling to enlighten the 'backward' and 'conservative' villager, but also to that of the selfish Party or state official who was indifferent to the villagers' plight at the hands of exploitative landlords.

What is more, given the spatial, numerical and temporal expansion of the People's Houses, the impact of such practices could not have been inconsequential. That is, the continuous existence in most cities and towns of Turkey for almost 20 years of an institution whose activities involved thousands certainly played a part in the shaping of social and gender identities in urban centres. This 'shaping', as we have seen, was not simply imposed by a coercive state, but also involved the active participation of people who were able to, and did, negotiate state desiderata. This negotiation was not obviously practised with the same intensity or results everywhere, and we should not overestimate it; nevertheless, it should not be overlooked either. Statist perspectives and modernization apologists have emphasized the state's strength and overlooked society, which is usually overlooked or at best considered passive, backward and in need of reforming. From such perspectives, state coercion was more or less vindicated as necessary. Equally, oppositional stances, although underlining the regime's oppression and authoritarianism, nevertheless treated the state of the single-party period as an entity isolated from society. Both perspectives seem to deny or at least overlook (the possibility of) interaction between the state apparatus and societal forces. In this book I have argued that, seen from below, the picture was less black and white.

Notes

Introduction

1   Şerif Mardin, 'Projects as Methodology: Some Thoughts on Modern Turkish Social Science', in Sibel Bozdoğan and Reşat Kasaba (eds), *Rethinking Modernity and National Identity in Turkey* (Seattle and London: University of Washington Press, 1997), 72–4.

2   Deniz Kandiyoti, 'Gendering the Modern. On Missing Dimensions in the Study of the Turkish Modernity', in Bozdoğan and Kasaba, *Rethinking*, 113.

3   Joel Migdal, 'Finding the Meeting Ground of Fact and Fiction. Some Reflections on Turkish Modernization', in Bozdoğan and Kasaba, *Rethinking*, 255.

4   Kandiyoti, 'Gendering the Modern', 113.

5   For a critique of modernization theory, see Dean Tipps, 'Modernization Theory and the Comparative Study of Societies: A Critical Perspective', *CSSH* 15 (1973). For a review of Lewis' book in relation to the literature on Turkey since its publication, see Erik Jan Zürcher, 'The Rise and Fall of "Modern" Turkey: Bernard Lewis's *Emergence* Fifty Years On', in idem, *The Young Turk Legacy and Nation Building: From the Ottoman Empire to Atatürk's Turkey* (London: I.B.Tauris, 2010), 41–53.

6   Mardin, 'Projects as Methodology', 64. For a compact presentation of the two approaches of modernization and dependency theory, see Atul Kohli and Vivienne Shue, 'State power and social forces: on political contention and accommodation in the Third World', in Joel Migdal, Atul Kohli and Vivienne Shue (eds), *State Power and Social Forces. Domination and Transformation in the Third World* (Cambridge: Cambridge University Press, 1994), 295–301.

7   Metin Heper, *The State Tradition in Turkey* (Hull: Eothen Press, 1985), 16, 149–50, 154.

8   Reşat Kasaba, 'A time and a place for the nonstate: social change in the Ottoman Empire during the "long" nineteenth century', in Migdal et al., *State Power and Social Forces*, 207–31. Cf. Reşat Kasaba, 'Do States Always Favor Stasis? The Changing Status of Tribes in the Ottoman Empire', 27–49, and Beatrice Hibou, 'Conclusion', in Joel Migdal (ed.), *Boundaries and Belonging. States and Societies in the Struggle to Shape*

Identities and Local Practices (Cambridge: Cambridge University Press, 2004).

9 Milen Petrov, 'Everyday forms of Compliance: Subaltern Commentaries on Ottoman Reform, 1864–1868', *CSSH* 46:4 (2004). There are a number of recent works on the reception of the Tanzimat reforms that focus on human agency. Cf. Yücel Terzibaşoğlu, 'Eleni Hatun'un Zeytin Bahçeleri: 19. Yüzyılda Anadolu'da Mülkiyet Hakları Nasıl İnşa Edildi?', *Tarih ve Toplum Yeni Yaklaşımlar* 4 (2006); Elizabeth Thompson, 'Ottoman Political Reform in the Provinces: The Damascus Advisory Council in 1844–45', *IJMES* 25:3 (1993); Huri İslamoğlu, 'Property as a Contested Domain: A Reevaluation of the Ottoman Land Code of 1858', in Roger Owen and Martin P. Bunton (eds), *New Perspectives on Property and Land* (Cambridge, MA: Harvard University Press, 2001); Cengiz Kırlı, 'Yolsuzluğun icadı: 1840 Ceza Kanunu, iktidar ve bürokrasi', *Tarih ve Toplum Yeni Yaklaşımlar* 4 (2006).

10 Yael Navaro-Yashin, *Faces of the State: Secularism and Public Life in Turkey* (Princeton, NJ: Princeton University Press, 2002); Nilüfer Göle, *The Forbidden Modern. Civilization and Veiling* (Ann Arbor: University of Michigan Press, 1997); articles in Bozdoğan and Kasaba (eds), *Rethinking*; and Deniz Kandiyoti and Ayşe Saktanber (eds), *Fragments of Culture: The Everyday of Modern Turkey* (New Brunswick: Rutgers University Press, 2002).

11 Quoted in Meltem Ahıska, 'Occidentalism: The Historical Fantasy of the Modern', *The South Atlantic Quarterly* 102:2/3 (2003), and Kandiyoti and Saktanber, *Fragments of Culture*, 367.

12 Reşat Kasaba, 'Kemalist Certainties and Modern Ambiguities', in Bozdoğan and Kasaba, *Rethinking*, 30.

13 Oral history studies have investigated similar issues by focusing on specific local contexts and the narrative of social actors. Cf. Ayşe Durakbaşa and Aynur Ilyasoğlu, 'Formation of Gender Identities in Republican Turkey and Women's Narratives as Transmitters of "Her story" of Modernization', *Journal of Social History* 35:1 (2001); Esra Üstündağ-Selamoğlu, 'Bir Sözlü Tarih Çalışması. Hereke'de Değişim', *Toplumsal Tarih* 8:45 (1997).

14 Joel Migdal, 'Finding the Meeting Ground of Fact and Fiction', in Bozdoğan and Kasaba, *Rethinking*, 255.

15 Aradhana Sharma and Akhil Gupta, 'Introduction: Rethinking Theories of the State in an Age of Globalization', in idem, *The Anthropology of the State* (Oxford: Blackwell, 2006), 6.

16 Michel-Rolph Trouillot, 'The Anthropology of the State: Close Encounters of a Deceptive Kind', *Current Anthropology* 42:1 (2001); David Nugent, 'Building the State, Making the Nation: The Bases and Limits of State Centralization in "Modern" Peru', *American Anthropologist* 96:2 (1994); Philip Abrahams, 'Notes on the Difficulty of Studying the State', *Journal of Historical Sociology* 1 (1988).

17 Timothy Mitchell, 'The Limits of the State: Beyond Statist Approaches and their Critics', *American Political Science Review* 85:1 (March 1991): 94–95.

18 The differentiation between practices and representations is of course analytical in nature as they are 'deeply co-implicated and mutually constitutive'. Sharma and Gupta, 'Introduction', 19.

19 Joel Migdal, *State in Society. Studying How States and Societies Transform and Constitute One Another* (Cambridge: Cambridge University Press, 2001). Cf. Migdal, 'The state in society: an approach to struggles for domination', in idem., *State Power and Social Forces*, 1–30.

20 A distinction reminiscent of Migdal's is the one offered by Bruce Berman and John Lonsdale, *Unhappy Valley* (London: James Currey, 1992), 5 and 11–39, where, commenting on the case of the colonial state of Kenya, they differentiate between 'state building' and 'state formation', the former defined as 'a conscious effort at creating an apparatus of control', while the latter represents 'an historical process whose outcome is a largely unconscious and contradictory process of conflicts, negotiations and compromises between diverse groups whose self-serving actions and trade-offs constitute the "vulgarization" of power'.

21 Migdal, *State in Society*, 15–17.

22 Mitchell, 'The Limits of the State', 94.

23 Akhil Gupta, 'Blurred Boundaries: The Discourse of Corruption, the Culture of Politics, and the Imagined State', in Sharma and Gupta, *The Anthropology of the State*, 211–41.

24 A similar perspective from an anthropological study of bureaucracy: Michael Herzfeld, *The Social Production of Indifference. Exploring the Symbolic Roots of Western Bureaucracy* (Chigaco: University of Chicago Press, 1992).

25 Influenced by Migdal, recent works have offered new insights into state–society relations, everyday forms of state power, and its limits in the Kurdish populated south-east of Turkey. Nicole F. Watts, 'Re-Considering State–Society Dynamics in Turkey's Kurdish Southeast', and Senem Aslan, 'Incoherent State: The Controversy over Kurdish Naming in Turkey', *EJTS* 10 (2009), URL: http://ejts.revues.org/4196 and URL: http://ejts.revues.org/4142 (accessed 14 March 2014); Senem Aslan, 'Everyday Forms of State Power and the Kurds in the Early Turkish Republic', and Ceren Belge, 'State Building and the Limits of Legibility: Kinship Networks and Kurdish Resistance in Turkey', *IJMES* 43:1 (2011).

26 Migdal, *State in Society*, 124–34.

27 By centre/central state, I refer to the top echelons of the ensemble of interconnected state (bureaucracy) and para-state (Party and state/

Party-controlled associations) institutional organizations and structures, mainly situated in the capital. I do not contend that what I term as the centre, i.e. these core-state bureaucratic, educational, financial, military, judicial and ideological structures, possess the ideological and organizational integration, coherence and sophistication which the 'images of the state' usually claim, or centre–periphery models imply. Here the term centre is not equated with the 'state' – however conceptualized – nor is it ontologically juxtaposed to an 'exterior' or to 'society', a juxtaposition that would imply a border separating these two entities.

28 Michel de Certeau, *The Practices of Everyday Life* (Los Angeles: University of California Press, 1988), xiii.

29 All extracts from de Certeau, *Practices*, xv–xviii.

30 Ibid., 31.

31 Ibid., xviii.

32 Ibid., 35–36.

33 Ibid., 37.

34 Necmi Erdoğan, 'Devleti "İdare Etmek"': Maduniyet ve Düzenbazlık', *Toplum ve Bilim* 83 (2000).

35 Sherry Ortner, 'Resistance and the Problem of Ethnographic Refusal', *CSSH* 37:1 (1995).

36 James C. Scott, *Seeing Like a State. How Certain Schemes to Improve the Human Condition Have Failed* (New Haven, CT, and London: Yale University Press, 1998). Scott has been extensively criticized for substantializing resistance and overestimating the role and power of the state under 'high modernism'. For an example of this critique, see Beatrice Hibou, 'Conclusion', in Migdal, *Boundaries and Belonging*.

37 Tactical in character, everyday practices and 'ways of operating': 'victories of the "weak" over the "strong", clever tricks, knowing how to get away with things, "hunter's cunning", maneuvers'. De Certeau, *Practices*, xix; Scott, *Seeing Like a State*, 309–41.

38 James C. Scott, *Domination and the Arts of Resistance. Hidden Transcripts* (New Haven, CT, and London: Yale University Press, 1990).

39 Ahıska, 'Occidentalism'. For Chakrabarty, 'historicism posited historical time as a measure of the cultural distance that was assumed to exist between the West and the non-West'. Dipesh Chakrabarty, *Provincializing Europe. Postcolonial Thought and Historical Difference* (Princeton, NJ, and Oxford: Princeton University Press, 2000), 7.

40 For an earlier usage of the term, see Christopher M. Hann, *Tea and the Domestication of the Turkish State* (Huntingdon: Eothern Press, 1990).

41 Kandiyoti, 'Gendering the Modern', 127.

Chapter 1: The People's House

1 Erik Jan Zürcher, *Turkey: A Modern History* (London: I.B.Tauris, 2003), 121-32; Carter V. Findley, *Turkey, Islam, Nationalism, and Modernity* (New Haven, CT, and London: Yale University Press, 2010), 194-8, 233-6.

2 Geoffrey Lewis, *The Turkish Language Reform. A Catastrophic Success* (Oxford: Oxford University Press, 1999), 75 ff.

3 Büşra Ersanlı Behar, *İktidar ve Tarih. Türkiye'de resmi tarih tezinin oluşumu 1929-1937* (Istanbul: Afa, 1992).

4 Findley, *Turkey*, 245-62, 283-4; Zürcher, *Turkey*, 166-79, 186-95.

5 Erik Jan Zürcher, 'Who were the Young Turks?', in idem, *The Young Turk Legacy and Nation Building* (London: I.B.Tauris, 2010), 95-109.

6 Şükrü Hanioğlu, *Preparation for a Revolution. The Young Turks 1902-1908* (Oxford: Oxford University Press, 2001), 308-11; Erik Jan Zürcher, 'The Ottoman Legacy of the Kemalist Republic', in Touraj Atabaki (ed.), *The State and the Subaltern. Modernization, Society and the State in Turkey and Iran* (London: I.B.Tauris, 2007), 105-10.

7 Especially in relation to the Ottoman-Turkish language. David Kushner, *The Rise of Turkish Nationalism 1876-1908* (London: Frank Cass, 1977), 56-80.

8 Niyazi Berkes, *Turkish Nationalism and Western Civilization. Selected Essays of Ziya Gokalp* (London: George Allen & Unwin, 1959), 127 and 259 where there is an extract from Gökalp's article 'Halka Doğru'.

9 The Turkish Society (*Türk Derneği*), Turkish Science Association (*Türk Bilgi Derneği*), National Instruction and Training Society (*Milli Talim ve Terbiye Cemiyeti*), Turkish Hearth (*Türk Ocağı*), Peasant Information Society (*Köylü Bilgi Cemiyeti*) and the Towards the People Society of Izmir (*İzmir Halka Doğru Cemiyeti*) were the more prominent societies. Masami Arai, *Turkish Nationalism in the Young Turk Era* (Leiden: Brill, 1992), 7-20; İsmayıl Hakkı Baltacıoğlu, *Halkın Evi* (Ankara: Ulus, 1950), 22-4; Francois Georgeon, 'Les Foyers Turks à l' époque Kemalist 1923-1931', *Turcica* XIV (1982): 169; *Köylü Bilgi Cemiyeti esas nizamnamesi* (Istanbul, 1330 (1914)); Zafer Toprak, 'Osmanlı Narodnikleri: Halka Doğru gidenler', *Toplum ve Bilim* 24 (1984): 75; Tarık Zafer Tunaya, *Türkiye'de Siyasal Partiler, Vol. 1: İkinci Meşrutiyet Dönemi* (Istanbul: Hürriyet Vakfı Yayınları, 1988), 414, 417-18, 475.

10 Rıdvan Akın, *Osmanlı İmparatorluğu'nun Dağılma Devri ve Türkçülük Hareketi 1908-1918* (Istanbul: Der, 2002), 202-3, 210-12. See works on *terbiye-yi avam* by educationalists Sati Bey (1909), Edhem Nejad and İsmail Hakkı (1913) in Mustafa Ergün, *II Meşrutiyet Devrinde Eğitim Hareketleri 1908-1914* (Ankara: Ocak, 1996), 142-4, 188; Baltacıoğlu, 18-28.

11 National Libraries (*Milli Kütüphane*) were established in Izmir, Konya and Eskişehir. For Izmir, see Erkan Serçe, *İzmir'de Kitapçılık 1839-1928* (Izmir: İzmir Büyükşehir Belediyesi Kültür Yayınları, 2002), 76 ff.

12 Şükrü Hanioğlu, 'The Second Constitutional Period, 1908–1918', in Reşat Kasaba (ed.), *The Cambridge History of Turkey*, vol. 4: *Turkey in the Modern World* (Cambridge: Cambridge University Press, 2008), 69–83.

13 Hakan Aydın, 'İttihat ve Terakki Mekteplerinin Yapısal Özellikleri Üzerine bir İnceleme', PhD thesis (Konya: Selçuk University, 2008), 22–38, 60, 75–84, 159–69. For similar activities by the Unionist Clubs of Aydın, Bursa and Ayntab, cf. Günver Güneş, 'Taşradan Meşrutiyede Bakış: Sosyal, Siyasal ve Ekonomi açıdan II. Meşrutiyet Döneminde Aydın Sancağı (1908–18)', Mine Akkuş, 'II. Meşrutiyet'in Yörel Düzlemde yansımalarına bir örnek: Bursa', and Celal Pekdoğan, 'Ayntab'da İttihat ve Terakki Kulübü'nün kurulması ve Ayntab'da etkisi', in Sina Akşin et al. (eds), *100. Yılında Jön Türk Devrimi* (Istanbul: İş Bankası Kültür Yayınları, 2010), 443, 468–72, 496–7. Akşin likens the Clubs to the Halkevi in his *Jön Türkler ve İttihat ve Terakki* (Ankara: İmge, 2001), 360.

14 Yücel Aktar, *İkinci Meşrutiyet Dönemi Öğrenci Olayları 1908–1918* (Istanbul: İletişim, 1990), 80.

15 Association for National Defence (*Müdafaa-i Milliye Cemiyeti*) in 1914; Ottoman Strength Clubs (*Osmanlı Güç dernekleri*) in 1914; Turkish Strength Association (*Türk Gücü Cemiyeti*) in 1913; Youth Societies (*Genç Dernekler*) in 1916. Handan Nezir Akmeşe, *The Birth of Modern Turkey. The Ottoman Military and the March to World War I* (London: I.B.Tauris, 2005), 163–72; Tunaya, 448–73.

16 For a list of the women's associations between 1908 and 1918, see Tunaya, 476–82.

17 Uluğ Iğdemir, *Yılların içinde* (Ankara: Türk Tarih Kurumu, 1976), 292. He was referring to the 1918 Peasantist Association (*Köycüler Cemiyeti*).

18 Tunaya, 455, 462–3.

19 Andrew Mango, *Atatürk* (London: John Murray, 1999), 150.

20 The first works depicting peasants appeared in the late 1910s. Carole Rathbun, *The Village in the Turkish Novel and Short Story 1920 to 1955* (The Hague and Paris: Mouton, 1972), 18–21; Ramazan Kaplan, *Cumhuriyet Dönemi Türk Romanında Köy* (Ankara: Akçağ, 1997), 33–63.

21 Journals stemming from the Turkish Hearth society, such as *Halka Doğru* (Towards the People) and *Türk Sözü* (Turkish Word), both published in 1913–14, unambiguously expressed the need to reach and educate the people. François Georgeon, *Aux origines du nationalisme Turc. Yusuf Akçura 1876–1935* (Paris: ADPF, 1980), 66–7; Erol Köroğlu, *Ottoman Propaganda and Turkish Identity: Literature in Turkey during World War I* (London: I.B.Tauris, 2007), 65.

22 Arai, *Turkish Nationalism*, 72–3; Tunaya, 432–44.

23 Füsun Üstel, *İmparatorluktan Ulus-Devlete Türk Milliyetçiliği Türk Ocakları 1912–31* (Istanbul: İletişim, 2004), 167.

24 Georgeon, 'Les Foyers Turks', 203.

25 For an example of the educational, propagandistic and cultural activities of one of the most active Hearths (Izmir), see Günver Güneş, 'Türk Devrimi ve İzmir Türk Ocağı', *Çağdaş Türkiye Tarihi Araştırmaları Dergisi* 8 (1998): 116–26.

26 Üstel, *Türk Ocakları*, 227.

27 Mete Tunçay, *Türkiye Cumhuriyeti'nde tek-parti yönetimin kurulması 1923–1931*, 3rd edn (Istanbul: Tarih Vakfı Yurt Yayınları, 1999), 317–18; Esat Öz, *Türkiye'de Tek-parti Yönetimi ve siyasal katılım 1923–1945* (Ankara: Gündoğan, 1992), 106–8.

28 For an eyewitness view, see Ahmet Hamdi Başar, *Atatürk ile üç ay ve 1930 dan sonra Türkiye* (Ankara: Ankara İktisadi ve Ticari İlimler Akademisi, 1981).

29 Mustafa Yılmaz and Yasemin Doğaner, *Cumhuriyet Döneminde Sansür 1923–1973* (Ankara: Siyasal, 2007), 7–9.

30 Taha Parla, *Türkiyede siyasal kültürünün resmi kaynakları. Tek parti ideolojisi ve CHP'nin 6 ok'u* (Istanbul: İletişim, 1992), 81–3; Tunçay, *Tek-parti*, 327–8;

31 Cemil Koçak, *İktidar ve Serbest Cumhuriyet Fırkası* (Istanbul: İletişim, 2006), 369 ff.

32 Mehmet Asım Karaömerlioğlu, 'The People's Houses and the cult of the peasant in Turkey', *MES* 34:4 (1998): 86; Çetin Yetkin, *Türkiye'de tek parti yönetimi* (Istanbul: Altın Kitaplar, 1983), 78–86.

33 Tunçay, *Tek-parti*, 307. Niyazi Altunya, *Türkiye'de öğretmen örgütlenmesi 1908–1998* (Ankara: Ürün, 1998), 40–2; Eyal Ari, 'The People's houses and the Theatre in Turkey', *MES* 40:4 (2004): 41–2. In communiqué no. 345 of 16 August 1934 the Party Secretary Recep Peker asked Party branches to warn those who attempt to open youth unions that they should avoid it and join the Houses. *Tebligat*, vol. 5 (Ankara: Ulus, 1935), 55; See Ö.A.A., 'Halkevleri-Muallimler', *Ülkü* 6:36 (February 1936): 462–3, where the author presented the voluntary closing down of teachers' unions to join the Halkevi as very reasonable and asking youth clubs to do the same.

34 Arzu Öztürkmen, *Türkiye'de Folklor ve milliyetçilik* (Istanbul: İletişim, 1998), 53–64.

35 Yiğit Akın, *'Gürbüz ve Yavuz Evlatlar' Erken Cumhuriyet'te Beden Terbiyesi ve Spor* (Istanbul: İletişim, 2004).

36 Yetkin, *Türkiye'de*, 72; Ali Arslan, *Darülfünün' dan Üniversiteye* (Istanbul: Kitabevi, 1995).

37 A number of reasons for the Hearths' dissolution have been proposed. They range from the Soviet Union's anxiety over the Hearths' pan-Turkic overtones to the support the Free Republican Party had received from members and executive of the Hearths. But probably the primary reason was the difficulty of exercising total hierarchical and effective control over

the rather decentralized Hearths especially given the powerful position of their president, Hamdullah Suphi. For a thorough discussion, see Üstel, *Türk Ocakları*, 321 ff; Günver Güneş, 'Serbest Cumhuriyet Fırkası Döneminde Türk Ocakları ve Siyaset', *Toplumsal Tarih* 65 (1999): 11–18.

38 *Cumhuriyet*, 2 January 1931, in Tunçay, *Tek-parti*, 306.

39 Tunçay, *Tek-parti*, 307–8, 327.

40 Neşe Yeşilkaya, *Halkevleri: ideoloji ve mimarlık* (Istanbul: İletişim, 1999), 135–6. Sharing the same dwelling was only one among many characteristics demonstrating the close affinity between Halkevi and *Türk Ocağı*. Most of the individuals who drafted the Halkevi by-laws had been active *Ocak* members. Anıl Çeçen, *Atatürk'ün kültür kurumu Halkevleri* (Ankara: Gündoğan, 1990), 95; Orhan Özacun, 'Halkevlerin dramı', *Kebikeç* 3 (1996): 89–90. The provincial cadres of both institutions were probably similar if not identical.

41 Işıl Çakal, *Konuşunuz Konuşturunuz. Tek Parti Döneminde Propagandanın Etkin Silahı: Söz* (Istanbul: Otopsi, 2004), 67–82; Hakan Uzun, 'Cumhuriyet Halk Fırkası Halk Hatipleri Teşkilâtı', *Cumhuriyet Tarihi Araştırmaları Dergisi* 11 (2010): 85–113.

42 *CHFHT*, 4.

43 *CHFHT*; *CHPHITT*; and *CHPHCT*.

44 13 March 1932 circular of the RPP General Secretary to provincial Party in *Tebligat*, vol. 1 (Ankara, 1933), 56–7.

45 The 1940 by-laws allowed the appointment of civil servants upon recommendation and if a suitable Party member candidate could not be found. *CHPITT*, § 35.

46 *CHFHT*, § 2. Also § 75 of the 1931 RPP statuses in Tunçay, *Tek-parti*, 317 and 439.

47 *CHP Tüzüğü* (Ankara: Ulus, 1935), § 49, in Yetkin, *Türkiye'de*, 267.

48 *CHFHT*, § 20.

49 *CHPITT*, § 43.

50 *CHPITT*, § 21.

51 *CHPITT*, § 26.

52 Sheila Fitzpatrick, 'Signals from Below: Soviet Letters of Denunciation of the 1930s', *Journal of Modern History* 68:4 (1996): 831–66.

53 Migdal, *State in Society*, 124–34. Here I completely disagree with Şimşek who argues that 'The relation between state and society remained largely unilateral' and considers the Houses as exclusively top-down instruments of political propaganda. Sefa Şimşek, '"People's Houses" as a Nationwide Project for Ideological Mobilization in Early Republican Turkey', *Turkish Studies* 6 (2005): 88.

54 *CHPHCT*, § 1–18.

55 *CHPHCT*, § 19–42.

56 Serdar Öztürk, '*Karagöz* Co-Opted: Turkish Shadow Theatre of the Early Republic (1923-1945)', *Asian Theatre Journal* 23:2 (2006): 292–313.

57 CHPHCT, § 43-52; Halkevleri 1932-1935, 103 Halkevi Geçen Yıllarda Nasıl Çalıştı (Ankara, 1935), 37-41. The first requirement from prospective authors at the Halkevi theatre competitions organized by the Party in the 1940s was to 'impregnate the principles of the revolution'. 'CHP Piyes, Hikâye Müsabakaları', Ülkü 11:67 (October 1938): 79, and 'CHP 1945 Sanat Mükafatı', Ülkü 70 (August 1944): 3, quoted in Nurhan Karadağ, Halkevleri tiyatro çalışmalar (Ankara: T.C. Kültür Bakanlığı, 1998), 109-11.

58 CHPHCT, § 53-65. Akın, Beden Terbiyesi, 131-70. The promotion of similar 'national sports' was among the duties of Bureau VI (Sport and Youth) of the Party General Secretariat as stated in Party communiqué no. 1123 of 17 February 1938 to provincial governors and Party chairmen. It described the working structure of the General Secretariat and asked the provincial branches to adopt a similar - although not identical - working structure in performing similar duties. Tebligat, vol. 12 (Ankara: Ulus, 1938), 19.

59 CHPHCT, § 66-78.

60 CHFHT, § 45-52; CHPHCT, § 79-88.

61 CHFHT, § 53-56; CHPHCT, § 89-103.

62 CHPHCT, § 90 and 94. The Party would issue lists of prohibited books that 'inculcate the idea of communism and similar foreign and false views'. See Party communiqués no. 1166, 8 April 1938, and no. 1206 of 25 June 1938 in Tebligat, vol. 12 (Ankara: Ulus, 1938), 74-5 and 100 respectively.

63 Party communiqué no. 1206, 25 June 1938 in Tebligat, vol. 12 (Ankara: Ulus, 1938), 100.

64 CHFHT, § 57-61; CHPHCT, § 104-112.

65 CHPHCT, § 113-117.

66 'Halkevlerinin Asgarî Çalışma Planı', in BCA, 490.01/ 846.348.1.

67 'Halkodaları', Ülkü 14:79 (1939): 78-80.

68 Donald Webster, The Turkey of Atatürk: Social Process in the Turkish Reformation (New York: American Academy of Political and Social Science, 1939), 144-5.

69 CHP 7. Büyük Kurultayı (Ankara: Ulus, 1948), 206 ff.

70 Şimşek, Bir ideolojik seferberlik, 204-14; Özacun, 'Halkevlerin dramı', 92-4.

71 Ahmet Yıldız, 'Recep Peker', in Tanıl Bora and Murat Gültekingil (eds), Modern Türkiye'de Siyasi Düşünce: vol. 2, Kemalizm (Istanbul: İletişim, 2001), 58-63.

72 Recep Peker, 'Halkevleri Açılma Nutku', Ülkü 1:1 (February 1933): 6.

73 Hamit Zübeyr [Koşay], Halk Terbiyesi (Ankara: Köy Hocası, 1931), 9.

74 Koşay, 'Halk terbiyesi', 152-3.

75 Şükrü Kaya, Halkevleri ve ödevimiz, TC Ordu ilbaylığı (Ordu: Gürses, 1938), 22.

76 In the 1930s and 1940s, intellectuals writing about people's education would also speak extensively of the 'engineering' (*inşa*) of the people, the villager, the youth. Tezcan Durna, *Kemalist Modernleşme ve Seçkincilik. Peyami Safa ve Falih Rıfkı Atay'da Halkın İnşası* (Ankara: Dipnot, 2009), 124-8.

77 Durna, *Kemalist Modernleşme*, 166-7.

78 It was not a coincidence then that the practitioners of *Halk Terbiyesi* were frequently depicted as self-sacrificing missionaries: Ertan Aydın, 'The Peculiarities of Turkish Revolutionary Ideology in the 1930s: the *Ülkü* version of Kemalism 1933-1936', *MES* 40:5 (2004): 70-1.

79 Füsun Üstel, *Makbul Vatandaşın Peşinde: II Meşrutiyetten Bugüne Vatandaşlık Eğitimi* (Istanbul: İletişim, 2004), 136-45.

80 Şimşek, 'People's Houses', 83.

81 Münir Hayriğ, 'Halk Eğitim Yolu-Kukla Tiyatrosu', *Ülkü* 6:31 (September 1925): 70-2.

82 Cennet Ünver, 'Images and Perceptions of Fascism among the mainstream Kemalist elite in Turkey, 1931-1943', MA thesis (Istanbul: Boğaziçi University, 2001), 55-66; Aydın, 'The Peculiarities of Turkish Revolutionary Ideology', 277-9.

83 Peker, 'Halkevleri açılma nutku', 6.

84 Funda Şenol Cantek, *Yabanlar ve Yerliler Başkent olma sürecinde Ankara* (Istanbul: İletişim, 2003), 87-94.

85 Levent Cantek, *Cumhuriyetin Bülüğ Çağı. Gündelik Yaşama Dair Tartışmalar 1945-1950* (Istanbul: İletişim, 2008), 83-8. For similar images in novels, see Deniz Kandiyoti, 'Slave Girls, Temptresses, and Comrades: Images of Women in the Turkish Novel', *Feminist Issues* 8:1 (1988): 38.

86 Koşay, 'Halk terbiyesi', 154; Cantek, *Yaban'lar ve Yerliler*, 34; Durna, *Kemalist Modernleşme*, 138-60, 177-9; Üstel, *Makbul Vatandaş*, 199-200.

87 Quoted in Meltem Ahıska, *Occidentalism in Turkey. Questions of Modernity and National Identity in Turkish Radio Broadcasting* (London: I.B.Tauris, 2010), 18.

88 Ahıska, *Occidentalism*, 39; idem, 'Occidentalism: The Historical fantasy of the Modern', *South Atlantic Quarterly* 102:2/3 (2003): 189.

89 Arzu Öztürkmen, 'The role of the People's Houses in the making of national culture in Turkey', *New Perspectives on Turkey* 11 (Fall 1994). For the influence of Halkevi festivals on the creation of a national repertoire of folk dances, see idem, 'I Dance Folkore', in Kandiyoti and Saktanber, *Fragments of Culture*, 131-5. For an attempt by the state in the 1930s to replace older popular books of folk stories with new chapbooks that would use the same folk literature heroes in novel stories in order to propagate the regime's ideology to the populace, see Serdar Öztürk, 'Cumhuriyetin İlk Yıllarında Halk Kitaplarını

Modernleştirme Çabaları', *Kebikeç* 21 (2006): 56; idem, 'Efforts to Modernize Chapbooks during the Initial Years of the Turkish Republic', *European Historical Quarterly* 40:1 (2010): 19 ff.

90 *CHP Genel Sekreteri R. Peker'in Söylevleri* (Ankara, 1935), 33. Oranges cannot grow on the rugged terrain of the Zigana Mountains in the Black Sea coast.

91 Nusret Kemal (Köymen), 'Halkçılık', *Ülkü* 1:3 (April 1933): 187.

92 Ahıska, *Occidentalism*, 7, 15, 38; Chakrabarty, *Provincializing Europe*, 7–10.

93 Ahıska, *Occidentalism*, 149.

94 Durna, *Kemalist Modernleşme*, 167–8.

95 To become a Party member one had to be 18 in 1927, or 22 years old in 1939, but the 1935 by-laws declared that all youths that had not yet reached the age of 'political activity' were considered natural Party members. Tuncay Dursun, *Tek Parti Dönemindeki Cumhuriyet Halk Partisi Büyük Kurultayları* (Ankara: Kültür Bakanlığı, 2002), 15, 37, 105.

96 *CHFHT*, § 15 (emphasis added).

97 In Ankara in the 1930s, policemen expelled those not 'properly' dressed from the new parts of the city that were occupied by state employees and elites. Cantek, '*Yaban'lar ve Yerliler*, 147.

98 Frederick Frey, *The Turkish Political Elite* (Cambridge, MA: MIT, 1965); Cemil Koçak, 'Parliament Membership during the Single-Party System in Turkey (1925–1945)', *EJTS* 3 (2005), URL: http://ejts.revues.org/497 (last accessed 5 August 2014). The number and importance of MPs with real ties to the provinces and non-state occupational backgrounds will increase only with multi-party politics after 1946.

99 Zürcher, 'Who were the Young Turks', 106–7.

100 The changes introduced by the 1927 Party Congress were a 'legitimization of the centralist–authoritarian structure' and laid the foundation of the one-party system. Öz, *Tek-parti*, 99–101.

101 Cemil Koçak, *Umumi Müfettişlikler 1927–1952* (Istanbul: İletişim, 2003).

102 Öz, *Tek-parti*; Dursun, *Tek Parti*, 24–5.

103 Cemil Koçak, 'Tek- Parti Döneminde Cumhuriyet Halk Partisi'nde Parti Müfettişliği', in *Tarık Zafer Tunaya'ya Armağan* (Istanbul: İstanbul Barosu, 1992); idem, 'Tek parti döneminde CHP parti müfettişliğine ilişkin ek bilgi(ler)', in Mehmet Alkan et al. (eds), *Mete Tunçay'a Armağan* (Istanbul: İletişim 2007), 675–81. The Party even published instructions for Party inspectors: *CHP Teftiş Talimatnamesi* (Ankara: Ulus, 1939); *CHP Teftiş Talimatnamesi* (Ankara: Sümer, 1943).

104 Next to the Party, there was a whole array of inspectors from many state offices cruising through the provinces. Even the rumour of an incoming *müfettiş* might have caused anxiety. The arrival of a *müfettiş*

and the panic that followed was apparently so widespread that it featured in Orhan Kemal's novel *Müfettişler Müfettişi* (Istanbul: Varlık, 1966) about a trickster who travels around Anatolia pretending to be 'the inspector' in order to extract bribes in exchange for not reporting frauds and wrongdoings. For the account of the visit of an inspector to investigate the case of an alleged communist teacher, compare Cevdet Kudret's autobiographical novel, *Havada Bulut Yok* (Istanbul: İnkilab ve Aka, 1976), 325 ff, and Fakir Baykurt's memoirs, *Köy Enstitülü Delikanlı* (Istanbul: Papirüs, 1999), 301-24. The similarities are impressive, suggesting the commonality of the experience.

105 Cemil Koçak, 'CHP-devlet kaynaşması (1936)', *Toplumsal Tarih* 118 (2003).

106 Speaking against the 125th article of the 1931 Party by-laws that allowed for free local Party elections, Alaeddin from Kütahya stated why the centre mistrusted the provincial Party: 'There are thirty thousand Party members in Kütahya. There would be no issue, if three thousand had comprehended the revolution's ideology; our Anatolian friends know that demagogy plays a major role in Anatolia. If we abolish it [the old system that allowed officially sanctioned - in practice appointed - candidates], as a result of propaganda of the type "he does not pray", "he does not fast", we won't see any youth that has accepted the revolution enter any administrative committee.' In *CHF Üçüncü Büyük Kongre Zabıtları* (Istanbul: Devlet Matbaası, 1931), 236.

107 On the historical roots of provincial elites and their relation with state elites see Ayşe Durakbaşa, 'Taşra burjuvazisinin tarihsel kökenleri', *Toplum ve Bilim* 118 (2010): 11-19; also Hakkı Uyar, 'Tek Parti İktidarın Toplumsal Kökenleri', *Toplumsal Tarih* 106 (2002).

108 Çağlar Keyder, *State and Class in Turkey: A Study in Capitalist Development* (London: Verso, 1987), 81-3.

109 *CHF Üçüncü Büyük Kongre*, 276. For the Party's decision in 1930-1 to curtail the power of local elites, see Avni Doğan, *Kurtuluş, Kuruluş ve Sonrası* (Istanbul: Dünya, 1964), 217.

110 For examples, see the second chapter. For a detailed presentation of the debate on the 126th article, see Koçak, *İktidar ve Serbest*, 294 ff.

111 Kazım Nami Duru, *Cumhuriyet Devri Hatıralarım* (Istanbul: Sucuoğlu, 1958), 46.

112 Öz, *Tek-parti*, 107. Alaeddin, delegate of Kütahya at the 1931 Party Congress, expressed this ambivalence regarding the *mutemet* (Party boss): 'We know that many *mutemet* are old *ağas* [landlords], wherever we may go, a *mutemet* comes out like a usurper [*mütegallibe*] of the old age.' In *CHF Üçüncü Büyük Kongre*, 231. The Unionist cadres had expressed the exact same feelings and pragmatism in their relations with local notables after 1908: although calling them usurpers and oppressors, they cooperated with and used local notables in their

'traditional' function, i.e. as mediators between state and local populace. Kudret Emiroğlu, *Anadolu'da Devrim Günleri*. *II Meşrutiyet'in İlanı* (Ankara: İmge, 1999), 229, 236, 301; Fevzi Demir, *Osmanlı Devleti'nde II. Meşrutiyet Dönemi Meclis-i Mebusan Seçimleri 1908-1914* (Ankara: İmge, 2007), 206, 272, 278-9.

113 Both letter and directive of 15 October 1936 in BCA, 490.01/3.13.74.

114 For Özbudun, it was only these social strata that the Kemalist regime ever tried to win over to its cause: Ergun Özbudun, 'The nature of the Kemalist political regime', in Ali Kazancıgil and Ergun Özbudun (eds), *Atatürk, Founder of a Modern State* (London: Hurst & Co, 1981), 93-4.

115 Civil servants were apparently considered natural elements of the Party. Koçak, *İktidar ve Serbest*, 197.

116 Communiqués by General Secretariat to the provincial Party and Halkevleri on the need to register teachers, students, lawyers, engineers, etc.: no. 67 of 25 May 1932, and no. 83 of 28 June 1932 in *Tebligat*, vol. 1 (Ankara, 1933), 92, 100; no. 1179 of 4 May 1938 in *Tebligat*, vol. 12 (Ankara: Ulus, 1938), 23; and no. 1/1987 of 24 January 1947 in *Tebligat*, vol. 18 (Ankara: Ulus, 1941), 5.

117 See Recep, 'Konuşunuz ve konuşturunuz', *Ülkü* 1:1 (February 1933): 27; 'Halkevi Açılma Nutku', 6-8.

118 Yahya Akyüz, *Türkiye'de öğretmenlerin toplumsal değişmedeki etkileri 1848-1940* (Ankara: Doğan, 1978), 251; Hürrem Arman, *Piramidin tabanı. Köy Enstitüleri ve Tonguç* (Ankara: Arkın Kitabevi, 1969), 208, 213, 240.

119 See directives urging the provincial Party to register new members: *Tebligat*, vol. 2 (Ankara: Hakimiyeti Milliye, 1933), 10; *Tebligat*, vol. 3 (Ankara: Hakimiyeti Milliye, 1934), 17; no. 1179, 4 May 1938, *Tebligat*, vol. 12 (Ankara: Ulus, 1938), 23; no. 1/1987, 24 January 1941, *Tebligat*, vol. 18 (Ankara: Ulus, 1941), 5; and women members: nos 413, 414, 420, *Tebligat*, vol. 5 (Ankara: Ulus, 1935), 21, 22, 29.

Chapter 2: People's Houses in Provincial Urban Centres

1 Kayseri and Balıkesir have been chosen because of their similarities, which assist in comparing data: both were provincial towns surrounded by a rural hinterland, and administrative centres with a substantial state presence, common characteristics of most Houses in provincial centres. In contrast, their demographic and cultural differences offer the opportunity to assess the extent to which local peculiarities affected the Houses.

2 TC Başbakanlık İstatistik Genel Direktörlüğü Genel nüfus sayımı 20 İlkteşrin 1935, *Kayseri Vilayeti*, vol. 33 (İstanbul: Hüsnütabiat, 1937), 6, 23, 26-32.

3   Kayseri Ticaret ve Sanayi Odası, *Sekizinci İzmir Fuarında Kayseri* (n.p., 1938), 23–7.

4   Necmettin Çalışkan, *Kuruluşundan Günümüze Kayseri Belediyesi* (Kayseri: Kayseri Büyükşehir Belediyesi Kültür Yayınları, 1995), 94–5.

5   Osman Köroğlu, '1923–1950 yılları arası Kayseri'nin ekonomik ve sosyal yapısı', MA thesis (Kayseri: Erciyes University, 1992), 18.

6   Ibid., 25–8.

7   Kayseri Party (30 June 1938 and 30 June 1939), BCA, 490.01/670.255.1 (unless otherwise mentioned all archival documents cited were sent to the Party's General Secretariat in Ankara); *CHP' nin Kayseri il kongresinde okunan geçmiş haller raporu* (Kayseri: Yeni Basımevi, 1936), 3.

8   In an autobiographical novel from the period, the Party fees are extracted from their wage. Cevdet Kudret, *Havada Bulut Yok* (Istanbul: İnkılap ve Aka, 1976), 235.

9   Kayseri Party (30 June 1938), BCA, 490.01/670.255.1; *Istatistik Yıllığı 1942–43* (Ankara: İstatistik umum Müdürlüğü, 1944), i–vii; Kayseri Party (June 1944), BCA, 490.01/671.261.1.

10   Many members were double-registered. Party Inspector Fuat Sirmen (15 February 1937), BCA, 490.01/623.46.1.

11   Kayseri Party (June 1944), BCA, 490.01/671.261.1.

12   BCA, 490.01/276.1106.2. Although the date of the original is not stated, the date of the copy is given (4 April 1941).

13   Esat Öz, *Türkiye'de tek-parti yönetimi ve Siyasal Katılım 1923–1945* (Ankara: Gündoğan, 1992), 186.

14   Party Inspector Hilmi Çoruh, BCA, 490.01/670.255.1.

15   Islamic colleges primarily teaching theology and religious law. In Turkey they were abolished in 1924.

16   Such as Osman Feyzioğlu, relative of Sait Azmi Feyzioğlu, lawyer and MP for Kayseri, and his son, MP and founder of the *Güven Partisi* in the 1970s, Turhan Feyzioğlu. Ali Rıza Önder, *Kayseri Basın tarihi 1910–1960* (Ankara: Ayyıldız, 1972), 153–4.

17   The Bar of Kayseri had 21 members in 1938; among them, three were MPs, five were Municipal Assembly members and one was the city's mayor. Kayseri Ticaret ve Sanayi Odası, *Sekizinci*, 48; Çalışkan, *Kayseri*, passim.

18   The Kayseri *Türk Ocağı* had been offering a number of courses (typing, foreign languages, new script) and staging theatrical plays and various conferences. Its chairman in 1925, Necmettin, was a member of a local elite family (Feyzioğlu) engaged in local politics and the Halkevi. İbrahim Karaer, *Türk Ocakları 1912–1931* (Ankara: Türk Yurdu Neşriyatı, 1992), 74, 87, 96 and 112; Mehmet Uzun, 'Kayseri Türk Ocağı', *Kayseri Türk Ocağı* 7:81 (2007): 12.

19   The Halkevi chairman was appointed by the local Party cadre: §1 of the *CHFHT*, 5.

20 Mustafa Şanal, 'Türk kültür tarihi içerisinde Kayseri Halkevi ve Faaliyetleri', *Milli Eğitim Dergisi* 161 (2004): 4–7.

21 1,399 for the first and 1,973 for the second semester of 1937. BCA, 490.01/837.310.2.

22 In 1931–2 there were 229 teachers in the Kayseri province, 88 of whom taught in the town of Kayseri. *Başvekalet istatistik umum müdürlüğü, Maarif istatistikleri 1923–1932* (Istanbul: Devlet matbaası, 1933), 82 and 93.

23 The female membership was always below 10 per cent in all Party sources. See membership statistics from 1932 to 1941 in *CHP Halkevleri ve Halkodaları 1932–1942* (Ankara: Alaadin, 1942).

24 Report no. 42 (3 March 1940), BCA, 490.01/671.263.1.

25 *Kayseri Halkevi Armağanı,* 3 (Kayseri: Yeni Matbaa, 1934), 49.

26 Kayseri Halkevi (28 January 1938), BCA, 490.01/837.310.2.

27 Report no. 42 (3 March 1940), BCA, 490.01/671.263.1.

28 Kayseri Halkevi (23 August 1950), BCA, 490.01/838.311.1.

29 Önder, *Kayseri Basın,* 109–10.

30 He published about visits to nearby villages (see Chapter 6), wrote on local history, and was habitually delivering speeches. Önder, *Kayseri Basın,* 165; BCA, 490.01/227.895.1.

31 Inspector Aga Sırrı Levend (16 July 1942), BCA, 490.01/671.259.1.

32 Tacettin Tacettinoğlu was the only merchant Halkevi executive who was active in both Halkevi and local political and economic life: Chamber of Commerce executive, Municipal Council member, and mayor in 1950.

33 Students staged theatrical plays (*Kayseri,* 15 October 1932 and 1 April 1940, 2; *Kayseri Lise Mecmuası,* 5 (April/May 1933, 19)); organized literature evenings and gave lectures (*Kayseri Lise Mecmuası,* 5 (April–May 1933), 20) and gymnastic shows in the Halkevi Hall; and registered in language, physics and chemistry courses opened for students in the House (*Erciyes,* 28 and 29 (May, June/July 1945)).

34 According to the Kayseri Halkevi (28 January 1938, BCA, 490.01/837.310.2), one out of three library users were students; teachers, civil servants, officers, students and professionals made up 70 per cent of library users in 1937.

35 TC Başbakanlık istatistik Genel Direktörlüğü. Genel Nüfus sayımı. 20 ilkteşrin 1935, *Balıkesir Vilayeti,* vol. 8 (Istanbul: Hüsnütabiat, 1936).

36 From 7.5 per cent of the overall local population in 1937 to 8.5 per cent in 1941 and 11.5 per cent in 1942. Party Inspector Fuat Sirmen (15 February 1937), BCA, 490.01/623.46.1; Öz, *Tek-Parti,* 182–3; Balıkesir Party (25 June 1942), BCA, 490.01/624.49.2. The sub-province membership ranged from 4.5 per cent in Susurluk to 11 per cent in Edremit.

37 Party Inspector Fuat Sirmen registered the names and occupations of 205 Party executives in the province and sub-provinces of Balıkesir (15 February 1937), BCA, 490.01/623.46.1.

38 Balıkesir Party structure (19 March 1941), BCA, 490.01/276.1106.1.

39   Öz, *Tek-parti*, 186.

40   Party chairman of Balıkesir province no. 27 (31 January 1944), BCA, 490.01/595.58.3.

41   Compared with the names in the report of Party Inspector Fuat Sirmen (15 February 1937), BCA, 490.01/623.46.1.

42   'Halkevi Faaliyete Geçiyor', *Türk Dili*, 20 December 1932; 'Halkevi Kütüphane ve Neşriyat ve Temsil şubeleri bugün toplanarak komitelerini seçeceklerdir', *Türk Dili*, 23 December 1932; 'Halkevi Şubeleri faaliyete', *Türk Dili*, 25 December 1932; 'Halkevi Güzel San'atlar Şubesi bu akşam toplanacaktır', *Türk Dili*, 26 December 1932.

43   'Balıkesir Halkevi Tesis Faaliyeti', *Kaynak* 1 (February 1933): 32.

44   Balıkesir Halkevi, *Sekiz ayda nasıl çalıştı ve neler yaptı* (Balıkesir: Balıkesir Vilayet Matbaası, n.d.), 27.

45   *Alkım*, Balıkesir Lisesi Dergisi, 18–22 (15 May–15 September 1938).

46   This must have been the reason for the vivacity of the Turkish Hearth before the establishment of the Halkevi in Balıkesir. The Halkevi inherited the building and personnel of the Hearth. Karaer, *Türk Ocakları*, 74, 87, 95, 113, 158–9 and 171.

47   Abdullah Yurdakök, *Balıkesir Basın Tarihi* (Balıkesir: Sonsöz Gazetesi, 1992), 290–1.

48   Nüfus sayımı 1935, *Balıkesir Vilayeti*, 42.

49   Balıkesir Halkevi, *Sekiz ay*, 30; 'Halkevimizin bir buçuk ayda yaptığı işler', *Kaynak* 3 (April 1933): 93–6.

50   Party Inspector Fuat Sirmen (15 February 1937), BCA, 490.01/623.46.1; Balıkesir Party (19 March 1941), BCA, 490.01/276.1106.1.

51   *Savaş*, 30 September 1934 and 14 October 1934. Artisans and merchants formed the majority of the elected.

52   'Halkevi Şubeleri Faaliyete', *Türk Dili*, 25 December 1932.

53   Balıkesir Halkevi, *Sekiz ayda*, 12–15; *Balıkesir*, 3 February 1936. Doctors and lawyers spoke on medical or legislative subjects. 'Konferans ve Nutuklar', *Kaynak* 10/11 (October 1933): 295.

54   '24 Şubat', *Kaynak* 2 (19 March 1933): 64. Four of the six actresses were teachers; the remaining two were the wives of two of the actors.

55   *Balıkesir*, 31 July 1933. Physics course for students at the Halkevi.

56   *Balıkesir*, 16 December 1935. Sewing courses for women at the Mithatpaşa school.

57   *Balıkesir*, 25 November 1935.

58   'Halkevimizin dördüncü üç aylık çalışması', *Kaynak* 22 (October 1934): 498. Four categories of readers are given: 'students', 'teachers', 'civil servants' and 'people'.

59   Report on local association by local Party (31 January 1944), BCA, 490.01/595.58.3.

60   644 teachers and civil servants in the Balıkesir province to just 237 teachers and civil servants in Kayseri. Başvekalet İstatistik Umum

müdürlüğü, *Vilayet Hususi İdareleri 1929–1936. Faaliyeti istatistiği.*
Varidat, masrifat, memurlar (Ankara: Receb Ulusoğlu, 1938), 92, 95. In
1932, Balıkesir had 229 teachers, Kayseri 88. Başvekalet istatistik umum
müdürlüğü, *Maarif istatistikleri 1923–1932*, 76–7, 82, 93. Some 10 per
cent of Balıkesir's population were students, only 6 per cent in Kayseri.

61   Adil Öztürk, 'Halkevleri ve Aydın Halkevi', *Tarih ve Toplum* 182
     (February 1999): 44; Resul Yiğit, 'Mersin Halkevi 1933–1951', MA
     thesis (Mersin: Mersin University, 2001), 35; Uşak *Halkevi, Bir Yıllık*
     çalışmaları, 2 (Istanbul: Resimli Ay, 1937), 20–1; İbrahim Azcan, *Türk*
     modernleşmesi sürecinde Trabzon Halkevi (Trabzon: Serander, 2003),
     76, 86, 97–122. *Gaziantep Halkevi Broşürü* (Gaziantep, 1935); 1941
     activities' report of Artvin Halkevi reproduced in Party circular no.
     5/2035 (19 March 1941) in *Tebligat*, vol. 18 (Ankara: Ulus, 1941), 80;
     Süleyman İnan, 'Denizli'deki Halkevleri ve Faaliyetleri (1932–1951)',
     Atatürk Yolu 7:25/26 (2001): 135–57; Hasan Kaş, 'İsparta Halkevi
     çalışmaları ve Ün Dergisi (1934–1950)', MA thesis (Ankara: Hacettepe
     University, 2007), 22–5; Osman Kaynar, 'Konya Halkevi'nin Türk
     Modernleşmesindeki Faaliyetleri (1932–1951)', MA thesis (Konya:
     Dumlupınar University, 2007), 85–98; Hikmet Pala, 'Cumhuriyet
     Modernleşme Projesinin bir aracı olarak Ordu Halkevi ve çalışmaları',
     MA thesis (Ankara: Gazi University, 2006), 16–23; *Halkevlerin 1933*
     senesi Faaliyet Raporları Hülasaları (Ankara: Hakimiyeti Milliye, 1934),
     82–115; Günver Güneş and Müslime Güneş, 'Cumhuriyet Döneminde
     Manisa'nın sosyo-kültürel yaşamında Halkevi'nin yeri ve önemi', *Çağdaş*
     Türkiye Tarihi Araştırmaları Dergisi 1:5 (2007): 57; Hakan Yaşar, 'Sinop
     Halkevi ve Faaliyetleri (1932–1951)', MA thesis (Tokat: Gaziosmanpaşa
     University, 2008), 77–86; Berna Kaya, 'Bir halk Eğitim Kurumu olarak
     İzmit Halkevi (1932–1951)', MA thesis (Sakarya University, 2008), 54–
     5, 149–51, 184–5; Necla Aslan, 'Bursa Halkevi Uludağ Dergisi ve Türk
     Devrimi', MA thesis (Istanbul: İstanbul University, 2007), 24–5; Gülsün
     Karakuzuoğlu, 'Kastamonu Halkevi ve Faaliyetleri', MA thesis (Aydın:
     Adnan Menderes University, 2008), 15–20, 101–9.
62   Yaşar, 'Sinop Halkevi', 66.
63   Üstel, *Türk Ocakları*, 173–83, 194–5, 202–5, 227–40, 290–307.
64   For a campaign against non-Turkish speakers, cf. Alexandros Lamprou,
     'Nationalist mobilization and state–society relations: the People's House's
     campaign for Turkish in Izmir June–July 1934', *MES* 49:5 (2013).
65   Undated list in BCA, 490.01/7.36.9. A similar list (26 December 1947)
     in BCA, 490.01/8.41.3.
66   Cemil Koçak, *Tek-Parti Döneminde Muhalif Sesler* (Istanbul : İletişim,
     2011), 197–9.
67   See emphasis on the spreading of the use of Turkish among the local
     Arab and Kurdish population by the Mardin Halkevi. Mardin Halkevi,
     Mardin (Istanbul: Resimli Ay, 1938), 89, 92–3, 101.

68   Behçet Kemal Çağlar, 'Halkevleri Haberleri', *Ülkü* 9:49 (March 1937): 75.

69   Uğur Üngör, *The Making of Modern Turkey: Nation and State in Eastern Anatolia 1913–1950* (Oxford: Oxford University Press, 2011), 205; Sevim Yeşil, 'Unfolding Republican Patriarchy: The case of Young Kurdish Women at the Girls' Vocational Boarding School in Elazığ', MA thesis (Ankara: METU, 2003), 86–91.

70   Canser Kardaş, 'Diyarbakır Halkevi ve *Karacadağ* Dergisinin Halkbilim açısından Değerlendirmesi (1932–1951)', MA thesis (Kayseri: Erciyes University, 2007), 33–44.

71   Üngör, *The Making of Modern Turkey*, 206. See reports by Party and state officials on the 'Kurdish Question' in Tuğba Yıldırım (ed.), *Kürt Sorunu ve Devlet. Tedip ve Tenkil Politikaları 1925–1947* (Istanbul: Tarih Vakfı Yurt Yayınları, 2011), and Tuba Akekmekçi and Muazzez Pervan (eds), *'Doğu Sorunu' Necmeddin Sahir Sılan Raporları 1939–1953* (Istanbul: Tarih Vakfı Yurt Yayınları, 2010), passim.

72   In his reports (11 November 1939, 11 November 1940, 21 December 1941, 11 November 1942 and 11 December 1943) about Bingöl and Tunceli, MP Necmeddin Sahir Sılay clearly and emphatically related the linguistic assimilation of the 'mountain Turks' (an euphemism employed to denote Kurds) to the work of Houses and schools. Akekmekçi, *Kürt Sorunu*, passim. The emphasis on the duty of Houses and schools to assist in the assimilation of Kurds was reiterated in most state and Party documents. Nizam Önen, 'Bir tek-parti dönemi politikacısının gözünden Cumhuriyet'in "Doğu" meselesi ve bürokrasinin hali: CHP Genel Sekreteri Memduh Şevket Esendal'ın Doğu gezisi', *Tarih ve Toplum Yeni Yaklaşımlar* 12 (2011): 161–4, 174; Bülent Varlık (ed.), *Umumi Müfettişler Konferansı'nda Görüşülen ve Dahiliye Vekaleti'ni İlgilendiren İşlere Dair Toplantı Zabıtları ile Rapor ve Hulasası 1936* (Ankara: Dipnot, 2010), passim.

73   Kemal Güngör (10 November 1940), BCA, 490.01/1006.882.1; Münir Soykam (7 January1941, 29 April 1941: 'take great care to eliminate the languages of these citizens [and] teach them how to read and write Turkish', 11, 12, 22 and 31 May 1941), BCA, 490.01/996.850.1, quoted in Üngör, *The Making of Modern Turkey*, 190, 193–7.

74   They did so by either collecting solely among refugees settled in the area and Turcoman villages, or by translating and presenting the material into Turkish, as in a collection of local folk songs published by the Diyarbakır Halkevi. Üngör, *The Making of Modern Turkey*, 191 and 200.

75   Senem Aslan, 'Everyday Forms of State Power and the Kurds in the Early Turkish Republic', *IJMES* 43:1 (2011): 85–6.

76   Kardaş, 'Diyarbakır Halkevi', 22, 30; Party report (3 January1941), BCA, 490.01/996.850.1, quoted in Üngör, *The Making of Modern*

Turkey, 190. Üngör identifies most local elite members as 'former CUP operatives and sympathisers' who conveyed a 'strong sense of continuity of Diyarbakır's local elites from the CUP era into the RPP era'. Among the local Halkevi executives were the notable Pirinççizade and Müftüzade families, notorious for their active participation in the Armenian massacres of 1915.

77   Suavi Aydın et al., *Mardin. Aşiret-Cemaat-Devlet* (Istanbul: Tarih Vakfı Yurt Yayınları, 2000), 370–82; *Mardin Halkevi* (Mardin: Ulus Sesi, 1935).

78   The People's Rooms of Ergani, Çermik and Kulp, and the People's House of Silvan, all in the Diyarbakır province, were also run by schoolteachers and civil officials. Münir Soykam (29 April 1941), BCA, 490.01/996.850.1, quoted in Üngör, *The Making of Modern Turkey*, 194–6.

79   The Party inspector for Diyarbakır, Ali Reşat Göksidar, reported (18 September 1943) that the Halkevi of the small town of Gerçüş was only frequented by civil servants who 'came to read a newspaper or a book and come together and discuss as a group', as nobody among the locals could speak Turkish. BCA, 490.01/841.925.02.

80   Aslan, 'Everyday Forms of State Power', 79; Sinan Ergen, 'Türkiye'de Halkevleri ve Elazığ örneği', MA thesis (Elazığ: Fırat University, 2007), 61–3, 70–1, 78, 112–18.

81   Aslan, 'Everyday Forms of State Power', 82–6.

82   Abdülhalik Renda to Interior Ministry (14 July 1925), in Yıldırım (ed.), *Kürt Sorunu*, 4; reports of Necmeddin Sahir in Akekmekçi, '*Doğu Sorunu*', passim.

83   Report to Premier İnönü (10 November 1934), BCA, 490.01/69.457.24, quoted in Üngör, *The Making of Modern Turkey*, 154.

84   Ergen, 'Elazığ', 74.

85   Kayseri Halkevi report (28 January 1938), BCA, 490.01/837.310.2. About Üzel, see Önder, *Kayseri Basın*, 55.

86   Sahir Üzel, 'Yüzler açılıp, çarlar çıkarılirken. 8 Eylül Pazar gününden itibaren çarşaf ve peçe kalktı', *Kayseri*, 9 December 1935.

87   The factory director expressed identical opinions about the educative and disciplinary potential and function of the factory on the local 'conservative' population. Lilo Linke, *Allah Dethroned. A Journey through Modern Turkey* (London: Constable & Co, 1937), 312.

88   Factory director (Linke, *Allah Dethroned*, 312) and Party Inspector Levent (14 July 1941), BCA, 490.01/671.262.1.

89   Quotes from Sahir Üzel, 'Kayseri Kadınları bu nimetten neden istifade etmiyorlar?', *Kayseri*, 11 May 1936.

90   Linke, *Allah Dethroned*, 312; also local governor to Interior Minister (26 April 1937), BCA, 490.01/837.310.2.

91   For example, Kemaleddin Kara Mehmet Ağa zade, *Erciyes Kayserisi ve Tarihine bir bakış* (Kayseri: Yeni Matbaa, 1934). Önder, *Kayseri Basın*, 169–70.

92 Kara Mehmet, *Erciyes*, v–vi.

93 BCA, 490.01/306.1249.1 and 490.01/307.1250.2.

94 Durakbaşa, *Taşra burjuvazisinin tarihsel kökenleri*, 12–19.

95 One of his forthcoming books doubtlessly served that purpose: *Et'in Ulus hayatında önemi ve ürünlerinden pastırma* (The importance of meat in the Nation's life and one of its products, *pastırma*). All information and quotes from his 1946 application in BCA, 490.01/307.1250.2.

96 For example, Recep Peker, 'Halkevleri Açılma Nutku', *Ülkü* 1:1 (February 1933): 6; idem, 'Ülkü niçin çıkıyor', *Ülkü* 1:1 (February 1933): 1.

97 Fahri Tümer, Ömer Sıtkı Erdi, Hamdi Uçok, Nazlı Gaspıralı. BCA, 490.01/306.1249.1 and 490.01/307.1250.2.

98 Kara Mehmet, *Erciyes*.

99 With a monthly wage he would probably be paid for all the days of the month instead of just the working days the daily wage covered. In other words, he was asking for an increase in his payment.

100 Thousands of youths were sent to Germany during the war either to study in schools and universities or receive training in factories. Mustafa Gençer, *Jöntürk Modernizmi ve 'Alman Ruhu': 1908–1918 Dönemi Türk-Alman İlişkileri* (Istanbul: İletişim, 2003), 304–29.

101 BCA, 490.01/838.311.1.

102 The reply (3 August 1938) by the General Secretariat to Şener's and Özsan's letters rejected their demand for mediation, reminding them that the petition had to be addressed to the Under-Secretariat of Defence. BCA, 490.01/838.311.1.

103 BCA, 490.01/478.1947.1.

104 Linke, *Allah Dethroned*, 303.

105 Communiqué no. 190 (18 November 1933) in *Tebligat*, vol. 3, (Ankara Hakimiyeti Milliye, 1934), 52–3.

106 Gaspıralı was a member of the Municipal Assembly in 1933–36 and 1946–50; Mamurhan Özsan, Naciye Özsan (both wives of Party men) and 'the daughter of the Mevlevi Şeyh Ahmet Remzi efendi' Zehra Karakaya in 1933–36. Çalışkan, *Kayseri Belediyesi*, 90–5, 106–7, 117–23, 133–4.

107 A prominent nationalist intellectual.

108 All extracts from her petition (11 February 1943) in BCA, 490.01/306.1249.1.

109 Party Inspector Hıfzı Oğuz Bekata (25 December 1944), BCA, 490.01/273.1094.1; Party Inspector Hilmi Çoruh (3 March 1940), BCA, 490.01/670.255.1; local Party reports (1 June 1944 and 1 June 1945), BCA, 490.01/671.261.1. In 1937 she participated in the Halkevi's village excursions. Kayseri Halkevi, *Germir Köyü*, 15, BCA, 490.01/837.310.1.

110 She means the Society for the Defence of the Rights of Anatolia and Rumelia (*Anadolu ve Rumeli Müdafaai Hukuk Cemiyeti*), established in 1919 to fight the partitioning of the Ottoman Empire. After the

establishment of the Republic of Turkey, the Society was transformed into the Republican People's Party. E. J. Zürcher, *Turkey. A Modern History* (London: I.B.Tauris, 2004), 133 ff.

111 BCA, 490.01/306.1249.1.

112 BCA, 490.01/478.1947.1.

113 Meltem Karadağ, 'Taşra kentlerinde yaşam tarzları alanı: Kültür ve ayrım', *Toplum ve Bilim* 118 (2010): 48; cf. Gül Özsan, 'Eşraf ailelerinin statü kazanma mücadelelerinde kadınların rölü', *Toplum ve Bilim* 118 (2010): 71–3.

114 Party members Ali Talaslıoğlu and Murat Şerbetçi (14 March 1939), BCA, 490.01/344.1440.4.

115 Özsan, 'Eşraf ailelerinin statü kazanma', 76.

116 The House had asked for a lady to be employed at the House's Library and apparently Zatiye, a non-local girl, was employed. 'Halkevi başkanlığından', *Kayseri*, 24 April 1939, 3.

117 BCA, 490.01/838.311.1.

118 Compensation in the form of a job or money was offered to lure women's participation in the Halkevi Theatre stage. Very few women volunteered, as women on stage were considered immoral. See Chapter 5.

119 Report of 3 March 1940, BCA, 490.01/671.263.1.

120 'Halkevi Temsilleri', *Kayseri*, 1 April 1940.

121 Letter to Kayseri Halkevi (19 September 1940), BCA, 490.01/671.263.1.

122 Kemal Karpat, 'A personal postscript' to the chapter 'The Hijra from Russia and the Balkans: the Process of self-definition in the late Ottoman State', in idem, *Studies on Ottoman Social and Political History* (Leiden: Brill, 2002), 709–11.

123 Nahid Sırrı Örik, *Anadolu'da yol notları, Kayseri Kırşehir Kastamonu, Bir Edirne Seyahatnamesi* (Istanbul: Arma, 2000).

124 This is an all too typical discourse of the period on the coffee house as a degenerate place of gathering. See Chapter 4.

125 This seems a 'make do', cunning practice, where social actors, unable to openly reject, invent ways to circumvent and evade the imposed order. N. Erdoğan, 'Devleti "Idare etmek": Maduniyet ve Düzenbazlık', *Toplum ve Bilim* 83 (2000).

126 My italics.

127 All above extracts from Örik, *Anadolu'da yol notları*, 90–116.

128 M. İğneci, 'Bir Geziden İntibalar', *Kayseri*, 2 March 1939.

129 Ibid., 16 March 1939.

130 Eating, drinking, smoking, shouting and cursing were very common among the audiences of theatre and cinema since the first days of cinema and theatre performances in the Ottoman Empire in the nineteenth century. The absence of a 'proper' and 'civilized' audience was also a very common complaint of intellectuals. Metin And, *Türk Tiyatrosunun Evleri* (Ankara: Turhan, 1983), 375–7.

131 M. İğneci, 'Bir Geziden İntibalar', *Kayseri*, 20 March 1939.

132 That is, the polarized and spatialized time of Orientalisms/ Occidentalisms. Chakrabarty, *Provincializing Europe*, 7-10.

133 Meltem Ahıska, 'Occidentalism', 351-79.

134 Kudret is mentioned for a speech he gave in 1938. BCA, 490.01/837.310.2, and 'Halkevinde Hamit Gecesi', *Kayseri*, 14 April 1938, 2.

135 İhsan Kudret and Apay Kabacalı (eds), *Cevdet Kudret'e saygı* (Ankara: Kültür Bakanlığı, 1993), 171; Ihsan Kudret, *İhsan benimle çalışır mısın?* (Istanbul: İnkilap, n.d.), 96.

136 Murat Yalçın (ed.), *Tanzimat'tan Bugüne Edebiyatçılar Ansiklopedisi* (Istanbul: Yapı Kredi, 2001), 524-5.

137 Interview with the author and Ali Rıza Önder, 'Cevdet Kudret ve anımsadıklarım', *Cumhuriyet*, 10 October 1992, both reproduced in Kudret and Kabacalı, *Cevdet Kudret'e saygı*, 171-2 and 121-2 respectively.

138 Kudret and Kabacalı, *Cevdet Kudret'e saygı*, 172. Kudret described himself as an idealist teacher much like the character of schoolteacher Feride in Güntekin's novel *Çalıkuşu* (Istanbul: İnkılâp Kitabevi, [1922] 2010) whose story influenced generations of teachers. It tells the struggle of a woman teacher from Istanbul to educate and enlighten the villagers. Arman, *Piramidin tabanı*, 185.

139 For a similar reference to the alienation of state functionaries in provincial towns, see Linke, *Allah Dethroned*: 150-1. 'Everybody drinks here. Life is so dull we couldn't bear it otherwise. On Sundays we start at three o'clock in the afternoon, on ordinary days at six.'

140 A very common ambition among Halkevi chairmen. See Hıfzı Veldet Velidedeoğlu, *Anıların izinde* (Istanbul: Remzi, 1977-9), 274; Şevket Beysanoğlu, 'Anılarımda Diyarbakır Halkevi', *Kebikeç* 3 (1996), 165; Nadir Nadi, *Perde Aralığından* (Istanbul: Çağdaş, 1964), 23.

141 Kudret, *Havada Bulut Yok*, 185-8. In 1936-37 the lawyer Naci Özsan was chairman and in 1946 he asked to be nominated as an MP candidate. BCA, 490.01/307.1250.2. We have already seen how incredible the Kayseri Halkevi membership statistics were.

142 Kudret, *Havada Bulut Yok*, 80-3. A Party (*Halk Hatipleri*) propaganda initiative. Çakal, *Konuşunuz*, 67-77.

143 Distribution of food and the registering of the poor occurred in 1945-46. Şanal, 'Kayseri Halkevi', 10.

Chapter 3: People's Houses and Local Politics

1 Letter of 14 March 1940, BCA, 490.01/844.337.2.

2 Examples of denunciation of Halkevi chairmen: Hakkı Özveren (Kütahya 15 November 1946), BCA, 490.01/839.319.1; Mustafa Dedeoğlu (Kırkağaç 7 May 1943) and anonymous (Akhisar 10 January

1947), BCA, 490.01/840.323.1; Hakkı Kunt (Edremit 19 July 1943), BCA, 490.01/825.265.2; Hasanoğlu Alitaş (Mardin 23 July 1943), BCA, 490.01/841.925.2; Hasan Öztürk (Eğrigöz 18 April 1949), BCA, 490.01/840.320.1; Salih Türkoğlu (Van 15 July 1939), BCA, 490.01/845.342.1; Mehmet Gülmen (Dereçine 4 May 1942), BCA, 490.01/733.1.1; Şemseddin Gürer (Doğubeyazit 15 February 1946), BCA, 490.01/733.2.2; Ali Karataş (Elaziğ 20 August 1939), BCA, 490.01/832.287.2; anonymous Halkevi member accusing Nazilli Halkevi chairman of continuously intimidating and oppressing the Halkevi executives (29 September 1948), BCA, 490.01/825.263.1.

3   Some letters from small towns complained about the occupation of the Halkevi by police or army officers: chairman of People's Room of Gölyaka (24 December 1945), BCA, 490.01/827.271.3; Şirnak Halkevi chairman (18 January 1950), BCA, 490.01/843.332.1; Party chairmen in Hopa (12 May 1948) and Bingöl (25 July 1951), BCA, 490.01/830.279.2, and BCA, 490.01/827.269.1 respectively.

4   Technically it was the gendarmerie (Jandarma) officer.

5   Sent on 1 January1950, BCA, 490.01/840.321.1.

6   The accusation pointed to widespread perceptions of theatre as an immoral or even 'infidel' activity, caused by the presence of women on stage. Women in travelling theatre companies, especially, were seen almost as prostitutes. To counter such perceptions, Halkevi members differentiated Halkevi theatre from 'ordinary', i.e. immoral, theatre. See Chapter 5.

7   Buldan Halkevi chairman (7 January 1943), BCA, 490.01/831.281.1.

8   BCA, 490.01/842.329.1.

9   Report no. 71 (3 August 1944) by Party Inspector Kemal Çelik, BCA, 490.01/842.329.1.

10   Letter of 31 October 1948, BCA, 490.01/825.263.1.

11   For instance, the denunciation by Party elites of the Kaymakam of Pınarbaşı (19 February 1947) and Tercan (12 January 1939), in BCA, 490.01/239.950.1, and 490.01/833.289.1, respectively.

12   Ilgaz Halkevi chairman (12 April 1940), BCA, 490.01/830.278.2.

13   Bulanık Halkevi chairman (19 January 1941), BCA, 490.01/841.326.2.

14   Kazım Özyurt (4 March 1947), BCA, 490.01/830.277.1.

15   Party Inspector Recai Güreli (17 May 1947), BCA, 490.01/830.277.1.

16   Deniz Kandiyoti, 'Gendering the Modern. On Missing Dimensions in the Study of the Turkish Modernity', in Sibel Bozdoğan and Reşat Kasaba (eds), Rethinking Modernity and National Identity in Turkey (Seattle and London: University of Washington Press, 1997), 113.

17   Horst Unbehaun, Türkiye kırsalında kliyentalizm ve siyasal katılım. Datça örneği: 1923-1992 (Ankara: Ütopya, 2006), 171-3.

18   Michael Meeker, A Nation of Empire: The Ottoman Legacy of Turkish Modernity (Berkeley and London: University of California Press, 2002), 306-8.

19 Signed by two civil servants and two teachers (12 September 1940), BCA, 490.01/830.279.2.

20 Accountant Mehmet Bilgetürt (25 February 1942), BCA, 490.01/ 830.279.2.

21 Bahri Curdan (n.d.), BCA, 490.01/830.279.2.

22 Report no. 260 of Party Inspector Cemal Karamuğla (1 October 1942), BCA, 490.01/830.279.2.

23 Yeşilkaya, *Halkevleri*, 140–7. Quite often Halkevi and Party shared the same building.

24 Founder of *Türkiye Sosialist Partisi* in 1946. Özgür Gökmen, 'Çok-Partili rejime geçerken sol: Türkiye sosyalizminin unutulmuş partisi', *Toplum ve Bilim* 78 (1998).

25 Party executive, merchant and journalist (1890–1942). *TBMM Albümü 1920–2010*, vol. I (Ankara: TBMM Basın ve Halkla İlişkiler Müdürlüğü, 2010), 104.

26 Aydın Ayhan, 'Esat Adil Müstecablıoğlu İlk Yazıları', *Yeni Haber*, 1994–95.

27 See his application for Party nomination in 1943, BCA, 490.01/291.1171.4; 'Balıkesir Halkevi Tesis Faaliyeti', *Kaynak* 1 (February 1933): 32; 'Vilayet Umumi Meclisi', *Kaynak* 2 (19 March 1933): 64; Balıkesir Halkevi, *Sekiz ayda*, 11; *Balıkesir Şehir Kulübü Nizamnamesi* (Balıkesir: Türk Pazarı, 1934), 11; 31 January 1944 report of Balıkesir Party with information on local associations, BCA, 490.01/595.58.3; Abdullah Yurdakök, *Balıkesir Basın Tarihi* (Balıkesir: Sonsöz Gazetesi, 1992), 324; Özgür Gökmen, 'Esat Adil Müstecaplıoğlu', in Tanıl Bora and Murat Gültekin (eds), *Modern Türkiye'de Siyasi Düşünce*, vol. 8: *Sol* (Istanbul: İletişim, 2007), 940–7. Emin Karaca, *Unutulmuş Sosialist: Esat Adil* (Istanbul: Belge, 2008).

28 Hürrem Arman, *Piramidin tabanı. Köy Enstitüleri ve Tonguç* (Ankara: Arkın Kitabevi, 1969), 139. Arman was a member of a group of recent university graduates visiting towns in western Turkey in 1934. About their visit, see also 'Enstitülü izciler şehrimize geldiler', *Savaş*, 23 July 1934. For a similar account by one of the visitors, see Hüseyin Avni, 'Görüşler ve Sezişler Balıkesir'de', *Savaş*, 26 July 1934.

29 The Halkevi assisted villagers in their dealings in town and cooperated with the Red Crescent and the Association for the Protection of Children 'to help the poor, the families in need, the children and the jobless.' 'Balıkesir Halkevi Tesis Faaliyeti', *Kaynak* 1 (February 1933): 32.

30 On *Kaynak*, see Yurdakök, *Balıkesir Basın*, 290–1.

31 *Savaş*, Günlük Siyasi Gazete. It was published from 1933 until 1935. Yurdakök, *Balıkesir Basın*, 40–3.

32 On his political views, see Gökmen, 'Esat Adil Müstecaplıoğlu'.

33 Esat Adil, 'Halkçılıkta Maarif', *Savaş*, 6 July 1934.

34 Esat Adil, 'Savaşçı gözile, Hapishanelerimiz', *Savaş*, 8 July 1934.

35 '[An answer] has to be given to the Turkish worker who is made to work fourteen hours a day deprived of all types of civil rights [...]

We have a law for obligatory primary education but thousands of city children are employed in the most heavy services.' Esat Adil, 'Savaşçı gözile, iş kanunu', *Savaş*, 11 July 1934.

36 He called them 'half men and pavement politicians' making 'a livelihood with the swindlers of hidden politics'. Esat Adil, 'Savaşçı gözile, Dürüst olalım', *Savaş*, 19 July 1934.

37 The newspaper *Türk Dili*, for instance, was owned by Hayrettin Karan, a rival of Esat Adil, local notable, Party boss and MP between 1927 and 1946. *TBMM Albümü*, 137, 244. The close relationship of his newspaper with the Party is attested by Party Inspector M. Bengisu (8 March 1940), BCA, 490.01/623.47.1.

38 Hasan Basri Çantay (1887–1964) was a Unionist, teacher, journalist and MP (1920–23). *TBMM Albümü*, 40.

39 Summary of Basri Çantay (20 February 1939), BCA, 490.01/344.1440.04.

40 *Savaş*, 14 October 1934.

41 'Yeni Adam'ın baş muharririmiz hakkında bir kadirşinaslığı', *Savaş*, 22 August 1934.

42 Esat Adil Müstecabi, 'İşçi sınıfına pey sürenler', *Gerçek* 7, 5 April 1950, 1, 4. I am indebted to Özgür Gökmen for bringing this article to my attention.

43 The former was prohibiting publications that hurt the honour of MPs, the Council of Ministers and state officials, and the latter communist propaganda.

44 'Gazetemiz aleyhine Müddeiumumilik dava açtı', *Savaş*, 23 July 1934.

45 'Muhakememiz dün başladı', *Savaş*, 20 August 1934; 'Karar bugün tefhim edilecek', *Savaş*, 22 August 1934; 'Beraat Ettik', *Savaş*, 23 August 1934.

46 Mustafa Yılmaz, Yasemin Doğaner, *Cumhuriyet Döneminde Sansür 1923-1973* (Ankara: Siyasal, 2007), 7-9.

47 Serdar Öztürk, 'Muhalif bir Gazete: Mücadele (1931)', *Selçuk İletişim* 3:4 (2005): 152-65.

48 According to the 126th article of the 1931 Party by-laws (*CHF Nizamnamesi*), those working in Party administrative committees could occupy only one position that brought profit (provincial General Assembly, Municipal Assembly, Chamber of Commerce). Those holding two positions were prohibited from 'holding voluntary duties' in other institutions like the Red Crescent. Esat Adil's resignation (23 October1934), just a week after his election to the Municipal Assembly, could have been a result of pressure from his opponents to abide by the by-laws, as he was also president of the local training club (*Balıkesir İdman yurdu*). On the 126th article, see Cemil Koçak, *İktidar ve Serbest Cumhuriyet Fırkası* (İstanbul: İletişim, 2006), 294-9.

49 The members of the standing committee were the only ones to receive a salary among Assembly members, and the competition was likely to have been more intense.

50 *Savaş*, 10 February 1935, reproduced in Esat Öz, *Türkiye'de Tek-parti Yönetimi ve siyasal katılım 1923–1945* (Ankara: Gündoğan, 1992), 204.

51 For a similar denunciation of Balıkesir Party elites, see Zühtü Özmelek (18 January 1943), BCA, 490.01/142.569.1.

52 Ayşe Ayata Güneş, *CHP Örgüt ve İdeoloji* (Ankara: Gündoğan, 1992), passim.

53 Decision of the Finance Ministry (18 October 1935), BCA, 030.11.1/99.34.14.

54 BCA, 490.01/344.1440.04. The summary of the denunciation by Basri Çantay was part of a document containing the summaries of over 100 denunciations of applicants for Party nomination for the National Assembly in 1939. In all probability, the file was composed in order to assist in the selection process. The last denunciation (19 March 1939) was sent four days before the Party leadership convened and announced the Party's list of candidates (24 March 1939). Cemil Koçak, *Türkiye'de Milli Şef Dönemi*, vol. 2 (Istanbul: İletişim, 2003), 33. The summary provided a registration number for every denounced candidate. If that was the registration number stamped on their application form (*Mebus Talebnamesi*) – and I believe it was for practical reasons – it was helpful for those composing the Party's candidate list because they could easily track the application of the person denounced. Esat Adil had applied in 1939, as a registration number was printed next to his name.

55 The literature on minority politics and persecution in the Republic of Turkey has grown in the last year. For the Jews of Turkey, see the work of Rıfat Bali, especially his *Cumhuriyet Yıllarında Türkiye Yahudileri: Bir Türkleştirme Serüveni 1923–1945* (Istanbul: İletişim, 2005). Uğur Üngör, *The Making of Modern Turkey: Nation and State in eastern Anatolia 1913–1950* (Oxford: Oxford University Press, 2011), is the most recent work on state minority policies in eastern Turkey. For a more general picture, see Soner Cagaptay, 'Race, Assimilation and Kemalism: Turkish Nationalism and the Minorities in the 1930s', *MES* 40:3 (2004): 86–101. As for the persecution of opposition the regime considered 'reactionary', see Cemil Koçak, *Tek-Parti Döneminde Muhalif Sesler* (Istanbul: İletişim, 2011), 33–91.

56 Novelists Fakir Baykurt and Yaşar Kemal are famous examples. For the Village institutions, see Mehmet Asım Karaömerlioğlu, 'The Village Institutes Experience in Turkey', *BJMES* 25:1 (1998).

57 A number of prominent intellectuals in the 1930s, including Şevket Süreyya Aydemir, biographer of Atatürk, İnönü and Enver paşa, were ex-members of the Turkish Communist Party. For their biography and contributions to an influential journal in the early 1930s, see Ilhan Tekeli and Selim Ilkin, *Bir Cumhuriyet Öyküsü, Kadrocuları ve Kadro'yu Anlamak* (İstanbul: Tarih Vakfı Yurt Yayınları, 2003).

58 For Ahmet Ağaoğlu, perhaps the most eminent liberal intellectual and politician in the 1930s, see A. Holly Shissler, *Between two Empires. Ahmet Ağaoğlu and the New Turkey* (London: I.B.Tauris, 2003). See also contributions in Bora and Gültekin (eds), *Modern Türkiye'de Siyasi Düşünce*, vol. 7: *Liberalizm* (Istanbul: İletişim, 2005).

59 See contributions to Bora and Gültekin (eds), *Modern Türkiye'de Siyasi Düşünce*, vol. 5: *Muhafazakârlık*, 3rd edn (Istanbul: İletişim, 2006).

60 Cennet Ünver, 'Images and Perceptions of Fascism among the mainstream Kemalist elite in Turkey 1931–1943', MA thesis (Istanbul: Boğaziçi University, 2001).

61 I draw on Victor Turner's work on social dramas, defined as 'public episodes of tensional irruption' performed by social actors in situations of conflict. Victor Turner, *Dramas, Fields, and Metaphors. Symbolic Action in Human Societies* (Ithaca, NY, and London: Cornell University Press, 1974), 33; idem, 'Social Dramas and Stories about Them', *Critical Inquiry* 7:1 (1980): 150.

62 BCA, 490.01/832.283.1.

63 'Because of his sick mind he does not find the time to oversee students and teachers. It is well-known that the second and third grade students under his instruction do not know how to multiply one by one.' Letter of 21 March 1935, BCA, 490.01/832.283.1.

64 Telegram of 4 April 1935, BCA, 490.01/832.283.1.

65 Letter of 26 May 1935, BCA, 490.01/832.283.1.

66 Turner, *Dramas, Fields*, 38–40.

67 Tevfik's telegram (4 April 1935), BCA, 490.01/832.283.1.

68 Joel Migdal, *State in Society. Studying How States and Societies Transform and Constitute One Another* (Cambridge: Cambridge University Press, 2001), 16–22.

69 Ömer Öner (December 1936), BCA, 490.01/832.283.1. İzzet Kılavuz was the *Kaymakam* of the previous incident.

70 *Kaymakam* of Silvan to Diyarbakır governor (8 December 1936), BCA, 490.01/832.283.1.

71 It is not a coincidence that ethnic differences made up a substantial part of the denunciations' accusatory repertoire. For instance, see the letter (8 March 1947) of Kemal Zülfikaroğlu, complaining about the mocking of the Bitlis accent in the Diyarbakır Halkevi: 'The people of Bitlis not only always speak Turkish everywhere, but also speak pure Turkish', BCA, 490.01/827.270.2; the letter of former secretary of Ağrı Halkevi and 'head of the Kara babk tribal confederation [*aşiret*]' Nusret Arslan (13 January 1945), BCA, 490.01/827.268.2; and the denunciation of the Gercüş Halkevi chairman for speaking Arabic and having Armenian relatives (23 July 1943 by Hasan oğlu Alitaş), BCA, 490.01/841.925.02.

72 Provinces of Elazığ, Tunceli, Bingöl, Urfa, Diyarbakır, Mardin, Hakkari, Siirt, Bitlis, Muş, Van and Ağrı according to *CHP Teşkilatı*

Kurulmamış Vilayetlerdeki Halkevleri ve Odaları Teftiş Talimatnamesi (Ankara: Zerbamat, 1940), 5. In default of Party structures, the Houses were under the direction of the first general inspector, a high-level bureaucrat in charge of a large Kurdish-populated area in the southeast. Cemil Koçak, *Umumi Müfettişlikler 1927–1952* (Istanbul: İletişim, 2003).

73   See contributions to David Gilmore, *Honor and Shame and the Unity of the Mediterranean* (Washington, DC: American Anthropological Association, 1987).

74   It was the state or ruler's duty to undo wrongdoings and protect his unjustly treated subjects (*mazlum*) from the oppression of his servants (*zülm*). The self-presentation of the petitioner as unjustly treated was a common theme of petition and complaint writing even before the establishment of the Ottoman state. See S. M. Stern, 'Petitions from the Ayyubid Period', *Bulletin of the School of African and Oriental Studies* 27:1 (1964): 9. On grievance administration as a state practice and discourse, see J.S. Nielsen, 'Mazalim', in C.E. Bosworth, E. van Donzel, W.P. Heinrichs and Ch. Pellats (eds), *Encyclopaedia of Islam*, vol. VI, 2nd edn (Leiden: Brill, 1991), 933.

75   In her study of the court records of Antep in the sixteenth century, Leslie Peirce has shown how the audience of a public act involving the state was also local. Especially in the case where 'honour was at stake, they [the litigants] were mindful that another audience was listening'. Thus many, especially women, might break the law or opt for a stance that would convict them in court in order to protect their threatened honour and thus appear socially absolved. L. Peirce, *Morality Tales. Law and Gender in the Ottoman Court of Aintab* (Berkeley and Los Angeles: University of California Press, 2003), 203.

76   Migdal, *State in Society*, 15–17.

77   Timothy Mitchell, 'The Limits of the State: Beyond Statist Approaches and their Critics', *American Political Science Review* 85:1 (March 1991), 94.

78   The suspicion targeted both elites and population – consider the demeaning *mütegallibe* (userper) or *cahil halk* (ignorant people) of bureaucratic papers.

79   Migdal, *State in Society*; Meeker, *A Nation of Empire*.

Chapter 4: People's Houses vs Coffee Houses

1   On the Oriental/Ottoman coffee house, see Ralph Hattox, *Coffee and Coffeehouses, The Origins of a Social Beverage in the Medieval Near East* (Seattle and London: University of Washington Press, 1996); Ekrem Işın, 'A Social History of Coffee and Coffeehouses', in Selahattin Özpalabıyıklar (ed.), *Coffee, Pleasures in a bean* (Istanbul: YKY, 2001);

Helene-Desmet Gregoire and François Georgeon (eds), *Doğuda Kahve ve Kahvehaneler* (Istanbul: YKY, 1999).

2   Uğur Kömeçoğlu, 'Historical and Sociological Approaches to Public Space: The Case of the Islamic Coffeehouse in İstanbul', PhD dissertation (Istanbul: Boğaziçi University, 2001), 46.

3   Cengiz Kırlı, 'The Struggle over Space: Coffeehouses of Ottoman Istanbul, 1780-1845', PhD dissertation (New York: State University of New York, 2000), 24.

4   Kırlı, 'The Struggle over Space', 283-4.

5   On the *kıraathane*/literary coffee houses of late Ottoman Istanbul, see Kömeçoğlu, 'Historical and Sociological Approaches to Public Space', 29-74 and 59-62.

6   François Georgeon, 'Osmanlı İmparatorluğu'nun Son Döneminde İstanbul Kahvehaneleri', in Gregoire and Georgeon, *Doğuda Kahve ve Kahvehaneler*, 72-7.

7   Serdar Öztürk, *Cuhmuriyet Türkiyesinde Kahvehane ve İktidar 1930-1945* (Istanbul: Kırmızı, 2005), 86-8.

8   The connection between idleness and coffee houses (especially civil servants sitting idle in coffee houses) was also a recurrent theme in the reports of Ahmed Şerif in the newspaper *Tanin* after the 1908 Revolution. Ahmet Şerif, *Anadolu'da Tanin* (Istanbul: Kavram, 1977), 14-15, 34, 40.

9   Öztürk, *Kahvehane*, passim., but especially, 111 ff.; Levent Cantek, *Cumhuriyetin Bülüğ Çağı. Gündelik Yaşama Dair Tartışmalar 1945-1950* (Istanbul: İletişim, 2008), 253-6.

10 Öztürk, *Kahvehane*, 183-267.

11 Ibid., 162-79.

12 Similar financial reservations were behind similarly inconclusive policies of the Ottoman state. Kırlı, 'The Struggle over Space', 58-62.

13 A small study about the villages in the area of Trabzon in the Black Sea published in 1934 reported that the government had closed down village coffee houses because villagers had been sitting idle there while the hazelnut fields were left uncultivated. Ömer Türkmen, 'Trabzon Köyleri', *Ülkü* 4:20 (October 1934): 159; for a similar state policy in Giresun in 1936, see Serdar Öztürk, 'The Struggle over Turkish Village Coffeehouses 1923-1945', *MES* 44:3 (2008): 443.

14 Öztürk, *Kahvehane*, 99-106, 357 ff. During the years of World War II, coffee-house frequenters were ridiculed for their ignorant know-it-all talking as 'coffeehouse diplomats or politicians'. Based on his own experience of the 15 days he spent hiding from the police, Rıfat İlgaz's novel *Karartma Geceleri* (Istanbul: Çınar, 1974) is a first-hand account of the close supervision of coffee houses and similar public spaces by spies and policemen in Istanbul during World War II.

15   Article 'Kahveler-Halkevleri' in Halkevi journal *Aksu*, 10 (October 1934), 16–17, quoted by Arzu Öztürkmen, *Türkiye'de Folklor ve milliyetçilik* (Istanbul: İletişim, 1998), 101.

16   Village rooms were common spaces of socialization where male villagers gathered in villages that did not usually have coffee houses.

17   Kemal Akça, 'Eski Köy Odaları', *Folklor Postası* 6 (1945): 3–4, in Öztürk, *Kahvehane*, 285.

18   Naşit Uluğ, 'Halkevlerinin Memleket Hayatına getirmiş olduğu büyük içtimai inkişaf', *Ulus*, 25 February 1940, in Öztürk, *Kahvehane*, 286.

19   *Akşam*, 17 January 1930, in Öztürk, *Kahvehane*, 186.

20   *Hakimiyeti Milliye*, 15 January 1932, in Öztürk, *Kahvehane*, 188, where more examples are given.

21   Report of Hikmet Işık on Kastamonu province Houses in 1936, BCA, 490.01/999.861.1, quoted in Gülsün Karakuzuoğlu, 'Kastamonu Halkevi ve Faaliyetleri', MA thesis (Aydın: Adnan Menderes University, 2008), 109.

22   See Chapter 1.

23   No. 2882 (21 August 1930), BCA 490.01/435.1804.2, quoted in Cemil Koçak, *İktidar ve Serbest Cumhuriyet Fırkası* (Istanbul: İletişim, 2006), 193–4.

24   Kırlı, 'The Struggle over Space', 50.

25   Ankara issued a series of directives to the provincial Party to enlist more women. See, for instance, communiqués no. 413, 414, 415 and 418 in *Tebligat*, vol. 5 (Ankara: Ulus, 1935), 21, 22, 23 and 27. On the low number of women members, see chapters 1 and 5.

26   Some Halkevi activities were apparently antagonistic to other enterprises as well. Consider the letter of the Yıldız cinema owner in Trabzon (20 June 1939) complaining that the free entrance cinema projections of the local Halkevi were damaging his business. BCA, 490.01/844.337.2. See also two similar petitions by a cinema owner in Aydın (10 November 1939 and 8 February 1939), BCA, 490.01/824.260.1.

27   Similar grievances were also voiced against the Turkish Hearths. The Izmir Hearth, for instance, was accused in 1930 of operating as a drinking tavern and gambling club. Günver Güneş, 'İzmir Türk Ocağı ve Hamdullah Suphi', *Tarih ve Toplum* 129 (1994): 170.

28   BCA, 490.01/840.322.2. Ahmet Kayaner, chairman of the Youth Club of Ceylanpınar, and 27 others (27 January 1950), protested that 'we have seen no activity in the People's Room apart from gambling. [If you do nothing] you will become the cause we and other youths like us get poisoned in the corners of the coffeehouse.' BCA, 490.01/844.340.2.

29   Sent on 3 February 1942, BCA, 490.01/842.331.2.

30   Letter of the chairman of the Theatre section of the Kula Halkevi (30 June 1935), BCA, 490.01/840.322.2.

31 Letter signed by ten members of the Theatre and Sport sections of İnegöl House (27 August 1943), BCA, 490.01/829.273.2.

32 Anonymous letter (27 November 1948) from İzmit, BCA, 490.01/839.316.1.

33 Mehmet Solmaz from Düzce (3 August 1939), BCA, 490.01/828.271.3.

34 BCA, 490.01/835.300.1. Sent on 27 September 1946 from Sariyer, Istanbul. For some more examples, see the article from the newspaper *Tasvir* of 30 September 1945 about the Kırşehir Halkevi, BCA, 490.01/838.314.1; the letter by Hüseyin Erkaya from Kadınhan, dated 10 November 1949, BCA, 490.01/840.320.1; and the letter of 22 March 1941 signed as 'yüzlerce bafra genci [hundreds of the youths of Bafra]', BCA, 490.01/842.330.2. The majority of the letters dealing with similar issues (coffee house, gambling) use similar expressions.

35 Riza from Kızılhisar (16 November 1947), BCA, 490.01/831.282.2.

36 Salih Peker from Elmalı to President İnönü (29 November 1947), BCA, 490.01/824.257.1.

37 In the order mentioned above, F. Doğaner (18 March 1948), BCA, 490.01/830.277.1; Sami Filibeli and Mehmed Dilmez (3 September 1941), BCA, 490.01/830.276.1; lycée principal Fuat Karal (26 November 1946), BCA, 490.01/842.331.2; Mustafa Timin (1 March 1948), BCA, 490.01/842.331.2; 'Halkodası değil, kahvehane', *Tasvir*, 29 September 1948, BCA, 490.01/830.279.2; telegram by Ahmet Umutlı (5 August 1948), BCA, 490.01/833.291.2; telegram to Premier Şükrü Şaraçoğlu by Nuri Gümedağ (18 March 1946), BCA, 490.01/836.305.1; Party boss Dr Sezai Yavaşça to Izmir Party branch (1 April 1944), BCA, 490.01/836.305.1; Ahmet oğlu Hamdi Gozluk and Sadettin (29 March 1949), BCA, 490.01/837.309.1; anonymous letter (27 November 1948), BCA, 490.01/839.316.1; Riza (16 November 1947), BCA, 490.01/831.282.2; two members of the Kula Halkevi Theatre section (30 June 1935), BCA, 490.01/840.322.2; RPP General Secretariat to Party branch of Mardin (23 June 1948, no. 7/12089), BCA, 490.01/841.325.2; anonymous (8 October 1949), BCA, 490.01/843.333.2; 'Gençlik', *Hürses* (an oppositional newspaper), 8 February 1946, 6, BCA, 490.01/843.336.2; Ali oğlu Mustafa (28 April 1941), BCA, 490.01/827.269.1; Tahir Atabay (9 February 1939); and Hasan Karabacak (4 May 1949) and Ahmet Yumuk (18 August 1941) to RPP general secretary and (15 September 1941) to Halil, MP for Zonguldak, BCA, 490.01/733.3.2; Ahmet Kayaner, president of Youth Club, and 27 people (27 January 1950), BCA, 490.01/844.340.2; Mehmet Akcan (5 February 1946), BCA, 490.01/844.340.2.

38 In small towns in the east or south-east of Turkey and among linguistic and ethnic minorities, the segregation of state officials from locals was probably more acute. The People's Houses and Rooms in the east, as we have seen in Chapter 2, were exclusively frequented by non-local state

employees, bureaucrats, teachers, judges and officers.

39   The occupation of the Halkevi by officers or other officials was a common theme of complaint letters and local politics as we have seen in Chapter 3.

40   Şakır Karataş from Gölyaka İmamlar (24 December 1945), BCA, 490.01/842.331.2.

41   Sent on 25 November 1939, BCA, 490.01/831.281.1.

42   İbrahim Kacar from Kızılcabölük (21 February 1940), BCA, 490.01/831.281.1. Similar letter by Mehmet Solmaz from Düzce (3 August 1939), BCA, 490.01/828.271.3.

43   Sent on 29 November 1945, BCA, 490.01/733.2.2.

44   Üzeyir Tüzün Köylüoğlu (17 October 1945), BCA, 490.01/827.268.2.

45   Sami Filibeli and Mehmed Dilmez (3 September 1941), BCA, 490.01/830.276.1.

46   Telegram, BCA, 490.01/836.305.1.

47   By 'friends', Party documents usually refer to the Party executive and, less frequently, members.

48   "'Münevver olmayan bir parça serkeş ve külhanbeyi geçinmek isteyen toylardır.'" BCA, 490.01/836.305.1. Emphasis added.

49   Nuri Gümedağ from Kemalpaşa to Premier Şükrü Saraçoğlu (18 March 1946), BCA, 490.01/836.305.1.

50   This compartmentalization of the Halkevi space in order to serve the civil servants' need to segregate from the locals has also been observed in the House's discursive rival, the coffee house. Referring to the coffee houses in Orf, Meeker mentioned the existence of inner rooms in some coffee houses that were reserved for the exclusive use of certain 'notables'. In a similar fashion, some coffee houses were frequented mainly by non-local civil servants and educated local youths, while others by locals, villagers, merchants and artisans. Michael Meeker, *A Nation of Empire: The Ottoman Legacy of Turkish Modernity* (Berkeley and London: University of California Press, 2002), 348, 350–2.

51   Ahmet oğlu Hamdi Gözlük and Sadettin (29 March 1949), BCA, 490.01/837.309.1.

52   *Balıkesir Şehir Kulübü Nizamnamesi* (Istanbul: Türk Pazarı, 1934), 2.

53   Serdar Öztürk, 'Bir Kurumun Tarihsel ve Sosyolojik İncelemesi: Şehir Kulüpleri (1923–1950)', *Galatasaray İletişim* 4 (August 2006): 94.

54   Communiqué no. 345 (16 August 1934), *Tebligat*, vol. 5 (Ankara: Ulus, 1935), 55.

55   For examples, see Öztürk, *Kahvehane*, 175–8, 240.

56   Öztürk, *Kahvehane*, 175.

57   The clubs that Unionists established between 1908 and 1918 were similarly accused of being solely occupied by state officials and teachers. Fevzi Demir, *Osmanlı Devleti'nde II. Meşrutiyet Dönemi Meclis-i Mebusan Seçimleri 1908–1914* (Ankara: İmge, 2007), 252.

58   BCA, 490.01/847.352.1 quoted in Öztürk, 'Şehir Kulüpleri', 111.

59 Report no. 354 (16 May 1941), BCA, 490.01/827.268.2.
60 Report no. 31 (8 February 1944), BCA, 490.01/842.331.2.
61 Communiqué no. 2882, 21 August 1930, BCA, 490.01/435.1804.2, in Koçak, *İktidar ve Serbest*, 193-4.
62 Letter of 15 September 1941, BCA, 490.01/837.309.1.
63 Communiqué no. 22328/10391 (23 December 1944), BCA, 490.01/ 847.352.1, in Öztürk, *Kahvehane*, 240.
64 Işıl Çakal, *Konuşunuz Konuşturunuz*. *Tek Parti Döneminde Propagandanın Etkin Silahı: Söz* (Istanbul: Otopsi, 2004), 205-7.
65 Some examples: Adil Öneren from Urfa (12 March 1936), BCA, 490.01/832.283.1; Aslan Kaynardağ from Kastamonu (7 March 1941), BCA, 490.01/837.308.2; from Düzce Party Inspector Ş. Karaca, BCA, 490.01/828.271.3; Public Prosecutor Hayrettin Sezine from Kayseri (24 May 1946), BCA, 490.01/338.311.1. During school plays and shows performed by students on the Halkevi stage, priority through invitation was probably given to the students' relatives, as was implied in the report of the Party chairman in Kayseri, Salih Avgın (11 June 1946), BCA, 490.01/338.311.1.
66 Talip Dereli from Izmir (29 March 1944), BCA, 490.01/836.305.01.
67 Nafia İzli from Gelibolu (31 May 1938), BCA, 490.01/ 830.276.1. For more examples, see next chapter.
68 Sent on 8 July 1942, BCA, 490.01/845.344.2. More examples include the lawyer Necati Erdem from Sinop (5 December 1947 and 23 February 1948), BCA, 490.01/843.333.2; ten Halkevi members from İnegöl (27 August 1943), BCA, 490.01/829.273.2; an anonymous letter from Tosya (22 March 1948), BCA, 490.01/837.309.1; a letter published on 6 February 1940 in the newspaper *Kars*, BCA, 490.01/837.306.2; Avni Kozak from Izmir (27 February 1943), BCA, 490.01/836.305.1. For a similar system, see Esra Üstündağ-Selamoğlu, 'Bir Sözlü Tarih Çalışması. Hereke'de Değişim', *Toplumsal Tarih* 45 (1997).
69 The invitation was attached to a complaint letter signed by university students, BCA, 490.01/836.305.1.
70 Meltem Ahıska, *Occidentalism in Turkey. Questions of Modernity and National Identity in Turkish Radio Broadcasting* (London: I.B.Tauris, 2010), 15, 17-18, 26, 56.
71 Other works on previous periods have attempted to gauge the degree of reception by ordinary people of the state's discourse and policies. See Milen Petrov, 'Everyday forms of Compliance: Subaltern Commentaries on Ottoman Reform, 1864-1868', *CSSH* 46:4 (2004): 730-59.
72 Paraphrasing Davies' 'speak Bolshevik' in Sarah Davies, *Popular Opinion in Stalin's Russia* (Cambridge: Cambridge University Press, 1997), 7.
73 Vladimir A. Kozlov, 'Denunciation and Its Functions in Soviet Governance: A Study of Denunciations and Their Bureaucratic Handling from Soviet Police Archives, 1944-1953', in Sheila Fitzpatrick and

Robert Gellately (eds), *Accusatory Practices. Denunciation in Modern European History, 1789-1989* (Chicago: University of Chicago Press, 1997), 136.

74 The social cleavage expressed in terms of 'us' and/against 'them' was a theme of the letters and has also been noticed in works based on similar sources (letters) for the same period. See Davies, *Popular Opinion*, 124-44.

75 Examples include letters from Biga (14 September 1941), BCA, 490.01/830.276.1: 'When a show is taking place, the people are ordered out and the civil servants in', and (3 September 1941), BCA, 490.01/830.276.1: 'the Halkevi invites only the civil servants and those ladies and gentlemen suiting their interests, while they do not even open the door to the people and the youths'; from Bulanik (21 May 1942), BCA, 490.01/841.326.2: 'Is the local People's House the "House of the civil servant"?'; from the newspaper *Kars*, 6 February 1940, BCA, 490.01/837.306.2: 'The people are denied access to the show because the invitations are distributed among notables such as civil servants and merchants'; from Kuşadası (3 November 1944), BCA, 490.01/836.305.1: 'Is the Halkevi the civil servants' club? Are the people to be kept away from there?'

76 'The Halkevi chairman does not lower himself to come to the Halkevi because there are citizens from a lower standing who are not civil servants. The invited to the ceremony were those favoured by our honourable chairman and his poker friends.' Anonymous from Tosya (22 March 1948), BCA, 490.01/ 837.309.1.

77 The same usage has been noticed by Davies, *Popular Opinion*, 8, where 'officially hallowed words such as "revolution" or "the people" were reclaimed for the expression of dissent. So, while the regime employed *narod* to denote "the whole people", and thereby to imply unity, dissenters used it in a divisive way to signify the powerless lower classes.'

78 Fahri Sakal, *Çok Partili Döneme Geçişte Tek Partinin Muhalefet Anlayışı* (Samsun: Etüt, 2008), 72, 107, 135, 154, 175-6.

79 Salih Peker from Elmalı (29 November 1947), BCA, 490.01/824.257.1.

80 Hüseyin Ekiz (19 February 1947), BCA, 490.01/824.257.1: 'They have turned this holy place into a brothel. Now, no serious and moral person can go there. It has become a place of masturbation.' Mustafa Kurtay from Eğridir (March 1943), BCA, 490.01/834.296.2: 'For years they have been bringing women and feeding prostitutes and dirty people.' Osmaniye school principal Fuat Kutal (22 November 1946), BCA, 490.01/842.331.2: 'It has become the drinking tavern of some Party notables and landlords, who sometimes bring prostitutes from Ankara.'

81 In one case the Halkevi women were presented as 'daughters of preachers and prayer leaders [*imam ve hatip*] and children of the

most honourable family': Faik Barım (13 January 1942), BCA, 490.01/825.265.2. There is a similar reference by Hakkı Özveren (15 November 1946), BCA, 490.01/839.319.1.

82   For a more rare expression ('under this sacred roof, which is the Kaaba of our holy Party'), see Mazhar Gençkurt (5 April 1944), BCA, 490.01/829.273.2.

83   Sheila Fitzpatrick, *Stalin's Peasants* (Oxford: Oxford University Press, 1994), 16-17, 200, 254-60.

84   Halil İnalcık, 'Şikayet Hakkı: "Arz-ı Hal ve Arz-ı Mahzar'lar"', *Osmanlı Araştırmaları* 7-8 (1988): 33-54.

85   Efi Avdela, *'For reasons of honour'*: *Violence, Sentiments, and Values in post civil-war Greece* (Athens: Nefeli, 2006), 42-3. (Εφη Αβδελά, 'Δια λόγους τιμής': Βία, Συναισθήματα και Αξίες στη Μετεμφυλιακή Ελλαδα (Αθήνα: Νεφέλη, 2006).) In Avdela's use, 'cultural scenarios' correspond to the culturally understood justifications for honour crimes in the 1950s and 1960s in Greece. The commonsensical character of the rhetoric schemes through which cultural scenarios are articulated ensures that anyone understands what they mean, whether one agrees or not.

86   On conservative intellectuals in the 1940s and 1950s, see Umut Azak, *Islam and Secularism in Turkey: Kemalism, Religion and the Nation State* (London: I.B.Tauris, 2010), 89-97.

87   Adnan Menderes, leader of the Democrat Party that ruled Turkey in the 1950s, habitually described the single party as a regime of domination and oppression. See Azak, *Islam and Secularism in Turkey*, 130.

88   Tanıl Bora and Necmi Erdoğan, '"Biz, Anadolu'nun Bağrı Yanık Çocukları": Muhafazakâr Populizm', in Tanıl Bora and Murat Gültekingil (eds), *Modern Türkiye'de Siyasi Düşünce*, vol. 5: *Muhafazakârlık* (Istanbul: İletişim, 2001), 636-43.

89   Fethi Açıkel, '"Kutsal mazlumluğun" psikopatolojisi', *Toplum ve Bilim* 70 (Fall 1996): 153-74.

90   In the popular music of Orhan Gencebay, for instance. Meral Özbek, *Popüler Kültür ve Orhan Gencebay Arabeski* (Istanbul: İletişim, 1991), 177.

91   Roughly half of the letters were anonymous or featured an illegible or false signature or name. Given their apparent knowledge of the Halkevi and, occasionally, their sophisticated writing style, most anonymous authors were probably middle-class urbanites as were most eponymous ones.

92   Yaşar Kemal, for instance, whose first book on folklore was published by the Adana Halkevi, worked in its library and also as a petition-writer. Alpay Kabacalı, *Bir Destan Rüzgarı: Fotoğraflarla Yaşar Kemal Yaşam Öyküsü* (Istanbul: Sel, 1997), 10. The Balıkesir Halkevi chairman wrote petitions for illiterates in 1934. Hürrem Arman,

Piramidin tabanı. Köy Enstitüleri ve Tonguç (Ankara: Arkın Kitabevi, 1969), 139. On petition-writers in the Ottoman context, see Gülden Sarıyıldız, *Sokak Yazıcıları, Osmanlıda Arzuhaller ve Arzuhalciler* (Istanbul: Derlem, 2011).

93 Letter-writing manuals, for instance, included examples of and instructions on petition-writing. Examples include Münir Naci, *Güzel İstid'a Nümuneleri* (Istanbul: n.p., 1929); Raif Necdet, *Küçük Mektup Nümuneleri* (Istanbul: Türk Neşriyat Yurdu, 1929); Muallim Fuat Şükrü, *Mükemmel Mektup Nümuneleri* (Istanbul: Anadolu Türk Kitaphanesi, 1931); Süleyman Tevfik, *Güzel Mektup nümuneleri* (Istanbul: Güneş, 1932); Selami Münir, *Yeni İstid'a Örnekleri* (Istanbul: n.p., 1934); and İsmet Tarti, *Yeni Mektup Örnekleri* (Istanbul: n.p., 1943).

94 For a critique of the recent literature on the 'Turkish Modernization' and the trend to view it as a failure or success, see Meltem Ahıska, *Radyonun Sihirli Kapısı. Garbiyatçılık ve Politik Öznellik* (Istanbul: Metis, 2005), 35–45.

Chapter 5: Women on the Halkevi Stage

1 Katz reminds us that 'national identities were formed and articulated against a field of gendered meanings'. Sheila Hannah Katz, '*Adam* and *Adama*, '*Ird* and *Ard*: En-gendering Political Conflict and Identity in Early Jewish and Palestinian Nationalism', in Deniz Kandiyoti (ed.), *Gendering the Middle East: Emerging Perspectives* (London: I.B.Tauris, 1996), 100.

2 Ayşe Durakbaşa, 'Kemalism as Identity Politics in Turkey', in Zehra Arat (ed.), *Deconstructing Images of 'the Turkish Woman'* (New York: Palgrave, 1999), 140.

3 Fatmagül Berktay, 'Osmanlı'dan Cumhuriyet'e Feminizm', in Tanıl Bora and Murat Gültekingil (eds), *Modern Türkiye'de Siyasi Düşünce*, vol. 1: *Tanzimat ve Meşrutiyet'in Birikimi* (Istanbul: İletişim, 2001), 353.

4 Deniz Kandiyoti, 'Emancipated but unliberated? Reflections on the Turkish case', *Feminist Studies* 13:2 (1987): 317–38.

5 Ibid., 'Slave Girls, Temptresses, and Comrades: Images of Women in the Turkish Novel', *Feminist Issues* 8:1 (1988): 47.

6 Ibid., 'Afterword: Some Awkward Questions on Women and Modernity in Turkey', in Lila Abu-Lughod (ed.), *Remaking Women: Feminism and Modernity in the Middle East* (Princeton, NJ: Princeton University Press, 1998), 282.

7 In Balıkesir, for example, the first actresses on the Halkevi stage were four teachers and the wives of two state functionaries who were also participating in the play. '24 Şubat', *Kaynak* 2 (19 March 1933): 64. Most of the female members of the People's Orator Organization were

also teachers. Hakan Uzun, 'Cumhuriyet Halk Fırkası Halk Hatipleri Teşkilâtı', *Cumhuriyet Tarihi Araştırmaları Dergisi* 11 (2010): 105.

8   In 1933, 26 of the 27 female members in Kastamonu were teachers; the other was a bank clerk. Karakuzuoğlu, 'Kastamonu Halkevi', 19.

9   Letter by chairman of a local Party branch, Ali Talaslıoğlu, and member Murat Şerbetçi (14 March 1939), in BCA, 490.01/344.1440.4.

10 In her study of the RPP in a small town in the province of Kayseri, Ayata shows that the only women participating in politics were the wives of educated men, usually non-local civil servants and local professionals with a Western lifestyle, educated in Ankara or Istanbul. Their participation was restricted to informal politics, that is, exchanging visits and tea parties with other women in an attempt to support their husbands' political careers. On the other hand, all male members of notable families had adopted a 'Western' outlook, but were keeping 'their' women secluded as they did not want to 'injure their honour/reputation'. Ayşe Ayata Güneş, *CHP Örgüt ve İdeoloji* (Ankara: Gündoğan, 1992), 144, 185.

11 Afsaneh Najmabadi, 'Authority and Agency: Revisiting Women's Activism during Reza Shah's Period', in Touraj Atabaki (ed.), *The State and the Subaltern. Modernization, Society and the State in Turkey and Iran* (London: I.B.Tauris, 2007), 168.

12 Sporadically there were directives – not questions – about women. See, for example, the directive of 5 July 1946 to the Halkevi chairmen to inform women Party members of the new, direct system of elections. BCA 490.01/6.30.26.

13 See Chapter 1.

14 Cemil Koçak, *İktidar ve Serbest Cumhuriyet Fırkası* (Istanbul: İletişim, 2006), 197–200. In Bursa in 1930 only eight women registered (page 370).

15 Nor is there a need for such an endeavour here: the place of women in the discourse of Turkish nationalism has been the subject of exemplary works by Kandiyoti, Arat, Durakbaşa and Berktay et al.

16 On the Halkevi theatre stage, see Nurhan Karadağ, *Halkevleri tiyatro çalışmaları* (Ankara: T.C. Kültür Bakanlığı, 1998), and Eyal Ari, 'The People's houses and the Theatre in Turkey', *MES* 40:4 (2004).

17 The Unionists also used the stage to disseminate their ideas and policies. Efdal Sevinçli, 'II. Meşrutiyet Döneminde Siyasal/Belgesel Tiyatro ve İlginç bir Yazar Örneği: Doktor Kamil Bey ve Oyunları', in Ferdan Ergut (ed.), *II. Meşrutiyet'i yeniden Düşünmek* (Istanbul: Tarih Vakfı Yurt Yayınları, 2009), 144–7; Kudret Emiroğlu, *Anadolu'da Devrim Günleri. II Meşrutiyet'in İlanı* (Ankara: İmge, 1999), 129, 199–200; Hakan Aydın, 'İttihat ve Terakki Mekteplerinin Yapısal Özellikleri Üzerine bir İnceleme', PhD thesis (Konya: Selçuk University, 2008), 159–63; Metin And, *Meşrutiyet döneminde Türk Tiyatrosu* (Ankara: Türkiye İş Bankası Kültür Yayınları, 1971), passim.

18   Donald Webster, *The Turkey of Atatürk: Social Process in the Turkish Reformation* (New York: American Academy of Political and Social Science, 1939), 188–9.

19   Karadağ, *Halkevleri tiyatro çalışmaları*, 109.

20   Vahap Kabahasanoğlu, *Faruk Nafiz Çamlıbel* (Istanbul: Toker, 1979), 16; the Turkish Hearths had also commissioned the writing of plays. Füsun Üstel, *İmparatorluktan Ulus-Devlete Türk Milliyetçiliği Türk Ocakları 1912–31* (Istanbul: İletişim, 2004), 233; Karadağ, *Halkevleri tiyatro çalışmaları*, 109–12.

21   Kenan Olgun, *Yöresel Kalkınmada Adapazarı Halkevi* (İstanbul: Değişim, 2008), 66; Karadağ, *Halkevleri tiyatro çalışmaları*, 103.

22   According to a Party communiqué (26 September 1946) to 29 Houses, the theatrical group of Atıf Kaptan and his wife Fatma Leman 'will arrive at your House to stage theatrical plays from the following repertoire'. BCA, 490.01/7.39.22.

23   *CHFHT*, § 38; *Tebligat*, vol. 4 (Ankara: Hakimiyeti Milliye, 1934), 30.

24   *CHPHCT*, 14. In the 1932 by-laws, this was not explicitly prohibited, but implied, one can argue, since this was the only part of the text where both 'men and women' were mentioned together and required to form the House's theatrical group.

25   It was even admitted in the Ankara Halkevi journal: 'Necip Ali Beyin Nutku', *Ülkü* 1:2 (March 1933): 113. An article in 1939 argued that even the Ankara Halkevi had difficulties in finding women volunteers because 'some morality conventions – not principles – portray those acting on stage negatively'. Ali Suha Delilbaşı, 'Halkevleri'nde Tiyatro Meselesi', *Ülkü* 14:81 (November 1939): 229–30.

26   Karadağ, *Halkevleri tiyatro çalışmaları*, 88–9, 109–10, 177–80. After the 1908 Revolution, Unionist attempts to stage plays and have women on stage caused open resistance, threats and violence from conservatives and the opposition. Emiroğlu, *Anadolu'da Devrim*, 129, 144, 167; Fevzi Demir, *Osmanlı Devleti'nde II. Meşrutiyet Dönemi Meclis-i Mebusan Seçimleri 1908–1914* (Ankara: İmge, 2007), 245; Fatma Denman Kılıç, *İkinci Meşrutiyet Döneminde Bir Jön Türk Dergisi: Kadın* (Istanbul: Libra, 2009), 77, 217; Aynur Demirdirek, *Osmanlı Kadınlarının Hayat Hakkı Arayışının bir Hikayesi* (Ankara: Ayizi, 2011), 28, 62.

27   'CHP Piyes Hikâye Müsabakaları', *Ülkü* 12:67 (September 1938): 79; 'CHP 1945 Sanat Mûkafatı', *Ülkü* 6:70 (August 1944): 3.

28   Some examples include 23 November 1939 letter of Party inspector of Bolu, BCA, 490.01/828.271.3; 25 July 1934 and 10 July 1934 letters of Karahisar Halkevi chairman on the refusal of local women teachers to participate in the Halkevi theatre, BCA, 490.01/833.293.1; letter of Izmir Party boss (1 November 1935) on the teachers' indifference towards the Halkevi and theatre, BCA, 490.01/836.303.1.

29   The Party inspector of Kütahya, Hasan Vasıf Somyürek (7 May 1943), complained that the chairman of the Manisa House had two men play female roles because two women teachers abandoned the rehearsals. BCA, 490.01/840.323.1. See also Üstel, *Türk Ocakları*, 182–5, for a similar response to the unwillingness of women to dance with men in the Turkish Hearth of Biga; women dancers were replaced by men dressed as women. Another case was reported in Giresun by an anonymous denunciation (31 December 1942), BCA, 490.01/833.293.1.

30   For an example, see dispatches no. 83 (28 June 1932), 66 (7 March 1932) and 67 (25 May 1932) in *Tebligat*, vol. 1 (Ankara, 1933), 56, 46 and 48.

31   *Tebligat*, vol. 1 (Ankara, 1933), 92.

32   In his report (7 August 1937) from Burhaniye, M. Sayman wrote that he gathered a number of teachers to explain their duties and the country's needs and to remind them of the circular of the Education Ministry. BCA, 490.01/623.46.1.

33   Yahya Akyüz, *Türkiye'de öğretmenlerin toplumsal değişmedeki etkileri 1848-1940* (Ankara: Doğan, 1978), 251.

34   'Halkevleri Postası', *Ülkü* 13:77 (July 1939): 468.

35   See, for instance, the letter of the Karahisar Halkevi chairman (16 March 1937), BCA, 490.01/833.293.1.

36   Hürrem Arman, *Piramidin tabanı. Köy Enstitüleri ve Tonguç* (Ankara: Arkın Kitabevi, 1969), 208, 213, 240.

37   In his letter (2 June 1939), the governor also asked for the Education Ministry's pressure on teachers to participate in the Halkevi plays. The Party (4 July 1939) and the Education Minister (13 July 1937) replied that the participation of female teachers could not be achieved through administrative order but through 'inspiration, and wide affection and respect'. BCA, 490.01/831.281.1.

38   Letter from the Iskilip Director of Education to the *Kaymakam* (11 November 1941), where five women teachers were obliged to sign a statement with their refusal. BCA, 490.01/831.280.2. For a similar case, see the letter (18 October 1935) of the Bergama Halkevi chairman and the minutes of a meeting (10 October 1935) with nine teachers in the Halkevi where their refusal to act on stage was discussed and recorded. BCA, 490.01/836.303.1.

39   See the example of a Halkevi where theatre could not be performed because women did not volunteer until a couple first climbed the stage together. Ziya Çevik, 'Bir Mektup: Eski bir Halkevliden Yeni bir Halkevliye', *Ülkü* 107 (March 1946): 2. Two among the first women on stage in Balıkesir were acting together with their civil servant husbands: '24 Şubat', *Kaynak* 2 (19 March 1933): 64.

40   Hikmet Pala, 'Cumhuriyet Modernleşme Projesinin bir aracı olarak Ordu Halkevi ve çalışmaları', MA thesis (Ankara: Gazi University, 2006), 162–3.

41 Apparently the Party was equally obliged to financially reward men and women who participated in another supposedly strictly volunteer-based Party activity, the People's Orators. Uzun, 'Halk Hatipleri Teşkilâtı', 103.

42 Edremit Halkevi chairman (3 January 1942), BCA, 490.01/825.265.2.

43 See Chapter 2.

44 BCA, 490.01/832.287.2. The Diyarbakır Halkevi chief asked the same. Canser Kardaş, 'Diyarbakır Halkevi ve Karacadağ Dergisinin Halkbilim açısından Değerlendirmesi (1932–1951)', MA thesis (Kayseri: Erciyes University, 2007), 35–6.

45 Letter by Mazhar Gençkurt (16 May 1942) and negative response by Party Inspector Zühtü Durukan (1 June 1942) in BCA, 490.01/829.273.2.

46 There were also many non-Muslim – usually Armenian – male actors. And, Meşrutiyet, 27–48.

47 In a parallel fashion to the Halkevi, women in the Turkish Hearths were typically mentioned either by virtue of their absence or their immorality. Üstel, Türk Ocakları, 182–5, 235. The same accusation appeared about 'common women' in Izmir as well: Günver Güneş, 'İzmir Türk Ocağı ve Hamdullah Suphi', Tarih ve Toplum 129 (1994): 170.

48 Metin And, A History of Theatre and Popular Entertainment in Turkey (Ankara: Forum, 1963–4), 77.

49 'Tuluat tiyatrosu', Türk Ansiklopedisi, vol. 31 (Ankara: Milli Eğitim, 1982), 483–4. For examples of eventful plays, see Metin And, Türk Tiyatrosunun Evreleri (Ankara: Turhan, 1983), 376–7.

50 'An outer garment covering a woman from head to foot and designed to hide her body form the view of men.' Redhouse Büyük Elsözlüğü (Istanbul, 2000).

51 Reşat Nuri Güntekin, Anadolu Notları (Istanbul: İnkılap va Aka, 1989), 132–3.

52 The notion that women performing on the tulûat stage were immoral or, plainly, prostitutes was so widespread that a short story about a travelling troupe that performed in the coffee house of a provincial town – although disapproving of the notion – was published in the journal of the Ankara Halkevi. Celâl Sıtkı, 'Hav ... Hav...', Ülkü 1:4 (May 1933): 318–21.

53 Letter of the Democrat Party leader in Eleşkirt (13 February 1950) about CHP's refusal to allow his Party to use the Halkevi. His use of the expression 'tiyatro kızları' underlines the gravity of the wrongdoing: 'Our show, organized for the benefit of our Party, was not permitted to take place in our Halkevi where the performance of theatre girls is permitted.' BCA, 490.01/733.2.2.

54 Letter of 5 April 1944, BCA, 490.01/829.273.2.

55 Hakkı Özveren (15 November 1946), BCA, 490.01/839.319.1.

56 BCA, 490.01/839.316.1. For another complaint about a prostitute performing on the Halkevi stage in Istanbul, see an undated (probably

1947) and handwritten letter with an illegible signature in BCA, 490.01/835.301.1.

57 Denouncing someone (or someone's wife or family) for not being Turkish (Kurd, Arab, Greek, but most commonly Armenian) was one of the most common accusations the letters employed next to corruption and immorality. What is more, ethnic and/or religious otherness was habitually paired with immorality. A typical example was to enhance the accusation of immorality of the person denounced by accusing his wife of being immoral and Armenian or Christian.

58 BCA, 490.01/839.316.1.

59 BCA, 490.01/839.316.1.

60 'Boğazlıyan Halkevinde neler oluyor', Tasvir, 11 December 1947, in BCA, 490.01/845.343.2.

61 Mustafa Timin from Bayramiç (1 March 1948), BCA, 490.01/830.277.1.

62 Dated 16 March 1937, BCA, 490.01/833.293.1.

63 Report (3 August 1944) and official record signed by five witnesses in BCA, 490.01/842.329.1.

64 Dated 5 April 1940, BCA, 490.01/829.273.2.

65 Anonymous (27 November 1948), BCA, 490.01/839.316.1.

66 Colonel Kutlu (20 March 1950), BCA, 490.01/839.316.1.

67 BCA, 490.01/833.289.1. The letter also accused the Kaymakam of extortion and profiteering. Corruption and immorality was a combination typical of many denunciations.

68 Anonymous (31 December 1942), BCA, 490.01/833.293.1.

69 Introduced in the 1920s when mixed-gender entertainment was on the increase, jazz was immediately associated with debauchery, moral decline and decadence. Carole Woodwall, '"Awakening a Horrible Monster": Negotiating the Jazz Public in 1920s Istanbul', CSSAAME 30:3 (2010): 574–82.

70 Quoted from Peyami Safa in Kandiyoti, 'Slave Girls, Temptresses, and Comrades', 44. Cf. Funda Şenol Cantek, Yabanlar ve Yerliler Başkent olma sürecinde Ankara (Istanbul: Iletişim, 2003), 151 ff.

71 Levent Cantek, Cumhuriyetin Bülüğ Çağı. Gündelik Yaşama Dair Tartışmalar 1945–1950 (Istanbul: İletişim, 2008), 230–1.

72 CHP Yedinci Kurultay Tutanağı (Ankara: Ulus, 1948), 211–12. A family meeting at the Çanakkale Halkevi was reportedly not executed properly because families were not taken in, jazz was played, and officers and civilians fought over who was going to dance with a girl. T. Ileri to local governor (12 August 1940), BCA, 490.01/830.276.1.

73 Fatmagül Berktay, 'Doğu ile Batı'nın Birleştiği Yer: Kadın imgesinin Kurgulanışı', in Tanıl Bora and Murat Gültekingil (eds), Modern Türkiye'de Siyasi Düşünce, vol. 3: Modernleşme ve Batıcılık (Istanbul: İletişim, 2002), 282.

74   BCA, 490.01/344.1440.4. The last letter was sent four days before the
      (24 March 1939) announcement of the nominations. The document
      was probably to assist in the selection. Cemil Koçak, *Türkiye'de Milli Şef
      Dönemi*, vol. 2 (Istanbul: İletişim, 2003), 33. Examples include 'his wife
      is loose', 'has a bad reputation', 'he was caught with the *Kaymakam*'s
      wife', 'he took his wife from a brothel and accepts all this dishonour by
      still being married to her', 'he frequently joins the governor's meetings
      with women and alcohol', 'the general tolerates his wife being a mistress',
      'he is tolerant to his young and beautiful wife's gracious postures', 'his
      French wife behaves like a mistress', 'he has an Armenian, a Greek, and
      a German wife'. Finally, the only female candidate had 'very low morals
      and character, the people regard her badly as she fulfilled the desires of
      the previous director of education and she has been witnessed doing
      the same thing with the dentist'.
75   BCA, 490.01/9.47.14.
76   On 17 May 1949, Party boss Esat Durusoy reported that supporters
      of the opposition shouted: 'We do not want a mayor who organizes
      theatre.' BCA, 490.01/440.1822.2, quoted in Fahri Sakal, *Çok Partili
      Döneme Geçişte Tek Partinin Muhalefet Anlayışı* (Samsun: Etüt, 2008),
      219. In the 1950s, similar opinions were expressed more outspokenly:
      local Democrat Party Congresses in 1951 and 1952 requested
      the banning of beauty contests and balls, the dismissal of female
      state employees, and the closing of City Clubs where officials were
      gambling and drinking. Umut Azak, *Islam and Secularism in Turkey:
      Kemalism, Religion and the Nation State* (London: I.B.Tauris, 2010),
      108–9.
77   Here I employ social script the way Ze'evi defines it in his work on sexual
      discourses in the Ottoman Middle East, influenced by John Gagnon
      and Jeffrey Weeks: 'a metaphor for the internal and external blueprints
      in our minds [...] like scripts for movies or plays, these outlines that
      suggest [...] the expected course of action, and the anticipated outcome
      of our actions. These scripts offer us a set of guidelines, which we do
      not necessarily follow but which allows us to recognize the parameters,
      the borders, within which we act and the points at which we transgress
      prescribed boundaries.' Dror Ze'evi, *Producing Desire: Changing Sexual
      Discourse in the Ottoman Middle East, 1500–1900* (Berkley: University
      of California Press, 2006), 10. The alternative term 'cultural scenario'
      also seems relevant in conceptualizing the culturally understood and
      anticipated notions and performances in relation to gender. See Efi
      Avdela, *'For reasons of honour': Violence, Sentiments, and Values in post
      civil-war Greece* (Athens: Nefeli, 2006), 42–3, where 'cultural scenarios'
      correspond to the culturally understood justifications for, and the
      rhetoric schemes used to justify, honour crimes in the 1950s and 1960s
      in Greece.

78   Saadet probably married Turgut Simer, as Mazhar Gençkurt's letter
      some years later (16 May 1942) mentioned a Saadet Simer, member of
      the Theatre section. BCA, 490.01/829.273.2.

79   Saadet Çırpan (7 March 1940), BCA, 490.01/829.273.2.

80   For a similar argument that 'women's constructions and interpretations
      of the past events are no different than those of men or their official
      presentations', see Zehra Kabasakal Arat, 'Where to look for the
      truth: Memory and Interpretation in Assessing the Impact of Turkish
      Women's Education', *Women's Studies International Forum* 26:1 (2003):
      58.

81   See the cases of three female members of Kayseri Halkevi in Chapter 2.

82   For a similar remark on the women supplicants' voices, see Natalie
      Zemon Davis, *Fiction in the Archives: Pardon Tales and Their Tellers
      in Sixteenth-Century France* (Cambridge: Polity Press, 1987), 103–4;
      L. Peirce, *Morality Tales. Law and Gender in the Ottoman Court of
      Aintab* (Berkeley and Los Angeles: University of California Press,
      2003), 199.

83   In his report on 5 April 1940, the Bursa Halkevi chairman even
      considered that the real author of the letter was not Saadet but Turgut
      Simer. BCA, 490.01/829.273.2.

84   Najmabadi has argued that the entrance of women into a heterosocial
      world necessitated the production of a new verbal and body language
      by women (and men) that imposed new forms of silence as the female
      voice became a 'veiled', disciplined voice. Afsaneh Najmabadi, *Women
      with Moustaches and Men without Beards: Gender and Sexual Anxieties
      of Iranian Modernity* (Berkley and Los Angeles: University of California
      Press, 2005), 152; idem, 'Veiled Discourse-Unveiled Bodies', *Feminist
      Studies* 19:3 (1993): 489.

85   Letter from the Director of Education of Iskilip to *Kaymakam*, 11
      November 1941, BCA, 490.01/831.280.2.

86   Pala, 'Ordu Halkevi', 164.

87   Interviews with Mehmet Şahin, 3 June 2005, and Zeki Özalay, 4 June
      2005, in Balıkesir.

88   Report of Kemal Çelik (3 August 1944), BCA, 490.01/842.329.1.

89   Kardaş, 'Diyarbakır Halkevi', 35–6.

90   For a similar note on the 'kinship idiom as a vehicle for easing
      social interaction and defusing tension', see Kandiyoti, 'Gendering
      the Modern', 126. For Baron, the kin idioms used by nationalists in
      Egypt and elsewhere reflected 'the transformations within families'
      and 'debates about gender relations'. Beth Baron, *Egypt as a Woman:
      Nationalism, Gender, and Politics* (Berkley: University of California
      Press, 2005), 4.

91   Berktay, 'Osmanlı'dan Cumhuriyet'e Feminizm', 353.

92   Kandiyoti, 'Slave Girls', 47.

93   Report no. 2/692 sent on 5 April 1940, BCA, 490.01/829.273.2.

94   Letter by Edremit Halkevi chairman (13 January 1942), BCA, 490.01/825.265.2.

95   Letter of Cevdet Kızılöz, Halkevi chairman, to the provincial Party on 7 January 1943 and a letter of the gendarmerie commander to the Buldan Halkevi chairman on 8 February 1943, both in BCA, 490.01/831.281.1.

96   The by-laws stated that the Halkevi was open for everyone while any denial of entry could only be applied for practical reasons, for example an overcrowded hall. Restrictions were stipulated only for unattended children and school students. See §§ 54–56 in *CHPHITT*, 12–13.

97   Party Inspector Muzaffer Akpınar (3 March 1942), BCA, 490.01/833.289.1.

98   Telegram to Prime Minister by Güney and Erdem from Bitlis (5 February 1940), BCA, 490.01/827.270.2.

99   Bitlis governor Hulusi Devrim (15 February 1940), BCA, 490.01/827.270.2.

100   Kırlı, 'The Struggle over Space', 41; Peirce, *Morality Tales*, 197–8.

101   Letter (28 November 1945) by R. Kılıç, Party chairman in Dursunbey, BCA, 490.01/825.265.2. Emphasis added.

102   Letter of 31 May 1938, BCA, 490.01/830.276.1.

103   Kandiyoti, 'Gendering the Modern', 126–8. In a similar tone, Arat writes that 'with Kemalism and modernization the preoccupation with *namus* (honour) [...] must have increased as a result of the desegregation of the sexes and the women's participation in public life'. Zehra Arat (ed.), *Deconstructing Images of the Turkish Woman* (New York: Palgrave, 1999), 26.

104   Dated 3 December 1945, BCA, 490.01/832.288.1.

105   Dated 8 May 1945, BCA, 490.01/829.273.2.

106   İlhan Tarsus, 'Adana Mektubu', *Ülkü* 2:39 (May 1943): 23.

107   Letter (3 April 1940) by 16 'Sarıgöl youths' who complain that 'women's evenings' (*kadın gecesi*) were organized on Mondays and 'a guard at the Halkevi entrance was only allowing women in'. BCA, 490.01/840.322.2.

108   Sewing courses for women organized by the Balıkesir House: *Balıkesir*, 16 December 1935; hat-making and flower-cultivation courses for women taught by women teachers in the Kastamonu Halkevi: 'Halkevleri Çalışmaları', *Ülkü* 13:78 (August 1939): 564.

109   He argued (4 September 1940) that with the courses 'I familiarize the people with the Halkevi but I also accomplish a women's advance as I assemble the young girls and ladies who stay idle at home.' BCA, 490.01/830.278.2.

110   Report no. 1356 by Governor Bayman (26 March 1937), BCA, 490.01/495.1994.1.

111 Erhan Sürme, 'Niğde Halkevi (1933–1951)', MA thesis (Niğde: Niğde University, 2009), 104. Also separate Turkish and foreign language courses for men and women, and reading-writing and sewing courses for women by the Mardin House. Mardin Halkevi, *Mardin* (Istanbul: Resimli Ay, 1938), 99.

112 Afsaneh Najmabadi, 'Hazards of Modernity and Morality: Women, State and Ideology in Contemporary Iran', in Deniz Kandiyoti (ed.), *Women, Islam and the State* (London: Macmillan, 1991), 66.

113 Zohreh Sullivan, 'Eluding the Feminist, Overthrowing the Modern? Transformations of Twentieth-Century Iran', in Abu-Lughod (ed.), *Remaking Women*, 236.

114 Michael Meeker, *A Nation of Empire: The Ottoman Legacy of Turkish Modernity* (Berkeley and London: University of California Press, 2002), 307; also in Hilmi Uran, *Meşrutiyet, tek Parti, çok Parti Hatıralarım 1908–1950* (Istanbul: Türkiye İş Bankası Kültür Yayınları, 2007), 188–9.

115 Interview with Mehmet Şahin, Balıkesir, 3 June 2005.

116 Asked about the Halkevi of her town, a woman recalled that 'there was shamelessness, we were not going there'. Arzu Öztürkmen, *Türkiye'de Folklor ve milliyetçilik* (Istanbul: İletişim, 1998), 69.

117 Azak, *Islam and Secularism*, 108–9.

118 Ayse Parla, 'The "Honour" of the State: Virginity Examination in Turkey', *Feminist Studies* 27:1 (2001): 66. Writing about the intersection of women, honour and the state in Egypt, Baron argues that 'family honour as an idea and set of practices was reinforced by state interventions in law, hygiene, education'. Beth Baron, 'Women, Honour, and the State: Evidence from Egypt', *MES* 42:1 (2006): 15.

119 In a very exceptional case, Tütüncü Mümin denounced his own wife (21 September 1940, BCA, 490.01/824.260.1): 'A young and beautiful woman is employed by the Nazilli Halkevi; she is known as a prostitute and her duty in the Halkevi is no other than to act as an instrument of pleasure for the chairman and secretary [...] This is my wife.'

120 Berktay argues that with regard to women the discourses of Kemalism and conservative patriarchy were quite homologous. The 'good-moral woman' of the conservative intellectual Peyami Safa shares the same characteristics as the ideal Kemalist woman, i.e. self-sacrifice and the 'double load' of domestic and social duty. Berktay, 'Doğu ile Batı'nın Birleştiği Yer', 284.

121 Deniz Kandiyoti, 'Women and the Turkish State: Political Actors or Symbolic Pawns?', in Niva Yuval-Davis and Floya Anthias (eds), *Women–Nation–State* (London: MacMillan, 1989), 143.

Chapter 6: People's Houses in the Countryside

1   A village(r) teacher who became very famous in the 1950s with
    his autobiographical book *Bizim Köy*, translated into English was
    Mahmut Makal, *A Village in Anatolia* (London: Vallentine Mitchell,
    1954).

2   Mahmut Makal, *Köye gidenler* (Istanbul: İnkılâp ve Aka, 1965), 70.

3   In Kudret's *Havada Bulut Yok*, the city poor in Kayseri did not know
    what the Halkevi was. Others considered the House a shameful place as
    we have seen in numerous complaint letters. See also Arzu Öztürkmen,
    Türkiye'de Folklor ve milliyetçilik (Istanbul: İletişim, 1998), 69.

4   Hıfzı Veldet Velidedeoğlu, *Anıların izinde* (Istanbul: Remzi, 1977–9),
    336. Kemal Karpat, 'The People's Houses in Turkey: establishment
    and growth', *Middle Eastern Journal* 17 (1963): 66; İlhan Başgöz
    and Howard Wilson, *Educational problems in Turkey 1920–1940*
    (Bloomington: Indiana University Press, 1968), 157; Donald Webster,
    The Turkey of Atatürk: Social Process in the Turkish Reformation
    (Philadelphia: American Academy of Political and Social Science,
    1939), 191; Mehmet Asım Karaömerlioğlu, 'The People's Houses and
    the Cult of the Peasant in Turkey', *MES* 34:4 (1998): 87.

5   İsmayıl Hakkı Baltacıoğlu, *Halkın Evi* (Ankara: Ulus, 1950), 20–8. See
    Chapter 1 for a more thorough presentation of the concept of people's
    education.

6   Ramazan Kaplan, *Cumhuriyet Dönemi Türk Romanında Köy* (Ankara:
    Akçağ, 1997), 33–63; Carole Rathbun, *The Village in the Turkish Novel
    and Short Story 1920 to 1955* (The Hague and Paris: Mouton, 1972),
    18–22; Mehmet Asım Karaömerlioğlu, 'The Peasants in Early Turkish
    Literature', *East European Quarterly* 36:2 (2002).

7   *CHFHT*, § 57–61.

8   Some examples include Ankara Halkevi, *Ankara Halkevi köycüler şübesi
    talimatnamesi* (Ankara: n.p., 1932); Tevfik Kılınçarslan, *Köy kütüğü*
    CHP Ankara Halkevi Büyük boy no. 25, Köycülük Şubesi (Ankara:
    n.p., 1939); Salahaddin Demirkan, *Köy nasıl tetkik edilmelidir?*,
    Istanbul Eminönü Halkevi Dil ve Edebiyat şubesi Neşriyatı: XX
    (Istanbul: Kültür, 1942); 'Ankara Halkevi Köycüler kolunun çalışması',
    Ülkü 4:24 (February 1935): 465; Salim Gündoğan, *Köycülük ve Köy
    Davası hakkında bir etüd. Aydın Halkevi Neşriyatından 25, Köycülük
    Şübesi* (Aydın: CHP Basımevi Raif Aydoğlu, 1944). See also Nusret
    Kemal, *Köycülük Rehperi* (Ankara: Çankaya, 1934), a compendium of
    most of his articles in *Ülkü*. For an elaborate reading of the regime's
    peasantist discourse in the 1930s, see Mehmet Asım Karaömerlioğlu,
    'The People's Houses and the Cult of the Peasant in Turkey', *MES* 34:4
    (1998).

9   'Köy Anketi', *Ülkü* 1:6 (June 1933): 362–4.

10 For instance, Dr Zeki Nasır, 'Köylerimizin sağlık işleri', *Ülkü* 2:5 (August 1933): 42-5; Salahattin Kandemir, 'Coğrafya bakımından köy', *Ülkü* 3:14 (April 1934): 153-60.

11 Kılıçarslan, *Köy kütüğü*, 1-47. For a similar plan of village research, see Kemal, *Köycülük Rehperi*, the part entitled 'Köyü nasıl tanımalı' (How the village should be known), 6-18.

12 CHP Kütahya Halkevi Köycülük Şuğbesi, *Köycünün defteri* (Kütahya: İl Basımevi, n.d.).

13 Demirkan, *Köy nasıl tetkik edilmelidir?*, 5.

14 Timothy Mitchell, *Rule of Experts. Egypt, Techno-Politics, Modernity* (Berkley and Los Angeles: University of California Press, 2002), 144.

15 Uluğ İğdemir, *Yılların içinde* (Ankara: Türk Tarih Kurumu, 1976), 292.

16 *Köylü Bilgi Cemiyeti esas nizamnamesi* (Istanbul, 1335 (1919)).

17 For de Certeau (Michel de Certeau, *The Practices of Everyday Life* (Los Angeles: University of California Press, 1988), 35-7), strategy is 'the calculation (or manipulation) of power relationships that becomes possible as soon as a subject with will and power (a business, an army, a city, a scientific institution) can be isolated. It postulates a *place* that can be delimited as its own and serve as the base from which relations with an *exteriority* composed of targets or threats can be managed. It would be also correct to recognize in these strategies a specific kind of knowledge, one sustained and determined by the power to provide oneself with its own place.' Italics in original.

18 Atatürk used this expression as early as 1922 at his inaugural address to the National Assembly. Sabri Akural, 'Kemalist Views on Social Change', in Jacob Landau (ed.), *Atatürk and the Modernization of Turkey* (Boulder, CO: Westview, 1984), 137.

19 In Egypt in the early twentieth century, the elites' images of the villager were transformed in a very similar way: from an object to be despised, the Egyptian villager 'emerged as a potent emblem of national identity'. Samah Selim, *The Novel and the Rural Imaginary in Egypt, 1880-1985* (New York and London: Routledge, 2004), 1.

20 Necmettin Çalışkan, *Kuruluşundan Günümüze Kayseri Belediyesi* (Kayseri: Kayseri Büyükşehir Belediyesi Kültür Yayınları, 1995), 17.

21 'Yeni Valimiz geldi', *Kayseri*, 3 September 1936, 1; Tavlusun village excursion, see 'Köy Gezintisi', *Kayseri*, 22 October 1936, 1.

22 'Germir gezintisi', *Kayseri*, 9 November 1936; 'Mimar Sinan gezintisi', *Kayseri*, 16 November 1936; 'Endürük köyünün kalkınması', *Kayseri*, 14 June 1937; 'Kıranardı köy Gezisi', *Kayseri*, 6 September 1937. Also see visits to Argıncık (22 November 1936) and Zencidere (13 December 1936) in governor's reports no. 4533/201 (8 December 1936) and no. 4741/214 (28 December 1936) to the Prime Minister, BCA, 030.10/199.360.16, and Kâzım Özdoğan, *Kayseri İlbay Adli Bayman Başkanlığı altında Yapılan Yaya Köy Gezileri Tetkik Notları, seri 4:*

Argıncık Köyü (Kayseri: Vilayet Matbaası, 1937). For excursions to Erkilet (21 November 1937), Molu (31 October 1937), Karahüyük (19 February 1938), Anbar (12 December 1937), Yamula (8 May 1938) and Ağırnas (15 May 1938), see Bayman's reports, BCA, 490.01/837.310.2.

23 Bayman (26 April 1937), BCA, 490.01/ 837.310.2.

24 Second biannual activities report of 1937 by the section's chairman, Fahri Tümer (28 January 1938), BCA, 490.01/837.310.2. For an almost identical description of a village excursion to Gesi before the arrival of Bayman, see 'Halkevi'nin Gesi Nahiyesine bir Gezi', *Kayseri*, 8 June 1936.

25 Kazım Özdoğan, *Kayseri Halkevi'nin Tertip Ettiği Yaya Köy Gezileri Tetkik Notları, Seri 2: Germir Köyü* (Kayseri: Vilayet Matbaası, 1937), 15.

26 The exact same people were mentioned in two other brochures of the Kayseri Halkevi. The women were again the same wives and daughters of the same state and Party officials. The male peasantists were also largely the same. Kazım Özdoğan, *Yaya Köy Gezileri Tetkik Notları, Seri 3: Mimarsinan Köyü* (Kayseri: Vilayet Matbaası, 1937), 13, and *Argıncık Köyü*, 41.

27 Mitchell has noted that similar notions and images of the exotic, child-like villager residing in nature and lacking education and culture abound in peasantist studies about the Egyptian villager. Mitchell, *Rule of Experts*, 127 ff.

28 Report no. 1177 (13 January 1937), BCA, 490.01/837.310.2. Bayman also sent copies of the same reports to the Prime Minister, BCA, 030.10/199.360.16.

29 Report no. 1046 (19 November 1936), BCA, 490.01/837.310.2.

30 The teacher Kazım Özdoğan spoke about Mimar Sinan, the famous Ottoman architect. The reasons why the villagers had to be enlightened about the name of their own village was that the village's name had just been changed to Mimar Sinan a year before, in 1935.

31 A few months prior to Bayman's appointment to Kayseri, the cooperation of Party and government was strengthened, with the June 1936 declaration of the Prime Minister İsmet İnönü, in accordance with which the Interior Minister also became Party General Secretary, and provincial governors became the heads of the provincial Party. Cemil Koçak, 'CHP-devlet kaynaşması (1936)', *Toplumsal Tarih* 118 (2003).

32 I could only locate three, about the villages of Germir, Mimarsinan and Argıncık.

33 F. Tümer, 'Hisarcık köyü', *Erciyes* 1 (March 1938): 27–30, and 'Hacılar köyü', *Erciyes* 4 (June 1938): 122–6.

34 Özdoğan, *Germir Köyü*.

35 Nevzat Yücel, Kemal Karamete, Hayri Özdemir and Melahat Erkmen. Melahat's husband was teacher Ekrem, chairman of the Library and

Publication section in 1940, and who probably participated in the excursion. BCA, 490.01/671.263.1, report no. 42 (3 March 1940) by Party Inspector Hilmi Çoruh.

36   M. Kılnamaz, 'Erkilet Gezisi', *Kayseri*, 1 February 1940, 1.

37   Sahir Üzel, 'Köy Gezileri intibalarından. İki asrı birbirine bağlıyan 130luk bir ihtiyar', *Erciyes* 6–8 (1938): 187.

38   The exotic and orientalist images of villagers and villages in Halkevi publications have also been noted by Öztürkmen, *Folklor ve Milliyetçilik*, 107–8.

39   Öztürkmen has also noticed similar romantic descriptions and the absence of the villager and of his/her voice in village studies from various Halkevi journals. Öztürkmen, *Folklor ve Milliyetçilik*, 125–7. The early Turkish cinema also offers similar romantic perceptions of villagers and village life. Levent Cantek, *Şehre Göçen Eşek: Popüler Kültür, Mizah ve Tarih* (Istanbul: İletişim, 2011), 266–9.

40   Both quotations from Özdoğan, *Mimarsinan Köyü*.

41   Ibid., 16.

42   Bureaucrat, intellectual and teacher, Kansu (1890–1949) published extensively on education. He was an MP from 1927 until his death in 1949, chairman of the Halkevi of Ankara and editor of its journal, *Ülkü*. Kansu also assumed several positions inside the Party bureaucracy.

43   Communiqué no. 1123 (17 February 1938) in *Tebligat*, vol. 12 (Ankara: Ulus, 1938), 18.

44   BCA, 490.01/837.310.2. Emphasis added.

45   Letter no. 1453 (26 April 1937), BCA, 490.01/837.310.2.

46   No. 5/1513 (10 May 1937), BCA, 490.01/837.310.2.

47   The Halkevi of Ankara was administered directly by the Party General Secretariat. Its publications and journal *Ülkü* gave guidelines on Halkevi activities.

48   Behçet Kemal Çağlar, 'Halkevleri Haberleri', *Ülkü* 9:51 (May 1937): 220. The subsequent issue also praised the Kayseri Halkevi's Sunday village excursions 'we read in the Halkevi's reports'. Behçet Kemal Çağlar, 'Halkevleri Haberleri', *Ülkü* 9:53 (July 1937): 388.

49   Articles series 'Halkevleri Dergileri' and 'Halkevleri Mecmuaları' in 1935–7, and 'Halkevleri Haberleri' in 1937–8. Quotes from 'Halkevleri Dergilerine Aylık Bakış', *Ülkü* 7:37 (March 1936): 77–8; 'Halkevleri Dergileri', *Ülkü* 6:33 (October 1935): 238.

50   Hürrem Arman, *Piramidin tabanı. Köy Enstitüleri ve Tonguç* (Ankara: Arkın Kitabevi, 1969).

51   Quoted in Karaömerlioğlu, 'The People's Houses and the Cult of the Peasant', 72.

52   For Kudret's short biography and information about his time in Kayseri, see Chapter 2.

53   The People's Rooms were established in 1940 as an extension of the People's Houses in villages. By the time of their abolition in 1950, almost 5,000 People's Rooms had been established. For their by-laws, see 'Halkodaları', *Ülkü* 14:79 (September 1939): 78–80.

54   Listening to complaints and receiving petitions and grievances was traditionally one of the Sultan's and state officials' obligations, as well as a tool to legitimize their authority. Halil İnalcık, 'Şikayet Hakkı: "Arz-ı Hal ve Arz-ı Mahzar'lar"', *Osmanlı Araştırmaları* 7–8 (1988): 33. During the single-party period, especially after the 1931 Party Congress, the management of petitions and grievances was meticulously organized and assumed a great significance due to the apparent lack of information from below but also because Party leaders saw it as a demonstration of the regime's democratic credentials. Tuncay Dursun, *Tek Parti Dönemindeki Cumhuriyet Halk Partisi Büyük Kurultayları* (Ankara: Kültür Bakanlığı, 2002), 24–5.

55   Cevdet Kudret, *Havada Bulut Yok* (Istanbul: İnkılap ve Aka, 1976), 108–11.

56   For a critique of the superficiality of village excursions in contemporary popular novels by Halkevi members, see Mükerrem Su, *İnandığım Allah* (Istanbul: Inkilâp, 1946), 33, quoted in Cantek, *Şehre Göçen Eşek*, 268. For a critique of the superficiality of the excursions products, i.e. village monographs, see Mediha Esenel, *Geç Kalmış Kitap. 1940'lı Yıllarda Anadolu Köylerinde Araştırmalar ve Yaşadığım Çevreden İzlenimler* (Istanbul: Sistem, 1999), 85–9, quoting from her article 'Genel Kanılardan gerçekçi gözlemlere', *Yurt ve Dünya* 1 (1941).

57   Lilo Linke, *Allah Dethroned. A Journey through Modern Turkey* (London: Constable & Co, 1937), 174.

58   Discussing the people's complaints in his reports of 8 August 1945, the Party Inspector Recai Güreli referred to the villagers' suffering at the hands of the gendarmes. BCA, 490.01/624.51.1.

59   Letter of Faik Barım, chairman of the House of Ayvalık (16 September 1942), BCA, 490.01/825.265.2, where he informed the Party of his intention to have some villagers brought by gendarmes to play music for the visiting Halkevi Inspector Adnan Saygun.

60   Özgür Balkılıç, 'Kemalist Views and Works on Turkish Folklore and Music during the Early Republican Period', unpublished MA thesis (Ankara: METU, 2005), 129–31.

61   Following villagers' requests, the teacher of the village of Çıtak in Denizli (24 April 1945, BCA, 490.01/831.281.1) complained of the customary and enforced carrying of the village's musical group by gendarmes to perform in the sub-district, as ordered by the Halkevi chairman and the town's mayor. In its reply to the teacher on 5 May 1945 (BCA, 490.01/831.281.1), the Party did not show the same sympathy for the coerced villagers: 'the calling of village musicians to the town to perform on national holidays is right and must be considered positively

because the happenings organized in the town become more national and more lively'. The Party turned a deaf ear to the use of force: 'it can be investigated by the responsible local authorities', in other words the local police, the very same people accused of using force.

62	Examples include 'The people of the village have robust and healthy bodies'; 'The people have big bodies, are sturdy, brave and hard working'; 'There is not even one weak among them.'

63	Naci Kum, 'Bir köy gezisinden örnek', Kayseri, 11 May 1939, 1.

64	'Our villages are valuable treasuries that have to be studied'; 'These two Turkish women are a valuable history to be read.'

65	Üzel, 'İki asrı', 189.

66	Karaömerlioğlu, 'The Peasants in Early Turkish Literature', passim.

67	Tümer, 'Hacılar köyü', 124.

68	CHP Kayseri İli 934-935 yılları Kongre dilekleri ve sonuçları (Kayseri: Yeni Basımevi, 1936); Kayseri ili içinde 934, 935, 936 ve 937 yıllarında arzedilmiş olan CHP nin kongrelerinde serdedilen dileklerin kovalama ve bitimleri (Kayseri: Vilayet matbaası, 1938). Requests from villages were by and large what the RPP elites would also condone: road construction, school buildings, telephone lines and the dispatching of teachers. Nevertheless, more sensitive issues were voiced: abolition or exception from forced labour; donation of seed; abolition of village scribes; lowering of the price of sugar and salt; payment of debts to the Agricultural Bank in instalments; the lowering of animal taxes; and the price of electricity. For the villagers' fear of the village clerks, see also Makal, A Village, 139-40.

69	After all they were compiled by local Party elites for the eyes of the supervising authority, the Party centre. Tunçay has argued that the published requests of Party Congresses were by and large expressing the demands and interests of provincial elites. Mete Tunçay, 'CHF'nın 1927 Kurultayının Öncesinde Toplanan İl Kongreleri', Siyasal Bilgiler Fakültesi Dergisi 36 (1981): 281-333.

70	The unintelligibility of the two languages, the one spoken by peasantists and the other by villagers, is mentioned by one of the pioneering peasantists in the 1930s in Turkey, Nusret Kemal Köymen, 'Köycülüğün daha verimli olması hakkında', Ülkü 13:73 (March 1939): 27. On the difference of the language spoken by peasantists and villagers, see also Esenel, 99.

71	Üzel, 'İki asrı', 189-90.

72	For Öztürkmen village studies contain the peasantists' voices not the peasant's. Öztürkmen, Folklor ve Milliyetçilik, 125-6.

73	This is very much in line with the modernist elite's discourses and images of the people as passive and naïve objects or children. Tezcan Durna, Kemalist Modernleşme ve Seçkincilik. Peyami Safa ve Falih Rıfkı Atay'da Halkın İnşası (Ankara: Dipnot, 2009), 138-45; Tanıl Bora and

Murat Gültekingil (eds), *Modern Türkiye'de Siyasi Düşünce*, vol. 3: *Modernleşme ve Batıcılık* (Istanbul: İletişim, 2002), 637–9.

74 Cantek, *Şehre Göçen Eşek*, 266–9.

75 Ibid., 266 ff.

76 Niyazi Berkes writes that Sabahattin Ali wrote a short story based on a real event Berkes had told him about. Niyazi Berkes, 'Kişisel anılar', in Filiz Ali Laslo and Atilla Özkırımlı (eds), *Sabahattin Ali* (Istanbul: Cem, 1979), 73.

77 Karaömerlioğlu, 'The Peasants in Early Turkish Literature', 138–44.

78 Rathbun, *The Village*, passim; Yakup Çelik, 'Roman 1920–1960', in Talât Sait Halman (ed.), *Türk Edebiyatı Tarihi*, vol. 4 (Istanbul: TC Kültür ve Turizm Bakanlığı, 2006), 252–68.

79 Güzine Dino, 'The Turkish Peasant Novel, or the Anatolian Theme', *World Literature Today* 60:2 (1986): 266–76.

80 Rathbun, *The Village*, 27, 50.

81 See the letter of the Edremit Halkevi chairman, dated 16 September 1943, about the visit of Halkevi Inspector Adnan Saygun and his friend Sabahattin Ali to Edremit and their use of the local Halkevi's facilities to visit nearby villages. BCA, 490.01/825.265.2.

82 See her request for Party nomination in the 1943 national elections in BCA, 490.01/ 291.1171.4, and the letter of the Balıkesir Halkevi chairman asking for the cancellation of her appointement elsewhere. No. 225 (22 July 1938), BCA, 490.01/825.265.1.

83 Apart from working in the Halkevi library in 1941–2, Yaşar Kemal also had his compilation of popular lamentations published by the Adana Halkevi: Kemal Sadık Göğceli, *Ağıtlar* (Adana: Türk Sözü, 1943).

84 Examples of village sociology include Niyazi Berkes, *Bazı Ankara Köyleri üzerine bir araştırma* (Ankara: n.p., 1942); Nermin Erdentuğ, *Hal köyünün etnolojik tetkiki* (Ankara: Türk Tarih Kurumu, 1956); İbrahim Yasa, *Hasanoğlan köyü* (Ankara: Doğuş, 1950). For a detailed bibliography, see Joseph Styliowicz, *Political Change in Rural Turkey. Erdemli* (Paris and The Hague: Mouton, 1966), 204–13.

85 Refik and Ziya, 'Bursa'nın Keles Köyü', *Ülkü* 3:15 (May 1934): 234–40. For a similar village study that criticized civil servants cf. Muallimi Nuri, 'Kütahya'da Alayund Köyü', *Ülkü* 2:8 (September 1933): 151–8.

86 The governor even did research to learn that the authors were the sons of two local peasants who were studying in the Agricultural Institute in Ankara: 'Keles Köyüne dair Bursa Valiliğinin bir Tavzihi', *Ülkü* 4:21 (November 1934): 238–40.

87 The single-party regime was not aiming at any major transformation of social relations in the countryside. Rather, 'the impetus for the transformation of rural life was believed to be in the struggle against nature, not in the struggle with social relations against surrounding

the peasants': Mehmet Asım Karaömerlioğlu, 'The Village Institute Experience in Turkey', *BJMES* 25 (1998): 63.

88 Başgöz described the Halkevi village activities as a complete failure. Başgöz and Wilson, *Educational problems in Turkey*, 156.

89 Between 1935 and 1941 at least 5,000 village excursions were reported. Sefa Şimşek, *Bir ideolojik seferberlik deneyimi, Halkevleri 1932-1951* (Istanbul: Boğaziçi Üniversitesi, 2002), 265. In 1935, only 495 excursions with 21,000 participants were reported: 'N. Kansu'nun Halkevleri hakkında söylevi', *Ülkü* 7:37 (March 1936): 7.

90 Özacun offers a rich catalogue of books published by the Houses and Party. A rather large part is related to villages and villagers. Orhan Özacun, *CHP Bibliografya denemesi* (Istanbul: n.p., 1993).

91 On Halkevi publications, see Kemal Karpat, 'The impact of People's Houses on the development of communication in Turkey 1931-1951', *Die Welt des Islams* 15 (1974); on Halkevi journals, see Nurettin Güz, *Tek parti ideolojisinin yayın organları: Halkevleri dergileri 1932-1950* (Ankara: Bilge Yapım, 1995).

92 I draw from de Certeau's study of the emergence of popular literature studies in nineteenth-century France. De Certeau, Julia and Revel argued that 'studies devoted to this sort of literature were made possible by the act of removing it from the people's reach and reserving it for the use of scholars and amateurs'. Michel De Certeau, Dominique Julia and Jacques Revel, 'The Beauty of the Dead: Nisard', in de Certeau, *Heterologies: Discourses on the Other* (Minneapolis: University of Minnesota Press, 2000), 119.

93 Karaömerlioğlu has also referred to the impact of peasantist ideology on the intellectuals in the 1930s. Karaömerlioğlu, 'The People's Houses and the Cult of the Peasant', 72. I am more interested in the impact of peasantist ideas *and practice* on the intellectuals of the era.

94 Fredrik Barth, 'Introduction', in Fredrik Barth (ed.), *Ethnic Groups and Boundaries. The Social Organization of Culture Difference* (Boston, MA: Little, Brown and Company, 1970). For a concise presentation of Barth's arguments, see 'Introduction', in Hans Vermeulen and Cora Govers (eds), *The Anthropology of Ethnicity. Beyond 'Ethnic Groups and Boundaries'* (Amsterdam: Het Spinhuis, 1994), 1.

95 Deniz Kandiyoti, 'Gendering the Modern. On Missing Dimensions in the Study of the Turkish Modernity', in Sibel Bozdoğan and Reşat Kasaba (eds), *Rethinking Modernity and National Identity in Turkey* (Seattle and London: University of Washington Press, 1997), 126-8. Also see the previous chapter for cases of habitual social and gender-based segregation in People's Houses.

96 In a similar vein, Mardin has remarked that 'the modernization of media and of cultural life in Turkey generally increased, rather than decreased, the gap between the "little" (periphery, society) and the "great" (state,

centre, bureaucracy) culture'. Şerif Mardin, 'Center–Periphery Relations: A Key to Turkish Politics?', *Daudelus* (Winter 1972/73): 179.

97   Mediha Esenel, 'Genel Kanılardan gerçekçi gözlemlere', *Yurt ve Dünya* 1:1 (1941), quoted in Esenel, *Geç Kalmış Kitap. 1940'lı Yıllarda Anadolu Köylerinde Araştırmalar ve Yaşadığım Çevreden İzlenimler* (Istanbul: Sistem, 1999), 85–9. See also Meltem Ağduk Gevrek, 'Yurt ve Dünya', *Toplum ve Bilim* 78 (1998): 255–6.

Chapter 7: Conclusions

1   İsmet İnönü *Hatıralarım. Genç Subay'ın Yılları 1884–1918* (Istanbul: Burçak, 1969), 112.

2   Metin Heper, *İsmet İnönü: The making of a Turkish Stateman* (Leiden: Brill, 1998), 78–81, 100. Andrew Mango, *Atatürk* (London: John Murray, 1999), 466.

3   Michel de Certeau, *The Practices of Everyday Life* (Los Angeles: University of California Press, 1988), xv–xviii.

4   George Marcus, 'Contemporary Problems of Ethnography in the Modern World System', in James Clifford and George Marcus (eds), *Writing Culture. The Poetics and Politics of Ethnography* (Berkley: University of California Press, 1986), 171–2.

5   Michael Meeker, *A Nation of Empire: The Ottoman Legacy of Turkish Modernity* (Berkeley and London: University of California Press, 2002) xxii and Chapter 6.

6   Nicole F. Watts, 'Re-Considering State–Society Dynamics in Turkey's Kurdish Southeast', *EJTS* 10 (Online) (2009). First published electronically on 31 December 2009. (Last accessed 14 March 2014). URL: http://ejts.revues.org/4196; Senem Aslan, 'Everyday Forms of State Power and the Kurds in the Early Turkish Republic', *IJMES* 43:1 (2011); Ceren Belge, 'State Building and the Limits of Legibility: Kinship Networks and Kurdish Resistance in Turkey', *IJMES* 43:1 (2011).

Bibliography

Archival Sources

Prime Minister Archives of the Republic of Turkey, Republican Period, BCA (TC Başbakanlık Devlet Arşivleri, Cumhuriyet Arşivi):

Bakanlar Kurulu Kararları 1920–44 (Decisions of Council of Ministers 1920–44): BCA, 030.18.11.

Bakanlıklar Arası Tayin Daire Başkanlığı (Inter-ministerial Department of Appointments): BCA, 030.11.1.

Cumhuriyet Halk Partisi (Republican People's Party): BCA, 490.01.

Muamelat Genel Müdürlüğü (Prime Minister General Secretariat): BCA, 030.10.

Newspapers and Periodicals

Alkım (Balıkesir Lisesi Dergisi).
Balıkesir (1933–34).
Erciyes.
Kaynak.
Kayseri (1936–7).
Türk Dili (1933–4).
Savaş (1934).
Ülkü.

Books and Articles

Abrahams, Philip, 'Notes on the Difficulty of Studying the State', *Journal of Historical Sociology* 1 (1988): 58–89.

Abu-Lughod, Lila (ed.), *Remaking Women: Feminism and Modernity in the Middle East* (Princeton, NJ: Princeton University Press, 1998).

Açıkel, Fethi, "'Kutsal mazlumluğun' psikopatolojisi'", *Toplum ve Bilim* 70 (Fall 1996): 153–99.

Ahıska, Meltem, 'Occidentalism: The Historical Fantasy of the Modern', *South Atlantic Quarterly* 102:2/3 (2003): 351–79.

—— Radyonun Sihirli Kapısı. Garbiyatçılık ve Politik Öznellik (Istanbul: Metis, 2005).

—— Occidentalism in Turkey. Questions of Modernity and National Identity in Turkish Radio Broadcasting (London: I.B.Tauris, 2010).

Ahmet Şerif, Anadolu'da Tanin (Istanbul: Kavram, 1977).

Akekmekçi, Tuba and Pervan Muazzez (eds), 'Doğu Sorunu' Necmeddin Sahir Sılan Raporları 1939–1953 (Istanbul: Tarih Vakfı Yurt Yayınları, 2010).

Akın, Rıdvan, Osmanlı İmparatorluğu'nun Dağılma Devri ve Türkçülük Hareketi 1908–1918 (Istanbul: Der, 2002).

Akın, Yiğit, 'Fazilet değil vazife istiyoruz: Erken Cumhuriyet Dönemi sosyal tarihçiliğinde dilekçeler', Toplum ve Bilim 99 (2003/2004): 98–128.

—— 'Gürbüz ve Yavuz Evlatlar' Erken Cumhuriyet'te Beden Terbiyesi ve Spor (Istanbul: İletişim, 2004).

—— 'Reconsidering State, Party, and Society in early Republican Turkey: Politics of Petitioning', IJMES 39:3 (2007): 435–57.

Akkuş, Mine, 'II. Meşrutiyet'in Yörel Düzlemde yansımalarına bir örnek: Bursa', in Sina Akşin et al. (eds), 100. Yılında Jön Türk Devrimi (Istanbul: İş Bankası Kültür Yayınları, 2010).

Akmeşe, Handan Nezir, The Birth of Modern Turkey. The Ottoman Military and the March to World War I (London: I.B.Tauris, 2005).

Akşin, Sina, Jön Türkler ve İttihat ve Terakki (Ankara: İmge, 2001).

Akşin, Sina, Sarp Balcı and Barış Ünlü (eds), 100. Yılında Jön Türk Devrimi (Istanbul: İş Bankası Kültür Yayınları, 2010).

Aktar, Yücel, İkinci Meşrutiyet Dönemi Öğrenci Olayları 1908–1918 (Istanbul: İletişim, 1990).

Akural, Sabri, 'Kemalist Views on Social Change', in Jacob Landau (ed.), Atatürk and the Modernization of Turkey (Boulder, CO: Westview, 1984).

Akyüz, Yahya, Türkiye'de öğretmenlerin toplumsal değişmedeki etkileri 1848–1940 (Ankara: Doğan, 1978).

Alçıtepe, A. Galip, 'Dranaz Sinop Halkevi dergisi bibliyografyası', Kebikeç 12 (2001).

Altunya, Niyazi, Türkiye'de öğretmen örgütlenmesi 1908–1998 (Ankara: Ürün, 1998).

Anastasopoulos, Antonis (ed.), Provincial elites in the Ottoman Empire, Halcyon Days in Crete V. A Symposium Held in Rethymnon, 10–12 January 2003 (Rethymnon: Crete University Press, 2005).

And, Metin, A History of Theatre and Popular Entertainment in Turkey (Ankara: Forum, 1963–4).

—— Meşrutiyet döneminde Türk Tiyatrosu (Ankara: Türkiye İş Bankası Kültür Yayınları, 1971).

—— Türk Tiyatrosunun Evreleri (Ankara: Turhan, 1983).

Arai, Masami, Turkish Nationalism in the Young Turk Era (Leiden: Brill, 1992).

Arat, Zehra, Deconstructing Images of 'the Turkish Woman' (New York: Palgrave, 1999).

Arat Kabasakal, Zehra, 'Where to look for the truth: Memory and Interpretation in Assessing the Impact of Turkish Women's Education', *Women's Studies International Forum* 26:1 (2003): 57–68.

Ari, Eyal, 'The People's houses and the Theatre in Turkey', *MES* 40:4 (2004): 32–58.

Arman, Hürrem, *Piramidin tabanı*. *Köy Enstitüleri ve Tonguç* (Ankara: Arkın Kitabevi, 1969).

Arslan, Ali, *Darülfünün' dan Üniversiteye* (Istanbul: Kitabevi, 1995).

Aslan, Necla, 'Bursa Halkevi Uludağ Dergisi ve Türk Devrimi', unpublished MA thesis (Istanbul: İstanbul University, 2007).

Aslan, Senem, 'Incoherent State: The Controversy over Kurdish Naming in Turkey', *EJTS* 10 (Online) (2009). First published electronically on 29 December 2009. (Last accessed 14 March 2014). URL: http://ejts. revues.org/4142).

—— 'Everyday Forms of State Power and the Kurds in the Early Turkish Republic', *IJMES* 43:1 (2011): 75–93.

Atabaki, Touraj (ed.), *The State and Subaltern: Modernization, Society and the State in Turkey and Iran* (London: I.B.Tauris, 2007).

Atatürk ve Halkevleri: Atatürkçü düşünce üzerine denemeler (Ankara: Türk Tarih Kurumu, 1974).

Avdela, Efi, 'For reasons of honour': Violence, Sentiments, and Values in post civil-war Greece (Athens: Nefeli, 2006) (Εφη Αβδελά, «Δια λόγους τιμής»: Βία, Συναισθήματα και Αξίες στη Μετεμφυλιακή Ελλαδα (Αθήνα: Νεφέλη, 2006)).

Ayata Güneş, Ayşe, *CHP Örgüt ve İdeoloji* (Ankara: Gündoğan, 1992).

Aydın, Ertan, 'The Peculiarities of Turkish revolutionary Ideology in the 1930s: the Ülkü version of Kemalism 1933–1936', unpublished PhD thesis (Ankara: Bilkent University, 2003).

—— 'The Peculiarities of Turkish revolutionary Ideology in the 1930s: the Ülkü version of Kemalism 1933–1936', *MES* 40:5 (2004): 55–82.

Aydın, Hakan 'İttihat ve Terakki Mekteplerinin Yapısal Özellikleri Üzerine bir İnceleme', unpublished PhD thesis (Konya: Selçuk University, 2008).

—— (ed.), *İkinci Meşrutiyet Devrinde Basın ve Siyaset* (Konya: Palet, 2010).

Aydın, Suavi, 'Türk tarih tezi ve halkevleri', *Kebikeç* 3 (1996): 107–30.

Aydın, Suavi, Kudret Emiroğlu, Oktay Özel and Süha Ünsal, *Mardin. Aşiret-Cemaat-Devlet* (Istanbul: Tarih Vakfı Yurt Yayınları, 2000).

Ayhan, Aydın, 'Esat Adil Müstecablıoğlu'nun ilk yazıları', 3rd part, 18/19, *Yeni Haber* (1995).

Azak, Umut, *Islam and Secularism in Turkey: Kemalism, Religion and the Nation State* (London: I.B.Tauris, 2010).

Azcan, Ibrahim, *Türk modernleşmesi sürecinde Trabzon Halkevi* (Istanbul: Serarder, 2003).

Bali, Rıfat, *Cumhuriyet Yıllarında Türkiye Yahudileri: Bir Türkleştirme Serüveni 1923–1945* (Istanbul: İletişim, 2005).

Balıkesir Halkevi, *Sekiz ayda nasıl çalıştı ve neler yaptı* (Balıkesir: Balıkesir Vilayet Matbaası, n.d.).

Balıkesir Şehir Kulübü Nizamnamesi (Balıkesir: Türk Pazarı Matbaası, 1934).

Balkılıç, Özgür, 'Kemalist Views and Works on Turkish Folklore and Music during the Early Republican Period', unpublished MA thesis (Ankara: METU, 2005).

Baltacıoğlu, İsmayıl Hakkı, *Halkın Evi* (Ankara: Ulus, 1950).

Baron, Beth, *Egypt as a Woman: Nationalism, Gender, and Politics* (Berkley: University of California Press, 2005).

Barth, Fredrik, 'Introduction', in Fredrik Barth (ed.), *Ethnic Groups and Boundaries. The Social Organization of Culture Difference* (Boston, MA: Little, Brown and Company, 1970).

Başar, Ahmet Hamdi, *Atatürk ile üç ay ve 1930 dan sonra Türkiye* (Ankara: Ankara İktisadi ve Ticari İlimler Akademisi, 1981).

Başgöz, İlhan and Howard Wilson, *Educational problems in Turkey 1920–1940* (Bloomington: Indiana University Press, 1968).

Başvekalet istatistik umum müdürlüğü, *Maarif istatistikleri 1923–1932* (Istanbul: Devlet matbaası, 1933).

—— *Vilayet Hususi İdareleri 1929–1936. Faaliyeti istatistiği. Varidat, masrifat, memurlar* (Ankara: Receb Ulusoğlu, 1938).

Baykurt, Fakir, *Köy Enstitülü Delikanlı* (Istanbul: Papirüs, 1999).

Belge, Ceren, 'State Building and the Limits of Legibility: Kinship Networks and Kurdish Resistance in Turkey', *IJMES* 43:1 (2011): 95–114.

Berkes, Niyazi, *Bazı Ankara Köyleri üzerine bir araştırma* (Ankara: Uzluk, 1942).

—— *Turkish Nationalism and Western Civilization. Selected Essays of Ziya Gokalp* (New York: Columbia University Press, 1959).

Berktay, Fatmagül, 'Osmanlı'dan Cumhuriyet'e Feminizm', in Tanıl Bora and Murat Gültekingil (eds), *Modern Türkiye'de Siyasi Düşünce*, vol. 1: *Tanzimat ve Meşrutiyet'in Birikimi* (Istanbul: İletişim, 2001).

—— 'Doğu ile Batı'nın Birleştiği Yer: Kadın imgesinin Kurgulanışı', in Tanıl Bora and Murat Gültekingil (eds), *Modern Türkiye'de Siyasi Düşünce*, vol. 3: *Modernleşme ve Batıcılık* (Istanbul: İletişim, 2002).

Berman, Bruce and John Lonsdale, *Unhappy Valley* (London: James Currey, 1992).

Beysanoğlu, Şevket, 'Anılarımda Diyarbakır Halkevi', *Kebikeç* 3 (1996): 161–7.

Bilgin, Çelik, 'Tek Parti döneminde Aydın'ın Sosyokültürel Yaşamında Halkevinin rolü', *Toplumsal Tarih* 66 (1999): 39–48.

Bora, Tanıl and Necmi Erdoğan, '"Biz, Anadolu'nun Bağrı Yanık Çocukları": Muhafazakâr Populizm', in Tanıl Bora and Murat Gültekingil (eds), *Modern Türkiye'de Siyasi Düşünce*, vol. 5: *Muhafazakârlık* (Istanbul: İletişim, 2006).

Bora, Tanıl and Murat Gültekingil (eds), *Modern Türkiye'de Siyasi Düşünce*, vol. 7: *Liberalizm* (Istanbul: İletişim, 2005).

Bozdoğan, Sibel and Reşat Kasaba (eds), *Rethinking Modernity and National Identity in Turkey* (Seattle and London: University of Washington Press, 1997).

Brockett, D. Gavin, 'Collective Action and the Turkish Revolution: Towards a Framework for the Social History of the Atatrk Era, 1923–1938', *MES* 34:4 (1998): 44–66.

Cagaptay, Soner, 'Race, Assimilation and Kemalism: Turkish Nationalism and the Minorities in the 1930s', *MES* 40:3 (2004): 86–101.

—— *Islam, Secularism, and Nationalism in Modern Turkey. Who is a Turk?* (London and New York: Routledge, 2006).

Çakal, Işıl, *Konuşunuz Konuşturunuz. Tek Parti Döneminde Propagandanın Etkin Silahı: Söz* (Istanbul: Otopsi, 2004).

Çalışkan, Necmettin, *Kuruluşundan Günümüze Kayseri Belediyesi* (Kayseri: Kayseri Büyükşehir Belediyesi Kültür Yayınları, 1995).

Cantek, Funda, *'Yaban'lar ve Yerliler. Başkent olma sürecinde Ankara* (Istanbul: İletişim, 2003).

Cantek, Levent, *Cumhuriyetin Bülüğ Çağı. Gündelik Yaşama Dair Tartışmalar 1945-1950* (Istanbul: İletişim, 2008).

—— *Şehre Göçen Eşek: Popüler Kültür, Mizah ve Tarih* (Istanbul: İletişim, 2011).

Çeçen, Anıl, *Atatürk'ün kültür kurumu Halkevleri* (Ankara: n.p., 1990).

Çelik, Yakup, 'Roman 1920-1960', in Talât Sait Halman (ed.), *Türk Edebiyatı Tarihi*, vol. 4 (Istanbul: TC Kültür ve Turizm Bakanlığı, 2006).

Certeau, Michel de, *The Practices of Everyday Life* (Los Angeles: University of California Press, 1988).

Certeau, Michel de, Dominique Julia and Jaques Revel, 'The Beauty of the Dead: Nisard', in Michel de Certeau, *Heterologies: Discourses on the Other* (Minneapolis: University of Minnesota Press, 2000).

Chakrabarty, Dipesh, *Provincializing Europe. Postcolonial Thought and Historical Difference* (Princeton, NJ, and Oxford: Princeton University Press, 2000).

CHF Üçüncü Büyük Kongre Zabıtları (Istanbul: Devlet Matbaası, 1931).

CHP VII Kurultay Tutanağı (Ankara: n.p., 1948).

CHP 18. Yıldönümünde Halkevleri ve Halkodaları (Ankara: n.p., 1950).

CHP Halkevleri çalışma talimatnamesi (Ankara: Zerbamat, 1940).

CHP Halkevleri ve Halkodaları 1932-1942 (Ankara: Alaadin, 1942).

CHP Halkevleri ve Halkodaları 1944 (Ankara: n.p., 1945).

CHP Halkevleri idare ve Teşkilat talimatnamesi (Ankara: Zerbamat, 1940).

CHP Halkevleri Yayımlarından Kılavuz Kitapları XXI, Halkevlerinde Müze, Tarih ve Folkor Çalışmaları Kılavuzu (Ankara: n.p., 1947).

CHP Kayseri İli 934-935 yılları Kongre dilekleri ve sonuçları (Kayseri: Yeni Basımevi, 1936).

CHP Kütahya Halkevi Köycülük Şuğbesi, *Köycünün defteri* (Kütahya: İl Basımevi, n.d.).

CHP Mardin Halkevi, *Mardin* (Istanbul: Resimli Ay, 1938).

CHP' nin Kayseri il kongresinde okunan geçmiş haller raporu (Kayseri: Yeni Basımevi, 1936).

CHP Teftiş Talimatnamesi (Ankara: Ulus, 1939).

CHP Teftiş Talimatnamesi (Ankara: Sümer, 1943).

CHP Teşkilatı kurulmamış Vilayetlerdeki Halkevleri ve odaları Teftiş Talimatnamesi (Ankara: Zerbamat, 1940).

CHP Yayımı Kılavuz Broşürler 2, CHP Halkevleri ve Halkodaları Türkçe Okuma ve Yazma Kursları için Kılavuz (Ankara: n.p., 1946).

CHP Yayımı Kılavuz Broşürler 3, Halkevlerinde Halk müziği ve Halk oyunları Üzerinde nasıl çalışmalı, neler yapmalı? (Ankara: n.p., 1946).

Çolak, Melek, 'Muğla Halkevi ve Çalışmaları', *Toplumsal Tarih* 73 (2000): 53–7.

Corrigan, Philip and Derek Sayer, *The Great Arch. English State Formation as Cultural Revolution* (Oxford: Basil Blackwell, 1985).

Cumhuriyet Halk Fırkası Halkevlerin Talimatnamesi (Ankara: n.p., 1932).

Cumhuriyet Halk Fırkası Katibiumumiliğinin Fırka Teşkilatına Umumi Tebligatı, vol. 1 (Ankara: n.p., 1933).

Cumhuriyet Halk Fırkası Katibiumumiliğinin Fırka Teşkilatına Umumi Tebligatı, İkinci Kanun 1933'ten Haziran nihayetine kadar, vol. 2 (Ankara: Hakimiyeti Milliye, 1933).

Cumhuriyet Halk Fırkası Katibiumumiliğinin Fırka Teşkilatına Umumi Tebligatı, Temmuz 1933'ten Birinci kanun 1933 sonuna kadar, vol. 3 (Ankara: Hakimiyeti Milliye, 1934).

Cumhuriyet Halk Fırkası Katibiumumiliğinin Fırka Teşkilatına Umumi Tebligatı, İkinci Kanun 1934'ten Haziran 1934 sonuna kadar, vol. 4 (Ankara: Hakimiyeti Milliye, 1934).

Cumhuriyet Halk Fırkası Katibiumumiliğinin Fırka Teşkilatına Umumi Tebligatı, Temmuz 1934'ten Birinci Kanun 1934 sonuna kadar, vol. 5 (Ankara: Ulus, 1935).

Cumhuriyet Halk Partisi Genel Sekreterliğin Parti örgütüne Genelgesi, İkinci Kanun 1938 den 30 Haziran 1938 tarihine kadar, vol. 12 (Ankara: Ulus, 1938).

Cumhuriyet Halk Partisi Genel Sekreterliğin Parti Teşkilatına Umumi Tebligatı, 1 Birinci Kanun 1941 den 30 Haziran 1941 tarihine kadar, vol. 18 (Ankara: Ulus, 1941).

Cumhuriyet Halk Fırkası Nizamname Projesi (Ankara: n.p., 1931).

Davies, Sarah, *Popular Opinion in Stalin's Russia. Terror, Propaganda and Dissent, 1934–1941* (Cambridge: Cambridge University Press, 1997).

Davis, Natalie Zemon, *Fiction in the Archives: Pardon Tales and Their Tellers in Sixteenth-Century France* (Cambridge: Polity Press, 1987).

Demir, Fevzi, *Osmanlı Devleti'nde II. Meşrutiyet Dönemi Meclis-i Mebusan Seçimleri 1908–1914* (Ankara: İmge 2007).

Demirdirek, Aynur, *Osmanlı Kadınlarının Hayat Hakkı Arayışının bir Hikayesi* (Ankara: Ayizi, 2011).

Demirkan, Salahaddin, *Köy nasıl tetkik edilmelidir?*, İstanbul Eminönü Halkevi Dil ve Edebiyat şubesi Neşriyatı XX (Istanbul: Kültür, 1942).

Denman Kılıç, Fatma, *İkinci Meşrutiyet Döneminde Bir Jön Türk Dergisi: Kadın* (Istanbul: Libra, 2009).

Dino, Güzine, 'The Turkish Peasant Novel, or the Anatolian Theme', *World Literature Today* 60:2 (1986): 266–76.

Doğan, Avni, *Kurtuluş, Kuruluş ve Sonrası* (Istanbul: Dünya, 1964).

Doğaner, Yasemin and Mustafa Yılmaz, *Cumhuriyet Döneminde Sansür 1923–1973* (Ankara: Siyasal, 2007).

Durakbaşa, Ayşe, 'Taşra burjuvazisinin tarihsel kökenleri', *Toplum ve Bilim* 118 (2010): 6–38.

——— 'Kemalism as Identity Politics in Turkey', in Zehra Arat (ed.), *Deconstructing Images of 'the Turkish Woman'* (New York: Palgrave, 1999).

Durakbaşa, Ayşe and Aynur İlyasoğlu, 'Formation of Gender Identities in Republican Turkey and Women's Narratives as Transmitters of "Her story" of Modernization', *Journal of Social History* 35:1 (2001): 195–203.

Durna, Tezcan, *Kemalist Modernleşme ve Seçkincilik. Peyami Safa ve Falih Rıfkı Atay'da Halkın İnşası* (Ankara: Dipnot, 2009).

Dursun, Tuncay, *Tek Parti Dönemindeki Cumhuriyet Halk Partisi Büyük Kurultayları* (Ankara: Kültür Bakanlığı, 2002).

Duru, Kazim Nami, *Cumhuriyet Devri Hatıralarım* (Istanbul: Sucuoğlu, 1958).

Emiroğlu, Kudret, *Anadolu'da Devrim Günleri: II Meşrutiyet'in İlanı* (Ankara: İmge, 1999).

——— 'Trabzon'da XIX. Yüzyıldan XX. Yüzyıla Kahvehane ve Kitabevi Bağlamında Toplumsal Tabakalanma, Kültür ve Siyaset', *Kebikeç* 10 (2000): 187–222.

Erdentuğ, Nermin, *Hal köyünün etnolojik tetkiki* (Ankara: Türk Tarih Kurumu, 1956).

Erdoğan, Necmi, 'Devleti "İdare Etmek": Maduniyet ve Düzenbazlık', *Toplum ve Bilim* 83 (2000): 8–31.

Ergen, Sinan, 'Türkiye'de halkevleri ve Elazığ örneği', unpublished MA thesis (Elazığ: Fırat University, 2007).

Ergün, Mustafa, *II Meşrutiyet Devrinde Eğitim Hareketleri 1908–1914* (Ankara: Ocak, 1996).

Ergut, Ferdan, *Modern Devlet ve Polis. Osmanlı'dan Cumhuriyet'e Toplumsal Denetimin Diyalektiği* (Istanbul: İletişim, 2004).

——— (ed.), *II. Meşrutiyet'i yeniden Düşünmek* (Istanbul: Tarih Vakfı Yurt Yayınları, 2009).

Ersanlı Behar, Büşra, *İktidar ve Tarih. Türkiye'de resmi tarih tezinin oluşumu 1929–1937* (Istanbul: Afa, 1992).

Esenel, Mediha, *Geç Kalmış Kitap. 1940'lı Yıllarda Anadolu Köylerinde Araştırmalar ve Yaşadığım Çevreden İzlenimler* (İstanbul: Sistem, 1999).

Findley, Carter Vaughn, *Turkey, Islam, Nationalism, and Modernity* (New Haven, CT, and London: Yale University Press, 2010).

Fitzpatrick, Sheila, *Stalin's Peasants. Resistance and Survival in the Russian Village after Collectivization* (Oxford: Oxford University Press, 1994).

—— 'Signals from Below: Soviet Letters of Denunciation of the 1930s', *Journal of Modern History* 68:4 (1996): 831–66.

—— 'Supplicants and Citizens: Public Letter-Writing in Soviet Russia in the 1930s', *Slavic Review* 55:1 (1996): 78–105.

Frey, Frederick, *The Turkish Political Elite* (Cambridge, MA: MIT Press, 1965).

Gaziantep Halkevi Broşürü (Gaziantep: n.p., 1935).

Gençer, Mustafa, *Jöntürk Modernizmi ve 'Alman Ruhu': 1908–1918 Dönemi Türk-Alman İlişkileri* (İstanbul: İletişim, 2003).

Georgeon, François, *Aux origines du nationalisme Turc. Yusuf Akçura 1876–1935* (Paris: ADPF, 1980).

—— 'Les Foyers Turks à l' époque Kemalist (1923–1931)', *Turcica* 14 (1982): 168–215.

—— 'Osmanlı İmparatorluğu'nun Son Döneminde İstanbul Kahvehaneleri', in Helene-Desmet Gregoire and François Georgeon (eds), *Doğuda Kahve ve Kahvehaneler* (İstanbul: Yapı Kredi Yayınları, 1999).

Gevrek, Meltem Ağduk, 'Yurt ve Dünya', *Toplum ve Bilim* 78 (1998): 255–72.

Göğceli, Kemal Sadık, *Ağıtlar* (Adana: Türk Sözü, 1943).

Gökmen, Özgür, 'Çok-Partili rejime geçerken sol: Türkiye sosyalizminin unutulmuş partisi', *Toplum ve Bilim* 78 (1998): 161–86.

—— 'Esat Adil Müstecaplıoğlu', in Tanıl Bora and Murat Gültekingil (eds), *Modern Türkiye'de Siyasi Düşünce*, vol. 8: *Sol* (İstanbul: İletişim, 2007), 940–7.

Göle, Nilüfer, *The Forbidden Modern. Civilization and Veiling* (Ann Arbor: University of Michigan Press, 1997).

Goloğlu, Mahmut, *Devrimler ve Tepkileri 1924–1930* (Ankara: Başnur Matbaası, 1972).

—— *Tek Partili Cumhuriyet 1931–1938* (Ankara: Kalite Matbaası, 1974).

Görener, Osman Kemal, *Halkevleri ve halkodaları* (Ankara: n.p., 1945).

Gregoire, Helene-Desmet and François Georgeon (eds), *Doğuda Kahve ve Kahvehaneler* (İstanbul: YKY, 1999).

Gündoğan, Salim, *Köycülük ve Köy Davası hakkında bir Etüt, Aydın Halkevi Neşriyatından 25, Köycülük Sübesi* (Aydın: CHP Basımevi Raif Aydoğlu, 1944).

Güneş, Günver, 'İzmir Türk Ocağı ve Hamdullah Suphi', *Tarih ve Toplum* 129 (1994): 169–74.

—— 'Türk Devrimi ve İzmir Türk Ocağı', *Çağdaş Türkiye Tarihi Araştırmaları Dergisi* 8 (1998): 115–35.

—— 'Serbest Cumhuriyet Fırkası Döneminde Türk Ocakları ve Siyaset', *Toplumsal Tarih* 65 (1999): 11–18.

—— 'Taşradan Meşrutiyede Bakış: Sosyal, Siyasal ve Ekonomi açıdan II. Meşrutiyet Döneminde Aydın Sancağı (1908–18)', in Sina Akşin et al. (eds), *100. Yılında Jön Türk Devrimi* (Istanbul: İş Bankası Kültür Yayınları, 2010).

Güneş, Günver and Müslime Güneş, 'Cumhuriyet Döneminde Manisa'nın sosyo-kültürel yaşamında Halkevi'nin yeri ve önemi', *Çağdaş Türkiye Tarihi Araştırmaları Dergisi* 5 (2007): 55–72.

Güntekin, Reşat Nuri, *Anadolu Notları* (Istanbul: İnkılap ve Aka, 1989).

Gupta, Akhil, 'Blurred Boundaries: The Discourse of Corruption, the Culture of Politics, and the Imagined State', in Aradhana Sharma and Akhil Gupta (eds), *The Anthropology of the State* (Oxford: Blackwell, 2006).

Güven, Ferit Celal, 'Halkevlerin kuruluş nedeni', in *Atatürk ve Halkevleri, Atatürkçü düşünce üzerine denemeler* (Ankara: Türk Tarih Kurumu, 1974).

Güz, Nurettin, *Tek parti ideolojisinin yayın organları: Halkevleri dergileri 1932–1950* (Ankara: Bilge Yapım, 1995).

Halkevleri 1932–1935, 103 Halkevi Geçen Yıllarda Nasıl Çalıştı (Ankara: n.p., 1935).

Halman, Talât Sait (ed.), *Türk Edebiyatı Tarihi*, vol. 4 (Istanbul: TC Kültür ve Turizm Bakanlığı, 2006).

Hanioğlu, Şükrü, *Preparation for a Revolution. The Young Turks 1902–1908* (Oxford: Oxford University Press, 2001).

—— 'The Second Constitutional Period, 1908–1918', in Reşat Kasaba (ed.), *The Cambridge History of Turkey*, vol. 4: *Turkey in the Modern World* (Cambridge: Cambridge University Press, 2008).

Hann, Christopher, *Tea and the Domestication of the Turkish State* (Huntingdon: Eothern Press, 1990).

Hattox, Ralph, *Coffee and Coffeehouses. The Origins of a Social Beverage in the Medieval Near East* (Seattle and London: University of Washington Press, 1996).

Heper, Metin, *The State Tradition in Turkey* (Hull: Eothen Press, 1985).

—— *İsmet İnönü: The making of a Turkish Stateman* (Leiden: Brill, 1998).

Herzfeld, Michael, *The Social Production of Indifference. Exploring the Symbolic Roots of Western Bureaucracy* (Chigaco and London: University of Chicago Press, 1992).

Hibou, Beatrice, 'Conclusion', in Joel Migdal (ed.), *Boundaries and Belonging. States and Societies in the Struggle to Shape Identities and Local Practices* (Cambridge: Cambridge University Press, 2004).

İğdemir, Uluğ, *Yılların içinde* (Ankara: Türk Tarih Kurumu, 1976).

Ilgaz, Rıfat, *Karartma Geceleri* (Istanbul: Çınar, 1974).

İnalcık, Halil, 'Şikayet Hakkı: "Arz-ı Hal ve Arz-ı Mahzar'lar"', *Osmanlı Araştırmaları* 7–8 (1988): 33–54.

İnan, Rauf, *Bir ömrün öyküsü* (Ankara: Öğretmen, 1986).

İnan, Süleyman, 'Denizli'deki Halkevleri ve Faaliyetleri (1932–1951)', *Atatürk Yolu* 7:25/26 (2001): 135–57.

İnönü, İsmet, *Hatıralarım. Genç Subay'ın Yılları 1884–1918* (Istanbul: Burçak, 1969).

Işın, Ekrem, 'A Social History of Coffee and Coffeehouses', in Selahattin Özpalabıyıklar (ed.), *Coffee, Pleasures Hidden in a Bean* (Istanbul: YKY, 2001).

İslamoğlu, Huri, 'Property as a Contested Domain: A Reevaluation of the Ottoman Land Code of 1858', in Roger Owen and Martin Bunton (eds), *New Perspectives on Property and Land* (Cambridge, MA: Harvard University Press, 2001).

İstanbul Eminönü Halkevi 1936–1938 (Istanbul: n.p., 1938).

İstatistik Yıllığı 1942–43 (Ankara: İstatistik umum Müdürlüğü, 1944).

Kabacalı, Alpay, *Bir Destan Rüzgarı: Fotoğraflarla Yaşar Kemal Yaşam Öyküsü* (Istanbul: Sel, 1997).

Kabahasanoğlu, Vahap, *Faruk Nafiz Çamlibel* (Istanbul: Toker, 1979).

Kandiyoti, Deniz, 'Emancipated but unliberated? Reflections on the Turkish case', *Feminist Studies* 13:2 (1987): 317–38.

——— 'Slave Girls, Temptresses, and Comrades: Images of Women in the Turkish Novel', *Feminist Issues* 8:1 (1988): 35–50.

——— 'Women and the Turkish State: Political Actors or Symbolic Pawns?', in Niva Yuval-Davis and Floya Anthias (eds), *Women–Nation–State* (London: MacMillan, 1989).

——— 'Afterword: Some Awkward Questions on Women and Modernity in Turkey', in Lila Abu-Lughod (ed.), *Remaking Women: Feminism and Modernity in the Middle East* (Princeton, NJ: Princeton University Press, 1998).

——— 'Islam, Modernity and the Politics of Gender', in Muhammad Khalid Masud, Armando Salvatore and Martin van Bruinessen (eds), *Islam and Modernity: Key Issues and Debates* (Edinburgh: Edinburgh University Press, 2009).

——— (ed.), *Women, Islam and the State* (London: Macmillan, 1991).

Kandiyoti, Deniz and Ayşe Saktanber (eds), *Fragments of Culture. The Everyday of Modern Turkey* (London: I.B.Tauris, 2002).

Kansu, Ceyhun Atuf, 'Halkevlerinin Kaynağı', in *Atatürk ve Halkevleri, Atatürkçü düşünce üzerine denemeler* (Ankara: Türk Tarih Kurumu, 1974).

——— '"Kemalizm" in Halk Okulları', in *Atatürk ve Halkevleri, Atatürkçü düşünce üzerine denemeler* (Ankara: Türk Tarih Kurumu, 1974).

Kaplan, Ramazan, *Cumhuriyet Dönemi Türk Romanında Köy* (Ankara: Akçağ, 1997).

Karaca, Emin, *Unutulmuş Sosyalist: Esat Adil Müstecaplıoğlu'nun Hayatı, Mücadelesi ve Eserleri* (Istanbul: Belge, 2008).

Karadağ, Meltem, 'Taşra kentlerinde yaşam tarzları alanı: Kültür ve ayrım', *Toplum ve Bilim* 118 (2010): 39–58.

Karadağ, Nurhan, *Halkevleri tiyatro çalışmaları* (Ankara: T.C. Kültür Bakanlığı, 1998).

Karaer, İbrahim, *Türk Ocakları 1912–1931* (Ankara: Türk Yurdu, 1992).

Karakuzuoğlu, Gülsün, 'Kastamonu Halkevi ve Faaliyetleri', unpublished MA thesis (Aydın: Adnan Menderes University, 2008).

Karaömerlioğlu, Mehmet Asım, 'The People's Houses and the cult of the peasant in Turkey', *MES* 34:4 (1998): 67–91.

—— 'The Village Institute Experience in Turkey', *BJMES* 25 (1998): 47–73.

—— 'Tek Parti döneminde Halkevleri ve Halkçılık', *Toplum ve Bilim* 88 (2001): 163–87.

—— 'The Peasants in Early Turkish Literature', *East European Quarterly* 36:2 (2002): 127–54.

—— *Orada bir Köy var Uzakta* (Istanbul: İletişim, 2006).

Kardaş, Canser, 'Diyarbakır Halkevi ve *Karacadağ* Dergisinin Halkbilim açısından Değerlendirmesi (1932–1951)', unpublished MA thesis (Kayseri: Erciyes University, 2007).

Karpat, Kemal, 'The People's Houses in Turkey: establishment and growth', *Middle Eastern Journal* 17 (1963): 55–67.

—— 'The impact of the People's Houses on the development of communication in Turkey 1931–1951', *Die Welt des Islams* 15 (1974): 69–84.

—— 'The *Hijra* from Russia and the Balkans: the Process of self-definition in the late Ottoman State', in Kemal Karpat, *Studies on Ottoman Social and Political History* (Leiden: Brill, 2002).

Kaş, Hasan, 'İsparta Halkevi çalışmaları ve Ün Dergisi (1934–1950)', unpublished MA thesis (Ankara: Hacettepe University, 2007).

Kasaba, Reşat, 'A time and a place for the nonstate: social change in the Ottoman Empire during the "long nineteenth century"', in Joel Migdal et al. (eds), *State Power and Social Forces. Domination and Transformation in the Third World* (Cambridge: Cambridge University Press, 1994).

—— 'Do States Always Favor Stasis? The Changing Status of Tribes in the Ottoman Empire', in Joel Migdal (ed.), *Boundaries and Belonging. States and Societies in the Struggle to Shape Identities and Local Practices* (Cambridge: Cambridge University Press, 2004).

Katz, Sheila Hannah, '*Adam* and *Adama*, *'Ird* and *Ard*: En-gendering Political Conflict and Identity in Early Jewish and Palestinian Nationalism', in Deniz Kandiyoti (ed.), *Gendering the Middle East: Emerging Perspectives* (London: I.B.Tauris, 1996).

Kaya, Berna, 'Bir halk Eğitim Kurumu olarak İzmit Halkevi 1932–1951', unpublished MA thesis (Sakarya: Sakarya University, 2008).

Kaya, Şükrü, *Halkevleri ve ödevimiz* (Ordu: Gürses, 1938).

Kaynar, Osman, 'Konya Halkevi'nin Türk Modernleşmesindeki Faaliyetleri 1932–1951', unpublished MA thesis (Konya: Dumlupınar University, 2007).

Kayseri Halkevi Armağanı 3 (Kayseri: Yeni Matbaa, 1934).

Kayseri ili içinde 934, 935, 936 ve 937 yıllarında arzedilmiş olan CHP nin kongrelerinde serdedilen dileklerin kovalama ve bitimleri (Kayseri: Vilayet matbaası, 1938).

Kayseri Ticaret ve Sanayi Odası, *Sekizinci İzmir Fuarında Kayseri* (n.p., 1938).

Kazancıgil, Alı and Ergun Özbudun (eds), *Atatürk, Founder of a Modern State* (London: Hurst & Co, 1981).

Kemaleddin, Kara Mehmet Ağa zade, *Erciyes Kayserisi ve Tarihine bir bakış* (Kayseri: Yeni Matbaa, 1934).

Kılınçarslan, Tevfik, *Köy kütüğü*, CHP Ankara Halkevi Büyük boy no. 25, Köycülük Şubesi (Ankara: n.p., 1939).

Kırlı, Cengiz, 'The Struggle over Space: Coffeehouses of Ottoman Istanbul, 1780–1845', unpublished PhD thesis (New York: State University of New York, 2000).

———'Yolsuzluğun icadı: 1840 Ceza Kanunu, iktidar ve bürokrasi', *Tarih ve Toplum Yeni Yaklaşımlar* 4 (2006): 45–119.

Koçak, Cemil, 'Tek-Parti Döneminde Cumhuriyet Halk Partisi'nde Parti Müfettişliği', in *Tarık Zafer Tunaya'ya Armağan* (Istanbul: İstanbul Barosu, 1992).

———'CHP–devlet kaynaşması (1936)', *Toplumsal Tarih* 118 (2003): 74–9.

———*Türkiye'de Milli Şef Dönemi 1938–1945* (Istanbul: İletişim, 2003).

———*Umumi Müfettişlikler 1927–1952* (Istanbul: İletişim, 2003).

———*İktidar ve Serbest Cumhuriyet Fırkası* (Istanbul: İletişim, 2006).

———'Parliament Membership during the Single-Party System in Turkey (1925–1945)', *EJTS* 3 (Online) (2005). First published electronically on 31 December 2005. http://ejts.revues.org/497 (last accessed 5 August 2014).

———'Tek parti döneminde CHP parti müfettişliğine ilişkin ek bilgi(ler)', in Mehmet Alkan, Murat Koraltürk and Tanıl Bora (eds), *Mete Tunçay'a Armağan* (Istanbul: İletişim 2007).

———*Tek-Parti Döneminde Muhalif Sesler* (Istanbul: İletişim, 2011).

Kohli, Atul and Shue Vivienne, 'State power and social forces: on political contention and accommodation in the Third World', in Joel Migdal et al. (eds), *State Power and Social Forces. Domination and Transformation in the Third World* (Cambridge: Cambridge University Press, 1994).

Kömeçoğlu, Uğur, 'Historical and Sociological Approaches to Public Space: The Case of the Islamic Coffeehouse in Istanbul', unpublished PhD thesis (Istanbul: Boğaziçi University, 2001).

Köroğlu, Erol, *Ottoman Propaganda and Turkish Identity: Literature in Turkey during World War I* (London: I.B.Tauris, 2007).

Köroğlu, Osman, '1923-1950 yılları arası Kayseri'nin ekonomik ve sosyal yapısı', unpublished MA thesis (Kayseri: Erciyes University, 1992).

Koşay, Hamit Zübeyr, *Halk Terbiyesi* (Ankara: Köy Hocası Matbaası, 1931).

Köylü Bilgi Cemiyeti esas nizamnamesi (Istanbul: n.p., 1335/1919).

Kozlov, Vladimir A., 'Denunciation and Its Functions in Soviet Governance: A Study of Denunciations and Their Bureaucratic Handling from Soviet Police Archives, 1944-1953', in Sheila Fitzpatrick and Robert Gellately (eds), *Accusatory Practices. Denunciation in Modern European History, 1789-1989* (Chicago: University of Chicago Press, 1997).

Kudret, Cevdet, *Havada Bulut yok* (Istanbul: Inkilap ve Aka, 1976).

Kudret, İhsan, *İhsan benimle çalışır mısın?* (Istanbul: İnkilap, n.d.).

Kudret, İhsan and Alpay Kabacalı (eds), *Cevdet Kudret'e saygı* (Ankara: Kültür Bakanlığı, 1993).

Kushner, David, *The Rise of Turkish Nationalism 1876-1908* (London: Frank Cass, 1977).

Lamprou, Alexandros, '"CHP Genel Sekreterliği Yüksek Makamına": 30'lu ve 40'lı yıllarda Halkevleri'yle ilgili CHP'ye gönderilen şikayet ve dilek mektupları üzerine kısa bir söz', *Kebikeç* 23 (2007): 381-92.

—— 'Nationalist mobilization and state-society relations: the People's House's campaign for Turkish in Izmir, June-July 1934', *MES* 49:5 (2013): 824-39.

Lewis, Geoffrey, *The Turkish Language Reform: A Catastrophic Success* (Oxford: Oxford University Press, 1999).

Linke, Lilo, *Allah Dethroned: A Journey through Modern Turkey* (New York: Alfred A. Knopf, 1937).

Makal, Mahmut, *A Village in Anatolia* (London: Vallentine Mitchell, 1954).

——*Köye Gidenler* (Istanbul: İnkılâp ve Aka, 1965).

Makdisi, Ussama, 'Ottoman Orientalism', *American Historical Review* 107:3 (2002): 768-96.

Mango, Andrew, *Atatürk* (London: John Murray, 1999).

Mardin, Şerif, 'Centre-Periphery Relations: A Key to Turkish Politics?', *Daedalus* 102:1 (1973): 169-90.

—— 'Centre-Periphery as a Concept for the Study of the Social Tranformation of Turkey', in D. Grillo (ed.), *Nation and the State in Europe. Anthropological Perspectives* (New York: Academic Press, 1980).

Mardin Halkevi (Mardin: Ulus Sesi, 1935).

Meeker, Michael, *A Nation of Empire: The Ottoman Legacy of Turkish Modernity* (Berkeley and London: University of California Press, 2002).

Metinsoy, Murat, 'Erken Cumhuriyet döneminde mebusların intihap dairesi ve teftiş bölgesi raporları', *Tarih ve Toplum Yeni Yaklaşımlar* 3 (2006): 103-69.

Migdal, Joel, *Strong Societies and Weak States: State–society Relations and the State Capabilities in the Third World* (Princeton, NJ: Princeton University Press, 1988).

—— 'Finding the Meeting Ground of Fact and Fiction. Some Reflections on Turkish Modernization', in Sibel Bozdoğan and Reşat Kasaba (eds), *Rethinking Modernity and National Identity in Turkey* (Seattle and London: University of Washington Press, 1997).

—— *State in Society: Studying how States and Societies Transform and Constitute one another* (Cambridge: Cambridge University Press, 2001).

—— (ed.), *Boundaries and Belonging. States and Societies in the Struggle to Shape Identities and Local Practices* (Cambridge: Cambridge University Press, 2004).

Migdal, Joel, Atul Kohli and Vivienne Shue (eds), *State Power and Social Forces. Domination and Transformation in the Third World* (Cambridge: Cambridge University Press, 1994).

Mitchell, Timothy, 'The Limits of the State: Beyond Statist Approaches and their Critics', *American Political Science Review* 85:1 (1991): 77–96.

—— *Rule of Experts. Egypt, Techno-Politics, Modernity* (Berkley and Los Angeles: University of California Press, 2002).

Muallim, Fuat Şükrü, *Mükemmel Mektup Nümuneleri* (Istanbul: Anadolu Türk Kitaphanesi, 1931).

Münir Naci, *Güzel İstid'a Nümuneleri* (Istanbul: n.p., 1929).

Müstecabi, Esat Adil, 'İşçi sınıfına pey sürenler', *Gerçek* 7, 5 April 1950.

Nadi, Nadir, *Perde Aralığından* (Istanbul: Çağdaş, 1964).

Najmabadi, Afsaneh, 'Veiled Discourse–Unveiled Bodies', *Feminist Studies* 19:3 (1993): 487–518.

—— *Women with Moustaches and Men without Beards: Gender and Sexual Anxieties of Iranian Modernity* (Berkley and Los Angeles: University of California Press, 2005).

—— 'Authority and Agency: Revisiting Women's Activism during Reza Shah's Period', in Touraj Atabaki (ed.), *The State and Subaltern: Modernization, Society and the State in Turkey and Iran* (London: I.B.Tauris, 2007).

Nalbandoğlu, Gülsüm Baydar, 'Urban Encounters with Rural Turkey', in Sibel Bozdoğan and Reşat Kasaba (eds), *Rethinking Modernity and National Identity in Turkey* (Seattle and London: University of Washington Press, 1997).

Navaro-Yashin, Yael, *Faces of the State: Secularism and Public Life in Turkey* (Princeton, NJ: Princeton University Press, 2002).

Neyzi, Leyla, 'Object or Subject? The Paradox of "Youth" in Turkey', *IJMES* 33:3 (2001): 411–32.

Nielsen, J. S., 'Mazalim', in C.E. Bosworth, E. van Donzel, W.P. Heinrichs and Ch Pellats (eds), *Encyclopaedia of Islam*, vol. VI, 2nd edn (Leiden: Brill, 1991): 933–34.

Nugent, David, 'Building the State, Making the Nation: The Bases and Limits of State Centralization in "Modern" Peru', *American Anthropologist* 96:2 (1994): 333–69.

Nusret, Kemal, *Köycülük Rehperi* (Ankara: Çankaya Matbaası, 1934).

Okutan, M. Çağatay, *Tek Parti Döneminde Azınlık Politikaları* (Istanbul: İstanbul Bilgi Üniversitesi, 2004).

Olgun, Kenan, *Yöresel Kalkınmada Adapazarı Halkevi* (Istanbul: Değişim, 2008).

Önder, Ali Rıza, *Kayseri Basın tarihi 1910–1960* (Ankara: Ayyıldız, 1972).

Önen, Nizam, 'Bir tek-parti dönemi politikacısının gözünden Cumhuriyet'in "Doğu" meselesi ve bürokrasinin hali: CHP Genel Sekreteri Memduh Şevket Esendal'ın Doğu gezisi', *Tarih ve Toplum Yeni Yaklaşımlar* 12 (2011): 153–98.

Or, Melda, 'Zonguldak halkevinden izlenimler: Karaelmas dergisi', unpublished MA thesis (Istanbul: İstanbul University, 2002).

Orhan, Kemal, *Müfettişler Müfettişi* (Istanbul: Varlık, 1966).

Örik, Nahid Sırrı, *Anadolu'da yol notları. Kayseri, Kırşehir, Kastamonu. Bir Edirne seyahatnamesi* (Istanbul: Arma, 2000).

Ortner, Sherry, 'Resistance and the Problem of Ethnographic Refusal', *CSSH* 37:1 (1995): 173–93.

Öz, Esat, *Türkiye'de Tek-parti Yönetimi ve siyasal katılım 1923–1945* (Ankara: Gündoğan, 1992).

Özacun, Orhan, *CHP Bibliografya denemesi* (Istanbul: n.p., 1993).

—— 'Halkevlerin dramı', *Kebikeç* 3 (1996): 87–97.

—— *CHP Halkevleri yayınları bibliyografyası* (Istanbul: n.p., 2001).

—— 'Halkevlerinin kuruluşu ve Atatürk döneminde İstanbul Halkevlerinin faaliyetleri (1932–1938)', unpublished PhD thesis (Istanbul: İstanbul University, 2002).

Özbek, Meral, *Popüler Kültür ve Orhan Gencebay Arabeski* (Istanbul: İletişim, 1991).

Özbudun, Ergun, 'The nature of the Kemalist Political Regime', in Ali Kazancıgıl and Ergun Özbudun (eds), *Atatürk, Founder of a Modern State* (London: Hurst & Co, 1981).

Özdoğan, Kâzım, *Kayseri Halkevi'nin Tertip Ettiği Yaya Köy Gezileri Tetkik Notları, Seri 2: Germir Köyü* (Kayseri: Vilayet Matbaası, 1937).

—— *Yaya Köy Gezileri Tetkik Notları, Seri 3: Mimarsinan Köyü* (Kayseri: Vilayet Matbaası, 1937).

—— *Kayseri İlbay Adli Bayman Başkanlığı altında Yapılan Yaya Köy Gezileri Tetkik Notları, seri 4: Argıncık Köyü* (Kayseri: Vilayet Matbaası, 1937).

Özmen, Müze, 'The activities of the People's House of Eminönü and its review: *Yeni Türk*', unpublished MA thesis (Istanbul: Boğaziçi University, 1995).

Özsan, Gül, 'Eşraf ailelerinin statü kazanma mücadelelerinde kadınların rölü', *Toplum ve Bilim* 118 (2010): 59–91.

Öztürk, Adil Adnan, 'Cumhuriyet ideolojisini Halka Yayma Girişimleri: Halkevleri ve Aydın Halkevi', *Tarih ve Toplum* 182 (1999): 42–51.

Öztürk, Serdar, 'Muhalif bir Gazete: "Mücadele" (1931)', *Selçuk İletişim* 3:4 (2005): 152–65.

——— 'Bir Kurumun Tarihsel ve Sosyolojik İncelemesi: Şehir Kulüpleri 1923–1950', *Galatasaray İletişim* 4 (August 2006): 89–115.

——— 'Cumhuriyetin İlk Yıllarında Halk Kitaplarını Modernleştirme Çabaları', *Kebikeç* 21 (2006): 42–72.

——— *Cumhuriyet Türkiyesinde Kahvehane ve İktidar 1930–1945* (Istanbul: Kırmızı, 2006).

——— 'Karagöz Co-Opted: Turkish Shadow Theatre of the Early Republic (1923–1945)', *Asian Theatre Journal* 23:2 (2006): 292–313.

——— 'The Struggle over Turkish Village Coffeehouses 1923–1945', *MES* 44:3 (2008): 435–54.

——— 'Efforts to Modernize Chapbooks during the Initial Years of the Turkish Republic', *European Historical Quarterly* 40:1 (2010): 7–34.

Öztürkmen, Arzu, 'The role of the People's Houses in the making of national culture in Turkey', *New Perspectives on Turkey* 11 (1994): 159–81.

——— *Türkiye'de Folklor ve milliyetçilik* (Istanbul: İletişim, 1998).

——— 'I Dance Folkore', in Deniz Kandiyoti and Ayşe Saktanber (eds), *Fragments of Culture. The Everyday of Modern Turkey* (London: I.B.Tauris, 2002).

Pala, Hikmet, 'Cumhuriyet Modernleşme Projesinin bir aracı olarak Ordu Halkevi ve çalışmaları', unpublished MA thesis (Ankara: Gazi University, 2006).

Parla, Ayse, 'The "Honour" of the State: Virginity Examination in Turkey', *Feminist Studies* 27:1 (2001): 65–88.

Parla, Taha, *Türkiye'de siyasal kültürünün resmi kaynakları. Tek parti ideolojisi ve CHP'nin 6 ok'u* (Istanbul: İletişim, 1992).

Peirce, Leslie, *Morality Tales. Law and Gender in the Ottoman Court of Aintab* (Berkeley: University of California Press, 2003).

Pekdoğan, Celal, 'Ayntab'da İttihat ve Terakki Kulübü'nün kurulması ve Ayntab'da etkisi', in Sina Akşin et al. (eds), *100. Yılında Jön Türk Devrimi* (Istanbul: İş Bankası Kültür Yayınları, 2010).

Peker, Recep, *CHP Genel Sekreteri R. Peker'in Söylevleri* (Ankara: n.p., 1935).

Petrov, Milen, 'Everyday forms of Compliance: Subaltern Commentaries on Ottoman Reform, 1864–1868', *CSSH* 46:4 (2004): 730–59.

Raif, Necdet, *Küçük Mektup Nümuneleri* (Istanbul: Türk Neşriyat Yurdu, 1929).

Rathbun, Carole, *The Village in the Turkish Novel and Short Story 1920 to 1955* (The Hague and Paris: Mouton, 1972).

Sakal, Fahri, *Çok Partili Döneme Geçişte Tek Partinin Muhalefet Anlayışı* (Samsun: Etüt, 2008).

Şakiroğlu, H. Mahmut, 'Halkevi dergiler ve neşriyatı', *Kebikeç* 3 (1996): 131–43.

Salmoni, Barak, 'The Teachers' Army and Its Miniature Republican Society: Educators' Traits and School Dynamics in Turkish Pedagogical Prescriptions, 1923-50', *CSSAAME* 21:1/2 (2001): 61-72.

Şanal, Mustafa, 'Türk Kültür tarihi içerisinde Kayseri Halkevi ve Faaliyetleri (1932-1950)', *Milli Eğitim Dergisi* 161 (2004): 37-60.

Şapolyo, Enver Behnan, 'Atatürk ve Halkevleri', in *Atatürk ve Halkevleri, Atatürkçü düşünce üzerine denemeler* (Ankara: Türk Tarih Kurumu, 1974).

Sarıyıldız, Gülden, *Sokak Yazıcıları, Osmanlıda Arzuhaller ve Arzuhalciler* (Istanbul: Derlem, 2011).

Satoğlu, Abdullah, *Kayseri Ansiklopedisi* (Ankara: Kültür Bakanlığı, 2002).

Scott, C. James, *Weapons of the Weak. Everyday Forms of Peasant Resistance* (New Haven, CT, and London: Yale University Press, 1985).

——— *Domination and the Arts of Resistance. Hidden Transcripts* (New Haven, CT, and London: Yale University Press, 1990).

——— *Seeing Like a State. How Certain Schemes to Improve the Human Condition Have Failed* (New Haven, CT, and London: Yale University Press, 1998).

Selami Münir, *Yeni İstid'a Örnekleri* (Istanbul: n.p., 1934).

Selim, Samah, *The Novel and the Rural Imaginary in Egypt, 1880-1985* (New York and London: Routledge, 2004).

Serçe, Erkan, *İzmir'de Kitapçılık 1839-1928* (Izmir: İzmir Büyükşehir Belediyesi Kültür Yayınları, 2002).

Sevinçli, Efdal, 'II. Meşrutiyet Döneminde Siyasal/Belgesel Tiyatro ve İlginç bir Yazar Örneği: Doktor Kamil Bey ve Oyunları', in Ferdan Ergut (ed.), *II. Meşrutiyet'i yeniden Düşünmek* (Istanbul: Tarih Vakfı Yurt Yayınları, 2009).

Sharma, Aradhana and Akhil Gupta, 'Introduction: Rethinking Theories of the State in an Age of Globalization', in Aradhana Sharma and Akhil Gupta (eds), *The Anthropology of the State* (Oxford: Blackwell, 2006).

Shissler, A. Holly, *Between Two Empires. Ahmet Ağaoğlu and the New Turkey* (London: I.B.Tauris, 2003).

Şimşek, Sefa, *Bir ideolojik seferberlik deneyimi, Halkevleri 1932-1951* (Istanbul: Boğaziçi Üniversitesi, 2002).

——— '"People's Houses" as a Nationwide Project for Ideological Mobilization in Early Republican Turkey', *Turkish Studies* 6 (2005): 71-91.

Stern, S.M., 'Petitions from the Ayyubid Period', *Bulletin of the School of African and Oriental Studies* 27:1 (1964): 1-32.

Styliowicz, Joseph, *Political Change in Rural Turkey. Erdemli* (Paris and The Hague: Mouton, 1966).

Su, Mükerrem, *İnandığım Allah* (Istanbul: Inkilâp, 1946).

Süleyman, Tevfik, *Güzel Mektup nümuneleri* (Istanbul: Güneş, 1932).

Sürme, Erhan, 'Niğde Halkevi (1933-1951)', MA thesis (Niğde: Niğde University, 2009).

Tamer, Aytül, 'İttihat ve Terakki kendini anlatıyor: Cemiyetin Propaganda Broşürleri', in Hakan Aydın (ed.), *İkinci Meşrutiyet Devrinde Basın ve Siyaset* (Konya: Palet, 2010).

Taner, Hasan, *Halkevlerin bibliyografyası* (Ankara: n.p., 1944).

Tarti, İsmet, *Yeni Mektup Örnekleri* (Istanbul: n.p., 1943).

TBMM Albümü 1920–2010, vol. I (Ankara: TBMM Basın ve Halkla İlişkiler Müdürlüğü, 2010).

TC Başbakanlık istatistik Genel Direktörlüğü. Genel Nüfus sayımı. 20 ilkteşrin 1935, *Balıkesir Vilayeti*, vol. 8 (İstanbul: Hüsnütabiat, 1936).

—— *Kayseri Vilayeti*, vol. 33 (İstanbul: Hüsnütabiat, 1937).

TC Başbakanlık İstatistik Genel Müdürlüğü, *Milli Eğitim Genel Kitaplıklar ve Müzeler ile Halkevleri, Halkodaları ve Okuma Odaları kitaplıkları istatistikleri 1944–45* (Ankara: Pulhan, 1946).

Tekel, İlhan and Selim İlkin, *Bir Cumhuriyet Öyküsü, Kadrocuları ve Kadro'yu Anlamak* (Istanbul: Tarih Vakfı Yurt Yayınları, 2003).

Tekeli, Ilhan and Gencay Şaylan, 'Türkiye'de halkçılık ideolojisinin evrimi', *Toplum ve Bilim* 6–7 (1978): 44–110.

Terzibaşoğlu, Yücel, 'Eleni Hatun'un Zeytin Bahçeleri: 19. Yüzyılda Anadolu'da Mülkiyet Hakları Nasıl İnşa Edildi?', *Tarih ve Toplum Yeni Yaklaşımlar* 4 (2006): 121–47.

Thompson, Elizabeth, 'Ottoman Political Reform in the Provinces: The Damascus Advisory Council in 1844–45', *IJMES* 25:3 (1993).

Tipps, Dean, 'Modernization Theory and the Comparative Study of Societies: A Critical Perspective', *CSSH* 15 (1973): 199–226.

Toprak, Zafer, 'Osmanlı Narodnikleri: Halka Doğru gidenler', *Toplum ve Bilim* 24 (1984): 69–81.

Trouillot, Michel-Rolph, 'The Anthropology of the State: Close Encounters of a Deceptive Kind', *Current Anthropology* 42:1 (2001): 125–38.

'Tuluat', *Türk Ansiklopedisi*, vol. 31 (Ankara: Milli Eğitim, 1982).

Tunaya, Tarık Zafer, *Türkiye'de Siyasal Partiler*, Vol. 1: *İkinci Meşrutiyet Dönemi* (Istanbul: Hürriyet Vakfı Yayınları, 1988).

Tunçay, Mete, 'CHF'nın 1927 Kurultayının Öncesinde Toplanan İl Kongreleri', *Siyasal Bilgiler Fakültesi Dergisi* 36 (1981): 281–334.

—— *Türkiye Cumhuriyeti'nde tek-parti yönetimin kurulması 1923–1931*, 3rd edn (Istanbul: Tarih Vakfı Yurt Yayınları, 1999).

Türkoğlu, Ömer, 'Halkevlerin kuruluş amaçları, örgütsel yapısı ve bazı uygulamaları', *Kebikeç* 3 (1996): 97–107.

Turner, Victor, *Symbolic Action in Human Societies* (Ithaca, NY, and London: Cornell University Press, 1974).

—— 'Social Dramas and Stories about Them', *Critical Inquiry* 7:1 (1980): 141–68.

Unbehaun, Horst, *Türkiye kırsalında kliyentalizm ve siyasal katılım. Datça örneği: 1923–1992* (Ankara: Ütopya, 2006).

Üngör, Uğur Ümit, *The Making of Modern Turkey. Nation and State in Eastern Anatolia, 1913–1950* (Oxford: Oxford University Press, 2011).

Ünver, Cennet, 'Images and Perceptions of Fascism among the mainstream Kemalist elite in Turkey, 1931–1943', unpublished MA thesis (Istanbul: Boğaziçi University, 2001).

Uran, Hilmi, *Meşrutiyet, tek Parti, çok Parti Hatıralarım 1908–1950* (Istanbul: Türkiye İş Bankası Kültür Yayınları, 2007).

Uşak Halkevi Bir Yıllık çalışmaları, 2 (Istanbul: Resimli Ay, 1937).

Üstel, Füsun, *İmparatorluktan Ulus Devlete Türk milliyetçiliği: Türk Ocakları 1912–1931* (Istanbul: İletişim, 1997).

—— *Makbul Vatandaş'ın Peşinde: II. Meşrutiyet'ten Bugüne Vatandaşlık Eğitimi* (Istanbul: İletişim, 2004).

Üstündağ-Selamoğlu, Esra, 'Bir Sözlü Tarih Çalışması. Hereke'de Değişim', *Toplumsal Tarih* 45 (1997): 28–37.

Uyar, Hakkı, 'İnkılap ve İstiklal Konferansları. Tek Parti Yönetiminin Halkevlerinde yürüttüğü propaganda işlerini anlamakta', *Toplumsal Tarih* 17 (1995): 52–6.

—— *Tek Parti Dönemi ve CHP* (Istanbul: Boyut, 1999).

—— 'Tek Parti İktidarın Toplumsal Kökenleri. İkinci seçmenler örneği 1935', *Toplumsal Tarih* 106 (2002): 54–7.

Uzun, Ahmet, *Tanzimat ve Sosyal Direnişler* (Istanbul: Eren, 2002).

Uzun, Hakan, 'Cumhuriyet Halk Fırkası Halk Hatipleri Teşkilâtı', *Cumhuriyet Tarihi Araştırmaları Dergisi* 11 (2010): 85–113.

Uzun, Mehmet, 'Kayseri Türk Ocağı', *Kayseri Türk Ocağı* 7:81 (2007): 11–13.

Varlık, Bülent, '*Bozok*: Yozgat Halkevi Dergisi bibliyografyası', *Kebikeç* 3 (1996): 193–9.

—— '*Devrimin sesi*: Bilecik Halkevi dergisi bibliyografyası', *Kebikeç* 6 (1998): 81–6.

—— '*Ülker*, Niksar Halkevi Kültür dergisi', *Kebikeç* 14 (2001).

—— (ed.), *Umumi Müfettişler Konferansı'nda Görüşülen ve Dahiliye Vekaleti'ni İlgilendiren İşlere Dair Toplantı Zabıtları ile Rapor ve Hulasası 1936* (Ankara: Dipnot, 2010).

Velidedeoğlu, Hıfzı Veldet, *Anıların izinde* (Istanbul: Remzi, 1977–9).

Vermeulen, Hans and Cora Govers, 'Introduction', in Hans Vermeulen and Cora Govers (eds), *The Anthropology of Ethnicity. Beyond 'Ethnic Groups and Boundaries'* (Amsterdam: Het Spinhuis, 1994).

Verner, Andrew, 'Discursive Strategies in the 1905 Revolution: Peasant Petitions from Vladimir Province', *Russian Review* 54 (1995): 65–90.

Watts, Nicole F., 'Re-Considering State–Society Dynamics in Turkey's Kurdish Southeast', *EJTS* 10 (Online) (2009). First published electronically on 31 December 2009. (Last accessed 14 March 2014). URL: http://ejts.revues. org/4196).

Webster, Donald, *The Turkey of Atatürk. Social Process in the Turkish Reformation* (Philadelphia: American Academy of Political and Social Science, 1939).

Weiker, Walter, *Political Tutelage and Democracy in Turkey* (Leiden: Brill, 1973).

Woodwall, Carole, '"Awakening a Horrible Monster"': Negotiating the Jazz Public in 1920s Istanbul', *CSSAAME* 30:3 (2010): 574–82.

Würgler, Andreas, 'Voices From Among the "Silent Masses": Humble Petitions and Social Conflicts in Early Modern Central Europe', *International Review of Social History* 46 (2001): 11–34.

Yalçın, Murat (ed.), *Tanzimat'tan Bügüne Edebiyat Ansiklopedisi* (Istanbul: YKY, 2001).

Yasa, İbrahim, *Hasanoğlan köyü* (Ankara: Doğuş, 1950).

Yaşar, Hakan, 'Sinop Halkevi ve Faaliyetleri (1932–1951)', unpublished MA thesis (Tokat: Gaziosmanpaşa University, 2008).

Yeşil, Sevim, 'Unfolding Republican Patriarchy: The Case of Young Kurdish Women at the Girls' Vocational Boarding School in Elazığ', unpublished MA thesis (Ankara: METU, 2003).

Yeşilkaya, Neşe Gurallar, *Halkevleri: ideoloji ve mimarlık* (Istanbul: İletişim, 1999).

Yetkin, Çetin, *Türkiye'de tek parti yönetimi* (Istanbul: Altın Kitaplar, 1983).

Yiğit, Resul, 'Mersin Halkevi 1933–51', unpublished MA thesis (Mersin: Mersin University, 2001).

Yıldırım, Tuğba (ed.), *Kürt Sorunu ve Devlet. Tedip ve Tenkil Politikaları 1925–1947* (Istanbul: Tarih Vakfı Yurt Yayınları, 2011).

Yıldız, Ahmet, *'Ne Mutlu türküm diyebilene' Türk Ulusal kimliğinin etnoseküler sınırları 1919–1938* (Istanbul: İletişim, 2001).

—— 'Recep Peker', in Tanıl Bora and Murat Gültekingil (eds), *Modern Türkiye'de Siyasi Düşünce*, vol. 2: *Kemalizm* (Istanbul: İletişim, 2001).

Yüksel, Ahmet, 'Merzifon Halkevi ve Taşan Dergisi', *Kebikeç* 3 (1996): 169–89.

Yurdakök, Abdullah, *Balıkesir basın tarihi 1886–1991* (Balıkesir: Sonsöz Gazetesi, 1992).

Ze'evi, Dror, *Producing Desire: Changing Sexual Discourse in the Ottoman Middle East, 1500–1900* (Berkley: University of California Press, 2006).

Zengin, Sabri, 'Yeni Tokat. Bir Halkevi Dergisi', *Tarih ve Toplum* 232 (2003): 33–9.

Zürcher, Erik Jan, *Turkey. A Modern History* (London: I.B.Tauris, 2003).

—— 'The Rise and Fall of "Modern" Turkey: Bernard Lewis's *Emergence* Fifty Years On', in idem, *The Young Turk Legacy and Nation Building. From the Ottoman Empire to Atatürk's Turkey* (London: I.B.Tauris, 2010).

Index